How the English Reformation was Named

How the English Reformation was Named

The Politics of History, c.1400–1700

BENJAMIN M. GUYER

OXFORD
UNIVERSITY PRESS

OXFORD
UNIVERSITY PRESS

Great Clarendon Street, Oxford, OX2 6DP,
United Kingdom

Oxford University Press is a department of the University of Oxford.
It furthers the University's objective of excellence in research, scholarship,
and education by publishing worldwide. Oxford is a registered trade mark of
Oxford University Press in the UK and in certain other countries

Published in the United States of America by Oxford University Press
198 Madison Avenue, New York, NY 10016, United States of America

British Library Cataloguing in Publication Data
Data available

Library of Congress Control Number: 2022932940

ISBN 978–0–19–286572–4

DOI: 10.1093/oso/9780192865724.001.0001

Printed and bound by
CPI Group (UK) Ltd, Croydon, CR0 4YY

For Rachel

Table of Contents

List of Figure and Table

Figure

Table

Gratis

The research and writing process behind the present volume were far greater than I ever anticipated. In retrospect, portions of this project extend very far back. Graduate work with Matthew Day and Sarah Irving-Stonebraker at Florida State University introduced me to monstrosity and inspired in me a deep awareness of the importance of nature as a moral and political category. I am further thankful that Darrin McMahon pushed me toward graduate work in history. As a doctoral student at the University of Kansas, I greatly profited from the oversight of Jonathan Clark. I also gleaned insights from Katherine Clark, Luis Corteguera, Steve Epstein, and Geraldo Sousa, the other members of my doctoral committee.

My understanding of religion within and beyond early modern England has benefited from conversations (and sometimes work) with Gregory Dodds, William Engel, David Scott Gehring, Torrance Kirby, Benjamin T.G. Mayes, Estelle Paranque, Brown Patterson, Richard Rex, Maximilian Scholz, Danielle Mead Skjelver, Keith Stanglin, Marjorie Swann, Darrick Taylor, and Elliot Vernon. I am grateful for general insights and suggestions made by Brad Gregory and Alec Ryrie on this project, as well as the more specific and sometimes critical comments made by the anonymous reviewers for OUP. My chair, David Coffey, has consistently supported my attendance at the Sixteenth Century Conference each year. Dana Breland of the Paul Meek Library at the University of Tennessee at Martin helped me secure various books and articles, not least during the difficult period of the COVID-19 pandemic. Alice-Catherine Carls, Kirk Essary, Bronwen McShea, and Vaughn Scribner assisted with developing my book proposal, and Karen Raith and Cathryn Steele made publication a painless process. Errors remain my own.

I thank Anupam Basu, Joseph Loewenstein, Martin Mueller, and Stephen Pentecost for helping me to better understand the *EarlyPrint Lab* and for permission to duplicate the N-gram on reformation (Figure I.1). I also thank Sharla Clute of SUNY Press for permission to print the quote by Martin Heidegger as the epigraph to my conclusion.

Finally and above all, I am wholly indebted to my wife Rachel, with whom I have learned the meaning of mutual delight.

And he that sat upon the throne said, Behold, I make all things new. And he said unto me, Write: for these words are true and faithful.

Revelation 21:5

Introduction

> It is singular, however, how long a time often passes before words
> embody things.
>
> Nathaniel Hawthorne (1850)[1]

Overview

It was a long time before the religious developments of sixteenth-century Europe
were known as "the Reformation." By then, Martin Luther had lived and died; the
label "Protestant" had spread across Europe, and was adapted in various ways and
in diverse locales; and other religious figures, today collectively termed "the
Reformers," had also passed away, bequeathing their theological tomes to later
generations. But for more than a century after his death, no one called Luther and
his legacy "the Reformation." No one spoke of a "Protestant Reformation" or a
Catholic "Counter-Reformation,"[2] just as no one wrote of a constellation of
smaller, national reformations that related to Luther's legacy like so many species
to their genus. The latter point matters most immediately here, for what is
predicated of the Reformation is no less true of its alleged descendants. It was a
long time before the religious developments of sixteenth-century England were
known as "the *English* Reformation."

In the pages that follow, I ask and answer a simple question: How did the
English Reformation get its name? Quite unlike the Luther-centric narrative that
defines so much of contemporary scholarship, I argue that reformation was an
international conciliar discourse that devolved to the local level in the mid-
sixteenth century. From here, competition within various kingdoms and regions
resulted in new, localized meanings for "reformation"; sometimes, competition
then also occurred between neighboring nations (e.g., England and Scotland); and
from all of this emerged the various tales of national reformation so familiar today.

---

[1] Nathaniel Hawthorne, *The Scarlet Letter and Other Writings*, ed. Leland S. Person (New York and
London: W.W. Norton & Company, 2005), Chapter XX, p. 143.

[2] The term "Counter-Reformation" dates to the late eighteenth century; see John W. O'Malley, *Trent
and All That: Renaming Catholicism in the Early Modern Era* (Cambridge and London: Harvard
University Press, 2000). Modern historiography about the Reformation as an event that began with
Luther is generally attributed to Veit Ludwig von Seckendorff's *Historical and Apologetic Commentary
on Lutheranism* (1688–92); see O'Malley, *Trent and All That*, pp. 18–19, and C. Scott Dixon, *Contesting
the Reformation* (Malden and Oxford: Wiley-Blackwell, 2012), p. 9.

How the English Reformation was Named: The Politics of History, c. 1400–1700. Benjamin M. Guyer,
Oxford University Press. © Benjamin M. Guyer 2022. DOI: 10.1093/oso/9780192865724.003.0001

Each ecumenical council between 1414 and 1563—Constance, Basel and its competing continuations, Lateran V, and Trent—described "reformation" as its duty and goal. The English sporadically participated in several of these councils, but when Queen Elizabeth I renewed her father's break with the papacy, and when the papacy ratified the same by excommunicating her in 1570, reformation was removed from the prescriptive, corporeal metaphors and institutional parameters that had long bound it to conciliar determinations. Initially, the English showed no interest in developing their own discourse of reformation, but by then, a very different approach had developed north of the Anglo-Scottish border—what John Knox and his associates called "reformatioun . . . be [by] force of armes."[3] Between the late 1550s and mid-1570s, Scotland thus saw two new discourses of reformation develop in rapid succession. The first pertained to revolt and the second to its historical narration. The central text of the latter discourse was Knox's *Historie of the Reformation of the Church of Scotland*, which detailed and defended the domestic evangelical rebellion that led to the extirpation of Catholicism and the instantiation of an especially militant and apocalyptic form of Protestantism. These developments polarized and defined English religious and political debate for more than a century. But it was only during the British civil wars of the 1640s that apologists for the Church of England advanced a distinctly historical discourse about an event that they variously termed "the English Reformation,"[4] "our English Reformation,"[5] or, most simply, "our Reformation."[6] The plural possessive indicates a contrast—but with the Scottish Reformation, not with anything done by Luther. Anglican authors argued that unlike its Scottish counterpart, the English Reformation was led by a succession of devout monarchs and largely accomplished without bloodshed. With the Restoration, apologetic narrative became historiographical habit and, eventually, historical certainty.[7]

---

[3] John Knox, *The History of the Reformation of the Church of Scotland*, in David Laing (ed.), *The Works of John Knox*, 6 Vols. (Edinburgh: The Wodrow Society, 1846), Vol. 1, p. 432; the modernized English quoted here comes from John Knox, *The History of the Reformation of the Church of Scotland*, 2 Vols., ed. William Croft Dickinson (New York: Philosophical Library, 1950), Vol. 1, p. 243.

[4] Charles I and Alexander Henderson, *The Papers Which Passed at New-Castle* (London, 1649; Wing/C2535), p. 16; Henry Ferne, *Of the Division Between the English and Romish Church upon the Reformation* (London, 1655; Wing/F796), p. 38.

[5] Henry Hammond, *A View of the New Directorie* (Oxford, 1645; Wing/H612), p. 6; Anonymous, *A Brief View and Defence of the Reformation of the Church of England by King Edward and Q. Elizabeth* (London, 1654; Wing/B4655), p. 68.

[6] Edward Boughen, *An Account of the Church Catholick* (London, 1653; Wing/B3812), p. 17; Thomas Fuller, *The Church-History of Britain* (London, 1655; Wing/F2416), Index, sig. [¶¶4].

[7] Due to difficulties presented by the COVID-19 pandemic, the present study was completed before I was able to secure a copy of Alexandra Walsham, Bronwyn Wallace, Ceri Law, and Brian Cummings (eds.), *Memory and the English Reformation* (Cambridge: Cambridge University Press, 2020). Some of the conclusions of that study parallel my own; others do not. I will have a review forthcoming in *The Sixteenth Century Journal*.

The Semantics of "Reformation"

There is no obvious reason why "reformation,"[8] originally a common noun, should have become a proper noun that denoted the transformations of religion across sixteenth-century Latin Christendom. For example, English monarchs occasionally passed laws for such matters as the "reformation" of clothing and coin,[9] two areas far removed from those issues now identified as central to early Protestant aims. Dictionaries tell a similar story, but with even greater detail. "Reformation" had an altogether positive meaning, but no necessarily religious referent. Thomas Elyot's bilingual Latin–English *Dictionary* of 1538 had no entry for "reformatio," but he defined "Reformo, mare" as "to refourme."[10] "Reformation" was included in Richard Huloet's dictionary of 1552, but Huloet's very short definition merely noted the Latin root "reformatio." His definition of "refourme" was slightly more developed. After giving the Latin etymology, Huloet offered an example, "Refourme a negligence wyth a better diligence, *Talum reponere*."[11] The Latin translates as "put back the die," a statement whose immediate relevance for understanding reform is opaque at best, but Huloet's entry had two precedents. Elyot had included *Talum reponere* in his dictionary under the letter "T," defining it as "to refourme that, whiche was negligently done, with more diligence."[12] More importantly, Erasmus of Rotterdam had included the Latin proverb in the 1533 edition of his *Adages*.[13] In a paragraph-long comment upon the saying, Erasmus upended its original meaning, which pertained to having a second try in a game. Citing the Greek orator Antiphon, who wrote that "One cannot cancel a move in life as one can a move in a game," Erasmus elaborated, "It is not granted us to replay life once it has passed." The most we can do is perform good works that might ameliorate the effects of earlier, negative actions.[14] Far from elaborate or extensive, Huloet's definition indicated that "refourme" could have morally weighty associations.

---

[8] Ethan H. Shagan, *The Rule of Moderation: Violence, Religion and the Politics of Restraint in Early Modern England* (Cambridge: Cambridge University Press, 2011), pp. 10–16, analyzes the semantics of moderation in large part by looking at dictionaries. The present study was written without having read Shagan's work. I thank the anonymous OUP reviewer for drawing my attention to *The Rule of Moderation*.

[9] See, e.g., Elizabeth I, *Articles for the Due Execution of the Statutes of Apparell, and for the Reformation of the Outragious Excesse Thereof* (London, 1562; STC 7947); James VI and I, *A Proclamation for Reformation of Great Abuses in Measures* (London, 1603; STC 8317); Charles I, *A Proclamation for the Better Execution of the Office of His Maiesties Exchanger, and Reformation of Sundry Abuses and Fraudes Practised vpon his Maiesties Coyness* (London, 1627; STC 8860). This brief list is indicative rather than exhaustive.

[10] Thomas Elyot, *The Dictionary* (London, 1538; STC 7659), sig. Xii.

[11] Richard Huloet, *Abcedarivm Anglico Latinvm* (London, 1552; STC 13940), sig. Bb.iiij. v.

[12] Elyot, *The Dictionary*, no page. Page numbers were rarely used in dictionaries, as seen in most of the citations in this section.

[13] CWE, Vol. 36, Adages IV iii to V ii 51, pp. 468–9.   [14] CWE, Vol. 36, p. 469.

Further insight comes from dictionaries published during Elizabeth's reign. Thomas Cooper, who later became bishop of Lincoln, published the first edition of his massive *Thesavrvs Lingvae Romanae & Britannicae* (Thesaurus of the Roman and British Languages) in 1565. Like Elyot, he too lacked an entry for "Reformatio," but Cooper defined "Reformo" as "To reforme: to renew: to bryng the olde state agayne." Latin uses of the word followed, such as "reformare & corrigere mores" ("to reform and correct customs or morals") and "Reformare ad exemplum," which Cooper glossed as "To amende a thyng accordynge to the example or paterne."[15] The subsequent editions of 1573, 1578, and 1584 maintained the same definitions and illustrations, but none included "reformatio" as a headword. Other dictionaries looked more directly to the Roman past and restricted definitions to what was gleaned from Latin literature. In John Higgins' 1572 revision of Huloet's work, "Reformation" appeared but its definition referred to the work of the Censor, the public office charged with monitoring and correcting morals in republican Rome. A "Reformer" was identified as the Censor, described as a "Reformer of maners, and of the gouernaunce of a commune wealthe." Higgins then defined the cognate "Refourme" as "to turn to a better state" ("Vertere in meliorem statum").[16] Similar was Baret's 1574 *An Aluearie or Triple Dictionarie*, where the headword "Reformation" simply read, "made by the censour." "Refourme" was explained as "agere censuram" ("to remove censure or blame").[17] For both Baret and Higgins, "reformation" could refer to improvements in *mores* imposed by lawfully constituted authority; doctrinal, devotional, or liturgical matters were unmentioned. The basic point is therefore worth repeating: in common parlance, "reformation" had no necessarily religious referent. Instead, "reforme" sometimes had more playful associations, as when Higgins retained both *Talum reponere* and the explication originally proffered by Elyot and Huloet. Rooted in less serious concerns, "reforme" could attain to a greater level of semantic sobriety, but the rhetorical force of *Talum reponere* wholly depended upon the Erasmian inversion of the otherwise ludic and frivolous.

"Reformation" was also not among the headwords used by the earliest authors and compilers of seventeenth-century dictionaries. Robert Cawdry's *A Table Alphabeticall*, the first monolingual English dictionary, appeared in 1604 without an entry for "reformation" or even "reform." The second edition of 1609, revised and expanded by Cawdry's son Thomas,[18] contained the barest of entries for "reforme," which he defined simply as "amend."[19] This definition was left untouched in the later editions of 1613 and 1617. John Rider's bilingual

---

[15] Thomas Cooper, *Thesavrvs Lingvae Romanae & Britannicae* (London, 1565; STC 5686), no page.; see the entry for "Reformo."

[16] Iohn Higgins (ed.), *Hvloets Dictionarie* (London, 1572; STC 13941), sig. Mm.iij. v.

[17] John Baret, *An Aluearie or Triple Dictionarie* (London, 1574; STC 1410), sig. Yy.iii.

[18] Janet Bately, "Cawdrey, Robert (b. 1537/8?, d. in or after 1604), Church of England clergyman and lexicographer," *ODNB*.

[19] Robert Cawdry, *A Table Alphabeticall* (London, 1609; STC 4884.5), sig. H3 v.

Latin–English dictionary, first published in 1589 as *Bibliotheca Scholastica*, was expanded only in its third edition of 1612 to contain entries for "reformatio," "reformo," "reformator," "reformatrix," and "reformatus, a, um."[20] "Reformatio" was defined as "A renuing" and "reformo" as "To renew, to reforme, to bring to the olde state again." "Reformator" and "reformatrix" were the masculine and feminine nouns used for those who brought about renewal,[21] while "reformatus, a, um" was the adjective applied to that which had been reformed.

But even if "reformation" was not among the earliest of seventeenth-century lemmata, once entered into a dictionary its definition remained consonant with sixteenth-century lexica. In his definition of "reformo," Rider largely followed Thomas Thomas' 1587 *Dictionarium*. The latter partially defined "reformo" as "To reforme, to renewe, to bring to the old state againe."[22] Rider borrowed this entirely, and in following Thomas he also followed Cooper, whose 1565 definition of "reformo" was taken directly into Thomas' own dictionary. Rider died in 1632, but his dictionary was revised and republished through 1659. The last edition maintained the five Latin entries added in 1612. The only changes were the inclusion of Greek etymological roots and the addition of "to transform" to the definition of "reformo."[23] The same consistency is found in other bilingual dictionaries, such as Randle Cotgrave's *A Dictionarie of the French and English Tongues* (1611), and John Florio's *Queen Anna's New World of Words, Or Dictionarie of the Italian and English Tongues* (1612), a revised version of his 1598 dictionary *A Worlde of Wordes*. Both authors noted cognates between their respective languages but only one entry carried a religiously themed definition; Cotgrave defined "reformez" as "Reformists, an Order of Franciscan Fryers."[24] These dictionaries were revised and republished into the last quarter of the seventeenth century, but their definitions remained unchanged. Once included in a dictionary, "reform" and "reformation" were not sites of semantic confusion but semantic stability, and were rarely used to describe, much less resolve, contemporary religious dispute. In England, "reformation" had no necessarily religious referent.

Methodology

As the section "The Semantics of 'Reformation'" indicates, the present volume is deeply informed by the "linguistic" approach to historical inquiry.[25] There is no

---

[20] John Rider and Francis Holyoake, *Riders Dictionarie* (Oxford, 1612; STC 21033), no page.

[21] Rider, however, describes "reformator" and "reformatrix" as verbs, not nouns. This remained true even in the 1659 edition of his work.

[22] Thomas Thomas, *Dictionarium Linguae Latinae et Anglicanae* (Cambridge, 1587; STC 24008), no page.

[23] John Rider and Francis Holyoake, *Riders Dictionarie* (London, 1659; Wing/R1443), no page.

[24] Randle Cotgrave, *A Dictionarie of the French and English Tongues* (London, 1611; STC 5830).

[25] See Quentin Skinner, *Visions of Politics*, 3 Vols., Vol. 1: *Regarding Method* (Cambridge: Cambridge University Press, 2002); J.G.A. Pocock, *Virtue, Commerce, and History: Essays on*

historical study without texts, and no texts without language—specifically, an author's vocabulary. When we study the past, we must attend closely to the lexicon used in and across surviving sources. As has been written elsewhere about a very different intellectual context, "vocabulary is often a sign of conceptual allegiances."[26] Discreet vocabularies may be the effectual signs of discreet communities—and "early modern" (as we call it) Europe was teeming with confessional groups in sometimes bloody competition with one another, oftentimes over terms that they otherwise shared (e.g., "Antichrist," "church," "reformation," etc.). Quentin Skinner rightly calls this "semantic confusion,"[27] and it was endemic to the period studied here. The Reformation is nonetheless treated as a coherent and formative episode in the development of modern Western history; it is generally assumed that it happened like we are so often told, with an unknown German monk in late 1517 unimpressively nailing up a set of theses for debate that, quite unexpectedly, changed the course of history.[28] And of course that was the beginning of "the" Reformation, for what else would we call Luther's act? (And of course the Reformation spilled over into wars of religion, which then resulted in the Enlightenment's secularizing tendencies, etc.) Allow me to gently counter that the meaning(s) of political and religious keywords—in this case, "reformation"—should be determined through investigation rather than assumed from the outset, just as the transformation(s) of meaning and its subsequent dissemination(s) should be approached as potentially unexpected developments. Such an approach yields a very different narrative of "early modern" religious change.

Digital databases such as Early English Books Online (EEBO) have facilitated this methodological shift. At first glance, the linguistic approach to history might appear the historiographical version of a Google search. Through EEBO, we can rapidly amass a vast number of "hits" on any given term, and by using the N-gram results of the online *EarlyPrint Lab*, we can generate indicative (but not exhaustive) visualizations of the same. The N-gram on reformation shown in Figure I.1 very much reflects the conclusions of this study.

Such research should be done; the tools are genuinely remarkable. However, a word of caution is also in order. It is not enough to use databases as a way of hunting for words or even phrases. Because vocabulary is not neutral, historians should attend to the metaphors and metonyms that pervade the sources under

---

Political Thought and History, Chiefly in the Eighteenth Century (Cambridge: Cambridge University Press, 1985), esp. ch. 1; J.G.A. Pocock, *Political Thought and History: Essays on Theory and Method* (Cambridge: Cambridge University Press, 2009).

[26] Ilaria L.E. Ramelli and David Konstan, *Terms for Eternity: Aiônios and Aïdios in Classical and Christian Texts* (Piscataway: Gorgias Press, 2013), p. 3

[27] Skinner, *Visions of Politics*, Vol. 1, p. 168.

[28] The accuracy of the story about Luther nailing up his Ninety-Five Theses has recently been questioned. See Peter Marshall, *1517: Martin Luther and the Invention of the Reformation* (Oxford: Oxford University Press, 2017); Thomas Albert Howard, *Remembering the Reformation: An Inquiry into the Meanings of Protestantism* (Oxford: Oxford University Press, 2017).

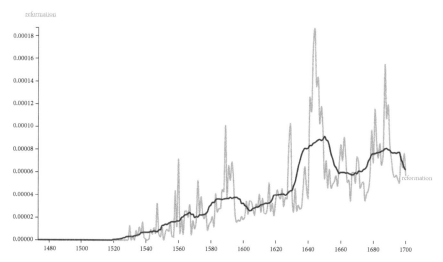

Figure I.1. The x-axis looks at twenty-year increments; the y-axis measures the word's relative frequency (how often it appears once divided by the total number of words in the corpus for that year). The black line is the rolling average per year, while the gray line is frequency per year. The graph is available online: http://earlyprint.wustl.edu/url/1622148819. Created May 26, 2021.

analysis.[29] Readers of this study will therefore find the "great men" of the time period, with their supposedly "great doctrines," placed firmly in the background. In the foreground they will instead find the acute apocalypticism that possessed Latin Christian literary culture between the fifteenth and seventeenth centuries, which debated without resolution the meaning of the social "body" and its monstrous converse. When the intellectual history of the Reformation focuses on matters such as soteriological speculation, it too often presumes that high intellectual debate should have priority.[30] But this is not always helpful. To borrow again from another, unrelated historical work, "Perhaps more than any seemingly inherent logic, the global history of concepts depends on how rival human actors choose to deploy them, for good or for ill."[31] Agency produces semantic transformations. Intellectual history is better studied by focusing neither on supposedly great men nor their allegedly great ideas, but upon "paradigm" or "discursive" shifts[32]—that is, the contingent development of new meanings, made possible

---

[29] In distinguishing thus, I am wholly indebted to George Lakoff and Mark Johnson, *Metaphors We Live By* (Chicago: The University of Chicago Press, 2003).

[30] A good example here is the immense amount published over the last half century on "Calvinism," "Arminianism," and "Anti-Calvinism" in early modern England.

[31] Samuel Moyn, *The Last Utopia: Human Rights in History* (Cambridge and London: The Belknap Press of Harvard University Press, 2010), p. 88.

[32] For paradigms, see Thomas Kuhn, *The Structure of Scientific Revolutions: 50th Anniversary Edition* (Chicago and London: The University of Chicago Press, 2012), ch. 5; for discourses, see Pocock, *Virtue, Commerce, and History*, ch. 1.

by historical actors, which then render further exercises of agency also comprehensible. In what follows, there is no such thing as the history of "ideas," only history as reconstructed from texts, the import of which then depends upon subsequent print history and/or the reception and development of a given text's vocabulary.

The reader will, I trust, agree that all of this is eminently practical. In fact, it yields a methodological opportunity. Moving forward, it would be helpful if historians would distinguish between *organic* and *synthetic* historical descriptors—or, to use terminology that has become common in pedagogy, we might also term the former *synchronous* and the latter *asynchronous*. *Organic* or *synchronous* descriptors are those that arose in the time period that they purport to describe. However, *synthetic* or *asynchronous* descriptors are those that arose at an unspecified period afterward; they were invented or crafted out of diverse and even dissimilar materials. To borrow from Hans-Georg Gadamer, a synthetic descriptor is produced by a "fusion of horizons,"[33] in which the concerns of a later era are used to render intelligible the events of an earlier period. To look briefly ahead, readers will find that the term "Scottish Reformation" was (and is) an *organic* historical descriptor because it was used by its protagonists. But "English Reformation" was (and is) a *synthetic* historical descriptor. It was first used a century after the events that it sought to describe, and was intended to not just elucidate the Tudor past, but to address the arguments that propelled the British civil wars of the 1640s. Gadamer believed that understanding always entailed a fusion of horizons, but he also argued that its value depended upon a larger interpretive community. "In a tradition this process of fusion is continually going on, for there old and new are always combining into something of living value, without either being explicitly foregrounded from the other."[34] Historical scholarship, however, is a descriptive rather than traditional endeavor. Historians should ask whether scholarship is well served by maintaining a *synthetic* historical descriptor ("the English Reformation") whose value derives from the normative commitments of a faith community (Anglican Christianity).

I am not claiming that it is wrong to use the term "English Reformation" to denote mid-Tudor religious history. Nor am I calling for the abandonment of "Protestant Reformation." However, historians need to recognize when and where our terminology embeds us within an interpretive tradition, and we should distinguish between that tradition and the period under analysis (in this case, "early modern" religious history). Two examples should help make this clear. First, it makes little sense to describe early modern religious change without primary reference to the conciliar councils of Constance, Basel, Lateran V, and

---

[33] Hans-Georg Gadamer, *Truth and Method*, second revised ed., translated by Joel Weinsheimer and Donald G. Marshall (London and New York: Continuum, 2004), pp. 300–5.
[34] Gadamer, *Truth and Method*, p. 305.

Trent; perhaps the largest international events of their day, and all foregrounded "reformation" as their singular keyword. If modern historians instead foreground the career and influence of Martin Luther, we have chosen to cultivate a distinctly Protestant historiographical tradition. There is no getting around it.

My second example turns to England. If Puritans had succeeded in their religious aims, we would most likely describe the mid-seventeenth, rather than the mid-sixteenth century, as the English Reformation. As I show in Chapter 4, many contemporaries termed the events of the 1640s as "reformation." What if we today used "English Reformation" to denote the religious developments of that unhappy decade? We might write that, patterned upon events in Scotland the previous century, the English Reformation was a failure; driven forward by civil war, it ground to a halt in 1660 with the Restoration of crown and miter. One possible benefit here is that we could drop from our historiographical lexicon the phrase "English Revolution," which reads the 1640s forward by focusing on the revolutions of the late eighteenth century. Some might consider this a strange proposal, but the simple fact of the matter is that describing Tudor religious history as the "English Reformation" perpetuates a distinctly Anglican historiographical tradition. So, should we maintain the Anglican practice, reject it for the Puritan attempt, or do something else entirely? Let us cultivate space for a conversation on whether to maintain historiographical traditions whose familiarity has obscured their value-laden origins. I am not inclined to terminological iconoclasm, but it is methodologically preferable to use organic descriptors. When unavailable, we should develop less value-laden modes of description.

Chapter Outline

The five chapters that now follow trace the history, in an English context, of three discourses: reformation by church council, reformation by revolt, and reformation as past historical event. The focus is upon perceptions and descriptions of religious change, rather than the content thereof; thus I offer the barest outline of developments during the reign of Edward VI, and nothing at all concerning religious changes during the reign of Charles I. Several themes thread the volume. First is the twofold conviction that it was violence—not theology—that drove Christian division, and it was apocalyptic—not soteriology—that vindicated violence.[35] Second, I lay far greater stress upon official confessional documents than

---

[35] My focus on apocalyptic rather than soteriological concerns is partially inspired by Richard Muller, *Christ and the Decree: Christology and Predestination in Reformed Theology from Calvin to Perkins*, new ed. (Grand Rapids: Baker Academic, 2008). Muller denies that predestination was the *principium* of Reformed theology. In this, his conclusions are quite different than the major trend in British historiography of the English Reformation, which has long argued that an initially "Reformed" consensus was challenged by an Arminian counterinsurgency that displaced soteriology for liturgy and

is standard within contemporary British historiography. Following Richard Muller, "confessions transcend individuals and provide ecclesial statement."[36] Importantly, confessions also help us avoid the "great man" approach too often characteristic of Reformation historiography. Finally, I offer recurring discussions of how English perceptions of Luther changed. This will enable the reader to contrast the perspectives of sixteenth- and seventeenth-century English authors with how we today tell the story of the English Reformation (and, by extension, the reformations of sixteenth-century Europe more broadly). In the words of Herbert Butterfield, "History is not the study of origins; rather it is the analysis of all the mediations by which the past was turned into our present."[37] We never view the past directly but see it only through its many historiographical mediations, some of which are older, while others are of more recent vintage.

The first chapter studies conciliar reformation. The councils of Constance and Basel strove for "reformation in head and members" ("reformatio in capite et membris"), bequeathing to the sixteenth century a vision of reformation defined by a distinctly corporeal "social imaginary."[38] When rightly ordered, the Church was described as a human body, but when disordered described as a monster, an image connoting divine judgment. Councils aimed to thread the eye of an apocalyptic needle, staving off divine wrath through the attainment of *reformatio*. Tracing this conciliar discourse through the Fifth Lateran Council and the Council of Trent, the first chapter sets more famous sixteenth-century episodes, such as Martin Luther's protest and the schism between Henry VIII and the papacy, within the same—inescapably apocalyptic—context.

Chapters 2 and 3 analyze English debates about reformation against the crucial backdrop of Scottish developments. To put the matter bluntly, under Elizabeth I and James I, the English produced no coherent narrative of "reformation." North of the border, however, Scottish evangelicals initially advocated reformation "by force of arms," which they used to justify the abrogation of papal authority, the mass, and a wide range of other religious ceremonies and practices. Then followed their historical apologetic. Knox's *Historie* was a historiographical watershed and the first account of a national reformation in the British Isles (and perhaps elsewhere, too). It must be recognized that Knox transformed *reformatio* by abandoning its conciliar institutional matrix, but he retained every vestige of long-familiar apocalyptic meaning. As with councils, so too with revolt, *reformatio*

sacraments. The classic statement of this view remains Nicholas Tyacke, *Anti-Calvinists: The Rise of English Arminianism c. 1590–1640*, new ed. (Oxford: Oxford University Press, 1990). All of this moves well outside the concerns of the present volume.

[36] Richard Muller, *Post-Reformation Reformed Dogmatics: The Rise and Development of Reformed Orthodoxy, ca. 1520 to ca. 1725*, second ed., 4 Vols. (Grand Rapids: Baker Academic, 2003), Vol. 2, p. 80.

[37] Herbert Butterfield, *The Whig Interpretation of History* (New York and London: W.W. Norton & Company, 1965), p. 47.

[38] Charles Taylor, *Modern Social Imaginaries* (Durham and London: Duke University Press, 2003).

sought to avert divine chastisement. However, between Elizabeth's accession and the death of James, no comparable historiography developed in England. To the contrary, the union of crowns only revealed the profound disparity between the religious cultures of each nation.

The fourth and fifth chapters encompass the reigns of Charles I and Charles II. As the civil wars instantiated apocalyptic violence in ways hitherto unknown in England, Anglican apologists coined "the English Reformation" to defend their church against domestic supporters of the Scottish Reformation, an event that contemporaries singled out for its violence and illegality. Anglicans used their neologism to denote select events from Tudor history, which they portrayed as peaceful and legal, and the total converse of events north of the border. Apocalypticism sought change in the present to avoid future judgment, but historical writing looked to the past to critique contemporary events. Effectively neutralizing the apocalyptic by fixing the bounds of reformation within the mid-sixteenth century, "the English Reformation" was a narrative that presented a pristine vision of the English past, and one that apologists endeavored to preserve in the 1640s and 1650s amidst civil war, regicide, and political oppression. Their novel apologetic blossomed into a rich but pointed historiography between 1660, when the monarchy and the British episcopal churches were restored, and 1685, when Charles II died. The English Reformation thus emerges as one of the most persuasive and skillfully crafted of all early modern religious polemics.

1

In Head and in Members

Discourses of Reformation, *c.*1414–1563

He [Henry VIII] plainly saw yt no waie there was to a reformacion,
but by this only meane, if the autoritie and usurped supremitie of the
See of Rome wer extirped, abolished, & clene extinct.

Nicholas Udall (1548)[1]

Introduction

Fifteenth- and sixteenth-century church councils described their work as *reformatio* ("reformation"). Between 1414, when the Council of Constance began, and 1563, when the Council of Trent concluded, *reformatio* was the keyword of dozens of conciliar resolutions. Because the Catholic church was the largest institution in Latin Christendom, its ecumenical councils were massive international events. Attendees came from every corner of Latin Christendom and sometimes beyond, thus rendering conciliar *reformatio* an international religious discourse familiar to all. Constance set the standard for later councils by publicly stating its desire to restore both unity and orthodoxy in the church,[2] but cohesion proved elusive. Rival papal allegiances tore the church apart between 1378 and 1417, and then again between 1439 and 1449. The latter half of the fifteenth century saw recurrent local schisms, particularly in the Holy Roman Empire,[3] and the sixteenth century saw the same throughout Latin Christendom from 1511 onward. With schism proliferating and the papacy often slow to respond, the Council of Trent ultimately commanded little support and could not secure international religious consensus. *Reformatio* eventually acquired new meanings in those locales, like England, that had separated from both the papacy and the councils of the Catholic church. But at least initially, in the wake of Tudor schism, the English did not articulate a comprehensive vision of domestic reformation.

[1] Erasmus, *The First Tome or Volume of the Paraphrase of Erasmus vpon the Newe Testamente* (London, 1548; STC 2854.3), sig. iii. v.

[2] DEC, Vol. 1, pp. 407 (unity; session 3), 411 (orthodoxy; session 8).

[3] An extensive overview is in Heiko A. Oberman, Daniel E. Zerfoss, and William J. Courtenay (eds.), *Defensorium Obedientiae Apostolicae et Alia Documenta* (Cambridge: The Belknap Press of Harvard University Press, 1968), pp. 1–59.

How the English Reformation was Named: The Politics of History, c. 1400–1700. Benjamin M. Guyer, Oxford University Press. © Benjamin M. Guyer 2022. DOI: 10.1093/oso/9780192865724.003.0002

The first section of this chapter offers a broad overview of how reformation was discussed from Constance to Trent. Consistent imagery, such as "reformation in head and in members," defined the conciliar goals during this 150-year period. Practically everyone, including Martin Luther, described reformation as the work of church councils. Explicating ideas of the ecclesial body, the chapter then traces how apocalyptic fears of monstrosity were intimately related to the schisms that Latin Christendom experienced. With reformation clearly defined as the work of church councils, the third section notes that neither Henry VIII nor Edward VI applied the same imagery and vocabulary to the English church after the 1534 break with the papacy—and this renders it unlikely that either monarch considered their actions the royal equivalent of conciliar reformation. The chapter concludes by analyzing the liturgical developments that took place under Edward VI. Where religious change did occur in mid-Tudor England, it was more sporadic and haphazard than contemporaries understood the term "reformation" to signify.

Conciliar Imaginaries

Conceptual continuity threaded the councils of Constance (1414–18), Basel (1431–49), Lateran V (1512–17), and Trent (1545–47, 1551–52, 1562–63).[4] Constance laid the thematic groundwork for its fifteenth- and sixteenth-century successors by describing the purpose of conciliar gathering as *reformatio*. At its third session, the bishops at Constance determined that the council "should not and may not be dissolved until the present schism has been entirely removed and until the church has been reformed [*reformata*] in faith and morals, in head and members."[5] Subsequent councils followed suit, with almost word-for-word consistency. At its second session, Basel affirmed its desire for "the extirpation of heresies and a general reformation [*reformatione*] of morals in the church in head and members."[6] Although more than half a century passed between the conclusion of Basel and the opening of Lateran V, the latter affirmed its hope for "the peace of the whole church, the union of the faithful, the overthrow of heresies and schisms, the reformation [*reformationem*] of morals, and the campaign against the

---

[4] Others also read these four councils together. See, e.g., Nelson H. Minnich, "Councils of the Catholic Reformation: A Historical Survey," in Gerald Christianson, Thomas M. Izbicki, and Christopher M. Bellitto (eds.), *The Church, the Councils, and Reform: The Legacy of the Fifteenth Century* (Washington, D.C.: The Catholic University of America Press, 2008), pp. 27–59. However, I do not read the century and a half between Constance and Trent as "the Catholic Reformation." Nor do I accept that rather teleological view that Trent concluded a long-term redefinition of an "early modern Catholicism." For the latter, see John W. O'Malley, *Trent and All That: Renaming Catholicism in the Early Modern Era* (Cambridge and London: Harvard University Press, 2000).
[5] DEC, Vol. 1, p. 407.   [6] DEC, Vol. 1, p. 457.

dangerous enemies of the faith."[7] Finally, the Council of Trent began in 1545 with aspirations cut from the same cloth:

> for the praise and glory of the holy and undivided Trinity, Father and Son and Holy Spirit, for the increase and advance in esteem of the faith and Christian religion, for the uprooting of heresies, for the peace and unity of the church, for the reformation [*reformationem*] of the clergy and the Christian people, for the crushing and complete removal of the enemies of the Christian name[.][8]

Formulaic descriptions reveal conceptual continuity. *Reformatio* was a discursive *longue durée* that evoked a range of values used time and again for more than a century.[9]

Metaphor enabled especially vivid articulations of conciliar goals. The Constance decree *Frequens* (1417), which called for decennial councils, expressed the importance of reformation through word play and agrarian metaphors; the verb *reformare* ("to reform") was presented as the means of fixing whatever deformed the church. "The frequent holding of general councils is a pre-eminent means of cultivating the Lord's patrimony. It roots out the briars, thorns and thistles of heresies, errors and schisms, corrects deviations, reforms [*reformat*] what is deformed [*deformata*] and produces a richly fertile crop for the Lord's vineyard."[10] Dependent upon Biblical imagery,[11] later councils imitated and explicated the same vocabulary. The early sessions of Basel often drew upon *Frequens*,[12] and Lateran V described itself as tending the field of God.[13] Trent rarely used agrarian imagery,[14] but as already noted, *reformatio* defined its aspirations as well. And, as later chapters will detail, the contrast of "reformed" with "deformed" remained a rhetorical commonplace well into the seventeenth century.

Of greater long-term import was Constance's detailed use of corporeal imagery. The councils from Constance to Trent inherited a richly detailed, metonymic vision of Christian harmony. The phraseology "in head and in members"

---

[7] DEC, Vol. 1, p. 595 (session 1).   [8] DEC, Vol. 2, e.g., p. 660 (session 1).

[9] Berndt Hamm, "Farewell to Epochs in Reformation History: A Plea," *Reformation & Renaissance Review*, Vol. 16, No. 3 (Nov., 2014), pp. 211–45; see also John Van Engen, "Multiple Options: The World of the Fifteenth-Century Church," *Church History*, Vol. 77, No. 2 (Jun., 2008), pp. 257–84; John Van Engen, "A World Astir: Europe and Religion in the Early Fifteenth Century," in J. Patrick Hornbeck II and Michael van Dussen (eds.), *Europe After Wyclif* (New York: Fordham University Press, 2017), pp. 11–45.

[10] DEC, Vol. 1, p. 438 (session 39).   [11] 1 Cor. 3:5–9.

[12] DEC, Vol. 1, e.g., pp. 455 (session 1), 457 (session 2), 466 (session 11), 481 (session 19).

[13] DEC, Vol. 1, e.g., pp. 604 (session 6), 605 (session 8), 610 (session 9), 626 (session 10), 651 (session 12). The *Libellus ad Leonem X*, the most extensive *reformatio* proposal at Lateran V, similarly described the church as a vineyard; see Stephen M. Beall and John J. Schmitt (eds. and trans.), *Libellus: Addressed to Leo X, Supreme Pontiff* (Milwaukee: Marquette University Press, 2016), p. 229.

[14] DEC, Vol. 2, p. 701 (session 13).

("in capite et in membris") indicated that *reformatio* pertained to the entire ecclesial body. From inception to conclusion, Constance regularly used the same somatic metaphor to articulate its expectations.[15] Although Basel split in 1437 and entered into a decade-long schism two years later, it initially maintained the corporeal imagery used by its more illustrious predecessor.[16] Lateran V and Trent presumed the priority of papal headship, but each council identified diverse areas in need of *reformatio*; among other matters, the former sought the *reformatio* of both preaching and the office of cardinal,[17] while the latter urged the *reformatio* of holy orders, especially the episcopal office, and sacramental rites.[18] All four councils sought the reformation of the entire Christian body.

Belief in a social "body" persisted through the fifteenth, sixteenth, and seventeenth centuries, but came from much older sources. By using human anatomy to describe collective life, corporate bodies—such as the church, the state, or voluntary civic organizations[19]—obscured any difference between metaphor and metonym. Christians had used such figures of speech since the mid-first century, when the apostle Paul described the church with a series of somatic images in his first (surviving) letter to Christians living in Corinth. As in the writings of Aristotle and Cicero, metonymy operated as a broad ethical guide for describing the interrelated character of community. "For just as the body is one and has many members, and all the members of the body, though many, are one body, so it is with Christ."[20] After framing a series of possible disputes between parts of the body—for example, the eye attempting to dispense with the hand, or the head attempting to dispense with the feet—Paul summarized his exhortation by writing, "Now you are the body of Christ and individually members of it."[21] From then on, the body occupied a privileged place in the Christian imaginary.

Three developments from later centuries necessitated the bifurcation that Constance and later councils presumed between "head" and "members."[22] First was the belief that the pope was *vicarius Christi* (vicar of Christ). This title was imperial in origin and referred to the idea, found in the Apocalypse in the New Testament, that Christ was a king who would someday return to earth and assume

---

[15] DEC, Vol. 1, e.g., pp. 408 (session 4), session 409 (session 5), 416 (session 12), 444 (session 40).

[16] DEC, Vol. 1, e.g., pp. 457 (session 2), 467 (session 11), 493 (session 22), 497 (session 23); see also p. 477 (session 18), where the council cites *Haec Sancta*, the decree passed at session 5 of Constance.

[17] DEC, Vol. 1, pp. 617–21 (on cardinals), 634–8 (on preaching).

[18] DEC, Vol. 2, e.g., pp. 698–701 (session 13), 714–18 (session 14), 728–32 (session 21), 737–41 (session 22), 744–59 (session 23), 759–73 (session 24).

[19] Alexander Russell, *Conciliarism and Heresy in Fifteenth-Century England: Collective Authority in the Age of the General Councils* (Cambridge: Cambridge University Press, 2017), ch. 3, esp. pp. 106–9.

[20] 1 Cor. 12:12 (NRSV).

[21] 1 Cor. 12:27 (NRSV).

[22] Christopher M. Bellitto, "The Reform Context of the Great Western Schism," in Joëlle Rollo-Koster and Thomas M. Izbicki (eds.), *A Companion to the Great Western Schism* (Leiden: Brill, 2009), pp. 303–31, here pp. 303–5; Francis Oakley, *The Conciliarist Tradition: Constitutionalism in the Catholic Church 1300–1870* (Oxford: Oxford University Press, 2003), pp. 22–31, 66–81; Phillip H. Stump, *The Reforms of the Council of Constance (1414–1418)* (Leiden: Brill, 1994), pp. 237–9.

direct sovereignty. The monarchs of Christendom were thus placeholders, exercising Christian rule until the time of Christ's second advent. In the mid-eleventh century, the monk Peter Damian used this imperial title to describe the papacy. Slowly but decisively, *vicarius Christi* became part of papal self-understanding, and beginning in the early twelfth century, some writers applied it exclusively to the papacy.[23] It remained just as central to advocates of papal sovereignty across the centuries studied here.[24] The second development occurred later in the twelfth century during the pontificate of Innocent III. An influential canon lawyer, Innocent sought to define the parameters of papal authority. Building upon the belief that the pope was *vicarius Christi*, Innocent further described the pope as the visible head of the visible church. Influenced by contemporary medical theory, which identified the head as source of life in the human body, the pope made physiological imagery an important facet of papal theology. He observed that "the fullness of all the senses exists as in the head, while in the other members [of the body] there is only a part of the fullness."[25] He applied this to the church and described the papal head as having *plenitudo potestatis*, the "plenitude of power."[26] Innocent's language did not absolve the head of responsibility, but was often used in later centuries to spur the pope toward *reformatio*. As two Camaldolese monks wrote to Pope Leo X during the Fifth Lateran Council, "All of the infirmities that exist in particular members, however, originate from the head, namely from the Supreme Pontiff, as anyone can see."[27] To exercise his office rightly, the pope could not rule by fiat but had to instead care for the entire church. Like other living bodies, the ecclesial body operated in a particular way. Head and members were interdependent.

The third development drew a corollary from the other two. In his 1302 bull *Unam Sanctam*, Pope Boniface VIII articulated an especially demanding vision of papal authority.[28] Like Innocent III, Boniface presumed that the church was a single body with a single head. The church, he wrote, "represents one mystical body whose head is Christ, while the head of Christ is God."[29] As the visible head of the visible church, the pope was "the vicar of Christ" for all Christians living on

---

[23] Agostino Paravicini-Bagliani, *The Pope's Body*, trans. David S. Peterson (Chicago and London: The University of Chicago Press, 2000), pp. 58–9.

[24] See, e.g., Beall and Schmitt, *Libellus*, p. 35.

[25] Innocent III, "On the Consecration of the Supreme Pontiff," in *Between God & Man: Six Sermons on the Priestly Office*, trans. Corrine J. Vause and Frank C. Gardiner (Washington, D.C.: The Catholic University of America Press, 2004), pp. 23–4; on Innocent III and medical theory, see Paravicini-Bagliani, *The Pope's Body*, pp. 179–80, 186–8.

[26] Paravicini-Bagliani, *The Pope's Body*, p. 60.   [27] Beall and Schmitt, *Libellus*, p. 201.

[28] Joëlle Rollo-Koster, *Avignon and its Papacy, 1309–1417: Popes, Institutions, and Society* (Lanham: Rowman & Littlefield, 2015), pp. 27–34. *Unam Sanctam* was, however, abrogated in 1306 by Clement V, successor of Boniface VIII.

[29] Boniface VIII, *Unam Sanctam*, in Brian Tierney (ed.), *The Crisis of Church and State 1050–1300* (Toronto: University of Toronto Press and the Medieval Academy of America, 1988), p. 188.

earth.[30] From these claims, Boniface deduced that the pope was necessary not only for ecclesial order but for the salvation of Christians. The pope concluded his bull in uncompromising terms: "we declare, state, define and pronounce that it is altogether necessary to salvation for every human creature to be subject to the Roman Pontiff."[31] Because Christ would someday have total spiritual dominion, the pope, as placeholder, wielded the same until Christ's return. Such dominion could no more be divided than the body decapitated. Although abrogated by his immediate successor Clement V, the argument of *Unam Sanctam* recurred throughout subsequent centuries. Predicated upon a basic biological datum, the apostle Paul's application of ancient political imagery to an early Christian community animated an extensive body of later theological reflection. By the time of Constance, metaphor had long since become metonym.

Anatomic precision gave church councils more than just a prescriptive vocabulary. For contemporaries, the harmonious proportionality of the rightly ordered body stood opposite monstrosity, which they understood most broadly as physical disorder or deformity. By invoking the body with such frequency, Constance and later councils also conjured its converse. When Boniface VIII addressed the unity of the church in *Unam Sanctam*, he contrasted it with monstrosity: "there is one body and one head . . . not two heads as though it [the church] were a monster."[32] Just as the body signified ecclesial, political, and voluntary forms of corporate order, monstrosity denoted disorder for the same forms of community—and, sometimes, a fear of divine judgment. Beginning in the fourteenth century, monstrosity acquired apocalyptic connotations, often directed against the papacy. Among the earliest such productions was *Genus Nequam* (The Beginning of Iniquity), a collection of disparate prophetic texts that alleged a connection between the papacy and the Antichrist. Consisting of both allusive artwork and written commentary, *Genus Nequam* circulated across all of Latin Christendom; it grew in popularity during the fifteenth century, and was printed throughout the two centuries that followed, including in Catholic countries.[33] The Great Schism seemed to confirm some of *Genus Nequam*'s worst predictions. According to contemporary commentators, a church divided between papal allegiances was under divine judgment, for it was a body with two heads—and thus a monster.[34] In the fifteenth century, the English priest John Wyclif and the Bohemian priest Jan Hus each described the papacy in monstrous terms, the former alleging that

[30] Boniface VIII, *Unam Sanctam*, p. 188.   [31] Boniface VIII, *Unam Sanctam*, p. 189.

[32] Boniface VIII, *Unam Sanctam*, p. 188. Such terminology was, however, older; see Paravicini-Bagliani, *The Pope's Body*, p. 146.

[33] See esp. Martha H. Fleming (ed.), *The Late Medieval Pope Prophecies: The Genus nequam Group* (Tempe: Arizona Center for Medieval and Renaissance Studies, 1999); Renate Blumenfeld-Kosinski, *Poets, Saints, and Visionaries of the Great Schism, 1378–1417* (University Park: The Pennsylvania State University Press, 2006), pp. 166–78, details the geographic and confessional spread of the document in "early modern" Europe.

[34] Blumenfeld-Kosinski, *Poets, Saints, and Visionaries of the Great Schism*, e.g., pp. 125–6.

the pope was joined to the "monstrous person of the Antichrist."[35] Constance condemned the polemics of both clergymen,[36] and yet shared the same metonymic assumptions. The church was called to union as a single, visible body with a single, visible papal head.

Monstrosity and its attendant apocalypticism became a moral vocabulary easily deployed by all sides in later ecclesiastical disputes. The papal continuation of the Council of Basel condemned its conciliar rival as "human monsters," soiled with "every stain of corruption."[37] When those still gathered in Basel elected their own pope, the Roman Pope Eugenius IV and his supporters, then meeting in Florence, countered that the new papal allegiance was a "most wicked monster" and the "first-born son of Satan."[38] Between 1439 and 1449, the church again possessed two rival heads. But it was not only high-ranking ecclesiastics who thought in such terms. Laity were equally inclined to discern monstrosity in the wider world. Even in the sixteenth and seventeenth centuries, Christians of diverse theological persuasions remained convinced that disruptions of the natural order indicated the imminent possibility of divine wrath. Generally classed as prodigies, the births of deformed children or animals, like the appearance of unusual cosmological phenomena, were ripe for apocalyptic interpretation.[39] Preternatural events sometimes inspired decades and even centuries of recurring apocalyptic speculation. Fifteenth-century opponents of the papacy reveled in such polemics, as did sixteenth-century evangelicals such as Martin Luther and Philip Melanchthon.[40] No more than 10 percent of Luther's writings were printed outside of German-speaking lands,[41] but among his small number of internationally significant works was the apocalyptic pamphlet *The Pope-Ass Explained* (1523). It drew upon the legend of a donkey discovered in 1495 whose disfigurement was widely believed to reveal divine displeasure. Luther and Melanchthon literally anatomized the beast for apocalyptic insights. For example, one of its hooves allegedly signified pastoral oppression, while the tail, reputedly so deformed that it looked like a dragon, exposed the papacy's manipulative use of fear. Readers across Latin Christendom proved an eager audience for such material. Through the end of the sixteenth

[35] DEC, Vol. 1, p. 423, n. 20 (session 15).
[36] For Wyclif, see DEC, Vol. 1, pp. 421–6; for Hus, see pp. 426–31 (both session 15).
[37] DEC, Vol. 1, p. 529 (session 7).   [38] DEC, Vol. 1, p. 562 (session 9).
[39] Katharine Park and Lorraine J. Daston, "Unnatural Conceptions: The Study of Monsters in Sixteenth- and Seventeenth-Century France and England," *Past & Present*, No. 92 (Aug., 1981), pp. 20–54; Lorraine Daston and Katharine Park, *Wonders and the Order of Nature 1150–1750* (New York: Zone Books, 1998), pp. 173–214.
[40] Lawrence P. Buck, "'Anatomia Antichristi': Form and Content of the Papal Antichrist," *The Sixteenth Century Journal*, Vol. 42, No. 2 (Summer, 2011), pp. 349–68; Lawrence P. Buck, *The Roman Monster: An Icon of the Papal Antichrist in Reformation Polemics* (Kirksville: Truman State University Press, 2014); Frances Courtney Kneupper, *The Empire at the End of Time: Identity and Reform in Late Medieval German Prophecy* (Oxford: Oxford University Press, 2016).
[41] Andrew Pettegree, "Print Workshops and Markets," in Ulinka Rublack (ed.), *The Oxford Handbook of the Protestant Reformations* (Oxford: Oxford University Press, 2017), pp. 373–89, at p. 383.

century, *The Pope-Ass Explained* saw at least twenty-three editions totaling more than twenty thousand copies in a half dozen languages.[42] When Constance called for later councils to reform "what is deformed,"[43] and when later councils adopted the same images and vocabulary for themselves, their language collectively and consistently blurred any distinctions between the prescriptive and the descriptive. Whatever its other stated goals, *reformatio* was also ecclesial monster hunting, and thus a matter of urgent necessity.

Conciliar Disparities

Although *reformatio* provided a shared vocabulary, imagery, and set of ideals for Latin Christendom, it was not enough for consensus. Attendance across councils was inconsistent. Constance was the gold standard. More than 2,200 official representatives participated, including bishops, theologians, canon lawyers, religious, and royal delegations.[44] Almost ten thousand more were present in an unofficial capacity,[45] and it has been estimated that, when combined with the number of occasional visitors and other pilgrims, perhaps as many as seventy thousand people attended the council at one point or another.[46] Basel was quite different. It opened with a single attendee and the pope tried to dissolve the council twice in just its first year.[47] The council's subsequent split, election of a rival pope, and ensuing decade-long schism all help explain why no council was called for the remainder of the fifteenth century. Lateran V saw greater episcopal participation. It is only a later stereotype, developed by Erasmus of Rotterdam, that the council was a failure.[48] Poor record keeping unwittingly aided his allegation; among other problems, names were misspelled and some attendees have never been successfully identified.[49] Nonetheless, Lateran V saw a majority of Latin Christendom's bishops in attendance; at least 350 episcopal sees were represented by 431 participants, making it more representative than any of the

[42] Buck, *The Roman Monster*, p. 160.   [43] DEC, Vol. 1, p. 438 (session 39).
[44] Phillip H. Stump, "The Council of Constance and the End of the Schism," in Joëlle Rollo-Koster and Thomas M. Izbicki (eds.), *A Companion to the Great Western Schism (1378–1417)* (Leiden: Brill, 2009), pp. 395–442, at p. 403, describes Constance as the "largest medieval Church council"; see Blumenfeld-Kosinski, *Poets, Saints, and Visionaries of the Great Schism*, p. 201, for official participants.
[45] Oakley, *The Conciliarist Tradition*, p. 21.
[46] Peter L. McDermott, "Nicholas of Cusa: Continuity and Conciliation at the Council of Basel," *Church History*, Vol. 67, No. 2 (Jun., 1998), pp. 254–73, at p. 259.
[47] Michiel Decaluwé and Gerald Christianson, "Historical Survey," in Michiel Decaluwé, Thomas M. Izbicki, and Gerald Christianson (eds.), *A Companion to the Council of Basel* (Leiden: Brill, 2017), pp. 8–37, at pp. 13–14.
[48] Nelson H. Minnich, *The Fifth Lateran Council (1512–1517)* (Aldershot and Brookfield: Variorum, 1993), Essay I, pp. 157–60.
[49] Minnich, *The Fifth Lateran Council (1512–1517)*, Essay I, pp. 165–74, esp. pp. 168, 172.

sessions that later occurred at Trent.[50] And yet, Trent's three sessions collectively exercised far greater long-term influence on Christian history. It opened with only twenty-nine of Europe's seven hundred Catholic bishops present. During the first ten sessions, the last of which occurred in 1547, and during the six sessions between 1551 and 1552, not more than a hundred bishops were present.[51] It was only in the last year of Trent's third session (1562–63) that attendance reached its maximum: 280 bishops, that is, approximately 40 percent of the Catholic episcopate. Such statistics reveal, at best, an idiosyncratic enthusiasm for conciliar gatherings.

More problematically, councils lacked a consistent vision of what needed reform. Each council appealed to unity and orthodoxy, and all were agreed on matters of longstanding consensus, such as the condemnation of simony,[52] but debates and decrees at one council were often either ignored or rejected by those that came later. For example, Constance passed *Frequens*, which Basel regularly cited, but decennial councils never became the norm; Lateran V witnessed discussion of *Frequens* but did not endorse it,[53] and Trent quietly set the decree aside.[54] So too, unlike later councils, Constance entertained extended discussion of indulgences. In a *reformatio* proposal sent with the English delegation, the University of Oxford complained of excessive fees charged by the Roman curia for "letters of indulgence, absolutions, favors, [and] provisions," alleging that "since all these things are judged for sale, they are all suspected of having been distorted by simony."[55] The committee that dealt with the matter showed considerable willingness to reject most indulgences,[56] arguing that they tended "more to the deception and derision of the Christian people than to the salvation of souls."[57] Indulgences given since 1378 were an especial target, but the outcome of these discussions is regrettably unknown; the text of the decree has been lost.[58] Basel and Lateran V, however, issued indulgences, and Trent defined and defended the same.[59]

---

[50] Minnich, *The Fifth Lateran Council (1512–1517)*, Essay I, pp. 181–97 (for participants) and pp. 197–204 (for sees represented).

[51] John W. O'Malley, *Trent: What Happened at the Council* (Cambridge and London: The Belknap Press of Harvard University Press, 2013), p. 4.

[52] For Constance, DEC, Vol. 1, p. 448 (session 43); for Basel, DEC, Vol. 1, pp. 471–2 (session 12), 473–4 (session 15), 498 (session 23); for Lateran V, DEC, Vol. 1, pp. 600–2 (session 5), 623 (session 9); for Trent, DEC, Vol. 2, pp. 768, 771 (session 24).

[53] Beall and Schmitt, *Libellus*, p. 221.   [54] O'Malley, *Trent*, pp. 270–1.

[55] David Wilkins, *Concilia Magnae Britanniae et Hiberniae*, 4 Vols. (London, 1737; ESTC T138837), Vol. 3, pp. 360–5, at p. 361; "literis super indulgentiis, absolutionibus, gratiis, provisionibus...sicque omnia judicantur venalia, et de simoniaca pravitate suspecta."

[56] Stump, *The Reforms of the Council of Constance*, pp. 67–72.

[57] Stump, *The Reforms of the Council of Constance*, p. 70.

[58] Stump, *The Reforms of the Council of Constance*, p. 70.

[59] For Basel, DEC, Vol. 1, pp. 506–7 (session 24); Lateran V, DEC, Vol. 1, p. 622 (session 9); Trent, DEC, Vol. 2, pp. 796–7 (session 25).

Matters left unresolved by one council sometimes provided fodder for later expressions of dissent. According to Aeneas Sylvius Piccolomini, who authored an eyewitness account of the breakdown at Basel, those who remained in Basel debated the merits of allowing the clergy, including bishops, to marry.[60] The failure of the continuing council rendered such discussions irrelevant, although considerations of clerical marriage circulated in later fifteenth-century texts, particularly in Germany.[61] Lateran V saw proposals for both vernacular liturgy and translations of the Bible,[62] but acted on neither. Trent allowed for vernacular translations of Scripture, provided that they were first vetted and found correct,[63] but it anathematized those who advocated vernacular worship.[64] The rejection of indulgences, the acceptance of clerical marriage, and the endorsement of vernacular worship and vernacular Bibles (even if of sometimes dubious quality) are now considered defining features of Protestantism—but all were the fruit of conciliar disquiet.

Print enabled fifteenth-century loose ends to unravel throughout the century that followed. The fragmentation of Basel had an especially wide orbit of literary influence. Some texts, such as the popular *Reformatio Sigismundi*, were primarily influential at the local level; in addition to seventeen surviving manuscripts, eight editions were printed between 1476 and 1522, all in German-speaking lands.[65] Other works had international influence. Piccolomini's history of the Council of Basel was first printed in the mid-1520s,[66] and later sixteenth-century editions appeared in 1535, 1551, and 1570. Although printed in German lands, it nonetheless shaped historical discourses abroad, such as John Foxe's *Actes and Monuments*;[67] seventeenth-century editions appeared elsewhere in Europe, including London in 1690.[68] Still more influential was Lorenzo Valla's 1440 polemic *On the Forged and Mendacious Donation of Constantine*. The Donation is an anonymously authored work that likely dates from the late eighth century. It claims that the fourth-century Emperor Constantine had given to the pope the western half of the Roman Empire; as the centuries progressed, Constantine came to be seen as an unwitting dupe whose newfound devotion to Christianity unwittingly facilitated the worst excesses of the papacy. Later incorporated into canon law, the Donation was long considered authentic, even among those who

---

[60] Aeneas Sylvius Piccolomini, *De Gestis Concilii Basiliensis Commentariorum Libri II*, ed. and trans. Denys Hay and W.K. Smith, rev. ed. (Oxford: Clarendon Press, 1967), pp. 247–9.

[61] See, e.g., "Reformatio Sigismundi," in Gerald Strauss (ed. and trans.), *Manifestations of Discontent in Germany the Eve of the Reformation* (Bloomington and London: Indiana University Press, 1971), pp. 3–31, at 14–15; for the dissemination of Piccolomini's *De Gestis*, see what follows.

[62] Beall and Schmitt, *Libellus*, pp. 167–71.   [63] DEC, Vol. 2, pp. 664–5 (session 4).

[64] DEC, Vol. 2, p. 736 n. 9 (session 22).   [65] Strauss, *Manifestations*, pp. 3–4.

[66] Piccolomini, *De Gestis*, pp. xxxii–xxxvi.

[67] Elizabeth Evenden and Thomas S. Freeman, *Religion and the Book in Early Modern England: The Making of Foxe's "Book of Martyrs"* (Cambridge: Cambridge University Press, 2011), pp. 176–7.

[68] Piccolomini, *De Gestis*, pp. xxx–xxxvi.

decried its influence.[69] Constance accepted its legitimacy and denounced Wyclif, among other reasons, for rejecting it,[70] and the Council of Basel witnessed recurrent dispute about the Donation as well.[71] Valla, however, used philology to show that the Donation was counterfeit.[72] His exposure of "linguistic barbarisms" revealed that the document's Latin postdated the reign of Constantine by centuries.[73] And, with Constantine's name now unburdened, his legacy became an inspiration—and sometimes a counterweight—to claims of papal authority. Valla's work remained in manuscript until 1506, but by the middle of the sixteenth century was available in its original Latin, as well as five other languages, including English.[74] The text helped convince Luther that the papacy was the Antichrist,[75] a theme elaborated in evangelical works such as his popular *Pope-Ass*. Much sixteenth-century religious history was merely the continuation of fifteenth-century conflict.

Above all, *reformatio* failed to provide a uniform framework for authority. The century and a half between Constance and Trent saw unresolved conflict over the location of ecclesial sovereignty. The four councils collectively entertained disparate and even contradictory determinations on point. At its fifth session, Constance passed *Haec Sancta*, one of its most influential decrees. Quite against the anthropomorphism of papal headship, the council defined itself as having "power immediately from Christ, and that everyone of whatever state or dignity, even papal, is bound to obey it in those matters which pertain to the faith, and the eradication of the said schism."[76] Constance thus subsumed the papacy to the wider ecclesial body. Basel was, at least initially, similar. Most of its decrees opened with a declaration such as, "The holy general synod of Basel, representing the church militant, for an everlasting record."[77] For fifteenth-century conciliarists, *plenitudo potestatis* did not come from the head but from the entire body.

After Basel split and a portion of the council joined the pope in Ferrara, a very different vision of authority was rapidly promulgated. The papal continuation of

---

[69] See esp. Robert Black, "The Donation of Constantine: A New Source for the Concept of the Renaissance?," in Alison Brown (ed.), *Language and Images of Renaissance Italy* (Oxford: The Clarendon Press, 1995), pp. 51–85.

[70] DEC, Vol. 1, p. 413, n. 33.

[71] Thomas A. Fudge, *The Magnificent Ride: The First Reformation in Hussite Bohemia* (Aldershot and Brookfield: Ashgate, 1998), pp. 241, 257; Nicholas of Cusa, *The Catholic Concordance*, ed. and trans. Paul E. Sigmund (Cambridge: Cambridge University Press, 1991), III.II, paras. 294–312, pp. 216–22.

[72] Salvatore I. Camporeale, "Lorenzo Valla's 'Oratio' on the Pseudo-Donation of Constantine: Dissent and Innovation in Early Renaissance Humanism," *Journal of the History of Ideas*, Vol. 57, No. 1 (Jan., 1996), pp. 9–26, at pp. 14–15.

[73] Lorenzo Valla, *On The Donation of Constantine*, trans. G.W. Bowersock (Cambridge and London: Harvard University Press, 2007), p. 73.

[74] Valla, *On The Donation of Constantine*, pp. ix–x.

[75] David M. Whitford, "The Papal Antichrist: Martin Luther and the Underappreciated Influence of Lorenzo Valla," *Renaissance Quarterly*, Vol. 61, No. 1 (Spring, 2008), pp. 26–52; see esp. pp. 28, 40.

[76] DEC, Vol. 1, p. 408 (session 5).   [77] DEC, Vol. 1, p. 456 (session 2).

that council rapidly inverted the formula that introduced so many of Basel's decrees, instead preferring incipits such as, "Eugenius, bishop, servant of the servants of God, for an everlasting record."[78] It was an argument both terse and blunt. Later sessions under the same pope decreed not only that "the Roman pontiff holds the primacy over the whole world" but that "he is the true vicar of Christ, the head of the whole church and the father and teacher of all Christians."[79] When Eastern Christians appealed to the pope for military aid against the Turks, Eugenius and his supporters required their assent to the papal *plenitudo potestatis*.[80] *Unam Sanctam* was thus restored in all but name, and sixteenth-century councils followed the same precedent. The decrees of Lateran V were also set forth in the name of the pope. "Julius, bishop, servant of the servants of God, with the approval of the sacred council, for an everlasting record."[81] It was a successful if unoriginal restatement of papal primacy.[82] At Lateran V, however, papal authority reemerged as a fractious issue, and although it became increasingly contested as the sixteenth century progressed, Trent neither defined the parameters of the papal head nor sought its reformation. The council wholly side-stepped the issue, arguably the most pressing theological question at the time.[83] Tridentine decrees first invoked the Trinity and then continued, "This holy ecumenical and general council of Trent, lawfully assembled in the Holy Spirit, with the same three legates of the apostolic see presiding."[84] At Trent, councils were not representative gatherings whose authority came from the wider body. Rather, papal authority was paramount. Trent saw the conciliar commitments of Constance and Basel placed decisively outside the bounds of Catholic orthodoxy.

Lateran V and Trent helped to further entrench papal primacy, but the fifteenth century had seen royal authority emerge as an important if primarily domestic counterweight to papal assertions. Constance and Basel were inseparable from the imperial legacy of the Holy Roman Emperor Sigismund, who led the way in calling both councils. Sigismund spent his last years working to prevent the breakdown of Basel,[85] and several texts produced during that council praised him by noting the role played by emperors in early Christian councils. In *The Catholic Concordance*, Nicholas of Cusa wrote that although councils in the early church met "with the consent of the Roman pontiff and of the other patriarchs," they were nonetheless "assembled by the emperors."[86] Cusa even advocated restoring *vicarius Christi* as an imperial title.[87] Sigismund's name was

---

[78] DEC, Vol. 1, p. 517 (session 3).   [79] DEC, Vol. 1, p. 528 (session 6).
[80] DEC, Vol. 1, e.g., pp. 557–8 (session 8), 581 (session 11).   [81] DEC Vol. 1, p. 595 (session 2).
[82] Minnich, *The Fifth Lateran Council (1512–1517)*, Essay II, p. 154.
[83] O'Malley, *Trent*, pp. 251–2.   [84] DEC, Vol. 2, p. 662 (session 3).
[85] Michiel Decaluwé, *A Successful Defeat: Eugene IV's Struggle with the Council of Basel for Ultimate Authority in the Church, 1431–1449* (Brussels: Institut Historique Belge de Rome, 2009), pp. 142–6.
[86] Cusa, *The Catholic Concordance*, II.VI, para. 85, p. 63.
[87] Cusa, *The Catholic Concordance*, III.V, paras. 340–42, pp. 233–4.

subsequently attached to the popular German text *Reformatio Sigismundi*, which prophesied a forthcoming emperor who, in messianic fashion, would reform both church and empire. The anonymous author credited Sigismund with calling Constance,[88] an oversimplification echoed by the English chronicler William Caxton.[89] When Erasmus later oppugned the outcome of Lateran V, he recalled an unnamed emperor "who at one time proclaimed them [councils] on his own,"[90] a clear reference to Sigismund. But by this time, other kings had also maneuvered to take greater control of the churches in their lands. France saw the Pragmatic Sanction of Bourges in 1438, which limited papal jurisdiction in France; the Holy Roman Empire concurrently entertained but ultimately failed to ratify a similar proposal.[91] In England, Henry VII placed on his coinage the image of a closed or "imperial" crown, which signified autonomy from the papacy.[92] England's common lawyers made the supporting claim that in England, the king's determinations were superior to those of the pope, and that appeals to the pope were forbidden.[93] Long before the schism with Rome, Henry VIII maintained his father's imperial convictions,[94] and after the split, imperialism became more central to his religious self-understanding. Lateran V secured the abrogation of the Pragmatic Sanction, but the ideas behind it had long since taken root.

Latin Christendom's threefold division of ecclesial authority between popes, kings, and councils proved incommensurable.[95] Each had supporters and each had detractors. Even as Valla's attack began to circulate through the medium of print, the Donation of Constantine became an important theme in papal visual propaganda. Leo X commissioned the school of Raphael to paint the Donation in the Vatican Palace, and Michelangelo painted the Donation in the Sistine Chapel. But Lateran V also saw considerable literary fallout when Erasmus anonymously published his sharp satire *Julius Excluded from Heaven*. Written as a dialogue about ecclesial authority between the apostle Peter and Julius II, who died in 1513, the late Pope was made the mouthpiece for an elaborate theology of papal

---

[88] Strauss, *Manifestations*, pp. 5, 31.

[89] William Caxton, *Polychronicon* (London, 1482; STC 13438), sig. CCCCix.

[90] CWE, Vol. 27, p. 182.   [91] Decaluwé, *A Successful Defeat*, pp. 290–4, 332–6.

[92] David Armitage, *The Ideological Origins of the British Empire* (Cambridge: Cambridge University Press, 2000), p. 34.

[93] Christopher Haigh, *English Reformations: Religion, Politics and Society under the Tudors* (Oxford: Oxford University Press, 1993), pp. 73–4; Decaluwé, *A Successful Defeat*, p. 311, sees the French Pragmatic Sanction and the German *Instrumentum Acceptationis* as akin to English laws against *praemunire*.

[94] Peter Marshall, *Heretics and Believers: A History of the English Reformation* (New Haven and London: Yale University Press, 2017), pp. 94–5; more broadly, see G.W. Bernard, *The Late Medieval English Church: Vitality and Vulnerability before the Break with Rome* (New Haven and London: Yale University Press, 2012), ch. 2.

[95] See, e.g., the documents collected in J.H. Burns and Thomas Izbicki (trans. and eds.), *Conciliarism and Papalism* (Cambridge: Cambridge University Press, 1997).

autonomy. Having heard Julius declare that "The supreme pontiff cannot be censured, even by a general council,"[96] Peter countered:

> But it is precisely because he is supreme that he must be removed: the greater he is, the more damage he can do. Civil laws can not only depose an emperor for misgovernment, but even sentence him to death; how unhappy is the condition of the church if it is obliged to tolerate a subversive pontiff at Rome and cannot by any means rid itself of such a public nuisance.[97]

Julius denied the validity of the comparison, and after running down a list of sins for which no pope could be deposed, he claimed that the pope could not be unseated even for heresy. Exasperated, Peter called for disobedience: "against such a man it is obviously not a general council that is needed, but a rising of the people, armed with stones, to remove him publicly from their midst as a public nuisance to the whole world."[98] The visual marvels of papal propaganda were restricted to those who visited Rome, but Erasmus' literary attack upon papal *plenitudo potestatis* circulated widely.

Sixteenth-century evangelicals thus traversed fault lines more than a century old. Protestantism is often described as advancing a new theology defined by new ideas about salvation,[99] but it may be more helpful to consider that, in light of the foregoing discussion, new soteriologies did not produce institutional fracture; rather, institutional fracture necessitated new soteriologies. Luther's soteriological speculations predated his arguments with the papacy, but his excommunication made the need for a new understanding of salvation quite urgent. If the papacy was either fraudulent or somehow related to the Antichrist, salvation had to be found elsewhere. Evangelicals could not agree upon a variety of doctrinal matters, but as diverse evangelical formations emerged—sometimes unwillingly, as in Luther's excommunication—soteriological convictions both shaped and were shaped by the creation of new confessional bodies. But this transition was slow, and risks occluding the fact that evangelicals initially discussed *reformatio* within a conciliar frame of reference shared entirely by their opponents. When relations with the papacy first soured, Luther began to openly repudiate the view, which Erasmus had placed into the mouth of Julius II, that "The pope and his see are not bound to be subject to Christian councils and decrees."[100] A council was the greatest possible counterweight to perceived papal excess, and for the next several

---

[96] CWE, Vol. 27, p. 178.   [97] CWE, Vol. 27, p. 179.   [98] CWE, Vol. 27, p. 180.

[99] Such is the tendency in, e.g., Rublack, *The Oxford Handbook of the Protestant Reformations*. Its first part, consisting of four chapters, is entitled "The New Theology." For a sometimes critical review of such an approach, see Benjamin M. Guyer, "The Protestant Reformation—A Review Article" (Review no. 2254), *Reviews in History* (June 2018). Available online: https://reviews.history.ac.uk/review/2254, accessed January 20, 2022.

[100] LW, Vol. 31, p. 385.

decades, evangelicals repeatedly stated their desire for conciliar consultation.[101] In his 1520 open letter *To the Christian Nobility of the German Nation Concerning the Reform of the Christian Estate*, Luther exclaimed, "Help us, O God, to get a free, general council which will teach the pope that he, too, is a man, and not more than God, as he sets himself up to be!"[102] Luther called into question the authority of the pope throughout his letter, and championed the rights of the German nation, especially the Holy Roman Emperor, even as he advocated the primacy of Scripture and the independence of councils. A decade later, the signatories of the Augsburg Confession promised that they would participate in "a general, free, Christian council,"[103] and in 1544, John Calvin sent a book-length letter to Emperor Charles V, urging him to convoke a council since the pope had not yet succeeding in doing so. Luther's most extended consideration of ecclesiastical authority appeared in his 1539 treatise *On the Councils and the Church*. Written against the background of Paul III's repeated inability to call a council, Luther rendered reformation and a council synonymous: "We see the necessity for a council or a reformation [eins Concilium oder Reformation] in the church."[104] It was hardly a new perspective. Whatever evangelicals' theological novelties, their equation of a council with *reformatio* was wholly mundane. Without a council, how could one possibly think about, let alone discuss, ecclesial reformation?

No Conciliar *Reformatio*

We now turn to England. Councils were a matter of general Christian respect, although this did not necessarily result in high participation. English attendance at conciliar gatherings fully bottomed out under Henry VIII, but this merely continued a trend in evidence since Basel. Despite the loss of key records surrounding their participation at Constance,[105] the English played an important part in several of its proceedings. They brought with them an extensive reform proposal, the University of Oxford's *Articles Concerning the Reformation of the Entire Church*,[106] and the committee in charge of dealing with indulgences was headed by the bishop of Bath and Wells, Nicholas Bubbewyth.[107] Constance was also

---

[101] Charles P. Arand, Robert Kolb, and James A. Nestingen, *The Lutheran Confessions: History and Theology of The Book of Concord* (Minneapolis: Fortress Press, 2012), 139–58.

[102] LW, Vol. 44, p. 169.

[103] The Augsburg Confession, Preface, 21, in Robert Kolb and Timothy Wengert (eds.), *The Book of Concord: The Confessions of the Evangelical Lutheran Church* (Minneapolis: Fortress Press, 2000), p. 34.

[104] LW, Vol. 41, p. 14; German text in *D. Martin Luthers Werke*, Kritische Gesamtausgabe, Vol. 50 (Weimar: Hermann Böhlaus Nachfolger, 1914), p. 514, l. 16.

[105] On the problem of sources, see Russell, *Conciliarism and Heresy in Fifteenth-Century England*, pp. 12–16.

[106] Stump, *The Reforms of the Council of Constance*, pp. 148–9; the *Articles* may be found in Wilkins, *Concilia Magnae Britanniae et Hiberniae*, Vol. 3, pp. 360–5.

[107] Stump, *The Reforms of the Council of Constance*, pp. 67–72.

important domestically. As manuscript copies of the council's *Acta* circulated, Henry Chichele, Archbishop of Canterbury, used the decrees of Constance as a model for his own domestic leadership in the early 1420s.[108] However, English participation in ecumenical councils later declined. The first English delegation to Basel arrived in 1432 but left the following year; a second delegation arrived in 1434 but left in 1435 as tensions rose between the pope and the council.[109] King Henry VI terminated English support in 1439.[110] However, the English also refused to attend Eugenius IV's council. Some of this was due to circumstance, as the papal envoy who carried the pope's invitation to England was kidnapped en route.[111] But non-participation was also a refusal to side either with the pope against the emperor, or with the emperor against the pope.[112] Fifteenth-century English historical works subsequently praised Constance while largely ignoring Basel.[113] English participation further decreased the following century. Only three English bishops attended Lateran V.[114] Because the first two sessions of Trent occurred after Henry VIII's break with the papacy, no invitation to participate arrived until Trent's third session, which occurred before the excommunication of Elizabeth I in 1570. But the queen, citing fears of domestic disturbance, refused to admit the papal nuncio to England.[115] Beginning with Henry VIII, and continuing with his children Edward VI and Elizabeth I, conciliar *reformatio*, with its international scope, was set aside in favor of an imperially circumscribed royal supremacy.

The English Parliament's 1534 declaration of Henry VIII as "supreme head" of the English church did not, however, automatically transfer papal or conciliar ideals to the king, his church, or his kingdom.[116] There was no precedent for applying the metaphors and ideals of conciliar *reformatio* at the local level without also presuming the continuity of the international framework of Latin

---

[108] Russell, *Conciliarism and Heresy in Fifteenth-Century England*, pp. 23–4.

[109] A.N.E.D. Schofield, "England, the Pope, and the Council of Basel, 1435–1449," *Church History*, Vol. 33, No. 3 (Sept., 1964), pp. 248–78.

[110] Decaluwé and Christianson, "Historical Survey," p. 27.

[111] Margaret Harvey, *England, Rome and the Papacy 1417–1464: The Study of a Relationship* (Manchester: Manchester University Press, 1993), p. 86.

[112] For a general overview, see Margaret Harvey, "England, the Council of Florence and the End of the Council of Basel," in Giuseppe Alberigo (ed.), *Christian Unity: The Council of Ferrara-Florence 1438/39–1989* (Leuven: Leuven University Press, 1991), pp. 203–25.

[113] Caxton, *Polychronicon*, sig. CCCCix; Peter J. Lucas (ed.), *John Capgrave's Abbreuiacion of Cronicles* (Oxford: The Early English Text Society and Oxford University Press, 1983), pp. 242–3, 249.

[114] Minnich, *The Fifth Lateran Council (1512–1517)*, Essay I, p. 176.

[115] O'Malley, *Trent*, p. 170.

[116] The Parliament that began in 1529 is widely known today as the "Reformation Parliament," but no one at the time referred to it as such. As far as I can tell, the proper noun "Reformation Parliament" entered into widespread academic usage with the publication of Andrew Amos, *Observations on the Statutes of the Reformation Parliament in the Reign of King Henry the Eighth* (London: V. & R. Stevens, & G.S. Norton and Cambridge: Deighton, Bell and Co., 1859). Seventeenth-century historians such as Herbert of Cherbury, Peter Heylyn, and Gilbert Burnet wrote of no such event, and searching for the term in the digital database Eighteenth Century Collections Online also yields no hits.

Christendom. Therefore, where domestic—in this case, English—discussions appear similar or even identical in themes and imagery, as in the concept of royal headship, we actually find idiosyncratic rather than consistent uses of a much older, more familiar, and more coherently elaborated discourse of conciliar *reformatio*. The desire for ecclesial reformation had long been articulated with the imagery of "head and members," a phrase curiously but tellingly absent across key religious texts published in England under Henry VIII and Edward VI. The reality of this aporia should hit us far harder than it does. One instead finds only sporadic and topical invocations of "reformation," which suggests that no one at the time could articulate a vision in which those known today as "reformers" aimed "to destroy one Church and build another."[117]

Royal supremacy was the overriding theme across numerous Henrician texts. It was rarely linked with *reformatio*. An especially vivid endorsement of royal headship was the frontispiece of the Great Bible, which portrayed Jesus looking down from Heaven upon Henry, as the latter gave his subjects copies of the Scriptures, then newly translated into English. The proposed canons of 1535 offered a textual approach to the same topic. Henry's Preface defined "Christian kings" as those "to whom not only secular and civil, but also ecclesiastical power has been given."[118] Such authority was "divinely established," and its papal usurpation "contrary to all divine and human right."[119] The doctrine of royal supremacy prefaced many subsequent religious works, such as the Ten Articles of 1536, the Bishops' Book of the following year, and its 1543 revision, also known as the King's Book.[120] *Reformatio* was mentioned far less often across the same texts. The canons called only for the "reformation" of monastic houses.[121] The Ten Articles were equally sporadic, denoting as "refourme" only the modifications of select religious practices. The sixth article affirmed images of saints as "represen-ters of vertue and good example," but then stated, "the rude people shulde not from henseforth take such superstition, as in tyme paste it is thought that the same hath used to do," but should instead "according to this doctrine refourme theyr abuses."[122] Henrician confessional documents emphasized the recent change "in capite" but offered comparatively little "in membris." In England (as else-where, no doubt), religious change was but a haphazard confluence of contingency and conviction.

---

[117] Diarmaid MacCulloch, *The Boy King: Edward VI and the Protestant Reformation* (Berkeley: University of California Press, 1999), p. 57; see also p. 8.

[118] Gerald Bray (ed.), *Tudor Church Reform: The Henrician Canons of 1535 and the* Reformatio Legum Ecclesiasticarum (Woodbridge and Rochester: The Boydell Press, 2000), p. 5.

[119] Bray (ed.), *Tudor Church Reform*, p. 7.

[120] For the Ten Articles, see The Church of England, *Articles Devised by the Kynges Highnes Maiestie* (London, 1536; STC 10033.6), sigs. A.ii–A.iii. v; hereafter, cited as *Ten Articles*. For the Bishops' and King's books, see Gerald Bray (ed.), *The Institution of a Christian Man* (Cambridge: James Clarke and Co., 2018), pp. 25–35.

[121] Bray (ed.), *Tudor Church Reform*, 11.22, p. 43.

[122] The Church of England, *Ten Articles*, sig. C.iv. v.

The international conciliar context of *reformatio* helps explain why Henry (and Edward after him) failed to articulate a comprehensive vision for domestic ecclesial reformation. Latin Christendom was sustained through both ecumenical councils and the papal court. By removing England from both, neither English king had any obvious reason, much less precedent, for drawing upon the vocabulary of *reformatio* that had long animated the conciliar imaginary. In this regard, one of the most important religious texts published during Henry's reign is also among the least studied. On April 8, 1537, the king published his response to the pope's intended council.[123] Henry affirmed that a council was desirable and even enthused that no one else "gladlyer wolde come to it" because "our forefathers inuented nothynge more holyer thanne generall councilles."[124] But he also admitted that because of the papal sentence against his divorce from Catherine of Aragon, he did not trust the pope as a fair arbiter. "The byshop of Rome is our great enemy...His honour, power, and primacie, whiche now are in question, shall they not all be establysshed, yf he being iudge, maye decide oure causes as hym lysteth?"[125] There could be no truly free and general council under papal headship, and even if one were had, the king of England would neither attend nor offer support. The letter concluded with a farewell that restated Henry's principal theological contention that kings, rather than popes, were the true leaders of the church: "Thus myghtye Emperoure fare ye moste hartely well, and ye Christen Prynces, the pyllers and staye of Chrystendome, fare ye hartely well."[126] Here was a remarkably brazen rejection of international Latin Christendom, and not just the papacy.

Several facets of Henry's religious convictions were carried over, without change, into Edward's reign. Like his father, Edward was wholly committed to the doctrine of royal supremacy. The imagery of "head and members" remained ready at hand, but we look in vain for any application of the same to the Edwardian church as a whole. An excellent example is an undated, five-page essay written by Edward entitled "A Discourse about the Reformation of my Abuses."[127] Reflecting contemporary assumptions and norms, the young king wrote that his realm was "divided into two parts, one Ecclesiastical, and the other Temporal."[128] The document's title reveals reformation as central to the king's concerns, but its application to both "parts" of the kingdom was revealingly lopsided; the church occupied merely two paragraphs totaling less than one page,

---

[123] Henry VIII, *An Epistle* (London, 1538; STC 13081).

[124] Henry VIII, *An Epistle*, sig. A.iii; see also sig. A.iiiii. v.

[125] Henry VIII, *An Epistle*, sig. A.iiiii.   [126] Henry VIII, *An Epistle*, sig. B.i. r–v.

[127] Wilhelm Pauck (ed.), *Melanchthon and Bucer* (Philadelphia: The Westminster Press, 1969), p. 171, dates the document to 1551.

[128] Edward VI, "A Discourse about the Reformation of my Abuses," in Gilbert Burnet, *The History of the Reformation of the Church of England* (London, 1681; Wing/B5798), A Collection of Records, Part II, Book II, pp. 69–73, at p. 69. The work is not paginated consecutively; the Collection of Records follows the Table at the end of Part II, Book III.

but discussion of the temporal realm was more than four times as long. The king said nothing specific about either theology or popular devotion, but instead mentioned just two matters: the need for an exemplary clergy and for unspecified liturgical changes. This was hardly religious reformation "in head and in members." Political reformation was, evidently, of greater concern. Edward embraced metonymic detail in the second section of his essay, which bore the subtitle "Temporal Regiment." Here the kingdom was fully anatomized. "The Temporal Regiment consisteth, in well-ordering, enriching, and defending the whole Body Politick of the Common-Wealth, and every part of the whole, to one Part, not the other." The young king compared the kingdom with "a Man's Body," describing "Gentlemen" as the arms that "aideth the whole Body, chiefly the Head."[129] Merchants and husbandmen were the organs of the body politic, chiefly the liver; "Vagabonds" were refuse, a "superfluous Humour of the Body" like "Spittle and Filth," which are "put out by the strength of Nature."[130] Although Edward pondered and advocated reformation in the sense of basic improvement, religion was neither his sole nor even his primary concern.[131]

The eccentric approach to councils found in Henry's 1537 letter also remained in place during Edward's reign. The gathering at Trent, however small, kept alive the longstanding connection between councils and *reformatio*. It matters little here that Trent's first two rounds of sessions were poorly attended. As already noted, continental evangelicals associated a council with *reformatio* and thus continued to share this common assumption with their Catholic opponents. But the English offered nothing similar. The boy king's council learned of conciliar developments and their attendant political tensions only through English diplomats. The correspondence of Richard Morysine in April and May 1551 revealed both concern and uncertainty as to whether Trent's next sessions would materialize,[132] and on June 9, Morysine wrote to the king's council that "The Assembly at Trent seems rather a privy conspiracy of a few in a corner, than anything like a General Council."[133] However, when the bishops at Trent passed their decree on the Eucharist that October, they again placed *reformatio* front and center by following the canons on the sacrament with a lengthy "Decretum super

---

[129] Edward VI, "A Discourse about the Reformation of my Abuses," A Collection of Records, Part II, Book II, p. 69.

[130] Edward VI, "A Discourse about the Reformation of my Abuses," A Collection of Records, Part II, Book II, p. 70.

[131] Like many works, Stephen Alford, *Kingship and Politics in the Reign of Edward VI* (Cambridge: Cambridge University Press, 2002), ch. 4, allows semantic slippage between Edwardian discussions of "reformation" and what is now called *the* English Reformation.

[132] "Edward VI: April 1551," in *Calendar of State Papers Foreign: Edward VI 1547–1553*, ed. William B. Turnbull (London: Her Majesty's Stationery Office, 1861), pp. 81–98 (Apr. 14, No. 319); "Edward VI: May 1551," in *Calendar of State Papers Foreign: Edward VI 1547–1553*, ed. William B. Turnbull (London: Her Majesty's Stationery Office, 1861), pp. 98–115 (May 5, No. 337). BHO.

[133] "Edward VI: June 1551, 1–15," in *Calendar of State Papers Foreign: Edward VI 1547–1553*, ed. William B. Turnbull (London: Her Majesty's Stationery Office, 1861), pp. 115–29. No. 377. BHO.

reformatione" ("decree on reformation") that addressed episcopal responsibility.[134] Another "Decretum super reformatione," passed at the fourteenth session, covered a range of disciplinary matters,[135] as did those ratified by later sessions in 1562 and 1563. As far back as October 1550, some English had discussed calling an international evangelical synod under Edward VI to resolve developing evangelical disagreements.[136] Archbishop Cranmer later wrote a series of letters to Heinrich Bullinger, John Calvin, and Philip Melanchthon, urging an evangelical gathering that would resolve longstanding disputes about doctrinal matters, especially concerning the Eucharist,[137] but nothing came from his endeavors. Perhaps an evangelical synod would have perpetuated among evangelicals the longstanding interrelationship of *reformatio* and councils, but with Edward's untimely death in 1553, the English were no longer positioned to take the lead in any such pursuit. As Chapter 2 will further detail, a very different understanding of *reformatio*, one divorced from conciliar consultation, soon developed in greater Britain.

The boy king's reign nonetheless witnessed occasional uses of "reformation" in proposals for religious change. One was Martin Bucer's lengthy *De Regno Christi* (*On the Kingdom of Christ*). Writing on ecclesial matters, Bucer sometimes drew upon themes and images more generally associated with fifteenth-century ecclesial history. He praised the example of Constantine,[138] a development made possible only by Valla's work. When discussing the English church, Bucer joined *reformatio* to *restitutio* ("renewal" or "restoration"). Advocating the "restoration of the ministers of the church" ("restitvtione ministeriorvm ecclesiae"), he identified "the need for reforming the order of bishops" ("reformando itaque episcoporum ordine") as the first order of business.[139] But following general linguistic usage, Bucer did not use *reformatio* in an exclusively theological or programmatically religious sense. He urged the young king to undertake the reformation of both schools ("de reformatione academiarvm")[140] and commerce ("de reformatione mercatvra").[141] However tantalizing some of this may seem, the full influence of the work was minimal at best, as Bucer passed away shortly after its completion. Unpublished during the remainder of Edward's reign, *De Regno*

---

[134] DEC, Vol. 2, p. 698 (session 13).   [135] DEC, Vol. 2, pp. 714–18.

[136] "Edward VI: October 1550," in *Calendar of State Papers Foreign: Edward VI 1547–1553*, ed. William B. Turnbull (London: Her Majesty's Stationery Office, 1861), pp. 56–60 (Oct. 27, Nos. 252–3). BHO.

[137] Thomas Cranmer, *Miscellaneous Writings and Letters of Thomas Cranmer*, ed. John Edmund Cox (The Parker Society/Cambridge University Press, 1846; repr. Vancouver: Regent College Publishing, n.d.), Vol. 2, n. 296, pp. 430–1 (Bullinger); n. 297, pp. 431–3 (Calvin); n. 298, pp. 433–4 (Melanchthon).

[138] François Wendel (ed.), *Martini Bvceri Opera Latina, Volumen XV: De Regno Christi Libri Dvo 1550* (Paris-VIe: Presses Universitaires de France, 1955), e.g., pp. 36–8, 130.

[139] Wendel (ed.), *De Regno Christi*, p. 118.   [140] Wendel, *De Regno Christi*, p. 107.

[141] Wendel, *De Regno Christi*, p. 247.

Christi was only printed in Basel in 1557,[142] and other than an excerpt on divorce translated and published by John Milton in 1644,[143] the work was largely neglected in the English-speaking world until the mid-twentieth century.[144]

Another vision of reformation came in a letter sent by John Calvin in 1549 to Duke Somerset, who then translated and printed the work for public dissemination. Calvin's letter is worth detailing because it came to have considerable if controversial import in the seventeenth century. The Genevan pastor foregrounded religious reformation as the best response to recent rebellions in England, arguing that true religion taught political obedience, but that superstition spurred revolt.[145] Calvin offered a detailed analysis of what reformation should—and should not—entail, and encouraged Somerset "to pursue a full & an entire reformacion of the Churche." Three points immediately followed. "The fyrste shalbe the meane to instructe ye people wel. The second shal be the taking away of the abuse yt hath beene of long tyme. The third with diligence to correct vices, & to kepe so good ordre that the slaunders & dysordres may not haue suche place as yt the name of god should be blasphemed."[146] Despite describing doctrine as "the soule of the churche,"[147] Calvin focused much on ceremonial matters. Conceding that it was both "conueniente to obserue some moderacyon" and "conuenient to use the ceremonies according to ye grosenes of ye people,"[148] Calvin also cautioned that moderation could invite divine wrath. If a purely "humayne prudence" sought to "moderate, or temper, or refourme" religion, it would only violate the divine will.[149] Reformation was thus no inherent good. Reforming the Church could result in divine benediction, but reformation also risked going awry, transforming Christianity into something less faithful to the Christian Gospel.

More common than Calvin's view was a developing domestic hagiography that lauded Henry for severing England's relationship with the papacy.[150] Continuity between Henry's reign and that of his son is worth underscoring. The recent past animated—and, conversely, constrained—how the new regime articulated its religious goals. Both the 1545 *Primer* and the 1538 translation of the Bible

---

[142] Martin Greschat, *Martin Bucer: A Reformer and His Times*, trans. Stephen E. Buckwalter (Louisville and London: Westminster John Knox Press, 2004), p. 240.

[143] John Milton, *The Ivdgement of Martin Bucer, Concerning Divorcement* (London, 1644; Wing/ B5270).

[144] The first critical edition was Wendel, *De Regno Christi*, in 1955. A largely complete English translation, based upon Wendel's work, may be found in Wilhelm Pauck (ed.), *Melanchthon and Bucer* (Philadelphia: The Westminster Press, 1969), pp. 174–394. For a broad analysis of Bucer in England, see Basil Hall, "Martin Bucer in England," in D.F. Wright (ed.), *Martin Bucer: Reforming Church and Community* (Cambridge: Cambridge University Press, 1994), pp. 144–60.

[145] John Calvin, *An Epistle* (London, 1550; STC 4408), e.g., sigs. A.[vi], B.iii, B.iiii v.

[146] Calvin, *An Epistle*, sig. B.[vii] r–v.   [147] Calvin, *An Epistle*, sig. D.[vi].

[148] Calvin, *An Epistle*, sig. C.[vii] r–v.   [149] Calvin, *An Epistle*, sig. D.ii r–v.

[150] For a broad discussion of early responses to Henry VIII's legacy, see Alec Ryrie, "The Slow Death of a Tyrant: Learning to Live without Henry VIII, 1547–1563," in Mark Rankin, Christopher Highley, and John N. King (eds.), *Henry VIII and His Afterlives: Literature, Politics, and Art* (Cambridge: Cambridge University Press, 2009), pp. 75–93.

remained in force, and the English translation of the New Testament *Paraphrases* of Erasmus, completed between 1548 and 1549, was a project begun under the patronage of Queen Catherine Parr.[151] Furthermore, the funeral for the late king was quite standard and the nine-year-old Edward ascended the throne with equally familiar rites.[152] Although Henry's church is sometimes described as "Catholicism without the pope,"[153] Edward's *Inivnccions* of late July 1547 offered no similar testimony. To the contrary, their description of the late king as Edward's "most derely beloued father, Kyng Henry the eighte, of moste famous memorie,"[154] suggests that the regime basked in the penumbra of a Henrician afterglow. Continuing the religious polemics first promulgated under his father, opposition to both idolatry and the papacy recurred throughout the *Inivnccions*. Rejection of one was consistently linked to rejection of the other. The papacy was expressly tied to idolatry in the first injunction, and the second and third injunctions articulated the need for casting idolatry out of England. The eleventh and twelfth injunctions were the same; the former deprecated idolatry while the latter attacked papal supremacy. The 1547 Book of Homilies opened on an equally anti-papal note, complaining of the "false usurped power of the bishop of Rome."[155] Edward's anti-papal polemic was Henrician in origin, and however selectively strategic, its retention indicates that the regime's praise of the recently deceased king was not merely superficial.

Henry's "moste famous memory" defined the comparatively small number of Edwardian texts that advocated reformation of one or another religious matter. The frontispiece of Archbishop Cranmer's 1548 translation of Justus Jonas' *Catechismus* offered a vivid ideological link between father and son. Imitating Henry on the frontispiece of the Great Bible, Edward now also gave the Bible to the bishops, who knelt before him holding their episcopal staffs, wearing copes and miters. In his Preface to the *Catechismus*, Cranmer claimed that Henry, with his "godly disposition and tender zele" had "moste diligently trauaylled for a trewe & a ryght reformation and a quiet concorde in Christes religion thorowout al hys

---

[151] Gregory D. Dodds, *Exploiting Erasmus: The Erasmian Legacy and Religious Change in Early Modern England* (Toronto: University of Toronto Press, 2009), p. 7; Alford, *Kingship and Politics in the Reign of Edward VI*, pp. 116, 122–3.

[152] Jennifer Loach, "The Function of Ceremonial in the Reign of Henry VIII," *Past & Present*, No. 142 (Feb., 1994), pp. 43–68; Jennifer Loach, *Edward VI*, ed. George Bernard and Penry Williams (New Haven and London: Yale University Press, 1999), pp. 29–38.

[153] This idea has come under recurrent criticism in recent work. See, e.g., G.W. Bernard, "The Dissolution of the Monasteries," *History*, Vol. 96, No. 4 (324) (Oct., 2011), pp. 390–409; G.W. Bernard, "Henry VIII: 'Catholicism without the Pope?'," *History*, Vol. 101, No. 2 (345) (Apr., 2016), pp. 201–21. Bernard, "Dissolution," p. 409, refines this to "Catholicism without the pope, without monasteries and without pilgrimages."

[154] Edward VI, *Inivnccions* (London, 1547; STC 10089), sig. a.ij.

[155] Gerald Bray (ed.), *The Books of Homilies: A Critical Edition* (Cambridge: James Clarke & Co. Ltd., 2015), p. 3.

dominions."[156] Cranmer encouraged the prince "perfytly to finyshe and brynge to passe, that your father dyd mooste Godlye begynne, do thynke that there is nothynge more necessarye, for the furtherance hereof, then that it myghte be forseen, howe the youthe & tender age of youre louynge subiectes, maye be broughte vp and traded in the trewth of Goddes holy worde."[157] We today are predisposed to read Cranmer's words as calling the prince to something like a "further" reformation, but in fact, the Preface identified only the unmet need for catechetical material oriented toward the young. When John Hooper preached on Jonah before the young king in 1550, he also called for "reformacion." Hooper praised the Israelite boy king Josiah, who "folowed the relygyon of hys father not Ammon the Idolater, but of Dauid," because he "destroyed not onlie the Images of his father, but also of Ieroboam, & of Solomon."[158] It is, however, difficult to argue that Henry's religious practice was the target of Hooper's words. Henry was often compared with David,[159] and Hooper's explicit focus was on bishop Stephen Gardiner and those like him, who argued against the recent Book of Common Prayer that, "As long as the kynge is in hys tender age hys councell shulde do nothinge in matters of religyon."[160] Hooper then directed the king, "reforme your Coleges in the Uniuersities, and se honest men to haue the leadynge and ouersyght of the youth."[161] In both Cranmer and Hooper, the apparent contrast with Henry's religious practice carried no connotations of reformation "in head and in members," but only denoted the improvement of individual, and primarily pedagogical, matters.

Henry was just as central to the Edwardian regime's most widely disseminated discussion of reformation, a lengthy essay by Nicholas Udall that celebrated Henry's separation from the papacy. Shot through with apocalyptic content, Udall's work appeared in 1548 as the Preface of the first translated volume of Erasmus' *Paraphrases*, which contained the four Gospels and Acts. The second volume, published in 1549, contained the rest of the New Testament excepting the Apocalypse, for which Erasmus composed no paraphrase. The popularity of both Erasmus and his *Paraphrases* is difficult to overstate, and the influence of the work was no less considerable. Perhaps as many as 30,000 copies were printed;[162] in the *Inivnccions*, Edward ordered clergy to purchase and study the work,[163] and every

---

[156] Thomas Cranmer and Justus Jonas, *Catechismus* (London, 1548; STC 5993), sig. ii. v.

[157] Cranmer and Jonas, *Catechismus*, sigs. ii. v–iii.; a similar concern with the "reformation" of education may be found in Cranmer, *Miscellaneous Writings and Letters*, pp. 418–20, at p. 419.

[158] John Hooper, *An Ouersight... vpon the Holy Prophete Jonas* (London, 1550; STC 13763), sig. +. iiiii.

[159] Micheline White, "The Psalms, War, and Royal Iconography: Katherine Parr's *Psalms or Prayers* (1544) and Henry VIII as David," *Renaissance Studies*, Vol. 29, No. 4 (Sept., 2015), pp. 554–75.

[160] Hooper, *An Ouersight... upon the Holy Prophete Jonas*, sig. +.iiiii.

[161] Hooper, *An Ouersight... upon the Holy Prophete Jonas*, fol. lxiii.

[162] Dodds, *Exploiting Erasmus*, pp. 10–11.   [163] Edward VI, *Inivnccions*, n. 07.

parish church was ordered to acquire it as well.[164] Through the broad geographical circulation of the *Paraphrases*, Udall's discussion of Henry's reformation was made available in every corner of the kingdom.

Drawing upon Biblical history, medieval hagiography, and common apocalyptic, Udall used florid praise of Henry to emphasize that Edward should maintain the changes wrought by his father. Udall variously described Henry as "an Englyshe Dauid" and "our Hercules,"[165] commemorated him with reference to Plato's philosopher king,[166] and commended him as "a most vigilaunt pastour" and "a moste christian Prince."[167] The thematic center of the essay was the struggle between king and pope, which Udall cast in broadly apocalyptic terms. Portraying Henry as St. Michael the Archangel, the king became "the Englishe Michael," who had "taken in hande to fight against the said draguon, and been strengthened of god with his Aungels the lordes, & godly prelates, to caste the said draguon that olden serpente and his Aungels out of Englande."[168] Biblical apocalypses such as Daniel and Revelation portrayed Michael as a principal adversary of the Antichrist, a belief restated in such popular later works as *The Golden Legend*.[169] Whether accepting this framework or simply borrowing it, Udall identified the pope as "the Romishe Antichryste."[170] But Udall worked just as freely within the world of Erasmian humanism, which accompanied his anti-papal invective and culminated in a sweeping attack upon "idolatrye."[171] Borrowing from Erasmus' attacks upon popular devotion, Udall described "the moste corrupt doctrine of the Romishe papacie" as including "vain ceremonies" and "supersticious weorkes," such as "pilgremages" and "transferryng the honour whiche was due to God alone, unto Sainctes and to feigned miracles."[172] Having been "chosen of God,"[173] Henry recognized that "no waie there was to a reformacion, but by this only meane, if the autoritie and usurped supremitie of the See of Rome wer extirped, abolished, & clene extinct."[174] Here was a thoroughly Henrician theme. By casting out "usurped" authority, Henry's kingdom would now flourish—and with it, true religion, guided by true ecclesiastical authority. Edward, if he so chose, could become not only Henry's successor but another Hercules, another David, another Michael. Here was no demand for "further" reformation but only an exhortation to follow in the footsteps of the heroic and pious.

---

[164] Edward VI, *Inivnccions*, n. 20.   [165] Erasmus, *The First Tome*, sigs. iii, iiii.
[166] Erasmus, *The First Tome*, sig. ii.   [167] Erasmus, *The First Tome*, sig. ii v, sig. iii.
[168] Erasmus, *The First Tome*, sig. iiii; the apocalyptic reflection begins on sig. iii. v.
[169] For a modern translation, see Jacobus de Voragine, *The Golden Legend: Readings on the Saints*, trans. William Granger Ryan (Princeton: Princeton University Press, 2012), n. 145, pp. 587–97.
[170] Erasmus, *The First Tome*, sigs. iiii v; (:) [iiii].
[171] Erasmus, *The First Tome*, e.g., sig. (:); see also, e.g., sig. (:) ii.
[172] Erasmus, *The First Tome*, sig. iii.   [173] Erasmus, *The First Tome*, sig. iiii.
[174] Erasmus, *The First Tome*, sig. iii v.

Liturgical Reformation

Nothing discussed thus far indicates that the English understood Henry's "reformation" as analogous to what councils sought to do "in head and in members." The same is true of Edward's reign; the areas identified for *reformatio* by the boy king and his council were discreet, such as education and liturgy. Only in retrospect, with the development of an Anglican tradition, does liturgical change appear the defining feature of what is now termed the English Reformation. And this creates a problem of interpretation. As the last two chapters of this book will show, the modern historiographical focus on the Book of Common Prayer began in the seventeenth century as an Anglican apologetic, although recent interpretations of Edwardian religious history are perhaps also influenced by the tendency of modern Anglicans to emphasize liturgy at the expense of other matters, such as canon law, in which Tudor church leaders took a more consistent interest. This chapter concludes by discussing liturgical change, not because those in the mid-sixteenth century believed that the Book of Common Prayer was the *sine qua non* of domestic religious improvement, but because after these vernacular liturgies became flashpoints of controversy under Elizabeth I, they also became central to the prescriptive aims that defined early historical writing on Tudor religious history.

Contemporary scholarship often interprets the liturgies of 1549 and 1552 in a teleological fashion, in which the English church was rapidly moved from a more ceremonial, if covertly evangelical liturgy, to a less ceremonial and even iconoclastic attack upon more elaborate forms of ritual.[175] Regrettably, the boy king's regime never articulated a summary of its liturgical goals, and initially made only occasional references to the need for otherwise undefined liturgical alteration. The first such public statement appeared in Edward's twenty-seventh injunction. Clergy were told to "instructe and teache in their cures, that no man ought obstinately, and maliciously, breake and violate, the laudable Ceremonies of the Churche, by the kyng commaunded, to be observed, and as yet not abrogated."[176] The last clause—"as yet not abrogated"—foreshadowed some sort of liturgical developments. Two royal proclamations published in 1548 were equally vague,

---

[175] See, e.g., MacCulloch, *The Boy King*, pp. 56, 57, 74 (an alleged policy of "gradualism"); Eamon Duffy, *The Stripping of the Altars: Traditional Religion in England 1400–1580*, second ed. (New Haven and London: Yale University Press, 2005), ch. 13; Gordon Jeanes, *Signs of God's Promise: Thomas Cranmer's Sacramental Theology and the Book of Common Prayer* (London and New York: T&T Clark, 2008), ch. 5, esp. pp. 193, 240; Kenneth Fincham and Nicholas Tyacke, *Altars Restored: The Changing Face of English Religious Worship, 1547–c. 1700* (Oxford: Oxford University Press, 2007), p. 8 ("a general policy of destruction" that was "planned"); Bryan D. Spinks, *The Rise and Fall of the Incomparable Liturgy: The Book of Common Prayer, 1559–1906* (London: SPCK, 2017), p. 1; Susan Wabuda, *Thomas Cranmer* (London and New York: Routledge, 2017), e.g., pp. 2, 71, 142, 163 (on Cranmer's longstanding "plans").

[176] Edward IV, *Inivnccions*, n. 27.

and although ambiguity may indicate a calculated strategy, it is just as possible that the full scope of liturgical transformation was unclear even to those most responsible for it. The first, dated February 6, stated that the Archbishop of Canterbury "hereafter shall declare" which liturgies would be "omitted or changed."[177] The second proclamation prefaced the 1548 *Order of Communion*, the first English-language liturgy for the celebration of the Eucharist. It exhorted subjects "to receaue this our ordinaunce, and mooste godly direction, that wee may be encouraged from tyme to tyme, further to trauell for the reformation, and settyng furthe of suche godly ordres, as maye be moost to goddes glory, the edifying of our subiectes, and for thaduancement, of true religion."[178] Perhaps this comparatively vague exhortation was the liturgical reformation that Edward had so briefly touched upon in "A Discourse about the Reformation of my Abuses."

As the only confessional texts of long-term importance produced between the late 1540s and early 1550s, the Book of Common Prayer, the Ordinal, and the Articles of Religion occupy an unusual position in the shifting religious terrain of sixteenth-century Latin Christendom. Although the Council of Trent was in session between 1545 and 1547, and again from 1551 to 1552, it was far from clear (as seen in the section "No Conciliar *Reformatio*"), that Trent would emerge as a tour-de-force, and that its norms would help spur what was termed, in the late eighteenth century, the "Counter-Reformation." The major Reformed confessions also date later, with the Belgic Confession written in 1561 and the Heidelberg Catechism in 1563; although Lutheran confessions first appeared in 1530 with the Augsburg Confession, the codification of Lutheran orthodoxy was a protracted process that only began to conclude in 1577 with the Formula of Concord. The development and use of confessional labels then remained idiosyncratic, variegated, and polemical into the seventeenth century. In Spain, for example, "Lutheran" was a catch-all insult for all kinds of religious deviancy, whether real or alleged;[179] "Lutheran" was no less vague in France, where it denoted any sort of evangelical faith.[180] Early seventeenth-century German Lutherans applied the term "reformed" exclusively to themselves, denying its applicability to evangelicals who rejected Lutheran confessional norms.[181] Meanwhile, and as Chapter 3 will further detail, the Scots debated whether Lutherans and English Episcopalians

[177] Cranmer, *Miscellaneous Writings and Letters*, pp. 508–9.

[178] The Church of England, *The Order of Communion* (London, 1548; STC 16457), sig. Aij. v.

[179] Henry Kamen, *The Spanish Inquisition: An Historical Revision*, third ed. (London: Weidenfeld & Nicolson, 1997), esp. pp. 98–9; Frances Luttikhuizen, *Underground Protestantism in Sixteenth Century Spain: A Much Ignored Side of Spanish History* (Göttingen: Vandenhoeck & Ruprecht, 2017), e.g., pp. 128, 134, 136; see also O'Malley, *Trent*, p. 13.

[180] Mack P. Holt, *The French Wars of Religion, 1562–1629*, second ed. (Cambridge: Cambridge University Press, 2005), p. 20.

[181] Benjamin T.G. Mayes, *Counsel and Conscience: Lutheran Casuistry and Moral Reasoning After the Reformation* (Göttingen: Vandenhoeck & Ruprecht, 2011), pp. 117–18.

were rightly termed "reformed"; some said yes, and others, no. The contentious nature of such exchanges should not obscure the fact that confessional description, whether for oneself or for others, was ambiguous precisely because it was so very fractious. It is therefore unhelpful to place upon the Prayer Book a single "confessional" label. Recent scholarship has often emphasized the "Protestant" influence upon the Edwardian Church of England, and especially those elements that later coalesced into the early "Reformed" tradition, but the simple fact of the matter is that the unsteady state of evangelicalism was decades away from yielding a clear division between "Lutheran" and "Reformed." Edwardian confessional documents actually drew upon a wide range of influences.

Although Edwardian religious developments are generally analyzed today with reference to evangelical movements elsewhere, it may be more helpful to begin with the fact that Henry VIII bequeathed no confessional alignment to his son. After his break with the papacy, Henry's refusal to join with the Lutheran princes made him a political and confessional *tertium quid*. Beginning in the mid-1530s, the output of English printing presses reveals domestic interest in religious debates on the European continent, even if unified only by a broadly anti-papal agenda. Valla's attack on the Donation of Constantine was printed in 1534;[182] *Julius Excluded from Heaven*, not yet ascribed to Erasmus of Rotterdam, was printed in 1534 and again in 1535.[183] Erasmus' *Enchiridion* was even more popular, with at least five complete editions and an abridgment published by 1545.[184] Henry inclined toward the humanist tendencies in German evangelicalism, which explains not only the translation of the Augsburg Confession during his reign[185] but both his 1534 invitation of Melanchthon to England, and Melanchthon's dedication to Henry of the 1535 revision of his influential work of systematic theology *Loci Communes* (Commonplaces).[186] Further exemplifying a broad if noncommittal interest in contemporary religious disputation, Henrician confessional texts sampled Lutheran soteriological ideas without fully accepting their conclusions.[187] Continuing in the same vein is the fact that comparatively little of Luther's work was printed at the time. During the reigns of both Henry and

[182] Lorenzo Valla, *A Treatyse of the Donation or Gyfte and Endowme[n]t of Possessyons, Gyuen and Graunted vnto Syluester Pope of Rhome, by Constantyne Emperour of Rhome* (London, 1534; STC 5641).

[183] Erasmus of Rotterdam, *The Dialoge Betwene Iulius the Seconde, Genius, and Saynt Peter* (London, 1534; STC 14841.5); Erasmus of Rotterdam, *The Dyaloge Bytwene Iullius the Seconde, Genius, and Saynt Peter* (London, 1535; STC 14842).

[184] Erasmus of Rotterdam, *Enchiridion* (London, 1533, 1534, 1541, 1544; STC 10479–10,480, 10,482–10,484); the abridgment was *A Shorte Recapitulacion or Abrigement of Erasmus Enchiridion*, abridged by Miles Coverdale (Antwerp, 1545; STC 10488).

[185] Philip Melanchthon et al., *The Confessyon of the Fayth of the Germaynes* (London, 1536 and 1538; STC 908–909).

[186] John Schofield, *Philip Melanchthon and the English Reformation* (Aldershot and Burlington: Ashgate, 2006), p. 61.

[187] For analyses of these broad trends, see Alec Ryrie, "The Strange Death of Lutheran England," *The Journal of Ecclesiastical History*, Vol. 53, No. 1 (Jan., 2002), pp. 64–92; Rory McEntegart, *Henry VIII,*

Edward, Luther's published writings were usually Biblical commentaries;[188] only a small number of controversial works appeared.[189] John Bale's edited collection of eyewitness accounts of Luther's death, published in 1546, went through just one edition.[190] The popular influence of such texts is difficult to gauge, as literacy limited their reach among England's largely illiterate population, but evangelical ideas circulated freely among the educated. As evangelicalism diversified, texts reflecting its increasing heterogeneity also appeared in England. But with his father having made no firm political alliances with evangelicals, Edward inherited a national church related only informally to evangelical regimes elsewhere.

Consequently, it should not be surprising that writings by select Catholic contemporaries sometimes remained quite popular in Edwardian England, including among evangelicals. Consider Erasmus. Through the *Paraphrases*, he became Europe's only recent religious controversialist whose writings received official approval from the Edwardian and Elizabethan governments. His 1530 letter on the Eucharist, written to Bishop Balthasar Mercklin, was translated and printed in 1547,[191] and having appeared often during Henry's reign, the *Enchiridion*, which also dealt extensively with the Eucharist, was reprinted in 1548 and again in 1552.[192] The *Paraphrases* contained lengthy disquisitions on the same, and with its expansive parochial ambit, Erasmian devotional assumptions and sacramental theology were given a privileged place in English religious culture. Another popular Catholic author was Hermann von Wied, the evangelical-sympathizing Archbishop of Cologne, who held his see from 1515

The League of Schmalkalden, and the English Reformation (Woodbridge: The Boydell Press, 2002); David Scott Gehring, "From the Strange Death to the Odd Afterlife of Lutheran England," *The Historical Journal*, Vol. 57, No. 3 (Sept., 2014), pp. 825–44.

[188] Under Henry, see Martin Luther, *A Very Excellent and Sweet Exposition* (London, 1537, 1538; STC 16999, 17000); Martin Luther, *An Exposition Vpon the Song of the Blessed Virgin Mary, Called Magnificat* (London, 1538; STC 16979.7). Under Edward, see Martin Luther, *A Ryght Notable Sermon... vppon the Twenteth Chapter of Iohan* (Ispwich, 1548; STC 16992); Martin Luther, *A Frutfull Sermon... vpon the. XVIII. Chapi. of Mathew* (London, 1548; STC 16983); Martin Luther, *A Frutefull and Godly Exposition and Declaracion of the Kyngdom of Christ and of the Christen Lybertye* (London, 1548; STC 16982).

[189] Under Henry, see Martin Luther, *Here After Ensueth a Propre Treatyse of Good Workes* (London, 1535; STC 16988); Martin Luther, *The Last Wil and Last Confession* (Wesel[?], 1543; STC 16984), was a translation of the Smalcald Articles. Under Edward, see Martin Luther, *The Chiefe and Pryncypall Articles of the Christen Faythe* (London, 1548; STC 16964), which contained, in the following order, translations of the Smalcald Articles, *Confession of the Lord's Supper*, an abbreviated form of *Against Hanswurst*(?), and *Three Symbols or Creeds of the Christian Faith*.

[190] John Bale (ed.), *The True Historie of the Christen Departynge of the Reuerende Man D. Martyne Luther* (Wesel, 1546; STC 14717). A consideration of Luther's early legacy in England is Ronald H. Fritze, "Root or Link? Luther's Position in the Historical Debate over the Legitimacy of the Church of England, 1558–1625," *Journal of Ecclesiastical History*, Vol. 37, No. 1 (Apr., 1986), pp. 288–302. I thank the anonymous reviewer for OUP for drawing the Fritze article to my attention.

[191] Erasmus of Rotterdam, *An Epistle... Concernynge the Veryte of the Sacrament of Christes Body, and Bloude* (London, 1549; STC 10490).

[192] Erasmus of Rotterdam, *Enchiridion Militis Christiani* (London, 1548 and 1552; STC 10485 and 10486).

until 1546, when Pope Paul III removed him from office. In 1543, when the likelihood of a church council still appeared small, von Wied published *Einfaltigs Bedencken* (*A Simple Consideration*). Cranmer owned the Latin translation of 1545,[193] *Simplex ac Pia Deliberatio* (*A Simple and Pious Deliberation*), and English translations based upon it followed. The first appeared in 1547 as *A Simple, and Religious Consultation*, and a second edition appeared the following year. The comprehensive volume by von Wied announced on its title page "a Christian reformation, and founded in Gods worde"[194] ("ein Christliche in dem wort Gottes gegründe Reformation"),[195] and the Preface conveyed his desire for "reformation of the church throughout the whole German nation" ("Reformation der kirchen durch ganze Teutsche Nation").[196] Written with several other theologians, most notably Bucer and Melanchthon,[197] von Wied described his goal as "general and godly concorde."[198] The *Deliberatio* heavily influenced Cranmer's *Order of Communion* and translated excerpts from the *Deliberatio* were also published in 1548 as *The Right Institucion of Baptisme*.[199] The 1549 edition of *The Right Instytucion of Baptisme* contained a further excerpt from Wied on burial,[200] and two editions of his pastoral guidance on marriage were published in 1553 as *A Brefe and a Playne Declaration of the Dewty of Maried Folkes*.[201] The Church of England freely borrowed from Catholic authors who either influenced or inclined toward evangelicals.

The Church of England's approach to the Eucharist offers a clear example of confessional hybridity and reveals the full spectrum of international influence upon the English church. Some Edwardian evangelicals had little desire to take sides on contentious matters, but instead believed that evangelicals needed to rapidly overcome their developing internal divisions. For example, Archbishop Cranmer was broadly evangelical in orientation and sympathy, and his presence on the councils of both Henry and Edward made his religious convictions, although not shared by the majority of the English population, disproportionately

---

[193] David G. Selwyn (ed.), *The Library of Thomas Cranmer* (Oxford: The Oxford Bibliographical Society, 1996), p. 41, n. 147; see further details at pp. xciii–xciv. Analyses of von Wied's influence may be found in, e.g., Bryan D. Spinks, "Treasures Old and New: A Look at Some of Thomas Cranmer's Methods of Liturgical Compilation," in Paul Ayris and David Selwyn (eds.), *Thomas Cranmer: Churchman and Scholar* (Woodbridge and Rochester: The Boydell Press, 1993), pp. 175–88; Diarmaid MacCulloch, *Thomas Cranmer* (New Haven and London: Yale University Press, 1996), pp. 393, 414–15; Jeanes, *Signs of God's Promise*, esp. pp. 100–10, 248–51, 260–1.

[194] Hermann von Wied, *A Simple, and Religious Consultation* (London, 1547; STC 13213).

[195] Hermann von Wied, *Einfaltigs Bedencken* (Cologne, 1543).

[196] von Wied, *Einfaltigs Bedencken*, sig. ij; for the 1547 English translation, von Wied, *A Simple, and Religious Consultation*, sig. a.ii r.

[197] Greschat, *Martin Bucer*, p. 189.

[198] von Wied, *Einfaltigs Bedencken*, sig. ij; here quoting von Wied, *A Simple, and Religious Consultation*, sig. a.ii.

[199] Hermann von Wied, *The Right Institucion of Baptisme* (London, 1548; STC 13211).

[200] Hermann von Wied, *The Right Instytucion of Baptisme* (London, 1549; STC 13212).

[201] Hermann von Wied, *A Brefe and a Playne Declaratyon of the Dewty of Maried Folkes* (London, 1553; STC 13208).

influential. In addition to encouraging an evangelical council as a counterweight to Trent, Cranmer developed links with diverse evangelical figures. He invited Melanchthon to England in 1547 and again in 1549/50,[202] and welcomed other evangelical refugees to England throughout Edward's reign. Quite opposite to the Archbishop's intentions, however, this only made international evangelical disputes a defining feature of England's own religious landscape. The influx of evangelical exiles produced significant debate over what sorts of religious ceremonies should be allowed, which, as Chapter 2 will show, helped determine some of the major fault lines that cut across Elizabeth's reign.

Nonetheless, the government condemned disputation on the sacrament in 1547.[203] It was a determination equally political and theological, and although it may have been a strategic stopgap eyeing the iconoclastic transformation of the English church, it may have also been a calculated intervention on the way, at least ideally, to greater evangelical concord. The print history of writings on the Eucharist is instructive here, and tilts toward the latter option. During Edward's reign, popular evangelical texts on the Eucharist included Melanchthon's work in support of utraquism, which saw two editions,[204] and Calvin's *Short Treatise on the Lord's Supper*, which went through four editions.[205] It is customary to describe Calvin as "Reformed," but in the 1540s he sought to steer a middle way between Luther and Zwingli, each of whom occupied, in his mind, opposite ends of the evangelical spectrum. Add to this the aforementioned writings of Erasmus and von Wied, and it becomes clear that interested English readers could sample a wide array of contemporary authors. The varied ideas of von Wied, Erasmus, Calvin, and Melanchthon were all present.

The short confessional document now known as the Forty-Two Articles of Religion reveals the same confessional bricolage—and this all the more so when compared with the bright lines of confessional division that developed in the latter half of the sixteenth century. Article 26, which introduced the sacraments, borrowed directly from the Augsburg Confession.[206] And, following centuries-old norms within scholastic theology, which the Council of Trent had recently restated, the Articles partially defined sacraments as "effectuall signes of

---

[202] Cranmer, *Works*, Vol. 2, n. 289, pp. 425–6; Schofield, *Philip Melanchthon and the English Reformation*, pp. 153–4 (1547 invitation), and additional correspondence with Cranmer is discussed at pp. 160–4.

[203] Edward VI, *A Proclamation Against the Vnreuerent Disputers and Talkers of the Sacramente of the Body and Blood of Christ* (London, 1547; STC 7812).

[204] Philip Melanchthon, *A Newe Work Concernyng Both Partes of the Sacrament* (London, 1548; STC 17795–17,796).

[205] John Calvin, *A Faythful and Moost Godlye Treatyse* (London, 1548; STC 4409.5–4412).

[206] For a more detailed discussion of these developments, see Benjamin M. Guyer, "'Sacrifices of Laud, Praise, and Thanksgiving': The Eucharist in Classical Anglican Formularies," in Daniel J. Handschy, Donna R. Hawk-Reinhard, and Marshall E. Crossnoe (eds.), *A Eucharist-Shaped Church: Prayer, Theology, Mission* (Lanham: Fortress Press/Lexington Books, 2022), ch. 2.

grace."[207] The Articles reveal a more complex relationship between the Church of England and the developing norms among evangelicals in Zurich and Geneva, who signed in 1549 a confessional agreement known today as the Consensus Tigurinus.[208] On the one hand, there were instances of disagreement. For example, the Consensus defined sacraments as "notes [*notae*] and tokens of Christian profession and society,"[209] but the Articles countered that sacraments were "not onely Badges, and tokens [*notae*] of Christien Mennes professione."[210] It was precisely here that the Articles then defined the sacraments in scholastic fashion— a conviction diametrically opposite the assertion of the Consensus that "sacraments do not confer grace" ("sacramenta non conferunt gratiam").[211] On the other hand, and continuing with Eucharistic doctrine, English evangelicals formally agreed with the Swiss on at least one issue. Against both Lutheran and Catholic confessional norms, the Articles, like the Consensus, denied that Christ was physically present in the Eucharist. Edwardian confessional norms reveal a diversity of influences.

The first Book of Common Prayer, published in 1549, illustrates all of this quite well. It sometimes followed long-familiar practice. Altars were still decorated with a white linen and two candles.[212] Communicants continued to receive the sacrament kneeling, and clergy wore the same vestments as when they had celebrated the Latin mass. However, the new Prayer Book changed things, too. An official set of liturgies imposed liturgical uniformity across England, abolishing the regional diversity that had defined English worship for centuries. Liturgical centralization was, at the same time, liturgical constriction. Alterations to the mass also went beyond mere translation. Previously, the clergy had performed the liturgy while the people followed along, praying their own individual prayers. The vernacular reading of the Gospel and the elevation of the Host were the only two moments when clergy and people participated in the same ritual act. The elevation was more important, because it was the miraculous moment when bread and wine became the body of blood of Christ. Popular devotion had long centered on sacramental spectacle, but the sacramental theology and piety of the new liturgies proffered a

---

[207] The Church of England, *Articles of Religion* (London, 1553; STC 10034), n. 26.

[208] The title "Consensus Tigurinus" was first used in the nineteenth century. See Emidio Campi, "The *Consensus Tigurinus*: Origins, Assessment, and Impact," *Reformation & Renaissance Review*, Vol. 18, No. 1 (Mar., 2016), pp. 5–24, at p. 5. The translations here are my own, but for a complete translation, see Torrance Kirby (trans.), "Consensus Tigurinus, 1549," *Reformation & Renaissance Review*, Vol. 18, No. 1 (Mar., 2016), pp. 34–44.

[209] John Calvin et. al., *Consensio Mutua in Re Sacramentaria* (Tiguri ex Officina Rodolphi Vuissenbachii, 1551[?]), p. 9, "notae sint ac tesserae Christianae professionis & societatis, sive fraternitatis."

[210] Church of England, *Articles*, n. 26; For the Latin text of the Articles, see The Church of England, *Catechismus Breuis* (London, 1553; STC 4808), sig. h.vi.

[211] Calvin et. al., *Consensio Mutua in Re Sacramentaria*, p. 14.

[212] See, e.g., William Durande of Mende, *The Rationale Divinorum Officiorum*, Book I, trans. Timothy M. Thibodeau (New York: Columbia University Press, 2007), 2.12 (p. 30; the linen), 3.27 (pp. 40–1; candelabra).

very different understanding of the mass. The Prayer Book barred the priest from elevating the bread and wine after their consecration, and instead directed him to invite the people to receive the sacrament. Private clerical communion, a centuries-old norm, was now forbidden, and clergy were directed to give both the bread and the wine, rather than just the bread, to all communicants. The new rituals represented a new symbolism predicated upon corporate participation.

Not all new developments tended consistently in a single direction. It thus bears repeating that religious change was but a haphazard confluence of contingency and conviction. Church seasons and major holy days such as Christmas, Easter, and Pentecost were retained in the Prayer Book, but the calendar of saints was almost completely gutted, and with the exception of All Saints (November 1), only the twelve apostles remained in the 1549 calendar. And yet, the 1553 *Primer* added to the calendar over 130 saints. The attempted canon law revision of 1552 followed older models even more closely, with perhaps as much as 95 percent of the text depending upon earlier canonical precedent.[213] Insofar as a shared legal culture had defined Latin Christendom for many centuries, reliance upon long-standing legal norms hardly indicates any desire to replace one church with another. Notably, even much of the canon law's sacramental doctrine appeared conventional. In its fifth chapter, which covered the sacraments, Baptism, Eucharist, ordination, marriage, and confirmation all received individual treatment. Confession and the anointing of the sick were left undefined, but it was also written, "Pastors of churches shall diligently visit the weak, afflicted and sick, and sustain them as far as they can by their prayers and consolations, in their most difficult and dangerous moments."[214] It is unclear whether confession and unction were now collapsed together into a single sacramental category, or if the pastoral act still encompassed two distinct sacramental rites, but either way, the legal and sacramental inheritance of the proposed Edwardian canon law was more expansive than is often realized. Nonetheless, it is undeniable The Book of Common Prayer and other authoritative documents fused new ideas with older practices, even as they undercut popular devotion by replacing familiar ritual acts with new sacramental standards.

Overlapping with liturgical change were recurrent attacks upon the idolatry perceived within English parishes. At the beginning of Edward's reign, the royal council sometimes condemned iconoclasm and ordered the replacement of destroyed images,[215] but images were soon removed by government order. Scholarship today has recognized the link between theology and iconoclasm, a conclusion well reflected by works published against idolatry at the time. The royal injunctions opened by calling for "the suppression of Idolatrie, and

---

[213] Bray, *Tudor Church Reform*, pp. lxiv–lxv.
[214] Bray, *Tudor Church Reform*, ch. 5, n. 9 (p. 231).
[215] Duffy, *The Stripping of the Altars*, pp. 453–4.

Supersticio[n]."[216] The Edwardian Book of Homilies elaborated upon the matter by attributing idolatry to greed, deception, and ignorance. Deeply embedded forms of Catholic devotion were described as "markets of merits, being full of their holy relics, images, shrines and works of supererogation ready to be sold."[217] In practice, it is sometimes more difficult to disentangle religiously motivated iconoclasm from acts of vandalism and theft, but all three intensified following political upheaval on the king's council. In the wake of protests against the 1549 Prayer Book, relations between Protector Somerset and the rest of the king's council broke down considerably; forced to tender his resignation, Somerset was locked in the Tower of London on October 13, 1550. Within weeks, iconoclasm and spoliation tore through many parishes. Following changes already imposed by the bishop of London in late 1549 and early 1550,[218] altars were destroyed and replaced with movable communion tables elsewhere in England. Attacks upon idolatry, articulated since the beginning of the reign, were now instantiated.

It may be surprising to note that, in the long run, two documents produced by the Edwardian regime ultimately helped facilitate a more muted understanding of liturgical change. First, in the regime's official response to a rebellion in Devonshire, the king described the Book of Common Prayer as containing "The self same woordes in Englishe, which were in Latin, savyng a fewe thynges taken out, so fonde that it had been ashame to haue heard them in Englishe."[219] The new liturgy was but the old, translated and restored to its pristine purity. "For the masse," he continued, "it is brought euen to the very vse as Christ left it, as thapostles vsed it, as holy fathers deliuered it, in dede some what altered, from that the Popes of Rome for their lucre brought to it."[220] Conventionally anti-papal, the letter bequeathed to later generations a vision of liturgical change at once unorig-inal and unimaginative. It may be recalled from the Introduction that mid-sixteenth century dictionaries variously defined "reformation" as "to bryng the olde state agayne,"[221] and "to refourme that, whiche was negligently done, with more diligence."[222] Interpreted through the lens of Edward's letter, the Prayer Book could be understood as an act of liturgical "reformation" that returned to better, older forms—and, consequently, quite opposite a "revolutionary" develop-ment. As will become clear beginning in Chapter 3, Stuart historians and theolo-gians took the boy king's response at face value.

---

[216] Edward VI, *Inivnccions*, sig. a.ii.   [217] Bray, *The Books of Homilies*, p. 49.
[218] Fincham and Tyacke, *Altars Restored*, pp. 19–21.
[219] Edward VI, *A Message Sent by the Kynges Maiestie, to Certain of His People, Assembled in Deuonshire* (London, 1549; STC 7506), sig. B.
[220] Edward VI, *A Message*, sig. B1r, v.
[221] Thomas Cooper, *Thesavrvs Lingvae Romanae & Britannicae* (London, 1565; STC 5686), no page; see the entry for "Reformo."
[222] Thomas Elyot, *The Dictionary* (London, 1538; STC 7659), no page.

A second legacy of Edwardian religious history was a critique of sacrilege. Some opponents of idolatry distinguished between the forcible restoration of true religion and the theft of silver, gold, and other valuables from England's parishes. Bucer concluded his lengthy analysis of the 1549 liturgies with a remonstrance against the "plundering of the churches."[223] Reflecting upon the pervasive unrest then present in England, as well as the experiences that predicated his own flight from the Holy Roman Empire, Bucer feared that divine judgment would be inflicted upon those who refused to recognize "how grave a sacrilege it is to gain or to repay the good graces of men by taking anything away from the churches of Christ for other purposes than those of the churches."[224] The proposed canon law further complained of "the scandalous and excessive greed of some people (who twist the good intensions of the law to suit themselves)."[225] It contained directions for the repair of dilapidated churches, and directed that clergy who participated in the alienation of goods should be deprived of their offices.[226] Again looking forward to future chapters of this study, arguments against sacrilege became an important feature in seventeenth-century historical writing. However, that development should not obscure the fact that equating Roman Catholicism with greater or lesser degrees of idolatry was a consistent feature of much English religious culture from the mid-sixteenth century onward.

The boy king's death on July 6, 1553 meant that the liturgical changes in the revised Book of Common Prayer, ratified November 1, 1552, were in use for barely seven months. Reflecting the absence of altars from many parishes, the new liturgies did not reference an altar but a table, albeit one still curiously vested like an altar, with a white linen and two candles. The word "mass" was also absent from the new Prayer Book, and the consecrated Eucharist was not described as the body and blood of Christ. Clergy were now expected to wear an alb and surplice, vestments traditionally associated not with the mass but with popular communion services that had developed in Germany and elsewhere in the fifteenth century.[227] It is customary in scholarship to see the 1552 liturgy as evidence of the fuller emergence of Protestant or proto-Reformed commitments. Intra-Anglican debates have often focused on this matter, but doing so risks missing the bigger picture. From at least 1549, the Book of Common Prayer envisioned a liturgical and devotional culture sometimes at considerable variance with the recent, but much deeper, past. The last word here should therefore belong to the regime's

---

[223] E.C. Whitaker, *Martin Bucer and the Book of Common Prayer* (Essex: The Alcuin Club, 1974), p. 160.
[224] Whitaker, *Martin Bucer and the Book of Common Prayer*, p. 162.
[225] Bray, *Tudor Church Reform*, chs. 15–16 (pp. 318–25).
[226] Bray, *Tudor Church Reform*, ch. 18, n. 1 (p. 325).
[227] Amy Nelson Burnett, "The Social History of Communion and the Reformation of the Eucharist," *Past & Present*, No. 211 (May, 2011), pp. 77–119.

ever-present advocacy of royal supremacy—and it is here that we return to ideas traditionally associated with conciliar *reformatio*. Article 22 of the Forty-Two Articles of Religion opened with the affirmation that "Generall counsailes maie not be gathered together without the commaundemente, and will of Princes." Marshaling against the Council of Trent fifteenth-century debates about conciliar authority,[228] the article bluntly stated that councils "maie erre, and sometimes have erred."[229] But where, then, was reformation to be found? Submerged by the floodwaters of Marian Catholic resentment, the Edwardian church bequeathed no coherent discourse or paradigm of *reformatio* to those who might follow.

[228] Russell, *Conciliarism and Heresy in Fifteenth-Century England*, p. 194.
[229] Church of England, *Articles*, n. 22.

2

Dangerous Positions

Debating Reformation, 1553–1603

> reformation cannot well come to our church without blood.
>
> Martin Marprelate (1589)[1]

Introduction

Between the accession of Mary I in 1553 and the death of her sister Elizabeth I fifty years later, contemporaries advanced a wide number of proposals for domestic *reformatio*. Whether papal or royal, conciliar or congregational, demands for reformation were at once assertions about who possessed the authority to identify, initiate, and conclude the work of ecclesial amelioration. Less contrapuntal than cacophonous, disparate calls for reformation articulated equally disparate theories of ecclesial sovereignty. The Marian church restored Catholicism and applied to England the vocabulary of reformation used by Trent and earlier church councils. The church under Elizabeth did not. By refusing papal obedience, the Elizabethan church, like that of Henry VIII and Edward VI, deprived itself of access to the same conciliar lexicon. Furthermore, by preferring the title "supreme governor" to "supreme head," Elizabeth undercut the applicability of corporeal metaphors to the Church of England. But even before Elizabeth's coronation, "reformation" had also begun to acquire a new meaning; both evangelicals and Catholics proved increasingly ready to give "reformation" a militant application. In July 1558, the Anglo-Scots reformer John Knox published a series of pamphlets that culminated in a call for reformation "[by] force of armes."[2] Catholics used the same language to defend rebellion against Elizabeth in 1569. For the next century, English debates about reformation thus doubled as debates about revolt.

---

[1] Joseph L. Black (ed.), *The Martin Marprelate Tracts: A Modernized and Annotated Edition* (Cambridge: Cambridge University Press, 2008), p. 197.

[2] John Knox, *The History of the Reformation of the Church of Scotland*, in David Laing (ed.), *The Works of John Knox*, 6 Vols. (Edinburgh: The Wodrow Society, 1846), Vol. 1, p. 432; the modernized English quoted here comes from John Knox, *The History of the Reformation of the Church of Scotland*, 2 Vols., ed. William Croft Dickinson (New York: Philosophical Library, 1950), Vol. 1, p. 243. Clarifying modernized English, when placed in brackets, comes from Dickinson.

How the English Reformation was Named: The Politics of History, c. 1400–1700. Benjamin M. Guyer, Oxford University Press. © Benjamin M. Guyer 2022. DOI: 10.1093/oso/9780192865724.003.0003

The fundamental theme of this chapter is resistance. It begins by charting the rise of resistance theory among the Marian exiles in Europe, with close attention paid to the writings of John Knox. The second section looks at how "reformation" acquired disruptive connotations in protest literature produced in the 1570s; the fifth section returns to this theme by focusing upon the backlash that developed in the 1590s against threats of martial revolt. The third and fourth sections bridge these decades by comparing and contrasting how the Marian and Elizabethan churches discussed recent Tudor history. The Marian regime advanced a coherent historiography that identified schism and heresy as the principal religious themes of Henrician and Edwardian England. Complimenting this historiography, Cardinal Pole offered a detailed plan for domestic *reformatio* that sought to uproot all erroneous doctrine and practice. The Elizabethan church advanced neither a historical counter-narrative nor its own vision for the reformation of the church. Ever on the defensive, the Elizabethan regime failed to develop its own discourse of reformation.

Reformation "[by] Force of Arms"

Evangelicals did not use "reformation" to articulate a theory of political revolt until Mary Tudor's last months on the throne, but from its very inception, her government associated the evangelical movement with treason. Immediately before his execution in 1553, the Duke of Northumberland repudiated his association with evangelicals, warning the crowd gathered at the scaffold "to beware of these seditiouse preachers, and teachers of newe doctryne."[3] The government immediately capitalized on Northumberland's disavowal by printing it, widely and effectively disseminating the view that evangelicals were not only untrustworthy but violent.[4] Evangelicals did themselves no favors, but time and again only vindicated their opponents' worst suspicions. January 1553/4 saw multiple risings associated with the plotting of Thomas Wyatt, an evangelical advised by John Ponet, the former bishop of Winchester.[5] Religious and political motivations were sometimes difficult to disentangle, as in the case of French support for an uprising by the evangelical Henry Dudley,[6] but the government had no difficulty alleging that it, too, was connected with Wyatt's rebellion.[7] An assassination

---

[3] John Dudley, *The Sayinge of John Late Duke of Northumberlande Uppon the Scaffolde* (London, 1553; STC 7283), no page.

[4] Eamon Duffy, *Fires of Faith: Catholic England under Mary Tudor* (New Haven and London: Yale University Press, 2009), p. 88.

[5] Anthony Fletcher and Diarmaid MacCulloch, *Tudor Rebellions*, sixth ed. (New York and London: Routledge, 2016), pp. 96–7.

[6] Mary I and Philip I, *By the Kyng and the Quene* (London, 1556; STC 7868.3).

[7] Mary I and Philip I, *By the Kyng and the Quene* (London, 1557; STC 7875).

attempt was made on the king in 1556,[8] and in early 1557, the king and queen promulgated their joint condemnation of Thomas Stafford, another evangelical who, having also joined Wyatt three years earlier, attempted yet another coup.[9] England's first queen remains popularly known as "bloody Mary" because she allowed the burning of Protestants. It is more accurate to write that Marian England saw unrepentant evangelical rebellion join an incendiary Catholic orthodoxy in a graceless, sometimes fatal, dance of violence.

Catholic polemicists recognized the political threat posed by militant religious dissenters. Miles Huggarde's 1556 exposé *The Displaying of the Protestantes* contained blistering attacks upon evangelicals as enemies of the state. Early in the work he mocked those who described men and women burned at the stake as martyrs. "Suche are our martyrs in these dayes, who in their lyfe tyme go aboute nothinge els but to sowe sedicion, either conspiracie againste their prince, and magistrates, or els to peruerte the innocent with their vaine perswasions & folishe talke."[10] Huggarde shared the widespread perception, among all religious factions, that a causal relationship existed between heresy and rebellion. When he attacked works of English evangelical theology, he focused on those that criticized Catholic practices, correlating their contents with recent political history. Beginning with unrest in Germany and continuing on with a catalogue of recent treatises by various Marian exiles, Huggarde concluded, as if goading his opponents, "the reste of your libelles and trumperie, are abhorred of your owne brethren. For they seyng your trayterie & horrible villanie used towardes your princes, do with hartes abhorre both you the authors, and your bokes by you deuised."[11] At the instigation of some evangelicals, the tangible reality of sedition transformed defenses of Catholicism into defenses of England. And as Huggarde's work left the press, evangelicals abroad began publishing works of political theology that justified his accusations.

---

[8] Geoffrey Parker, *Imprudent King: A New Life of Philip II* (New Haven and London: Yale University Press, 2014), pp. 293–4.

[9] Mary I and Philip I, *A Proclamation... Agaynste Thomas Stafforde* (London, 1557; STC 7874); Michael Hicks, "Stafford, Thomas (c. 1533–1557), Rebel," *ODNB*. The queen suspected French involvement here, too, but this is far from clear; see Peter Marshall, *Heretics and Believers: A History of the English Reformation* (New Haven and London: Yale University Press, 2017), pp. 411–12.

[10] Miles Huggarde, *The Displaying of the Protestantes* (London, 1556; STC 13558), p. 42 v; for background, see Duffy, *Fires of Faith*, pp. 174–8.

[11] Huggarde, *Displaying of the Protestantes*, p. 118 v. The works named were "Horne's Apologie, Bales vocation, Poynetes folysh confutacion against the lerned treatyse of doctor Martin stande in no steade, Noxes doctrinall of the Masseboke, and your newe reuiued practyse of prelates" (pp. 118 r–v). See Robert Horne, *Certain Homilies of M. Ioan Calvine Conteining... an Apologie of Robert Horne* (Rome [Wesel?], 1553; STC 4392); John Bale, *The Vocacyon of Iohan Bale* (Rome [Wesel?], 1553; STC 1307); John Ponet, *An Apologie* (Strasbourg, 1555; STC 20175); John Knox, *The Copie of a Letter* (Wesel, 1556; STC 15066). Presumably, the "newe reuiued practyse of prelates" refers to William Tyndale, *The Practyse of Prelates* (London, 1549; STC 24467); earlier editions had appeared in 1530 and 1548. "Noxes doctrinall of the Masseboke" likely denotes Knox's sermon against the mass appended to his *Copie of a Letter*.

English evangelical rationales for armed revolt developed out of disputes that began among exiles who settled in Frankfurt after the death of Edward VI. Surviving correspondence between émigrés reveals that an early debate over possible liturgical revision developed into further controversies about ecclesial and civil authority, including political relations with their host cities and the Holy Roman Empire.[12] The Frankfurt "troubles," as they came to be known under Elizabeth,[13] saw evangelicals deploy anti-Catholic invective against one another. Writing to exiles in Zurich on November 15, 1554, the English congregation in Frankfurt announced, in a telling phrase, that it would not allow "thunprofitable ceremoneys" retained in the 1552 Book of Common Prayer.[14] On December 11, several members sent to John Calvin a highly critical description of the Prayer Book. The authors derided morning and evening prayer services as "papsticall dregs,"[15] and accused the marriage rite of containing "petty ceremonies" and "absurdities";[16] the officiant at the Eucharist was mocked as a "sacrificer," and lest Calvin miss the referent, they clarified that other elements of the English rite also remained "as with the papists."[17] Later letters by members of the Frankfurt community were equally harsh,[18] and émigrés critical of these developments sometimes found themselves on the defensive against accusations of impiety.[19] In the short term, the Frankfurt community split between those who hoped to retain the liturgy and those who desired its alteration. The long-term effects of this division, which include the development of English religious dissent and its acceptance of political resistance, will inform the remaining chapters of this study.

That winter, John Bale, another Frankfurt exile, defended the Prayer Book by countering that its opponents aimed at political subversion. He singled out "Their

---

[12] Jane E.A. Dawson (ed.), *Letters from Exile: Documents of the Marian Exile* (The University of Edinburgh, School of Divinity, 2012). Available online: http://www.marianexile.div.ed.ac.uk/, accessed January 20, 2022. Citations take the form *Letters from Exile*, followed by the author, date, and MS reference. For a recent revision of the timeline of these events, see Timothy Duguid, "The 'Troubles' at Frankfurt: A New Chronology," *Reformation & Renaissance Review*, Vol. 14, No. 3 (Dec., 2012), pp. 243–68. A general overview may be found in Jane E.A. Dawson, *John Knox* (New Haven and London: Yale University Press, 2015), ch. 7. For an insightful overview of exiles in Frankfurt, see Maximilian Miguel Scholz, *Strange Brethren: Refugees, Religious Bonds, and Reformation in Frankfurt, 1554–1608* (Charlottesville and London: University of Virginia Press, 2022). I thank Dr. Scholz for sharing his research with me prior to publication.

[13] The key work in this terminological development is Anonymous [William Whittingham?], *A Brieff Discours off the Troubles Begonne at Franckford* (Heidelberg[?], 1574; STC 25442).

[14] Dawson, *Letters from Exile*, English Congregation at Frankfurt, November 15, 1554, DD/PP/839, pp. 39–40, at p. 39.

[15] Dawson, *Letters from Exile*, English Congregation at Frankfurt, December 11, 1554, DD/PP/839, pp. 65–8, at p. 66.

[16] Dawson, *Letters from Exile*, English Congregation at Frankfurt, December 11, 1554, DD/PP/839, pp. 65–8, at p. 67.

[17] Dawson, *Letters from Exile*, English Congregation at Frankfurt, December 11, 1554, DD/PP/839, pp. 65–8, at p. 67.

[18] Dawson, *Letters from Exile*, e.g., Supporters of John Knox at Frankfurt, c. March 21, 1555, DD/PP/839, pp. 48–9; Dawson, *Letters from Exile*, Christopher Goodman, n.d. aft. March 28, 1555, DD/PP/839, pp. 50–2 [letter 1], 56–8 [letter 2].

[19] Dawson, *Letters from Exile*, Richard Cox, April 15, 1557, DD/PP/839, pp. 61–2.

Scote Knoxe," whose "sedicious, barbarouse and scismatycall pratlynges hath reported the sayde booke [the 1552 Book Common Prayer] unperfect, uncleane, unpure, damnable and full of sup(er)stition deservinge also death, plague and exile."[20] Two points mitigate Bale's seemingly intemperate prose. First, Knox's ideas about revolt developed haphazardly. As late as 1556, his public, printed position was that "the victory of God's people" was not in bloodshed, but "in quietness, silence and hope."[21] However, Knox later urged revolt against multiple Catholic authorities, and if he had openly considered the acceptability of such acts in late 1554, then his well-known disdain for the Prayer Book enabled Bale to draw a line of connection between opposition to the English liturgy and support for political violence. Those guilty of the former were, through their association with Knox, guilty of the latter as well. Second, a number of émigrés agreed with Bale. They argued that Knox's 1554 pamphlet *A Faythfull Admonition* demanded rebellion not only against Queen Mary in England but against the Holy Roman Emperor Charles V as well.[22] Because a number of English exiles had fled to imperial cities, any hint of sedition risked carrying, at best, the penalty of still further exile. In the words of his critics, Knox was guilty of "speaking against Idolators, and howe they oght by thexpresse commaundement of God to be putt to deathe."[23] With idolatry and its synonyms among the major keywords of anti-Catholic polemic, Knox's language was understood as instigating opposition against local Catholic leaders. His defenders initially dismissed the accusation of sedition, believing it a subterfuge; in a letter composed in late March 1554/5, they did not discuss the political charges against him, but instead repeated and agreed with his negative assessment of the Prayer Book.[24] But fearing negative consequences over Knox's pamphlet, the Frankfurt city council sided with his critics and exiled him from the city.

When Marian exiles countenanced revolt, they broke both with the political orthodoxy of the Edwardian regime, which allowed only passive resistance, and with other theological authorities past and present. Centuries earlier, and like his contemporaries, Thomas Aquinas had flatly denied that "apostolic doctrine" allowed private persons to rebel, offering the general observation that "it would be a perilous thing, both for a community and its rulers, if anyone could attempt

---

[20] Dawson, *Letters from Exile*, John Bale, Winter of 1554–1555, Inner Temple Library, London, Petyt MSS, 538/47, f. 473.

[21] John Knox, *The Copy of a Letter Delivered to the Lady Mary, Regent of Scotland*, in Roger A. Mason (ed.), *Knox: On Rebellion* (Cambridge: Cambridge University Press, 1994), p. 49.

[22] Dawson, *John Knox*, pp. 104–5.

[23] Dawson, *Letters from Exile*, Edward Isaac, Edmund Sutton and Henry Parry et al., March 15, 1555, DD/PP/839, p. 45; Dawson, *Letters from Exile*, Christopher Goodman, n.d. aft. March 28, 1555, DD/PP/839, pp. 50–2, at p. 51.

[24] Dawson, *Letters from Exile*, Supporters of John Knox at Frankfurt, c. March 21, 1555, DD/PP/839, pp. 48–50.

to slay even tyrannical rulers simply on his own private presumption."[25] When tyranny proved unbearable, the responsibility fell upon the magistrates—lesser government officials—to remove the offending party.[26] Officials who took such steps were innocent of wrongdoing.[27] John Calvin agreed,[28] and identical restrictions remained normative in many other works of evangelical political theory.[29] It is unclear how many exiles refused the ideological temptation of justifying rebellion, but they certainly published less than their more militant coreligionists. John Olde, one of the translators of Erasmus' *Paraphrases*, may have been the only émigré who opposed revolt in print.[30] Published in Emden, his 1555 apologetic *The Acquital or Purgation of the Moost Catholyke Christen Prince, Edwarde the. VI.* was, in part, a disavowal of evangelical violence.[31] Olde aimed to dissociate reformation from rebellion—a concern that raises the possibility that the relationship between reformation and revolt, explicitly detailed in printed works from the late 1550s, was already a topic of open discussion among at least some exiles. The title page of the *Acquital* declared Olde's desire to defend "the Churche of Englande refourmed and gouerned under hym [Edward VI], against al suche as blasphemously and traitorously infame hym or the sayd Church of heresie or sedicion."[32] Creedal orthodoxy proved more important to Olde than political theology, but in a brief excursus on the latter, he drew upon 1 Peter 2 and Romans 13, two Biblical texts used in the Edwardian homily on political obedience. Olde also went further, applying to his own day the condemnation of heretical leaders found in 2 Peter 2. He described "wycked teachers" as those who "despyse autoritie." True evangelicals, he countered, taught differently. "[W]e therefore abhorying that kynde of doctrine, & condemning that ambicious, stubburne, presumptuous, and raylyng rebellion of those men, doo hartely honour Princes and magistrates, and teach all other to doo the like."[33] True gospelers were good subjects. Olde's opponents, whether Catholic or evangelical, disagreed.

More elaborate calls for revolt soon appeared. No idea was more subversive than the justification of popular regicide. The earliest extended English-language consideration on point was John Ponet's 1556 volume *A Shorte Treatise of Politike Pouuer*. Writing from Strasbourg, Ponet was evidently unconcerned with the

[25] Thomas Aquinas, "The Treatise 'De Regimine Principum' or 'De Regno'," in R.W. Dyson (ed.), *Aquinas: Political Writings* (Cambridge: Cambridge University Press, 2002), pp. 5–52, at p. 19.
[26] Aquinas, "De Regimine Principum," pp. 19–20.   [27] ST 2a2ae q. 42, art. 2, ad 3.
[28] John Calvin, *Institutes of the Christian Religion*, 2 Vols., ed. John T. McNeill (Philadelphia: Westminster John Knox Press, 1960), Vol. 2, Book IV.XX.31, pp. 1518–21.
[29] Dawson, *John Knox*, pp. 145–6; for a broader survey, see Quentin Skinner, *The Foundations of Modern Political Thought*, 2 Vols. (Cambridge: Cambridge University Press, 1978), Vol. 2, ch. 7.
[30] At the very least, Olde's is the only such work I have found. Evangelicals who returned to Catholicism, such as Northumberland, were more ready to associate their former convictions with political upset.
[31] John Olde, *The Acquital or Purgation of the Moost Catholyke Christen Prince, Edwarde the. VI.* (Waterford, 1555; STC 18797), sig. A.
[32] Olde, *The Acquital*, sig. A.   [33] Olde, *The Acquital*, sig. [E6].

recent fallout surrounding Knox's work. Drawing from the Old Testament book of Judges, he told his readers:

> I think it can not be maintened by Goddes worde, that any priuate man maie kill, except (wher execucion of iuste punishment vpon tirannes, idolaters, and traiterous gouernours is either by the hole state vtterly neglected, or the prince with the nobilitie and counsail conspire the subuersion or alteracion of their contrey and people) any priuate man haue som special inwarde commaundement or surely proued mocion of God: as Moses had to kill the Egipcian, Phinees the Lecherours, and Ahud king Eglon, with suche like[.][34]

Ponet then recounted the story of Ahud for his audience. An "Idolatrous persone and a wicked [king], called Eglon,"[35] was killed by the Israelite Ahud, who "thrust his dagger so harde in to the kinges fatte paunche, that ther laie king Eglon dead, and Ahud fled awaie." As with Knox, Ponet's invocation of idolatry resounded with contemporary referents, denoting Catholicism and, among English evangelicals, Mary Tudor. Recognizing that some would protest his interpretation, Ponet countered, "the scripture saieth, that Ahud (being a priuate persone) was stered vp only by the spirite of God."[36] Having already supported revolt in 1553/4, Ponet again vindicated violence by now commending Ahud's brutal actions.

Chapter 1 showed that conciliar discourses of *reformatio* depended upon apocalyptic ideas about monstrosity. The Marian exiles followed in much of this; although they dissociated reformation from the work of councils, they retained its association with the preternatural, and included detailed discussions on point alongside their politically disruptive readings of Scripture.[37] When Ponet concluded his *Shorte Treatise* with a jeremiad that catalogued recent "monstrous maruailes on the earthe, and horrible wonders in thelement,"[38] he did far more than introduce shock value into his work. Assuming the role of prophetic interpreter, he explicated for his readers two recent stories of deformed children born in England. The first, a newborn with two heads, signified imminent civil war; the second child, born with an underdeveloped body, and with arms and legs weighed down with the jewelry worn by the aristocracy, revealed a country unable to defend itself.[39] Incredulous that anyone would deny the obvious meaning of such phenomena, he asked, "how should they be taken, that doo not beleue

---

[34] John Ponet, *A Shorte Treatise of Politike Pouuer* (Strasbourg, 1556; STC 20178), pp. 109–10.
[35] Ponet, *Treatise*, p. 119.   [36] Ponet, *Treatise*, p. 121.
[37] For the historiographical background to discussions of monstrosity in this chapter, see esp., Katharine Park and Lorraine J. Daston, "Unnatural Conceptions: The Study of Monsters in Sixteenth- and Seventeenth-Century France and England," *Past & Present*, No. 92 (Aug., 1981), pp. 20–54; Lorraine Daston and Katharine Park, *Wonders and the Order of Nature 1150–1750* (New York: Zone Books, 1998); Kathryn Brammall, "Monstrous Metamorphosis: Nature, Morality, and the Rhetoric of Monstrosity in Tudor England," *The Sixteenth Century Journal*, Vol. 27, No. 1 (Spring, 1996), pp. 3–21.
[38] Ponet, *Treatise*, p. 148.   [39] Ponet, *Treatise*, p. 150.

the manifest workes of God?"[40] Monsters, like eclipses, famine, and disease, proclaimed impending judgment. So did comets and other celestial phenomena, wonders of especial fascination and urgency that, in ancient times, had preceded the fall of Jerusalem during the Jewish War. Likely borrowing from the first-century historian Josephus, Ponet ruminated, "Before the last and vtter destruction of the citie of Ierusalem, ther was sene hanging in thelement of the temple a burning sweorde almost the space of a hole yeare."[41] As in past times, so too in the present, God disrupted the normal course of nature with signs of profound disorder. Ahud's divinely inspired actions pointed the way to deliverance.

Monstrosity was equally important to Knox's pamphlet *The First Blast of the Trumpet Against the Monstrous Regiment of Women*. Published in January 1557/8, it became one of the principle works of sixteenth-century resistance theory.[42] An attack upon female political headship appears today as sexist,[43] but it is more contextually sensitive to read the text as an urgent if abrasive reflection upon monstrosity as a sign of divine displeasure. Deploying a wide range of philosophical, legal, Biblical, and patristic sources,[44] Knox sought to delegitimate Mary Tudor's rule by arguing that "the order of nature," a concept found throughout the work,[45] prohibited women from holding political office. "For who would not judge that body to be a monster where there was no head eminent above the rest, but that the eyes were in the hands, the tongue and mouth beneath in the belly and the ears in the feet?" The answer struck directly at the viability of all queens regnant: "no less monstrous is the body of that commonwealth where a woman beareth empire."[46] With his broad argument established, Knox turned to the specific case of England. He endorsed regicide by explicating the Biblical story of the idolatrous Queen Athaliah, who was deposed after "Jehoiada the high priest called together the captains and chief rulers of the people"—those who were, in effect, the chief magistrates of ancient Judah. Knox applied his interpretation to England in no uncertain terms: "The same is the duty as well of the estates as of the people that hath been blinded."[47] The English had but one choice, and following Biblical precedent, the magistrates were called to lead.

[40] Ponet, *Treatise*, p. 152.
[41] Ponet, *Treatise*, p. 152. Ponet did not identify a source, but see Josephus, *The Jewish War*, trans. H. St.J. Thackeray, Loeb Classical Library 210 (Cambridge and London: Harvard University Press, 1928), Book VI.288–300 (pp. 262–5).
[42] Dawson, *John Knox*, pp. 145–6.
[43] See, e.g., Adrian Streete, "Christian Liberty and Female Rule: Exegesis and Political Controversy in the 1550s," in Victoria Brownlee and Laura Gallagher (eds.), *Biblical Women in Early Modern Literary Culture, 1550–1700* (Manchester: Manchester University Press, 2015), pp. 59–74.
[44] Knox, *The First Blast of the Trumpet*, in Mason, *Knox: On Rebellion*, pp. 9–18.
[45] Knox, *The First Blast*, pp. 23, 27, 44; more general appeals to nature are made at pp. 8, 9, 11; the "order of creation" is identified as God's own at, e.g., pp. 8, 11, 22, 23.
[46] Knox, *The First Blast*, p. 23.   [47] Knox, *The First Blast* p. 44.

But when the kairotic moment broke forth, it dawned quite unexpectedly upon Scotland.[48] The transformation of "reformation" into a militant rather than conciliar summons received its first clear articulation across a series of pamphlets that Knox published in July 1558. This shift is key. Knox developed a unique political vocabulary that positioned "reformation" against "tyranny." The same pairing was absent from other contemporary British resistance theorists, such as Christopher Goodman and Anthony Gilby; the former revealed no interest in the terminology of reformation, while the latter never connected reformation with revolt.[49] Knox, however, carried his vocabulary forward into future works, most notably his posthumously published *Historie of the Reformation of the Church of Scotland*. The July pamphlets reveal that Knox then wrestled quite seriously with whether to maintain the magisterial limitation upon resistance. He initially lacked ideological clarity and did not apply to Scotland his endorsement of resistance in England,[50] but as Knox scanned Scotland's body politic from head to toe, his acceptance of traditional political orthodoxy progressively broke down. He began with the royal head by expanding his 1556 *Letter to the Regent* into a lengthier demand for Mary of Guise to reform the church. Using "idolatry" to signify Catholicism, Knox exhorted the queen to follow the examples of "the most godly princes Josiah, Hezekiah and Jehosaphat," who, "seeking God's favour to rest upon them, and upon their people, before all things began to reform the religion."[51] Religious reformation would reveal the queen's "motherly pity upon your subjects"—an evident necessity because, Knox believed, religion "within your realm is so deformed that no part of Christ's ordinances remain in their first strength and original purity."[52] The queen mocked Knox's original letter. Her response in 1558 is unknown.

Whether impatient or disillusioned, Knox rapidly turned to the limbs of the body politic, the nobles. His second pamphlet that July was *The Appellation*. Although formally addressed to the bishops, he primarily addressed his religious demands to the Scottish Parliament. Again citing the examples of Josiah and Hezekiah, his wording remained remarkably similar: "ought you, my Lords, all delay set apart, to provide for the reformation of religion in your dominions and bounds, which now is so corrupt that that no part of Christ's original institution remaineth in the original purity."[53] Knox recognized that his words demanded violence, and he now defended the same.

---

[48] Alec Ryrie, *The Origins of the Scottish Reformation* (Manchester: Manchester University Press, 2006), ch. 7.

[49] Christopher Goodman, *How Superior Powers Oght to be Obeyd* (Geneva, 1558; STC 12020), pp. 151–2, is the only use of "reformation" in the text but has no militant connotation; Anthony Gilby, *An Admonition to England and Scotland*, in John Knox, *The Appellation of Iohn Knox* (Geneva, 1558; STC 15063), pp. 59–77, at pp. 68 v, 69 v, 71 r, uses "reformation" in the standard sense of improvement.

[50] Ryrie, *Origins of the Scottish Reformation*, pp. 148–9.

[51] Knox, *The Letter to the Regent*, in Mason (ed.), *Knox: On Rebellion*, p. 61.

[52] Knox, *Letter to the Regent*, p. 61.   [53] Knox, *The Appellation*, p. 91.

True it is, God hath commanded kings to be obeyed, but like true it is that in things which they commit against His glory, or when cruelly without cause they rage against their brethren, the members of Christ's body, He hath commanded no obedience, but rather He hath approved, yea, and greatly rewarded, such as have opponed themselves to their ungodly commandments and blind rage.[54]

The *Letter to the Commonalty*, Knox's third and far shorter work, expanded upon this theme by giving the entire citizenry, long imagined as the feet of the realm, an active if limited role to play. Encompassing the largest portion of Scotland's population, Knox wrote in a marginal note that "Reformation of religion belongeth to all that hope for life everlasting."[55] All citizens were now political and spiritual actors, and Knox hoped that the common people would work together with their magistrates toward the shared end of reformation. Turning his polemic against Scotland's religious hierarchy into a sweeping condemnation, Knox further wrote, "I further desire that ye, concurring with your nobility, would compel your bishops and clergy to cease their tyranny"—that is, "their vain religion, false doctrine, wicked life and slanderous conversation."[56] Reformation in Scotland would thus be a magisterial revolt, but one in which the "commonalty" fully participated.

The Wars of the Congregation broke out the following year. The acute apocalypticism that possessed Knox's pamphlets did not reflect the views of most Scottish evangelicals, let alone Catholics,[57] but the last months of 1558 saw a continued escalation of invective. In a protestation made to the Scottish Parliament that December, evangelicals made the threat of popular armed violence openly: "yf any tumult or uproare shall aryise amanges the membres of this realme for the diversitie of religioun, and yf it shall chance that abuses be violentlie reformed, that the cryme thairof be not impute to us, who most humlie do now seak all thinges to be reformed by ane ourder."[58] Ensuring that his opponents would not misunderstand, when Knox later incorporated this passage into his *Historie*, he appended a marginal note that read, "Lett the Papists observe." War commenced with Knox preaching against idolatry in May 1559. Evangelicals subsequently tore through Perth, vandalizing churches and forcibly overthrowing Catholicism. Mary of Guise deployed 1,800 troops with French assistance, but they were outnumbered by an evangelical force of 2,500.[59] Scotland's evangelical

---

[54] Knox, *The Appellation*, p. 95.

[55] Knox, *Letter to the Commonalty*, in Mason (ed.), *Knox: On Rebellion*, p. 118.

[56] Knox, *Letter to the Commonalty*, p. 116.

[57] Ryrie, *Origins of the Scottish Reformation* pp. 150–1; Pamela Ritchie, "Marie de Guise and the Three Estates, 1554–1558," in Keith M. Brown and Roland J. Tanner (eds.), *Parliament and Politics in Scotland, 1235–1560* (Edinburgh: Edinburgh University Press, 2004), pp. 179–202, at pp. 201–2.

[58] Knox, *History*, in Laing, *Works*, Vol. 1, p. 314; Ryrie, *Origins of the Scottish Reformation*, p. 154.

[59] Jane E.A. Dawson, *Scotland Re-Formed: 1488–1587* (Edinburgh: Edinburgh University Press, 2007), pp. 204–8.

junta, now calling itself the Lords of the Congregation, wrote to the Queen Regent later that year and asked, "quhat [what] godlie man can be offendit that we sall seik reformatioun of thir enormities, (yea, evin be force of armes, seing that uthirwayis it is denyit unto us;)?"[60] Previous theories of reformation by council were now challenged by an uncompromising theology of reformation by righteous revolt.

Reformation as Present Necessity

Elizabeth thus ascended the English throne in a fraught domestic context. Her first decade began with threats of armed uprising and concluded with rebellion. Opposition came from both evangelicals and Catholics. Unfortunate timing greeted the publication of *The First Blast of the Trumpet*, and the sudden death of Mary Tudor resulted in Knox's pamphlet unwittingly demanding revolt against Elizabeth. The new queen responded by banning Knox from ever returning to England. Making matters still worse, in 1560, Marian exiles completed the Geneva Bible, a translation named after its city of publication.[61] The front cover indicated that it contained "moste profitable annotations vpon all the hard places,"[62] thereby enabling readers to better understand the text. But as with other sixteenth-century Bible translations, the Geneva Bible was sometimes more the product of prescriptive theology than careful philology. Elizabeth's bishops responded negatively to its endorsement of political resistance,[63] but even after the translation of the "Authorized" or King James version in 1611, the Geneva Bible remained an easily accessible inspiration for political opposition.

On the Catholic side, in early 1559, Mary, Queen of Scots, began appropriating the arms of England in public displays, thereby stating in vivid fashion her claim to England's throne.[64] The English Crown interpreted her actions as a symbolic but very real threat, and only the signing of a treaty in July 1560 caused Mary to stop using English insignia. But this was not all. In 1567, Mary Stuart's flight from Scotland led to speculation that Catholics at home and abroad might aid her in taking the English throne by force.[65] The fear materialized, albeit briefly, in late 1569 with a failed Catholic revolt in northern England. The rebels accused the Crown of being Protestant and heretical. Those on the receiving end began to

---

[60] Knox, *History*, in Laing (ed.), *Works*, Vol. 1, p. 432.

[61] Alister McGrath, *In the Beginning: The Story of the King James Bible and How It Changed a Nation, a Language, and a Culture* (New York: Anchor Books, 2001), pp. 114–23.

[62] William Whittingham et al., *The Bible* (Geneva, 1560; STC 2093).

[63] McGrath, *In the Beginning*, pp. 141–8.

[64] Steven Thiry, "'In Open Shew to the World': Mary Stuart's Armorial Claim to the English Throne and Anglo-French Relations (1559–1561)," *English Historical Review*, Vol. CXXXII, No. 559 (Dec., 2017), pp. 1405–39.

[65] Parker, *Imprudent King*, p. 206.

equate Catholic convictions with political treachery,[66] and the queen surpassed her Catholic opponents in violence by executing perhaps as many as 600 participants.[67] Pope Pius V's excommunication of Elizabeth in 1570 inspired further dread by attempting to absolve English subjects of their loyalty to the queen. Neither an idle nor a passing threat, the pope subsequently supported the invasion of England. A failed plot to assassinate Elizabeth in 1584 exposed the involvement of Don Bernardino de Mendoza, Spain's ambassador to England,[68] and when the Spanish Armada set sail in 1588, the pope republished his bull of excommunication. The effects of international religious division were all too tangible.

Evangelical confessional developments elsewhere proved equally disruptive and need some explication in order to fully frame the dynamics of Elizabethan debates about reformation. After ratification of the Peace of Augsburg in 1555, a theological free-for-all broke out within the tightly constrained confessional context of the Holy Roman Empire.[69] Intended to enable religious toleration between Catholics and evangelicals, the Peace of Augsburg used the Augsburg Confession to set the parameters of acceptable evangelical belief. Problematically, Philip Melanchthon had revised the Augsburg Confession multiple times since 1530; his many alterations, collectively known as the *Variata*, reflected his attempts at negotiating between rival evangelical personalities and convictions. For example, unlike the original 1530 text, soon termed by its defenders the *Invariata*, a revision made in 1540 did not define the body and blood of Christ as present "under the Form" ("unter Gestalt") of the bread and wine of communion. Because the Empire's new law failed to identify which version of the Augsburg Confession was normative, political peace failed to spur theological peace. Sacramental doctrine and the allowable extent of liturgical ceremony proved especially acrimonious points of contention, and redounded as arguments about not only the confession's theological pliability but also the legal limits of toleration. The late 1550s and early 1560s consequently saw multiple confessional documents written within and beyond imperial borders. Confessions composed within the Empire directly addressed debates over the Peace of Augsburg. The Heidelberg Catechism, a text with considerable long-term influence among those later termed Reformed Protestants, rejected ceremonies and endorsed the sacramental theology in Melanchthon's revision of 1540.[70] Confessions written outside

---

[66] K.J. Kesselring, *The Northern Rebellion of 1569: Faith, Politics and Protest in Elizabethan England* (New York: Palgrave Macmillan, 2007), e.g., pp. 59 and 115 (accusations of Protestantism and heresy), 156 (the equation of Catholicism with treachery); MacCulloch and Fletcher, *Tudor Rebellions*, ch. 8.

[67] Kesselring, *Northern Rebellion of 1569*, pp. 124–6, presents extensive statistics; Fletcher and MacCulloch, *Tudor Rebellions*, p. 108, estimate 450.

[68] Parker, *Imprudent King*, p. 280.

[69] For general background, see Thomas A. Brady, *German Histories in the Age of Reformations, 1400–1650* (Cambridge: Cambridge University Press, 2009), ch. 12.

[70] Lyle D. Bierma, "The Sources and Theological Orientation of the Heidelberg Catechism," in Lyle D. Bierma (ed.), *An Introduction to the Heidelberg Catechism: Sources, History, and Theology* (Grand Rapids: Baker Academic, 2005), pp. 75–102, at p. 101.

of the Germanic lands addressed major topics of theological debate as well as the Empire's new religious toleration. The Belgic Confession, originally printed in Rouen in 1561,[71] was submitted in 1566 to the Diet of Augsburg, but in a revised version that emphasized obedience to the governing authorities. The mixture of theological and political debate slowly redefined the evangelical movement after 1555, and by the late 1570s, distinct "Lutheran" and "Reformed" churches had come into existence, neither of which accepted the other's confessional distinctives.

This shifting confessional context shaped the Elizabethan church in multiple ways. Notably, the queen sent her first diplomatic embassy to the Lutheran princes of the Empire,[72] and she joined them in lobbying the emperor to call a new ecumenical council.[73] Widely recognized as sympathetic to Lutheranism by Catholic diplomats,[74] Elizabeth expressed the same in correspondence with Lutheran heads of state. On July 3, 1559, the queen wrote to John Frederick II, duke of Saxony, that she desired for the Church of England to have something "like the Confession of Augsburg" ("iuxta formulam Confessionis Augustanae").[75] Alterations made to England's confessional texts gave her precisely that. Most tangibly, the 1559 revision of the Book of Common Prayer restored to the communion rite an affirmation of Christ's physical presence in the Eucharistic elements. But the queen's diplomatic interests moved in a direction opposite of those who, over the course of the 1560s, came to be known as "Reformed" Protestants (at least, in some parts of Latin Christendom). The earliest use of "Reformed" as a confessional self-descriptor has not yet been identified, but British evangelicals who settled in Geneva described themselves as such after the Frankfurt congregation broke apart in the mid-1550s. Having rejected the Book of Common Prayer, they composed their own "forme and order of a reformed churche."[76] The authors of the new service assured their readers that its contents and directives were not unique because the "best reformed churches haue receyued the same."[77] Among British evangelicals, uses of "reformed" slowly but consistently grew. In a telling terminological move not paralleled by the Church of

[71] Nicolaas H. Gootjes, *The Belgic Confession: Its History and Sources* (Grand Rapids: Baker Academic, 2007), p. 30.

[72] David Scott Gehring, *Anglo-German Relations and the Protestant Cause: Elizabethan Foreign Policy and Pan-Protestantism* (New York: Routledge, 2013), p. 28.

[73] Hirofumi Horie, "The Lutheran Influence on the Elizabethan Settlement, 1558–1563," *The Historical Journal*, Vol. 34, No. 3 (Sept., 1991), pp. 519–37, at pp. 526–9.

[74] Martin A.S. Hume (ed.), April 29 (1559), No. 29, in *Calendar of State Papers, Spain (Simancas), Volume 1: 1558–1567*. BHO. Additional consideration of this and other related correspondence may be found in John Schofield, *Philip Melanchthon and the English Reformation* (Aldershot and Burlington: Ashgate, 2006), pp. 190–2.

[75] E.I. Kouri, *Elizabethan England and Europe: Forty Unprinted Letters from Elizabeth I to Protestant Powers* (London: Bulletin of the Institute of Historical Research, 1982), p. 23.

[76] The English Congregation at Geneva, *The Forme of Prayers and Ministration of the Sacraments* (Geneva, 1556; STC 16561), p. 9.

[77] The English Congregation at Geneva, *Prayers and Ministration*, p. 19.

England, the Latin translation of the 1560 Scots Confession identified the Church of Scotland as "Ecclesiam Reformatam" (translatable as either "the church having been reformed" or, more simply, as "the Reformed Church").[78] The early pursuit of Lutheran amity,[79] and the revision of English confessional and liturgical texts to accord with those aims, initially returned less theologically refined evangelical convictions to the Church of England. But over the course of Elizabeth's reign, international evangelicalism was redefined from within. By the time of the queen's death, the English church was increasingly out of step, albeit in different ways, with the developing orthodoxies of the Lutheran and Reformed churches.

Against this extended domestic and international background, "reformation" became the keyword for articulating the theological and political frustrations of Elizabethan religious dissent. Returning to England in the early years of Elizabeth's reign, Marian exiles strongly opposed wearing the vestments required by the Book of Common Prayer. Robert Crowley denoted vestments "garmentes of the popish churche" and applied to them a curse found in Psalm 31, "I haue hated all those, that holde of superstitious vanities."[80] Anthony Gilby described vestments as forms of "Idolatrye."[81] Correspondence between Christopher Goodman and John Knox was much the same, with Knox describing vestments as "Anticrists clothing."[82] English editions of evangelical works published abroad sometimes followed the same thematic direction. A Confession of Fayth, first published in 1568 and republished three years later,[83] contained translations of the First Helvetic Confession of 1536, the Gallican Confession of 1559, and the 1565 Epistle dedicatory of Theodore Beza's bilingual (Greek and Latin) edition of the New Testament. Addressed to Louis, prince of Condé, the original dedication otherwise had no title, but the English translation added to it the running header, "An Exhortation to the Reformation of the Churche."[84] Beza wrote against those who defined "reformation" as "a restorynge agayne of those rites, whiche were in use in the florishyng time of the Church, as they terme it (taking awaye some thinges which by the wickednes of times haue bene abused) the whiche except we doo receyue, they crie that the Churche is transformed, and depriued utterly of hir

---

[78] The Church of Scotland, *Confessio Fidei et Doctrinae per Ecclesiam Reformatam Regni Scotiae Professe* (Andreapoli, 1572; STC 22028), sig. A.

[79] Gehring, *Anglo-German Relations*, studies the entirety of Elizabeth's diplomatic efforts with the German Lutheran princes.

[80] Robert Crowley, *A Briefe Discourse Against the Outwarde Apparell and Ministring Garmentes of the Popishe Church* (Emden[?], 1566; STC 6079).

[81] Anthony Gilby, *To My Louynge Brethren* (Emden[?], 1566; STC 10390), sig. [Aiii] v.

[82] Jane E.A. Dawson, Lionel K.J. Glassey, and John Knox, "Some Unpublished Letters from John Knox to Christopher Goodman," *The Scottish Historical Review*, Vol. 84, No. 218, Part 2 (Oct., 2005), pp. 166–201, at p. 194.

[83] Theodore Beza et al., *A Confession of Fayth* (London, 1568; STC 23554).

[84] For the Latin original, see Theodore Beza, *Novum Testamentum* (Henricus Stephanus, 1565), sig. ¶.ii.ff. Regrettably, the English translator identified him- or herself only as "I.O." *Early English Books Online* assigns the translation to John Olde, who sometimes signed as "I.O.," but Olde died in 1557.

beautie and comelinesse."[85] Reflecting an increasingly normative position among the "Reformed," both the Gallican and Belgic confessions had denounced the continued use of ceremonies among Christians, teaching that Christ had abolished them.[86] Originally directed against Roman Catholics and the more ceremonial evangelical churches, Beza's polemic was easily assimilated by those who now sought the abolition of the Book of Common Prayer.

Works of English theological controversy soon reflected the anti-ceremonial and, increasingly, anti-episcopal demands of some evangelicals. The Parliament of 1571 witnessed a series of forceful public demands for reformation. William Strickland called for the "reformacion" of "The Booke of Commen Prayer," which "althoughe (God bee praised) it is drawne very neere to the sinceritie of the truth, yet are there somthinges inserted more superstitious or erroneous then in soe highe matters bee tolerable."[87] More detailed was the sweeping set of arguments for reformation contained in *An Admonition to the Parliament*, an anonymously published work authored by the clergymen John Field and Thomas Wilcox. Perhaps the most influential set of demands advanced during Elizabeth's reign, the authors desired to align the Church of England with "the best reformed Churches throughout Christendome."[88] Like the Gallican and Belgic confessions, Field and Wilcox rejected ceremonies because "the office of Priesthood is ended, Christ being the last Priest that ever was."[89] Anti-episcopal sentiment yielded a sustained demand for Presbyterian ecclesial order, and the abolition of priesthood and its ceremonial functions. Enacting the *Admonition* would have placed the English church in confessional harmony with Scottish and French evangelicals, whose churches the authors held up as models for emulation. They asked, "Is a reformation good for *France*, and can it be euill for *England*? Is Discipline meet for *Scotland*, and is it vnprofitable this Realme?"[90] When Parliament failed to heed the *Admonition*, Field and Wilcox sought out other avenues for the propagation of their message.

For many decades, scholars have argued that the authors and supporters of the *Admonition* advocated "further reformation."[91] In order for this claim to be true, evangelical critics of the Church of England would have needed to believe that

[85] Beza, "An Exhortation to the Reformation of the Churche," in *A Confession of Fayth*, sig. Diii v.

[86] On the relationship of these two confessions and their shared view of ceremonies, see Gootjes, *The Belgic Confession*, pp. 64–6.

[87] T.E. Hartley (ed.), *Proceedings in the Parliaments of Elizabeth I*, Vol. 1: 1558–1581 (London and New York: Leicester University Press, 1981), p. 200.

[88] John Field and Thomas Wilcox et al., *An Admonition to the Parliament* (Leiden[?], 1617; STC 10849), sig. A v.

[89] Field and Wilcox et al., *An Admonition*, p. 11 (no. 5).

[90] Field and Wilcox et al., *An Admonition*, p. 7.

[91] See, e.g., Peter Lake, *Moderate Puritans and the Elizabethan Church* (Cambridge: Cambridge University Press, 1982), pp. 19, 86, 243, 268; Stephen Alford, *Kingship and Politics in the Reign of Edward VI* (Cambridge: Cambridge University Press, 2002), pp. 185, 207; Tony Claydon, *William III and the Godly Revolution* (Cambridge: Cambridge University Press, 1996), p. 40; John Craig, "The

some sort of reformation had already taken place within England. Historians today think this way because we have inherited the seventeenth-century historiographical concept "the English Reformation," but in fact, Elizabethan evangelicals had no such framework; calls for "further" reformation were almost wholly absent from *Admonition* and the other texts later published with it. The *Admonition* instead opened by declaring that "nothing in this mortall life is more diligently to be sought for, and carefully to bee looked vnto then the restitution of true Religion and reformation of Gods Church."[92] The authors demanded a number of changes, each of which they associated with the abolition of "all popish remnants, both in ceremonies and regiment."[93] They described the liturgy for the consecration of bishops as "blasphemous," they called the required liturgical vestments "popish and Antichristian," and they complained about reciting the Nicene Creed.[94] When the *Admonition* was printed for public perusal in 1572, the editors joined to it several other treatises. The most systematic new text was "A View of Popish Abuses yet Remaining in the English Church." Nearly two dozen "corruptions & abuses" were identified. The marriage service was denigrated for its use of a wedding ring and its inclusion of communion, select facets of the funeral service were lampooned as "supersticious and heathenish," and the liturgy for the churching of women after childbirth was said to "smelleth of Iewish purification."[95] Other controversial matters were as diverse as kneeling to receive communion, celebrating holy days, and praying for the salvation of all people.[96] Field, Wilcox, and their associates sought sweeping change in the Church of England. From the standpoint of its critics, the Elizabethan church did not need "further" reformation but reformation itself.[97]

The same volume contained *A Second Admonition to the Parliament*. Like its namesake, it called for "that reformation of Religion which is grounded vpon

---

Growth of English Puritanism," in John Coffey and Paul C.H. Lim (eds.), *The Cambridge Companion to Puritanism* (Cambridge: Cambridge University Press, 2008), pp. 34–47, at pp. 35, 45; Gregory D. Dodds, *Exploiting Erasmus: The Erasmian Legacy and Religious Change in Early Modern England* (Toronto: University of Toronto Press, 2009), e.g., pp. 40, 136; Ethan H. Shagan, *The Rule of Moderation: Violence, Religion and the Politics of Restraint in Early Modern England* (Cambridge: Cambridge University Press, 2011), pp. 111, 166. No shortage of other references could easily be added.

[92] Field and Wilcox et al., *An Admonition*, p. 1.

[93] Field and Wilcox et al., *An Admonition*, p. 1.

[94] Field and Wilcox et al., *An Admonition*, pp. 2, 4.

[95] Field and Wilcox et al., *An Admonition*, pp. 12–13 (nos. 9, 11, 12).

[96] Field and Wilcox et al., *An Admonition*, pp. 9 (no. 1), 11 (no. 3), 14 (no. 13).

[97] Another critique, made by William Fuller, was that the Church of England was "halflie" reformed. Patrick Collinson drew attention to Fuller, whose words were used to title the second chapter of *The Elizabethan Puritan Movement* (Oxford: The Clarendon Press, 1967), pp. 29–44. Further analysis of Fuller may be found in Robert Harkins, "Elizabethan Puritanism and the Politics of Memory in Post-Marian England," *The Historical Journal*, Vol. 57, No. 4 (Dec., 2014), pp. 899–919, at pp. 913–19. However, Fuller's critique went unpublished until 1915, which means that drawing attention to him risks giving his writings and their descriptive metaphors undue influence for understanding the major trends within Puritanism. I thank Alec Ryrie for the Harkins reference.

Gods boke." Opposite were "the deformities of our English reformation."[98] It is tempting to assume that a phrase like this indicates periodization—as if "*our* English reformation" then denoted what we today call "*the* English Reformation"—but as seen in Chapter 1, the contrast between "reformed" and "deformed" was a venerable rhetorical move, and accusations of "deformation" had become a common polemic widely used in religious disputation. As the next section, "Marian Historiography," will show, Marian Catholics freely drew upon the same dichotomy. So did the Elizabethan Book of Homilies.[99] The *Second Admonition* is, in fact, nothing more than a detailed elaboration of the same fifteenth-century commonplace. Early on, the author(s) explained that they "craue redresse of the great abuses in our reformation of Religion," but they later claimed that the English church had "scarce come to the outward face of a Church rightly reformed."[100] The contrast set up the text's central question, "Is this to professe Gods word? is this a reformation?"[101] The authors' answer was clearly negative, for having either misused or misunderstood Scripture by retaining the Book of Common Prayer, the English church had only "this deformed reformation."[102] Almost every page of the *Second Admonition* called for reformation—but not "further" reformation. Other, similar works followed suit.[103] An absolute dichotomy existed between the Church of England and "the best reformed churches." Because erroneous reformation was no reformation at all, reformation was yet to come.

Marian Historiography

The semantics of "reformation" shifted in England against a clearly bifurcated historiographical backdrop. Here we study how Catholics, especially under Mary, understood the religious developments of the immediate past. In the section "Elizabethan Historiographies," we will turn to Elizabethan perspectives, which dissented from the Marian consensus but failed to arrive at a historiographical consensus of their own. Almost overnight, Marian Catholics developed a consistent perspective on the religious history of England under Henry VIII and Edward VI. They argued that what began as schism under Henry devolved into heresy under his son. According to Cardinal Pole, although 1534 saw "schism," it was only "after the rejection of the obedience of the Roman pontiff" that "false teachers

---

[98] Field and Wilcox et al., *An Admonition*, p. 33; the same contrast is made on p. 35.
[99] Gerald Bray (ed.), *The Books of Homilies: A Critical Edition* (Cambridge: James Clarke & Co. Ltd., 2015), pp. 533, 534.
[100] Field and Wilcox et al., *An Admonition*, pp. 39, 40.
[101] Field and Wilcox et al., *An Admonition*, p. 40.
[102] Field and Wilcox et al., *An Admonition*, p. 55; see also pp. 42, 54.
[103] See, e.g., Robert Browne, *A Booke which Sheweth the Life and Manners of all True Christians* (Middelburgh, 1582; STC 3910.3).

began to be both admitted and listened to."[104] The regime's official collection of homilies, edited by bishop Bonner and published in 1555, advanced the same basic declension narrative. Of its thirteen sermons, four were dedicated to the doctrine of the church; the latter two pertained to papal headship. The second sermon on the papacy cited Byzantine and German history to justify the continued need for papal obedience. John Harpsfield, its author, concluded that "very experience hath this thousand years proved that such, as disobeyed the see of Rome, did fall soon after into abominable heresy and thereupon into division amongst themselves, and consequently to destruction."[105] Harpsfield then turned to England, encouraging listeners to consider "what miseries have befallen amongst us since our disobedience against the see of Rome."[106] At the time, Catholics believed that accepting the truth of their declension narrative might yet spur a happy ending.

Because councils since the fifteenth century had used "reformation" as an antonym for both heresy and schism, Catholics had no reason use the same term when describing what they considered evangelical religious error. Marian Catholics instead kept with long-familiar usage, with *reformatio* denoting the resolution of schism and the restoration of orthodoxy. In a letter sent to bishop Bonner and dated March 4, 1553/4, Mary used "reformation" to denote the reversal of religious alterations made during her brother's reign. Since Edward's death, "diuers notable crimes, excesses, and faultes, with sondrie kindes of heresies, simonie, aduoutrye [sic], and other enormities" had continued "withoute any correction or reformation at all."[107] She directed Bonner to "reforme the same,"[108] and enclosed a series of eighteen articles that directed future religious practice. Fully contiguous with the conciliar history sketched in Chapter 1, under Mary *reformatio* retained its corporeal connotations, eliding the difference between metaphor and metonym. With papal obedience among the major topics of contention between Catholics and evangelicals, Mary's church had to offer a cogent apologetic for its restoration of Roman primacy. The holistic and ameliorative function of *reformatio* thus became a prominent feature in the literature of Marian Catholicism. The first homily on papal primacy described heresy as a "poison."[109] Extending the metaphor of illness by referencing the apostle Paul and the church father Cyprian, the homily maintained that once weakened by schism, the ecclesial body was incapable of fighting heretical sickness. Quoting St. Augustine, Harpsfield argued that papal headship would make England whole, because "He (meaning Christ) doth cure in the very head of the church (meaning Peter) the disease of the whole body and in the very crown or top of his head, he

---

[104] Gerald Bray (ed.), "The Legatine Constitutions of Cardinal Pole, 1556," in Bray (ed.), *The Anglican Canons, 1529–1947* (Woodbridge and Rochester: The Boydell Press, 1998), pp. 68–161, at p. 77; see also, e.g., pp. 71, 75, 111, 139.

[105] Bray, *The Books of Homilies*, p. 176.   [106] Bray, *The Books of Homilies*, p. 178.

[107] Mary I, *A Copie of a Letter wyth Articles* (London, 1553; STC 9182), sig. A v.

[108] Mary I, *Letter wyth Articles*, sigs. A v-[A2] r.   [109] Bray, *The Books of Homilies*, p. 168.

frameth the health of all the members."[110] The papal *plenitudo potestatis* was not just medicine, but the very order of the ecclesial body. The new regime believed itself well positioned to accomplish what its immediate predecessor, because of errors both inherited and discreet, could not.

The most detailed Catholic proposal for domestic reformation was the *Reformatio Angliae ex decretis Reginaldi Poli Cardinalis* (The Reformation of England from the Decrees of Cardinal Reginald Pole). In its most recent English translation, Pole's work is entitled "The Legatine Constitutions of Cardinal Pole," but the Latin title explicitly identified *reformatio* as the document's goal.[111] As Pole expressed his hopes for the future, he drew upon a familiar descriptive contrast: "this Church of England, which from the misfortune of the past schism had been very much deformed [*deformata*] both in doctrine and practice, might be reformed [*reformaretur*] again on the model of the ancient fathers and of the sacred canons."[112] Pole organized the *Reformatio Angliae* into twelve individual decrees collectively patterned upon the human body. After an opening decree on thanksgiving, Pole began with the papal head (second decree), continued on with the bishops (third and fourth decrees), and then turned to the clergy (fifth through eleventh decrees). The text concluded with instructions on episcopal visitations, thus returning to the duties of the episcopate while also identifying the laity as a vital part of the ecclesial body. In tandem with other leaders in the Marian church, Pole believed that "the greatest amount of error has arisen on those points which relate to the doctrine of the head of the church and the sacraments."[113] The Cardinal adapted statements on the papacy and the sacraments first passed during the papal continuation of the Council of Basel.[114] The discussion on the sacraments came from the 1439 Bull of Union with the Armenians, and a single, short paragraph about the papacy stated quite unambiguously that the pope "holds the primacy over the whole world" as "the true vicar of Christ, the head of the whole church, and the father and teacher of all Christians."[115] The *Reformatio Angliae* was a detailed blueprint for domestic ecclesial reformation that articulated a level of systematic clarity evinced by no one in either the Henrician or Edwardian church.

The broader terrain of Catholic historiography was, however, sometimes less confident. Notes of self-blame could be heard as early as the Marian regime's 1555 homily collection. Henry Pendleton, author of the seventh and eighth homilies, did not fault evangelicals alone for recent history. He lamented, "If the bishops and priests in time past and also the laity had learned and practiced their duties and vocations by this example, surely the church of Christ should not have come

---

[110] Bray, *The Books of Homilies*, p. 172.   [111] Bray, "The Legatine Constitutions," pp. 68–161.
[112] Bray, "The Legatine Constitutions," p. 71; I have slightly altered Bray's translation.
[113] Bray, "The Legatine Constitutions," p. 81.
[114] DEC, Vol. 1, pp. 523–8 (session 6; papacy); pp. 540–50 (session 8; sacraments).
[115] Bray, "The Legatine Constitutions," p. 81.

to such great disorder as we see."[116] No figure emerged more central to English Catholic self-critique than Cardinal Thomas Wolsey. As William Roper wrote in his biography of Thomas More, Wolsey enslaved himself to one of the most disconcerting but frequently noted vices of the period, for he was "a man very ambitious."[117] It proved the beginning of a tradition of historiographical description that later Catholic and evangelical authors further developed. Hungering for the papacy and bitterly disappointed, Wolsey blamed Charles V, and out of a desire for "revengement" against the emperor, worked to secure Henry's divorce from Catherine of Aragon.[118] Some Catholics even saw Wolsey as instigator of the schism between England and Rome.[119] George Cavendish's much lengthier *Life and Death of Cardinal Wolsey* allowed its subject to expressly repudiate the accusation,[120] but criticism nonetheless possessed the last word. Immediately after narrating Wolsey's death, Cavendish commented, "Here is the end and fall of pride and arrogancy of such men, exalted by Fortune to honor and high dignities; for I assure you in his time of authority and glory he was the haultest man in all his proceedings that then lived."[121] Later English Catholics wrote that the cardinal was "overcome by his passions" and "domineered by his lust of power."[122] In their text, Catherine of Aragon even identified Wolsey as the principle instigator of her divorce,[123] and he admitted the same before bishop Stephen Gardiner.[124] Vindicating Pendleton's criticism of pastoral neglect, the bitter fruit of Wolsey's career only underscored the dire need for truly Catholic *reformatio*.

Through the end of the century, the Marian historiographical consensus proved amenable to further elaboration and embellishment. The most influential work of sixteenth-century English Catholic historical polemic was written during Elizabeth's reign by two exiles living in Europe. Entitled *De Origine ac Progressu Schismatis Anglicani* (On the Origin and Development of the Anglican Schism), its principal author was Nicholas Sanders.[125] He did not live to complete his study but covered only the reigns of Henry, Edward, and Mary. Edward Rishton, another Catholic émigré, edited and expanded *Schismatis Anglicani* to encompass

---

[116] Bray, *The Books of Homilies*, p. 164.

[117] William Roper, "The Life of Sir Thomas More," in Richard S. Sylvester and Davis P. Harding (eds.), *Two Early Tudor Lives* (New Haven and London: Yale University Press, 1962), pp. 195–254, at p. 213; J. Patrick Hornbeck II, *Remembering Wolsey: A History of Commemorations and Representations* (New York: Fordham University Press, 2019), e.g., pp. 28, 33, 60, 81.

[118] Roper, "Sir Thomas More," p. 213.   [119] Hornbeck, *Remembering Wolsey*, pp. 22–31.

[120] George Cavendish, "The Life & Death of Cardinal Wolsey," in Sylvester and Harding, *Two Early Tudor Lives*, pp. 1–193, at pp. 85–6.

[121] George Cavendish, "Cardinal Wolsey," p. 186.

[122] Nicholas Sander, *Rise and Growth of the Anglican Schism*, trans. David Lewis (London: Burns and Oates, 1877), p. 34.

[123] Sander, *Rise and Growth*, p. 45.   [124] Sander, *Rise and Growth*, p. 74.

[125] Sanders' last name was sometimes also written "Sander." The latter spelling is normative in academic literature today. However, I will retain the former, which was more common, particularly among Sanders' opponents.

the early years of Elizabethan England. He published the final product in 1585.[126] The Elizabethan government outlawed *Schismatis Anglicani* and Sanders' other writings, and although a translation may have been in process in the mid-1590s, it was not until 1877 that an English translation was published. From 1585 onward, however, the work proved influential among European Catholics; it was translated into a half dozen languages and became the basis for much later Catholic historiography.[127]

Sanders and Rishton worked quite firmly within the bounds of Marian Catholic historiography. As their title indicates, they interpreted the reigns of Henry, Edward, and Elizabeth through the lens of schism, not reformation. The central argument of *Schismatis Anglicani* was that lay interference had severed the English church from its papal head. In and of itself, it was not an original thesis. Opposition to royal control had been a central, if occasionally contested, Catholic conviction since the eleventh-century Gregorian reforms;[128] more recently, the Council of Trent had anathematized those who claimed that valid ordination depended upon the consent of secular authority.[129] In his expansion of Sanders' original, Rishton explained that God "brought it about that the government of the Church in England should fall first into the hands of no other layman than Henry VIII, who was a most impious and sacrilegious tyrant; then after him to those of the boy Edward; and then of Elizabeth, a woman."[130] Here was another declension narrative—from lay man, to lay boy, to lay woman. However, Sanders and Rishton expressed further opposition to lay control through their negative evaluation of Parliamentary involvement in English religious affairs. Henry VIII severed his relationship "by the authority of a lay assembly,"[131] Parliament altered the liturgy under Edward VI,[132] and Elizabeth inherited the throne through an act of Parliament as well.[133] Most importantly and most offensively, the royal supremacy was enacted through Parliament. England's bishops were thus "parliamentary bishops,"[134] and its creed was a "royal or parliamentary belief."[135] As future

---

[126] For general background, see John Vidmar, O.P., *English Catholic Historians and the English Reformation, 1585–1954* (Brighton and Portland: Sussex Academic Press, 2005), pp. 10–22; Christopher Highley, "'A Pestilent and Seditious Book': Nicholas Sander's *Schismatis Anglicani* and Catholic Histories of the Reformation," *The Huntington Library Quarterly*, Vol. 68, Nos. 1, 2 (Mar., 2005), pp. 151–71; Victor Houliston, "Fallen Prince and Pretender of the Faith: Henry VIII as Seen by Sander and Persons," in Thomas Betteridge and Thomas Freeman (eds.), *Henry VIII and History* (Burlington and Farnham: Ashgate, 2012), pp. 119–34; T.F. Mayer, "Sander [Sanders], Nicholas (c.1530–1581), religious controversialist," *ODNB*.

[127] Highley, "'Pestilent and Seditious Book',", p. 154; Duffy, *Fires of Faith*, p. 202.

[128] Uta-Renate Blumenthal, *The Investiture Controversy: Church and Monarchy from the Ninth to the Twelfth Century* (Philadelphia: University of Pennsylvania Press, 1988); Kathleen G. Cushing, *Reform and the Papacy in the Eleventh Century: Spirituality and Social Change* (Manchester: Manchester University Press, 2005).

[129] The Council of Trent, Session 23 (15 July 1563), DEC, Vol. 2, p. 744, nn. 7–8.

[130] Sander, *Rise and Growth*, p. 237; for a similar statement, see p. 168.

[131] Sander, *Rise and Growth*, p. 107.   [132] Sander, *Rise and Growth*, p. 173.

[133] Sander, *Rise and Growth*, p. 230.   [134] Sander, *Rise and Growth*, p. 276.

[135] Sander, *Rise and Growth*, p. 309.

chapters will further detail, apologists for the Church of England responded by attacking these claims throughout the seventeenth century.

Sanders and Rishton perpetuated the longstanding interrelationship between reformation and monstrosity, but much like Knox and Ponet, they gave it a political application far removed from strictly conciliar meanings. *Schismatis Anglicani* argued that both Henry and his second queen were models of excess and sin, and Sanders alleged against Queen Anne that perversion manifested itself physically. She was a living monster, "rather tall of stature, with black hair, and an oval face of a sallow complexion, as if troubled with jaundice. She had a projecting tooth under the upper lip, and on her right hand six fingers." Her character was just as bad: "she was full of pride, ambition, envy, and impurity."[136] Henry's divorce from Catherine of Aragon was due to equally distorted appetites. Divorce and schism mapped one another when Henry chose to "renounce the faith together with his wife, rather than live without Anne Boleyn."[137] From their union was born not just the princess Elizabeth, but a stillborn child that Sanders described as yet another monster—in his words, "a shapeless mass of flesh."[138] With moral and spiritual monstrosity the disorders of the day, Catholic martial resistance was proposed as a viable option.[139] The political intent animating *Schismatis Anglicani* appeared in the last paragraph of the work, where Rishton vowed, "For the present, let this suffice to show the nature of the lay supremacy, and that the supremacy of a woman, and the troubles it has brought forth; our intention was to be brief. If, however, that supremacy shall again bring forth evil upon the world, we shall not keep silence."[140] Rejecting and thus negating the political concerns of the government, Rishton argued that Catholics executed in the wake of the Northern Rebellion of 1569 were not rebels but martyrs.[141] By glorifying those who transgressed the bounds of civil law, *Schismatis Anglicani* justified similar acts by Catholics who remained in England.

Elizabethan Historiographies

Against the challenges posed by Catholic historiography, English evangelicals advanced no shared historical narrative. Elizabethan apologetics subsequently witnessed no association between schism and reformation. When the Church of England rejected Catholic accusations of the former, it did not appeal to the latter as its justification. Finding itself on the defensive may have prevented Elizabethans from developing a coherent historiography of Tudor religious developments, but

---

[136] Sander, *Rise and Growth*, p. 25.   [137] Sander, *Rise and Growth*, p. 50.
[138] Sander, *Rise and Growth*, p. 132.   [139] Kesselring, *Northern Rebellion of 1569*, pp. 117, 173.
[140] Sander, *Rise and Growth*, p. 338.
[141] Sander, *Rise and Growth*, p. 314; see through p. 317 for other martyrs.

the same truth bound evangelicals and Catholics equally in the 1560s: "reformation" had never before denoted a past historical event. There was no obvious reason why, during Elizabeth's reign, evangelicals would have redefined the same word. The semantic contest between English evangelicals and their Catholic opponents instead concerned the meaning of "Catholic," rather than "reformation" and other words now associated with it, such as "evangelical" and "Protestant." In his popular *Apology of the Church of England*, John Jewel, bishop of Salisbury, aimed to show that "we have not without just cause left these men, and rather have returned to the apostles and old catholic fathers."[142] The bishop complained that although his opponents were "called catholics,"[143] the truth was that "our doctrine" was in fact "Christ's catholic doctrine."[144] The argument continued for decades, resulting in one of the most popular defenses of the Church of England, Williams Perkins' 1597 volume *A Reformed Catholike*.[145] Perkins defined his key term as "any one that holds the same necessarie heades of religion with the Romane Church: yet so, as he pares off and reiects all errours in doctrine whereby the said religion is corrupted."[146] Unusually, Perkins joined "Catholic" to "Reformed," and some English Christians used the compound noun through the seventeenth century.[147] The semantics of "Catholic" and "schism" are outside the scope of the present study, but they returned together in the mid-seventeenth century, shortly after the first halting steps were taken to develop historical accounts of a distinctly English reformation. As we will see, it was only in the 1650s that "our English reformation"—a phrase increasingly popular that decade—was used to counter accusations of schism by celebrating an alleged sixteenth-century return to the norms of the early church.

There were, nonetheless, a scattering of instances where Elizabethan authors used "reformation" to describe recent history, but even if read together, no unified perspective emerges across these works. Quite indifferent to the historiographical habits that we take for granted, even during Mary's reign, few evangelicals described Edwardian religious change with the terms common today. John Olde's *Acquital* may have been the earliest work to deploy the same vocabulary that we now use, but as with his opposition to evangelical violence, his was an

---

[142] John Jewel, *An Apology of the Church of England*, ed. John E. Booty (Charlottesville: University Press of Virginia, 1963, repr. New York: Church Publishing, 2002), p. 17; an expansive notion of Christian antiquity, containing both the Scriptures and the Church Fathers, is present throughout Jewel's volume, e.g., pp. 35, 68, 91, 121.

[143] Jewel, *Apology*, p. 17.   [144] Jewel, *Apology*, p. 85.

[145] For statistics on Perkins' popularity, see W. Brown Patterson, *William Perkins and the Making of a Protestant England* (Oxford: Oxford University Press, 2014), pp. 42, 60.

[146] William Perkins, *A Reformed Catholike* (Cambridge, 1598; STC 19736), sig. [¶3] v.

[147] See, e.g., Richard Baxter, *The Safe Religion* (London, 1657; Wing/B1381); Richard Baxter, *Full and Easie Satisfaction* (London, 1674; Wing/B1272); Roger L'Estrange, *The Reformed Catholique: Or, The True Protestant* (London, 1679; Wing/L1289). "Reformed Catholic" may have been used on the European continent as well; see Inhabitant of Rochill, *The Reformed Catholicque, against the Deformed Jesuit* ([Netherlands?], 1621; STC 4830.5).

unusual perspective at the time. He argued that "the Churche of Englande refourmed and gouerned under Kyng Edwarde the. vi. was no heretical, schismatical, nor sedicious Church."[148] However, despite the apparent clarity of his apologetic aims, Olde offered no detailed discussion of the boy king's reforms. *The Acquital* instead reads as an Erasmian encomium, cut from the same rhetorical cloth as Nicholas Udall's preface to the English translation of Erasmus' *Paraphrases*. Perhaps revealing its defensive orientation against Marian criticism, Olde's major emphasis was upon the "catholic" nature of the boy king's reformation. The Edwardian church maintained "the catholike understanding" of the Bible, doctrine, and the sacraments,[149] just as adherents of Edwardian orthodoxy "deuysed no newe doctrine of fayth, but embrace & confesse the olde faythe with all theyr hartes."[150] Like Erasmus and other humanists, Olde encouraged the study of ancient languages,[151] criticized monasticism and prayers to saints,[152] and advanced a definition of Catholic orthodoxy that encompassed later Christian authors, creeds, and councils.[153] Olde's concept of orthodoxy points to an early episode in the decades-long semantic contest for the word "Catholic," but the success of his persuasive appeal is perhaps best revealed by the fact that his work went through only one edition under Mary and was never reprinted under Elizabeth. Olde's *Acquital* was not a historiographical watershed but a rhetorical flop.

Translations of works by continental authors are amenable to the assumption that under Elizabeth there emerged a cogent narrative, akin to our own, about sixteenth-century religious reformation. One example is the 1561 publication of *A Famous and Godly History*, a volume containing biographies of Martin Luther, Johannes Oecolampadius, and Ulrich Zwingli.[154] The title page collectively identified its subjects as "renowned reformers of the Christian Church." The long-term importance of the work is probably the fact that it contained Melanchthon's biography of Luther, in which the former revealed his ambivalence about the latter's propensity for abusive language. In seventeenth-century English historical writing, this became the most commonly mentioned facet of Luther's life and legacy. Otherwise, despite the glowing endorsement of the title *A Famous and Godly History*, of the three "reformers," only Luther evoked recurring interest during Elizabeth's reign. Under the initial oversight of John Foxe,[155] Luther's commentary on Galatians was printed in 1575, reprinted in 1577 and 1580,

---

[148] Olde, *The Acquital*, sig. [A6].   [149] Olde, *The Acquital*, e.g., sigs. B5, D4, E4–E5.
[150] Olde, *The Acquital*, sig. D5 v.   [151] Olde, *The Acquital*, sig. B1.
[152] Olde, *The Acquital*, e.g., sigs. C–C3 v, D4 v, E3 v–E4.
[153] Olde, *The Acquital*, sig. B3 (mispag. as B5); for still other Church Fathers, see, e.g., sigs. C3 v–C4 v.
[154] Henry Bennett (ed. and trans.), *A Famous and Godly History* (London, 1561; STC 1881).
[155] Elizabeth Evenden and Thomas S. Freeman, *Religion and the Book in Early Modern England: The Making of John Foxe's "Book of Martyrs"* (Cambridge: Cambridge University Press, 2011), pp. 248–55.

twice in 1588, and again in 1602.[156] His *Fourteen Points* saw three editions under Elizabeth; *The Liberty of a Christian* saw two,[157] as did his commentary on the fifteen gradual Psalms and a short sermon collection.[158] Melanchthon and Luther's works on monstrosity were printed once in a joint edition,[159] as were a small number of other sermons, treatises, and Biblical commentaries. But by 1561, only one sermon by Oecolampadius had appeared in England,[160] and nothing of his was printed for the remainder of the sixteenth century. Zwingli had little better fortune, with the translation of a lone letter to Luther on the Eucharist and a single printing of *A Brief Rehersal of the Death, Resurrection, and Ascension of Christ*.[161] In England, it appears that Luther overshadowed his Swiss contemporaries—and yet, *A Famous and Godly History* saw only one edition.

Another possible example of a developing historiography of reformation is Johann Sleidan's *Commentaries on the State of Religion and the Republic of Emperor Charles the Fifth*. Translated into English and published in 1560 as *A Famovse Cronicle of Oure Time, Called Sleidanes Commentaries*,[162] Sleidan portrayed the recent history of Latin Christendom as the unfulfilled pursuit of reformation. In his opening pages, he complained "how oftentimes the Bishops of Rome haue bene in hand with the Emperour and other Kinges, how oft they have put them in hope of a reformation and of a counsel."[163] Throughout, he discussed a diversity of possible reformations, each rooted in a discreet site of ecclesiastical authority. One option was archiepiscopal reformation. Near the end of his tenth book, Sleidan discussed Hermann von Wied, Archbishop of Cologne, who "of long tyme intending a reformation of his churche, holdeth at this tyme [1536] a counsell of his owne province."[164] The Archbishop was put into contact with Martin Bucer who, as noted in the last chapter, helped him prepare *Einfaltigs Bedencken*.[165] Von Wied's association with a known evangelical produced considerable controversy, but also raised further questions about authority, and whether local or international reformation should have priority. His critics

---

[156] Martin Luther, *A Commentarie of M. Doctor Martin Luther vpon the Epistle of S. Paul to the Galathians* (London, 1575; STC 16965; 16966 [1577], 16967 [1580], 16968 and 16969 [1588], 16970 [1602]; 16973 [1616]).

[157] Martin Luther, *A Treatise, Touching the Libertie of a Christian* (London, 1579; STC 16995 and 16996).

[158] Evenden and Freeman, *Religion and the Book*, p. 255.

[159] Philip Melanchthon and Martin Luther, *Of Two Wonderful Popish Monsters* (London, 1579; STC 17797).

[160] Johann Oecolampadius, *A Sarmon, of Ihon Oecolampadius, to Yong Men, and Maydens* (London, 1548; STC 18787).

[161] Ulrich Zwingli, "Vpon the Euchariste," in Anonymous, *A Paraphrase Vppon the Epistle of the Holie Apostle S. Paule to the Romanes* (London, 1572; STC 19137.5), fos. 68 r–69 r; Ulrich Zwingli, *A Brief Rehersal of the Death, Resurrectio[n], & Ascension of Christ* (London, 1561; STC 26135).

[162] Johannes Sleidanus, *A Famovse Cronicle of Oure Time, Called Sleidanes Commentaries* (London, 1560; STC 19848).

[163] Sleidanus, *A Famovse Cronicle*, sig. A.iiii. v.   [164] Sleidanus, *A Famovse Cronicle*, fol. cxlj. r.

[165] Sleidanus, *A Famovse Cronicle*, fol. ccxvi. r.

asked "that he woulde staye vntyll the counsell, or at the leste vntill the conuention of thempire"[166]—a convention that, as the emperor soon stated, would defer religious matters to the pope's forthcoming council.[167] Conciliar reformation thus remained an option. However, resolution proved elusive. In his sixteenth book, Sleidan explained that arguments about reformation only undermined relations between Pope Paul III and Emperor Charles V. In 1544, the pope complained that the emperor "hath nothing to doe with the reformation of Churches but the same to be longe vnto hys [the pope's] office chyefly, whom God hath geuen authorytie to bynde and loose."[168] The antinomy generated by rival reformations—archiepiscopal or conciliar, imperial or papal—further exacerbated Latin Christendom's breakdown in ecclesial authority.

It may seem surprising, but much like Olde's *Acquital* and the biopics of the "three renowned reformers," the English edition of Sleidan's *Commentaries* saw but one edition. The disparity between Elizabethan historical perceptions and our own is fully revealed by the comparative unpopularity of such seemingly crucial publications. Sleidan's work provides an excellent example. At the time of its English translation, forty-seven other editions had also been printed, encompassing not only the Latin original, but French, German, and Italian translations. By 1600, it had seen ninety-five editions and a further translation into Dutch.[169] In England, however, Sleidan's great historical work was never as popular. Other than a brief excerpt published in 1643,[170] the *Commentaries* was not reprinted again until 1689.[171] Only confirmation bias enables us to interpret the printing of this and other such works as evidence that Elizabethan evangelicals believed themselves the heir of an already-accomplished religious reformation.

Reformation by royal authority did, however, become an important theme in some Elizabethan historical writing. Elizabeth restored the Edwardian requirement that all parishes own Erasmus' *Paraphrases*, thus again ensuring that every English citizen could read Nicholas Udall's narrative of Henry's reformation.[172] John Foxe's *Actes and Monuments*, which went through four editions between 1563 and 1583, continued in the same vein. In 1571, Canterbury Convocation decreed that every cathedral should purchase a copy of the second, revised edition of 1570, and that all clergy should own the work as well. Foxe's vision was therefore, like Udall's, disseminated to every corner of the kingdom. But unlike

---

[166] Sleidanus, *A Famovse Cronicle*, fol. ccxvi. r.

[167] Sleidanus, *A Famovse Cronicle*, fol. ccxviij. r.

[168] Sleidanus, *A Famovse Cronicle*, fol. ccxv. r.

[169] Alexandra Kess, *Johann Sleidan and the Protestant Vision of History* (Aldershot and Burlington: Ashgate, 2008), pp. 2, 74.

[170] Johannes Sleidanus, *Martin Luther's Declaration to His Countrimen* (London, 1643; Wing/ L3511).

[171] Johannes Sleidanus, *The General History of the Reformation of the Church* (London, 1689; Wing/ S3989).

[172] Dodds, *Exploiting Erasmus*, ch. 3.

Udall, the *Actes and Monuments* identified no singular moment of reformation. Foxe instead presented reformation as a recurring episode in the life of the church. Like so many dawns differentiated only by passing dusk, reformation broke forth again and again. The fourteenth century, when John Wyclif lived, was "the time wherin the Lord, after long darckenes beginneth some reformation of his churche, by the diligent industrye of sondry his faythfull and learned seruauntes."[173] The fifteenth century saw reformation during the council of Constance,[174] and the sixteenth century saw reformation as well. Foxe was so enamored with the idea of recurring reformation that he was sometimes free in his editorial practices. In his 1570 transcription of Henry VIII's royal injunctions, Foxe labeled them "The kinges Articles and Iniunctions, for reformation of religion."[175] In the original document, however, no such title appeared. Something similar was true of the boy prince, whose reign was entitled "Reformatiō by K. Edward."[176] And yet, as seen in Chapter 1, Edward's reign saw nothing so coherent. It all seems so familiar today. But here too we risk reading Foxe through our own historiographical lenses. Reformation happened many times, in many places, and among many people. Reformation did not mean for Foxe what it means for us.

Simply stated, in the *Actes and Monuments*, "reformation" was a rhetorical exhortation rather than a historiographical category. With every new reformation, Foxe hit out against papal authority and rendered royal reformation central to his narrative of recurring purification. For example, he foregrounded royal authority in his narrative of the councils of Constance and Basel.

> Here is also to be remēbred the worthy saying of themperor Sigismond, when talk was ministred as touching the reformation of the spiritualtye, and some said ɸ oporteat incipere a minoritis, that is þᵉ reformation ought first to begin at þᵉ minorites. Themperor answered againe. Non a minoritis sed a maioritis, that is not wyth the Minorites saith he but wᵗ the Maiorites. Meaning þᵉ reformation ought first to begin with the pope, cardinals & bishops & other superior states of the church, & so to discend after to the inferiors.[177]

---

[173] Foxe, *Actes and Monuments* (1570 ed.), Book 5, section 2, p. 515. All citations of the *Actes and Monuments* come from *The Unabridged Acts and Monuments Online* or *TAMO* (HRI Online Publications, Sheffield, 2011). Available online: http://www.johnfoxe.org, accessed January 20, 2022.

[174] Foxe, *Actes and Monuments* (1563 ed.), Book 2, section 19, p. 236. Each subsequent edition retained this story. See Foxe, *Actes and Monuments* (1570 ed.), Book 5, section 41, p. 728; Foxe, *Actes and Monuments* (1576 ed.), Book 5, section 39, p. 596; Foxe, *Actes and Monuments* (1583 ed.), Book 5, section 41, p. 617.

[175] Foxe, *Actes and Monuments* (1570 ed.), Book 8, section 23, p. 1285.

[176] Foxe, *Actes and Monuments* (1570 ed.), Book 9, section 3, p. 1525.

[177] Foxe, *Actes and Monuments* (1563 ed.), Book 2, section 19, p. 236. Each subsequent edition retained this story. See Foxe, *Actes and Monuments* (1570 ed.), Book 5, section 41, p. 728; Foxe, *Actes and Monuments* (1576 ed.), Book 5, section 39, p. 596; Foxe, *Actes and Monuments* (1583 ed.), Book 5, section 41, p. 617.

Royal wisdom was, unlike papal perfidy, a trustworthy guide. Turning to Basel, Foxe proceeded to then limit the reach of papal power by partially translating and partially summarizing Piccolomini's history of that council's breakdown. Foxe was especially partial to the argument that *Haec Sancta* was a constitutional declaration that gave councils final authority over "all men of what estate or condicion soeuer they were, yea althoughe that they were Poopes them selues to be bounde vnder the obedience and ordinaunces of the sacred generall Councels."[178] Foxe praised the Emperor Sigismund, as well as the king of France and those bishops who sought "to represse the ambition of the bishoppes of Rome, which exalting them selues aboue the vniuersal church, thought it lawful for them to do all thynges what they would."[179] With the Council of Trent having concluded in 1563, Foxe's narrative acquired even greater urgency in the wake of Elizabeth's 1570 excommunication. In his hands, earlier eras revealed reformation as a simple dichotomy, setting the papacy against true Christian monarchy. The *Actes and Monuments* exhorted the queen to stay the course and recapitulate the same righteous pattern.

Disparate uses of reformation mapped disparate perceptions of Martin Luther's import. Unlike their Catholic opponents, English evangelicals did not portray Luther as the catalyst for sixteenth-century religious developments. By describing reformation as a cyclical occurrence, Foxe mitigated the likelihood that English apologists would fasten upon Luther as the pivotal figure of recent religious history. He introduced Luther in the 1570 edition of *Actes and Monuments* by writing, "Here beginneth the reformation of the Churche of Christ, in the tyme of Martin Luther," a header retained in the editions of 1576 and 1583.[180] Centuries later, we expect and agree with Foxe's portrayal of Luther, but it was, in fact, unusual; by way of comparison, in Knox's *Historie* Luther was mentioned only in passing. But even in the *Actes and Monuments*, and in keeping with Foxe's more general practice, Luther appeared as but one of many figures through whom reformation came. Whereas Foxe neutralized Luther's uniqueness, Catholics did the opposite. Publishing multiple attacks against the German evangelical rendered him an exceptional heresiological target. When a 1521 sermon by John Fisher against Luther was reprinted in 1554, the title page identified its contents as "concerning the heresies of Martyne Luther, whiche he had raised vp against the church, wherin it may appeare howe men sithens that tyme haue gone astray."[181] Bishop Bonner's homily collection similarly described Luther as the "ringleader"

---

[178] Foxe, *Actes and Monuments* (1563 ed.), Book 2, section 26, p. 313.
[179] Foxe, *Actes and Monuments* (1563 ed.), Book 2, section 27, p. 372.
[180] Foxe, *Actes and Monuments* (1570 ed.), Book 7, section 8, p. 1005; Foxe, *Actes and Monuments* (1576 ed.), Book 7, section 8, p. 837; Foxe, *Actes and Monuments* (1583 ed.), Book 7, section 8, p. 864.
[181] John Fisher, *A Sermon Very Notable* (London, 1554; STC 10896).

of contemporary evangelical movements.[182] For Catholics, Luther was, in the worst of ways, extraordinary.

Identifying Luther as a heretic enabled Catholics to connect subsequent Protestant history with a much larger narrative of successive but failed heretical attacks upon their church. In a terminological move unusual for the time, Marian Catholics named their domestic opponents "Protestant." Edwardian evangelicals had not identified as such, and evangelicals under Elizabeth also failed to do so; "Protestant" became a self-descriptor among the English only in the seventeenth century.[183] By assimilating English gospellers to German Lutherans, Marian Catholics imposed—or, from their perspective, detected—a constellation of heretical connections. Like Foxe, therefore, some Catholics also used Luther to advance a cyclical narrative—but one preoccupied with religious error, rather than reformation. Miles Huggarde saw Luther as the most recent reference point for other, earlier heretics, beginning with "Luthers graundfather Simon Magus, Cherinthus, Ebion, Basilides, Arrius, with a thousand moe."[184] However, the English Catholic focus on Luther simply did not reflect English evangelicals' perceptions of the history that animated domestic religious developments. Luther's writings were steady sellers, but hardly best sellers, in Elizabethan England. Future chapters will continue to show that English "Protestants" consistently denied that Luther was central to their own history. As the decades passed, they responded with increasing incomprehension to Catholic allegations of Luther's import.

Historical publications in Elizabethan England yielded neither political nor cultural consensus. Matters were quite different north of the border. In the early 1570s, as he neared the completion of his *Historie*,[185] Knox—however unwittingly—effected yet another transformation in the semantics of "reformation." Having denoted armed revolt since the late 1550s, "reformation" now also denoted a past event. From the very beginning of the work to its very end, Knox recounted a tale of apocalyptic proportions in which proponents of true religion fought against "the generatioun of Sathan."[186] Knox's focus was largely domestic, and although he began with Wyclif and Hus, he traced his story through the Lollards of Kyle before focusing on the Scottish evangelical Patrick Hamilton. Knox wrote, "it pleased God of his great mercy, in the year of God 1527, to raise up

[182] Bray, *The Books of Homilies*, p. 176.

[183] On Edwardian uses of the term, see Diarmaid MacCulloch, *The Boy King: Edward VI and the Protestant Reformation* (Berkeley and Los Angeles: University of California Press, 1999), p. 2; for a broad overview, see Peter Marshall, "The Naming of Protestant England," *Past and Present*, No. 214 (Feb., 2012), pp. 87–128.

[184] Huggarde, *Displaying of the Protestantes*, p. 16 r.

[185] Dawson, Glassey, and Knox, "Some Unpublished Letters from John Knox to Christopher Goodman," pp. 200–1. The print history is complicated. See Robert M. Healey, "John Knox's 'History': A 'Compleat' Sermon on Christian Duty," *Church History*, Vol. 61, No. 3 (Sept., 1992), pp. 319–33, at pp. 319–20, esp. n. 3, and pp. 331–3, esp. nn. 50–2; Dawson, *John Knox*, pp. 251–7.

[186] Knox, *History*, in Laing, *Works*, Vol. 1, p. 6.

his servand, Maister Patrik Hammyltoun, at whome our Historie doith begyn."[187]
A former abbot, Hamilton came into contact with evangelical theology while
journeying through Europe in the 1520s. After returning to Scotland, he began
to preach publicly. James Beaton, Archbishop of St. Andrews, learned of
Hamilton's preaching and brought him to a conference at St. Andrews. Initially
appearing sympathetic, Knox recounted that Beaton and "his bloddy boucheris
[butchers], called Doctouris,"[188] conspired to burn Hamilton at the stake, thereby
transforming him into a "blessed martyre."[189] According to Knox, the wider
Scottish nation did not respond well. Some friars soon began preaching "against
the pride and idile lief of Bischoppis";[190] other friars preached "against the vices of
preastis," and still others opposed "the corrupt doctrin of the Papistrye."[191] Recent
scholarship disputes the accuracy of this portrait,[192] but what matters here is that
Knox's *Historie* recounted, for the first time in the English-speaking world, the
story of a discreet national reformation.

Several themes in the *Historie* reverberated across the Anglo-Scottish border.
One, already touched upon, was Knox's defense of armed violence. Furthermore,
and like evangelical dissenters in England, the Lords of the Congregation, whom
Knox denoted "the Brethren," opposed two things: idolatry, which encompassed
religious ceremonies and popular devotion, and episcopacy, which Knox repeatedly described as tyrannical. Knox's *Historie* added nothing to the diatribes
against bishops found in earlier works such as the *Appellation*, but the *Historie*
reveals much about his understanding of liturgical ceremony. Immediately after
he preached his first sermon in 1547, Knox entered into a dispute with Friar
Arbuckle, Subprior of St. Andrews. As reported in the *Historie*, the debate made
Knox shine.[193] The friar asked, "Why may nott the Kirk, (said he,) for good causes,
devise Ceremonies to decore the Sacramentis, and other [of] Goddis service?"
Knox responded, "It is not yneucht [enough] that man invent a ceremonye, and
then give it a significatioun, according to his pleasur...it man [must] have the
word of God for the assurance."[194] The friar then asked, "Will ye bynd us so strait,
that we may do nothing without the expresse word of God? What! and I ask a
drynk? think ye that I sinne? And yitt I have nott Goddis word for me." Knox
answered in the affirmative: "yf ye eyther eat or drynk without assurance of
Goddis worde, that in so doing ye displease God, and ye sinne into your verray

---

[187] Knox, *History*, in Laing, *Works*, Vol. 1, p. 13. For general background, see Ryrie, *Origins of the
Scottish Reformation*, pp. 31–3.
[188] Knox, *History*, in Laing, *Works*, Vol. 1, p. 15.
[189] Knox, *History*, in Laing, *Works*, Vol. 1, p. 17.
[190] Knox, *History*, in Laing, *Works*, Vol. 1, p. 36.
[191] Knox, *History*, in Laing, *Works*, Vol. 1, pp. 44–5.
[192] See, e.g., Ryrie, *Origins of the Scottish Reformation*, pp. 139–60; Dawson, *John Knox*, pp. 177–91.
[193] Dawson, *John Knox*, pp. 46–50.
[194] Knox, *History*, in Laing, *Works*, Vol. 1, p. 195; Dickinson, Vol. 1, p. 88.

eatting and drynking."[195] The two then entered into a debate where the friar tried to prove that Catholic ceremonies were "ordeyned by God."[196] Knox dissented, and henceforth inveighed against ceremonies. More than a decade later, when the brethren offered their protestation in Parliament, they complained "that our consciences ar burdened with unprofitable ceremonies, and are compelled to adhear to idolatrie."[197] John Willock, one of Knox's colleagues, believed that the Devil had invented the Mass, and Knox identified the Devil as the primary force behind the hostility of the queen and her fellow Catholics toward evangelicals.[198] While Knox never missed an opportunity to lambast the episcopate, their perceived failures were primarily moral. Ceremonies, as the visible and effectual signs of Antichrist, were quite different.

Knox did not live to complete his work, and although it eventually encompassed five books, his narrative of reformation culminated at the end of book three, when, on July 10, 1560, Parliament abolished the mass and terminated the authority of the pope.[199] He then included the entirety of the 1560 Book of Discipline, a revised version of the 1556 service composed by the English exiles in Geneva. Some Scots, most notably Queen Mary, maintained their Catholic practices, but Knox asserted that she "perfytlie [perfectly] understood, that within this Realme thair was a Reformed Churche."[200] In 1560, Scotland's reformation was complete, and at least some of its members believed that the Church of Scotland was now "the best reformed kirk."[201] But the English had no comparable narrative and no comparable self-understanding.

Resisting Reformation

By the early 1570s, "reformation" encompassed two divergent religious visions in greater Britain. The first was unique to Catholics, for whom "reformation" denoted the determinations of church councils. Theirs was a very old meaning, but because the most recent council was Trent, Catholic reformation specifically entailed the instantiation of Tridentine decrees. The second definition was unique to "Reformed" Protestants, for whom "reformation" denoted the extirpation of Catholic practices. Most often, liturgical rites were expressly tied to Catholicism— hence their frequent denigration as "popish"—but Reformed Protestants used the same vocabulary against evangelicals with greater ceremonial inclinations.

---

[195] Knox, *History*, in Laing, *Works*, Vol. 1, p. 196.
[196] Knox, *History*, in Laing, *Works*, Vol. 1, p. 197.
[197] Knox, *History*, in Laing, *Works*, Vol. 1, p. 313.
[198] Knox, *History*, in Laing, *Works*, Vol. 1, p. 390–1.
[199] Knox, *History*, in Laing, *Works*, Vol. 2, pp. 123–5.
[200] Knox, *History*, in Laing, *Works*, Vol. 2, p. 296; Dickinson, Vol. 2, p. 26.
[201] Knox, *History*, in Laing, *Works*, Vol. 2, p. 189.

Elizabeth refused to allow either group to determine the liturgical and confessional norms of the Church of England, thus placing her church consistently on the defensive. But the English church was forced to engage in far more than just apologetic counterarguments. Militants, both Catholic and Reformed, gave "reformation" a violent application, one that often intersected events immediately north. Like Scottish evangelicals a decade earlier, the Catholic leaders of the Northern Rebellion used "reformation" in an aggressive fashion. As the Earl of Northumberland confessed in 1572, "Our first object in assembling was the reformation of religion and preservation of the person of the Queen of Scots, as next heir, failing issue of Her Majesty."[202] In the *Admonition* and its attendant explications, English evangelicals had professed their own Scottish inspiration; Catholics now also confessed something similar. The influential antiquarian John Stow understood the message, and in his *Chronicles* described the Northern rising as guilty of "pretending for conscience sake to seeke to reforme Religion."[203] For the remainder of Elizabeth's reign, English discussions and debates about reformation were made with both Scottish and domestic religious militancy in mind.

One response to the Catholic uprising was the composition of "An Homily Against Disobedience and Wilful Rebellion," a widely disseminated six-part treatise soon included in the second Book of Homilies.[204] By giving official recognition to less conciliatory uses of "reformation," the sermon rendered the term questionable. The homily began by meditating upon metaphysical order. God, angels, humanity, and nonhuman creatures constituted a fixed but sublime hierarchy. Following a Biblical outline, the homily identified the Devil as the instigator of metaphysical defiance, asserting that as among the angels in heaven and then again in paradise with Adam and Eve, disobedience was diabolically inspired.[205] In both heavenly and earthly realms, order therefore preceded rebellion. God, however, instantiated new forms of hierarchy to lessen the destructive effects of disorder. Among these was political authority, and although not salvific, there was "similitude" between "the heavenly monarchy and earthly kingdoms well governed."[206] Inverting the kingdom, rebels of every sort were "the express similitude of hell," and their leaders "the ungracious pattern of Lucifer and Satan, the prince of darkness."[207] Political revolt recapitulated the Devil's own. The middle portion of the homily advanced a detailed hermeneutic of suspicion drawn, perhaps cryptically, from "so many rebellions of old time, and some yet fresh in memory."[208] While the 1569 rebellion was the immediate target, the sermon's phraseology all but invited consideration of other recent insurrections, such as that in Scotland. The homily explained that because rebels "would pretend

[202] MacCulloch and Fletcher, *Tudor Rebellions*, p. 168.
[203] John Stow, *The Chronicles of England* (London, 1580; STC 23333), p. 1137.
[204] Bray, *The Books of Homilies*, p. 519, describes the sermon as a "treatise."
[205] Bray, *The Books of Homilies*, e.g., pp. 525, 530–1.   [206] Bray, *The Books of Homilies*, p. 513.
[207] Bray, *The Books of Homilies*, p. 529.   [208] Bray, *The Books of Homilies*, p. 533.

sundry causes," including "reformation of religion,"[209] their stated goals were a "pretence."[210] Like the Devil, rebels used deception. Good citizens needed to recognize the potentially dubious meanings that often drove the claims of political agitators. Emphasizing the point, the homily twice warned, with that most common of comparisons, that alleged "reformation" could actually lead to "deformation."[211] Through "An Homily Against Disobedience and Wilful Rebellion," the Elizabethan government not only recognized the terminology used by its Catholics opponents but condemned the same with language rapidly applicable to other forms of confessionally-inspired opposition. "Reformation" was now an inherently suspect term.

Did the domestic evangelical demand for reformation connote the same threat of martial action made by religious militants elsewhere? A series of disruptive events, following in close succession between 1587 and 1591, answered in the affirmative. The first came from the resistance theories of Scottish evangelicals. George Buchanan, tutor to James VI, published *De Iure Regni* (*On the Law of Kingship*) in 1579 after circulating the work in manuscript on both sides of the Anglo-Scottish border.[212] Unlike earlier works of resistance theory, Buchanan made no appeal to Biblical precedent, but instead grounded his arguments upon natural law and Scottish history.[213] The Scottish Parliament banned *De Iure Regni* in 1584,[214] but by then it had seen three editions printed in Scotland and two in England.[215] England's government took no action against Buchanan's work, but the same was not true of Knox's *Historie*. When John Whitgift, Archbishop of Canterbury, learned in 1587 of its imminent publication in London, he had it pulled from the press. Incomplete and manuscript copies nonetheless circulated. As opposition to Presbyterianism mounted in the 1590s, the writings of Knox and Buchanan became principle exemplars of the threat that militant evangelicalism posed to the English church and nation.

A series of seven pamphlets were then published between October 1588 and September 1589 under the pseudonym Martin Marprelate. Like other seditious works that demanded fundamental alterations in church and state, the Marprelate tractates identified neither its printer nor its city of publication. Marprelate used Knox's anti-episcopal vocabulary to animate his own demands for the reformation of liturgy and episcopacy. The first pamphlet, known as the *Epistle*, described bishops as "petty antichrists, petty popes, proud prelates, intolerable withstanders of reformation, enemies of the gospel, and most covetous wretched priests."[216]

---

[209] Bray, *The Books of Homilies*, p. 532.   [210] Bray, *The Books of Homilies*, p. 533.
[211] Bray, *The Books of Homilies*, pp. 533, 534.
[212] Roger A. Mason and Martin S. Smith (eds.), *A Dialogue on the Law of Kingship among the Scots: A Critical Edition and Translation of George Buchanan's De Iure Regni apud Scotos Dialogos* (Aldershot and Burlington: Ashgate, 2004), p. xli.
[213] Mason and Smith, *A Dialogue*, p. xxxvii.   [214] D.M. Abbott, "Buchanan, George," *ODNB*.
[215] Mason and Smith, *A Dialogue*, p. lxxxiii.   [216] Black, *The Martin Marprelate Tracts*, p. 10.

Marprelate specified five demands: the promotion of preaching, the printing of Presbyterian works, the freedom for clergy to refuse liturgical dress and rituals, the freedom for laity to refuse kneeling at the communion, and that bishops not "slander the cause of reformation, or the furtherers thereof."[217] The rhetorical violence of the *Epistle* spurred both a year-long search for the perpetrators and multiple printed defenses of the Church of England. The queen intervened in February 1588/9 with "A Proclamation against certaine seditious and Schismatical Bookes and Libels," but it did not prevent the publication of additional pamphlets.[218] Before the search for "Martin Marprelate" successfully concluded, the final pamphlet advanced noticeably harsher rhetoric. As cited in the epigraph of this chapter, Marprelate insisted that *"reformation cannot well come to our church without blood."*[219] "Reformation" was now an inherently threatening term.

Works attacking the Marprelate tracts were published for several more years, their continued relevance justified by investigation, subsequent arrests, and ultimately a failed uprising in 1591 by the evangelical William Hacket.[220] Apologists for the English church and state subsequently drew the Hacket and Marprelate conspiracies together.[221] Unlike the Marprelate controversy, which relied upon secrecy, Hacket openly declared Elizabeth's reign illegitimate and episcopacy invalid. Quite audaciously, he claimed to have received from God the title "king ouer all *Europe*,"[222] and he vowed to fight and defeat the papal Antichrist. For support, he appealed to divine inspiration and angelic visions,[223] and even claimed to "participate" in "the humane nature of *Iesus Christ*."[224] Although some scholarship believes Hacket a convenient scapegoat for the unjustified fears of English episcopalians,[225] it is less clear that contemporaries, living in the wake of Marprelate's call for bloodshed, agreed. The ecclesiastical lawyer Richard Cosin

[217] Black, *The Martin Marprelate Tracts*, p. 34.

[218] Elizabeth I, *A Proclamation Against Certaine Seditious and Schismatical Bookes and Libels* (London, 1588; STC 8182).

[219] Black, *The Martin Marprelate Tracts*, p. 197; emphasis in original.

[220] The most recent general overview is Michael P. Winship, "Puritans, Politics, and Lunacy: The Copinger-Hacket Conspiracy as the Apotheosis of Elizabethan Presbyterianism," *The Sixteenth Century Journal*, Vol. 38, No. 2 (Summer, 2007), pp. 345–69. See also Alexandra Walsham, "'Frantick Hacket': Prophecy, Sorcery, Insanity, and the Elizabethan Puritan Movement," *The Historical Journal*, Vol. 41, No. 1 (Mar., 1998), pp. 27–66; Austen Saunders, "The Hacket Rebellion and Henry Arthington's Manuscript Annotations to his own Pamphlet," *The Review of English Studies*, New Series, Vol. 64, No. 266 (Sept., 2013), pp. 594–609.

[221] See, e.g., Richard Cosin, *Conspiracie, for Pretended Reformation* (London, 1592; STC 5823), p. 85; Richard Bancroft, *Davngerovs Positions and Proceedings* (London, 1593; STC 1344.5), discusses Marprelate at pp. 136–41, and Hacket at pp. 143–68, returning to Marprelate at p. 162. For contemporary scholarship on point, see Walsham, "Frantick Hacket," pp. 40–1; Winship, "Puritans, Politics, and Lunacy," pp. 348–50.

[222] Cosin, *Conspiracie, for Pretended Reformation*, p. 24; emphasis in original.

[223] Cosin, *Conspiracie, for Pretended Reformation*, e.g., pp. 7 (divine inspiration), 14, 47, 78 (angelic vision).

[224] Cosin, *Conspiracie, for Pretended Reformation*, p. 70.

[225] Walsham, "Frantick Hacket," p. 51, describes Richard Bancroft as "waiting" for someone like Hacket.

described Hacket as "the most dangerous firebrand of sedition, most detestable traitor, most hypocriticall seducer, and most execrable blasphemous helhound, that many ages euer sawe, or heard of, in this lande."[226] Hacket was tried, found guilty of sedition, and executed. His last words were a question addressed to the hangman. "Ah, thou bastards childe, wilt thou hange *William Hacket* thy king?"[227] One supporter, Edmund Copinger, died in prison shortly thereafter; a second follower, Henry Arthington, was eventually freed, but only after renouncing his involvement and alleging that Hacket's inspiration was satanic in origin. "Reformation" was now an inherently guilty term.

Polemics against Marprelate and Hacket drew heavily upon the hermeneutic of suspicion found in "An Homily Against Disobedience and Wilful Rebellion." Anti-Martinist literature comprised a number of genres, ranging from pamphlets of satirical poetry and prose to lengthier, more learned rebuttals. Marprelate was initially seen as a threat to ecclesiastical stability. As John Lyly asked in a polemical poem of more than four pages in length, "What is it not that Martin doth not rent?/[. . .] He teares withal the Church of Christ in two."[228] Some pamphlets further identified Marprelate's attack on the church as a threat to the state,[229] but his consistent preference for ridicule meant that apologists for the Church of England had no reason to suspect Marprelate's harsh and even violent rhetoric of hiding other meanings. It was more strategically beneficial to take Marprelate at his word. The response to Hacket, however, further developed the apologetic vocabulary found in "An Homily Against Disobedience and Wilful Rebellion." The title of Cosin's work was itself an argument: *Conspiracie, for Pretended Reformation: viz. Presbyteriall Discipline.* The phrase "pretended reformation" appeared multiple times,[230] and Cosin also used "pretended" to describe various facets of the plot, such as Hacket's "pretended zeale,"[231] and his many "pretended" revelations.[232] Time and again, Cosin's word choice cast doubt upon Hacket's message; the latter possessed a "counterfeit holines,"[233] and his supporters a "pretence" of the same.[234] Tracking with the Elizabethan homily against disobedience, Cosin's Preface repeatedly identified the Devil as not only the

---

[226] Cosin, *Conspiracie, for Pretended Reformation*, p. 72.

[227] Cosin, *Conspiracie, for Pretended Reformation*, p. 72; emphasis in original.

[228] John Lyly, *Rhythmes against Martin Marre-Prelate* (London, 1589; STC 17465), sig. A3; see also Anonymous, *Mar-Martin* (London, 1589; STC 17461.5), sig. A.ii. v.

[229] Thomas Nash, *A Countercuffe Giuen to Martin Iunior* (London, 1589; STC 19456.5), esp. sig. A. iij. v; Thomas Nash, *An Almond for a Parrat* (London, 1589; STC 534), p. 5; Thomas Cooper, *An Admonition to the People of England* (London, 1589; STC 5683), is concerned with sedition throughout.

[230] Cosin, *Conspiracie, for Pretended Reformation*, e.g., sig. a2 v, pp. 57, 78; see also, e.g., pp. 1 and 28 ("which they falsely call Reformation"), 46 ("a supposed Reformation"), 85 ("pretence of Reformation").

[231] Cosin, *Conspiracie, for Pretended Reformation*, p. 3; see also p. 26 ("shewe of zeale pretended").

[232] Cosin, *Conspiracie, for Pretended Reformation*, e.g., pp. 8, 11, 89, 97, 98.

[233] Cosin, *Conspiracie, for Pretended Reformation*, p. 7; see also p. 25 (mispag. as p. 23).

[234] Cosin, *Conspiracie, for Pretended Reformation*, p. 36.

instigator of rebellion[235] but also "the deceiuing enemie of mankind,"[236] and an agent of spiritual seduction.[237] Through Hacket, the ways of Satan were made all too tangible.

Cosin's more advanced hermeneutic of suspicion paved the way for further attacks on reformation. In 1593, two especially influential works were published. The first, *Davngerovs Positions and Proceedings*, was not reprinted again until 1641, but the work helped propel its author, Richard Bancroft, to the See of London in 1594, and then to the See of Canterbury a decade later. The second work was printed more regularly. Of all the Elizabethan literature published either for or against reformation, Richard Hooker's multi-volume *Of the Lawes of Ecclesiasticall Politie* had the greatest afterlife. In the seventeenth century, it saw seven editions before the civil wars, and four more after the Restoration. The *Lawes* was the most philosophically dense of all the material related to these debates. It was also among the longest; the most recent edition totals more than 1,000 pages. Its print history is, however, quite complicated. Hooker intended the *Lawes* to comprise eight books. The first four were published together with a preface in 1593, and the fifth book, published in 1597, was larger than the sum total of those published four years earlier. The remainder of the *Lawes* was incomplete when Hooker died in 1600, but manuscript drafts of the remaining three books were preserved, circulated, and eventually printed over the course of the mid-seventeenth century.[238] Because the print history of the last three books is so intricate, and because they did not influence debate until they were printed, the following discussion does not include them.

Bancroft and Hooker applied Cosin's hermeneutic of suspicion to a much larger international context by tracing the development and transmission of erroneous religious ideas from Geneva through Scotland and finally to domestic religious dissent. Individual national reformations were thus recognized, but also became qualitatively different. Until this point, John Calvin had inspired no historiographical reflection in England, even among his most ardent English devotees. Advancing a pattern that later authors would draw upon, Bancroft and Hooker's criticism of Geneva enabled criticism of Calvin and his alleged influence upon critics of the English church. However, it is unhelpful to describe such works as "anti-Calvinist." Calvin was not the target but a casualty of an intra-English dispute ultimately preoccupied with a far more proximate—and far more disconcerting—influence, namely that of Scotland. It is easy to miss this, for as Bancroft told the story, "the Genevian rules of Reformation" were predicated upon

[235] Cosin, *Conspiracie, for Pretended Reformation*, sigs. a3 v, [a4], [a4] v, B, b2, b2 v.

[236] Cosin, *Conspiracie, for Pretended Reformation*, sig. a3 v.

[237] Cosin, *Conspiracie, for Pretended Reformation*, sigs. B, b2 v.

[238] For a helpful overview of these issues with special reference to the seventeenth century, see Michael Brydon, *The Evolving Reputation of Richard Hooker: An Examination of Responses 1600–1714* (Oxford: Oxford University Press, 2006).

regicide, which rendered its proponents "contrary to the iudgement of all other reformed Churches."[239] Influenced by Marian émigrés such as Knox, who spent time in Geneva, Scotland then rejected the same peaceful consensus, setting out "by a violent and forcible course to reforme Religion."[240] Perhaps drawing upon Cosin's own vocabulary, Bancroft alleged that Scotland and Geneva inspired England's "pretended reformers," who advocated a "pretended discipline."[241] They were motivated by "pretence of religion" and "more political then Christian practises."[242] It all sounds anti-Calvinist, but attending to Bancroft's references reveals something different. *Davngerovs Positions and Proceedings* consisted of lengthy excerpts from, and scathing commentary upon, Knox's *Historie*,[243] Buchanan's *De Iure Regni*,[244] the Admonitions,[245] and the Marprelate pamphlets,[246] but only a scattering of works by continental "Reformed" authors.[247] Calvin was quoted once and cited twice,[248] unlike Knox and Buchanan, whose writings were cited dozens of times. Bancroft's focus was almost entirely upon the newly reformed Church of Scotland and its English sympathizers. Noting that "our English reformers, and their imitation of the Ministers in *Scotland*" had failed to bring about reformation,[249] Bancroft asked, "You see indeede their hearts. And is it not then euident whereat they ayme?"[250] His question was as urgent as it was rhetorical.

Hooker addressed his work "To them that seeke (as they tearme it) the reformation of Lawes, and orders Ecclesiasticall, in the Church of England."[251] Like Bancroft, the *Lawes* began with a discussion of the relationship between Geneva and Scotland, but Hooker aimed to do more than point out the subversive nature of his opponents' demands. Accusations of "pretended reformation" rarely appeared in the *Lawes*.[252] Rather, and not unlike the 1570 homily against disobedience, Hooker began his discourse with a lengthy metaphysical meditation. His subject was law, and he followed Aquinas in distinguishing between different kinds of law, all of which ultimately originated in God.[253] The first eternal law

---

[239] Bancroft, *Davngerovs Positions*, p. 9.   [240] Bancroft, *Davngerovs Positions*, p. 10.

[241] Bancroft, *Davngerovs Positions*, for "pretended reformers," see e.g., pp. 3, 5, 14, 44, 47; for "pretended discipline," see e.g., pp. 53, 88, 94–5, 96, 176; see also pp. 128, 136 for "pretended reformation."

[242] Bancroft, *Davngerovs Positions*, pp. 23, 62.

[243] Bancroft, *Davngerovs Positions*, e.g., pp. 10–15, 18–20, 33, 40, 45, 177–82.

[244] Bancroft, *Davngerovs Positions*, e.g., pp. 11, 15–17, 29, 141.

[245] Bancroft, *Davngerovs Positions*, e.g., pp. 47–8, 50, 55–6, 60.

[246] Bancroft, *Davngerovs Positions*, e.g., pp. 46, 48, 49, 56, 57, 59–60, 125, 126.

[247] Bancroft, *Davngerovs Positions*, e.g., pp. 29 (Bullinger), 141 (Beza); the pseudonymous *Vindiciae Contra Tyrannos* was cited on pp. 18, 141.

[248] Bancroft, *Davngerovs Positions*, e.g., pp. 8 (quoted), 41, 42 (cited).

[249] Bancroft, *Davngerovs Positions*, p. 128.   [250] Bancroft, *Davngerovs Positions*, p. 138.

[251] Hooker, *Lawes*, Preface; FLE, Vol. 1, p. 1.

[252] Hooker, *Lawes*, Preface, 8.8 and IV.7.4; FLE, Vol. 1, pp. 46, 295.

[253] ST 1a2ae q. 91; W.J. Torrance Kirby, *Richard Hooker, Reformer and Platonist* (Aldershot and Burlington: Ashgate, 2005), chs. 4 and 5.

concerned God, while the second eternal law comprised the various laws that direct creation. Within the life of a *polis*, a twofold distinction held between divine law, which was "not knowen but by speciall revelation from God," and "humane law" which came "out of the law either of reason or of God," and which human beings could use to order their respective communities.[254] Hooker concluded the first book with a hymn to law, whose "seate is the bosome of God, her voyce the harmony of the world." This was the order of nature itself, where "all thinges in heaven and earth doe her [law] homage," because they recognize her "as the mother of their peace and joy."[255] With such a vision, Hooker's theology allowed nothing in the way of immediate, sudden, or violent change.

Quite unusually for the time, Hooker maintained that the Church of England was *already* reformed. Bancroft's work contained a small number of statements that tended in the same direction,[256] but Hooker, in his conceptual tug of war with his opponents, repeatedly described England's reformation as complete. Out of this conviction, however, Hooker constructed not a detailed historiography but an extensive heresiological argument: "there hath arisen a sect in England, which... seeketh to reforme even the French reformation, and purge out from thence also dregs of popery."[257] Hooker conceded the existence of "some Churches reformed before ours,"[258] but argued, like both Bancroft and "An Homily Against Disobedience and Wilful Rebellion," that there were different "kinds of reformation." One was "this moderate kind, which the Church of England hath taken," but the other was "more extreme and rigorous."[259] Consequently, reformation remained, at best, suspect. In defending the Book of Common Prayer, Hooker argued that opposition to Rome, especially in the form of "extreme dissimilitude,"[260] risked error. In a section of the *Lawes* entitled "That the example of the eldest Churches is not herein against us,"[261] Hooker discussed the third-century church father Tertullian, who joined the Montanists, a charismatic movement that the wider church condemned as heretical. Drawing a line of connection between the Montanists and "them that favour this pretended reformation,"[262] Hooker complained that just as Tertullian rejected the shared judgment of the wider church, those who rejected the approved ceremonies of the Church of England also situated themselves against longstanding consensus. Still worse, Hooker drew attention to the "reformed Churches of Poland," which had so repudiated Roman Catholicism that they had even rejected the doctrine of the Trinity, alleging it "part of Antichristian corruption."[263] In no uncertain terms, Hooker asserted that the "blasphemies of Arrians" had been "renued" by those who embraced "the

---

[254] Hooker, *Lawes*, I.3.1; FLE, Vol. 1, p. 63.   [255] Hooker, *Lawes*, I.16.8; FLE, Vol. 1, p. 142.
[256] Bancroft, *Davngerovs Positions*, pp. 41, 46.   [257] Hooker, *Lawes*, IV.8.4; FLE, Vol. 1, p. 301.
[258] Hooker, *Lawes*, IV.13; FLE, Vol. 1, p. 327.
[259] Hooker, *Lawes*, IV.14.6; FLE, Vol. 1, pp. 342–3.
[260] Hooker, *Lawes*, IV.8.1; FLE, Vol. 1, p. 298.   [261] Hooker, *Lawes*, IV.7.4; FLE, Vol. 1, pp. 293.
[262] Hooker, *Lawes*, IV.7.4; FLE, Vol. 1, pp. 295.   [263] Hooker, *Lawes*, IV.8.2; FLE, Vol. 1, p. 299.

course of extreame reformation."[264] Already suspected of a metaphysical affront through their rejection of law, advocates of reformation risked committing the ultimate theological outrage: subverting Christ himself.

But yet again, however seemingly familiar, Hooker's terminology inspired no sudden change in apologetic tactics and Elizabeth's last years saw no attendant historiographical development. If anything, the wider national upset caused by the Marprelate controversy and the Hacket conspiracy dampened the reforming ardor of recent decades. Because of Elizabeth's refusal to marry, it became clear that her successor would have to come from beyond England. With the Virgin Queen's death and the accession of the Scottish King James VI to England's throne, the Scottish Reformation became increasingly central to English understandings of sixteenth-century religious history. It proved an unhappy union.

---

[264] Hooker, *Lawes*, V.42.13; FLE, Vol. 2, p. 177. See Field and Wilcox et al., *An Admonition*, p. 57, where they reject saying the Athanasian Creed.

3

That Damned Dialogue

The Reformations of Jacobean Britain, 1603–25

I will tell you a tale. After that the Religion restored by King *Edwarde the sixt* was soone ouerthrowne, by the succession of Queene *Marie*, here in *England*, wee in *Scotland* felt the effect of it. Whereupon *Mas. Knoxe*...and his adherents were brought in, and well setled, and by these meanes, made strong enough, to vndertake the matters of *Reformation* themselues.

James VI and I (1604)[1]

Introduction

Shortly after King James VI of Scotland became James I of England, he declared himself "King of Great Brittaine."[2] Despite making England and Scotland appear united, the king belied the accuracy of his newly acclaimed title by spending much of his reign trying to unite his kingdoms across lines of religious difference, suspicion, and hostility. Jacobean apologists for the Church of England increasingly described their church as "Protestant," but their historiography was out of step with that proffered by Protestants elsewhere. Lutheran and Reformed Protestants in Germany celebrated the Luther centenary in 1617, while Scottish Protestants continued to identify 1560 as "our reformation."[3] Having inherited neither a historiographical consensus nor a discreet discourse of reformation from Elizabethan authors, Jacobean historiography developed in such a way that it felt no need to privilege, much less defend, Tudor religious developments. Neither Henry VIII nor Martin Luther were figures of singular importance. Historical works published during James' reign described select Tudor religious changes as "reformation," but only sporadically, and usually with little reference to the larger European theological theater. However, across their historical accounts, Jacobean

---

[1] William Barlow, *The Svmme and Svbstance of the Conference* (London, 1604; STC 1456.5), pp. 80–1.
[2] James VI and I, *By the King* (London, 1604; STC 8361), sig. A v.
[3] David Calderwood, *Perth Assembly* (Leiden, 1619; STC 4360), p. 19.

How the English Reformation was Named: The Politics of History, c. 1400–1700. Benjamin M. Guyer, Oxford University Press. © Benjamin M. Guyer 2022. DOI: 10.1093/oso/9780192865724.003.0004

authors laid the groundwork for a vision of sixteenth-century religious change defined by a dependence upon monarchical legality and Christian antiquity.

This chapter analyzes the increasingly fractious relations between the national churches of England and Scotland. The focus is therefore domestic. James VI and I strove to shape international Christian relations;[4] for example, he attempted but failed to arrange a marriage between Charles I and the Spanish infanta,[5] and he sent a delegation to the Synod of Dort.[6] But insofar as the goal here is to further elucidate the semantics of "reformation," such international overtures, however otherwise important, illuminate little. What matters is that the Jacobean union of crowns only intensified debate about reformation. The section "The Hampton Court Conference" looks at how James VI of Scotland, newly crowned in 1603 as king of England, embraced his new church by developing new confessional standards intended to safeguard it from becoming like the Church of Scotland. The sections "The Articles of Perth" and "The Luther Centenary" work in tandem by comparing English interest in religious developments elsewhere. Protestants in Germany celebrated the Luther centenary that year, but the Church of England took no notice. The king was more concerned, from 1616 onward, with using the English church to set the standard for how religion in his other kingdoms would ideally operate. Central here were the Articles of Perth, which required the Church of Scotland to adopt select devotional practices normative in the Church of England. Because opponents saw the Articles as a betrayal of the Scottish Reformation, "reformation" returned to British political vocabulary. The chapter concludes with a survey of Jacobean historiography on Tudor England. Setting the stage for Chapter 4, this section notes that early Stuart historians not only failed to see Tudor religious history as one of reformation but also actually advanced the first negative appraisals of the sacrilege that took place under Henry VIII and Edward VI.

The Hampton Court Conference

The first year of James' reign brought to the fore key differences between the English and Scottish churches. In April 1603, as he traveled south to London for his coronation, a group of clergy presented him with a petition for reformation. Known as "The Millenary Petition" because of its claim to represent "more then a

---

[4] W.B. Patterson, *James VI and I and the Reunion of Christendom* (Cambridge: Cambridge University Press, 1997).

[5] Glyn Redworth, *The Prince and the Infanta: The Cultural Politics of the Spanish Match* (New Haven and London: Yale University Press, 2003).

[6] Much helpful material may be found in Anthony Milton (ed.), *The British Delegation and the Synod of Dort (1618–1619)* (Woodbridge and Rochester: The Boydell Press, 2005).

thousand" of the king's subjects,[7] the authors and supporters of the supplication were optimistic about securing their desired end. The petition identified and ranked four matters for reformation: liturgical ceremonies, the requirements for the ordained ministry, the problem of pluralism, and the need for church discipline. Their sequential order revealed significant thematic continuity with the debates of recent decades.[8] In the Millenary Petition, like its Elizabethan predecessors, the rites contained within the Book of Common Prayer comprised the principal matter of offense. Complaints concerning the ordained ministry and ecclesiastical discipline followed the same Elizabethan models. Pluralism, however, was a very old concern, and calls for its reformation date from before the Fifth Lateran Council.[9] Assuring the king that they desired "not a disorderly innovation, but a due and godlie Reformation," the authors offered to present more detailed information either in writing or "by conference among the learned."[10] The king chose the latter course and in January 1604 called a conference at Hampton Court. Its outcome laid the foundation for all later Stuart conceptions of orthodoxy.[11]

Before the meeting took place, the heads of the University of Oxford published *The Answere*, a pointed response to the petition. Much like Bancroft and Hooker, the Oxford heads articulated a consistent sense of misgiving. *The Answere* derided the Millenary Petition as a "Conspiracy for pretended Reformation" and "libell."[12] The university decried the petition's authors as "factious Schismatikes" and "factious Puritaines," and further denied the petitioners' claim to represent more than a thousand ministers.[13] They even referenced James' own political writings, using Scotland as evidence that reformation would lead to rebellion in England, just as it had in Scotland.[14] Positioning itself as conciliatory, *The Answere* proclaimed on its cover page that the university's conclusions were "Agreeable, undoubtedly, to the ioint and Vniforme opinion, of all the Deanes and Chapters, and all other the learned and obedient Cleargy, in the Church of England." The

---

[7] "The Humble Petition," in The University of Oxford, *The Answere of... the Vniversitie of Oxford* (Oxford, 1603; STC 19011), pp. 1–5, at p. 2 (sig. A v). The work is not paginated consecutively. A slightly modernized version may be found as "The Millenary Petition, 1603" in J.P. Kenyon (ed.), *The Stuart Constitution 1603–1688: Documents and Commentary* (Cambridge: Cambridge University Press, 1969), pp. 132–4.

[8] Frederick Shriver, "Hampton Court Re-visited: James I and the Puritans," *Journal of Ecclesiastical History*, Vol. 33, No. 1 (Jan., 1982), pp. 48–71, at p. 50–1.

[9] Jennifer Mara DeSilva, "Pluralism, Liturgy, and the Paradoxes of Reform: A Reforming Pluralist in Early Sixteenth-Century Rome," *The Sixteenth Century Journal*, Vol. 43, No. 4 (Winter, 2012), pp. 1061–78.

[10] "The Humble Petition," pp. 5, 4.

[11] See especially Alan Cromartie, "King James and the Hampton Court Conference," in Ralph Houlbrooke (ed.), *James VI and I: Ideas, Authority, and Government* (Hampshire and Burlington: Ashgate, 2006), pp. 61–80.

[12] The University of Oxford, *The Answere*, p. 27, sig. ¶3 v.

[13] The University of Oxford, *The Answere*, sig. [¶4].

[14] The University of Oxford, *The Answere*, p. 9.

University of Cambridge concurred and soon endorsed the Oxford response.[15] By late 1603, the impending conference between the king and the petitioners was a national matter of both ecclesial and academic interest and concern.

Knowledge of recent Scottish history made rebellion within England appear a distinct possibility to several conference participants, and none more so than the new king, who dominated the proceedings. Reflecting upon his experiences in his northern kingdom, James would not allow the Church of Scotland to become a model for its southern neighbor. He rejected the petitioners' request to limit the authority of bishops, believing it an attempt at imposing Presbyterianism on England. In his words, Presbyterian order "as well agreeth with a Monarchy, as God, and the Diuell."[16] Arguing for the maintenance of episcopal order in the English church, James declared his *bon mot*, "No Bishop, no King."[17] Although the petitioners protested their adherence to the royal supremacy, James suspected the contrary. He pointed out that John Knox and his associates had opposed the Scottish bishops despite declaring their adherence to the Scottish monarchy. In a telling phrase, the king explained that when Knox and his associates saw fit, they even ventured "to vndertake the matters of *Reformation* themselues."[18] Their actions undermined the royal authority of James' mother, and thereby revealed that their earlier protestations of loyalty had been insincere. Autobiographical reminiscence animated James' approach to the English petitioners: "How they vsed that poore Lady my mother, is not vnknowne, and with griefe I may remember it."[19] James was unwilling to allow his Scottish experiences to be repeated in England. As he told the bishops, "But if once you were out, and they in place, I knowe what would become of my *Supremacie*. *No Bishop, no King*, as before I sayd."[20] At the beginning of the conference, James described England as "the promised land, where Religion was purely professed." This contrasted with Scotland, where he was "a King without state, without honor, without order."[21] Quite unexpectedly for all involved, the new monarch fully vindicated English fears of Scottish anarchy.

The king's historical understanding was both a product of and a response to his Scottish Protestant tutelage. James entered England, and thus began the conference, with the conviction that sixteenth-century ecclesiastical history took a divinely authored turn in Scotland, but he also looked ambivalently upon its

---

[15] Patrick Collinson, "The Jacobean Religious Settlement: The Hampton Court Conference," in Howard Tomlinson (ed.), *Before the English Civil War: Essays on Early Stuart Politics and Government* (London: Macmillan Press, 1983), pp. 27–51, at pp. 30–1, 188 n. 11.

[16] Barlow, *Svmme and Svbstance*, p. 79.

[17] Barlow, *Svmme and Svbstance*, p. 36. For a broader analysis of the place of episcopacy at the Hampton Court Conference, see Benjamin M. Guyer, "'From the Apostles' Time': The Polity of the British Episcopal Churches, 1603–62," in Elliot Vernon and Hunter Powell (eds.), *Church Polity and Politics in the British Atlantic World, c. 1635–66* (Manchester: Manchester University Press, 2020), pp. 17–37, esp. pp. 20–2.

[18] Barlow, *Svmme and Svbstance*, p. 81. [19] Barlow, *Svmme and Svbstance*, p. 81.

[20] Barlow, *Svmme and Svbstance*, p. 82. [21] Barlow, *Svmme and Svbstance*, p. 4.

end result. His 1599 political work *Basilicon Doron* contained a brief comparison between "the reformation of Religion in *Scotland*" and those elsewhere. Although "extraordinarily wrought by God," in Scotland "many things were inordinately done by a popular tumult and rebellion, of such as blindly were doing the worke of God, but clogged with their owne passions and particular respects." James desired a different model of reformation, and he endorsed those "proceeding from the Princes order, as it did in our neighbor countrey of *England*, as likewise in *Denmarke*, and sundry parts of *Germanie*."[22] In an obverse way, Scotland's reformation thus defined those that happened elsewhere. Scottish reformation happened against its monarch, but non-Scottish reformations, which James classified together, happened by their monarchs. Notably, the king did not discuss the doctrinal issues widely associated today with "the Reformation," a seeming lacuna that enables us to clearly see that, for James, monarchical authority was the fundamental theological issue. He was wholly committed to maintaining "the Princes order" in England. In his opening remarks, the king set forth his understanding of the royal supremacy, explaining that he called the conference by "no nouell deuise, but according to the example of all Christian Princes, who, in the commencement of their raigne, usually take the first course for the establishing of the Church, both for doctrine and policie."[23] James identified Tudor history as his precedent: "in this land King *Henry* the eight, toward the ende of his raigne; after him King *Edward* the 6. who altered more, after him Queene *Marie*, who reuersed all; and the last Queene of famous memory ... who setled it as now it standeth."[24] Devoid of specific historical detail, one matter remained fully clear. England's "reformation" was monarchical, and its church would remain so.

In the short term, the Hampton Court Conference spurred the rapid publication of multiple works that followed the king's lead. William Barlow, Dean of Chester, published an account of the conference's proceedings that had considerable influence, and helped disseminate the new king's understanding of the differences between his two British churches.[25] First published in 1604 and immediately translated into French, it was reprinted in 1605 and 1625; it also appeared at two later crucial moments, first in 1638, during the Bishops' Wars in Scotland, and again in 1661, as Charles II and his supporters began turning against Presbyterians on both sides of the Anglo-Scottish border. James recognized the import of the work almost immediately, granting it royal approval and promoting Barlow to the bishopric of Rochester.[26] Barlow's narrative was a proud display of

[22] James VI and I, *Basilicon Doron*, in Johann P. Sommerville (ed.), *King James VI and I: Political Writings* (Cambridge: Cambridge University Press, 1994), pp. 1–61, at pp. 25–6.
[23] Barlow, *Svmme and Svbstance*, p. 3.   [24] Barlow, *Svmme and Svbstance*, pp. 3–4.
[25] A good overview of Barlow may be found in Cromartie, "Hampton Court Re-visited," pp. 68–71; more skeptical is Collinson, "The Jacobean Religious Settlement," p. 37. Shriver, "Hampton Court Revisited," pp. 64–5, emphasizes Barlow's import. Helpful comments on the historiography of the conference are in Patterson, *James VI and I*, pp. 43–8.
[26] Shriver, "Hampton Court Re-visited," p. 64; C.S. Knighton, "Barlow, William (d. 1613)" *ODNB*.

James' political erudition and theological orthodoxy. The king not only connected reformation with rebellion but also defended creedal orthodoxy by arguing that the petitioners could use their theological arguments to ultimately reject the doctrine of the Trinity.[27] According to Barlow, participants repeatedly praised the king's decisions. The most effusive example came from Barlow himself, who believed that during the conference, the king had fulfilled the words of Christ. Although "brought vp among *Puritans*, not the learnedst men in the world, and schooled by them," James had not adopted their theology. Rather, "as the Sauiour of the world said, *Though he liued among them, he was not of them.*"[28] Exalted comparisons did not stop here. Barlow later enthused, "I haue often hearde and read, that *Rex est mixta persona cum sacerdote* [the *persona* of the king is mixed with that of the priest], but I neuer saw the truth thereof, till this day."[29] Aided by the strategic timing of subsequent reprintings, Barlow publicized a vision of James' reign defined by the king's own anti-Scottish apologetic.

The years immediately following the conference saw repeated public statements of English orthodoxy, all of which further defined the Church of England against the Scottish church and its English supporters. Sermons that explained and defended English religious ceremonial were preached and printed,[30] as were sermons that maintained and buttressed episcopal authority.[31] In late September 1606, James became a proactive participant in the drafting and promulgation of such apologetics. He invited four English clergy—William Barlow, Lancelot Andrewes, John Buckeridge, and John King—to preach before a Scottish delegation at Hampton Court in defense of the episcopate and the royal supremacy. The king was pleased with the outcome; all four sermons were printed and the four clergy spent the remainder of their lives in the royal favor. Barlow was promoted yet again, this time to the see of Lincoln in 1608. Buckeridge became bishop of Rochester in 1610, and King bishop of London in 1611; Andrewes was promoted from the see of Chichester to Ely in 1609, and in 1618 to Winchester, at which time he also became Dean of the Chapel Royal. James' enthusiasm for the episcopate yielded tangible results for those who supported the same, although Presbyterians were unmoved by such overtures.

Long-term developments also followed the Hampton Court Conference. One was the ratification of a new canon law in 1604, which was rapidly used to remove

---

[27] Barlow, *Svmme and Svbstance*, pp. 66, 81-2 (reformation and rebellion), 73 (the Trinity).

[28] Barlow, *Svmme and Svbstance*, p. 20. The allusion is to John 1:10-11.

[29] Barlow, *Svmme and Svbstance*, p. 84.

[30] Roger Hacket, *A Learned Sermon Handling the Qvestion of Ceremonies* (London, 1605; STC 12588); Roger Hacket, *A Sermon Principally Entreating of the Crosse in Baptisme* (London, 1606; STC 12591); Richard Milbourne, *Concerning Imposition of Hands* (London, 1607; STC 17917).

[31] Francis Mason, *The Avthoritie of the Chvrch in Making Canons and Constitutions Concerning Things Indifferent* (London, 1607; STC 17595); Francis Holyoake, *A Sermon of Obedience* (Oxford, 1610; STC 13622); John Gordon, *Eirenokoinonia: The Peace of the Commvnion of the Chvrch of England* (London, 1612; STC 12056). Anthony Hugget, *A Diuine Enthymeme of True Obedience* (London, 1615; STC 13909).

up to a hundred nonconforming ministers from their offices.[32] The canon law's opening section, entitled "Of the Church of England," contained twelve canons. They collectively defined the church's authority structures and the bounds of liturgical and theological orthodoxy. The first canon affirmed the royal supremacy and the second canon prescribed excommunication for those who rejected it: "let him be excommunicated *ipso facto*, and not restored but onely by the Archbishop after his repentance and publike reuocation of those his wicked errours."[33] Each of the remaining ten canons in this section concluded with the same anathema. Instantiating the new norms throughout the nation, every parish was required to purchase a copy of the canon law by Christmas of that year. At Hampton Court, the king had emphasized conformity, affirming, "I will haue one Doctrine and one discipline, one Religion in substance, and in ceremonie."[34] With nonconformity deprived of any canonical foothold, the royal supremacy worked in tandem with newly ratified canonical norms to effect dozens of deprivations.

The second major development was the publication in 1611 of the Authorized Version of the Bible. When participants discussed Bible translation at the Hampton Court Conference, James did not hesitate to describe the Geneva Bible as "the worst" translation then available. He stipulated that in the new translation, "no marginall notes should be added, hauing found in them, which are annexed to the *Geneua* translation . . . some notes very partiall, vntrue, seditious, and sauouring too much, of daungerous, and trayterous conceites."[35] The Authorized Version followed through on the king's concerns. It contained neither an editorial apparatus nor substituted "king" with "tyrant" in translation,[36] and it maintained traditional ecclesiastical words such as "bishop" and "church." The prefatory material consisted solely of a lengthy introductory epistle, "The Translators to the Reader," followed by a far briefer dedication to the king. The former emphasized the importance of royal care for the church and the latter concluded with a prayer for James' continued prosperity. In 1614, the crown began to strongly discourage the printing of the Geneva Bible,[37] and its last legally printed edition appeared two years later.[38] Between 1604 and 1611, a Jacobean "settlement" of the church came about through the imposition of new, and by no

---

[32] Estimates slightly vary. Collinson, "The Jacobean Religious Settlement," p. 45, estimates "perhaps as many as a hundred"; Kenneth Fincham and Peter Lake, "The Ecclesiastical Policy of King James I," *The Journal of British Studies*, Vol. 24, No. 2 (Apr., 1985), pp. 169–207, at p. 177, estimate "some ninety." More broadly, see Charles W.A. Prior, "Ecclesiology and Political Thought in England, 1580–c. 1630," *The Historical Journal*, Vol. 48, No. 4 (Dec., 2005), pp. 855–84, at pp. 868–70.

[33] The Church of England, *Constitvtions and Canons Ecclesiasticall* (London, 1604; STC 10070), Canon II.

[34] Barlow, *Svmme and Svbstance*, p. 71.   [35] Barlow, *Svmme and Svbstance*, pp. 46–7.

[36] Alister McGrath, *In the Beginning: The Story of the King James Bible and How It Changed a Nation, a Language, and a Culture* (Anchor Books, 2001), p. 143.

[37] Gordon Campbell, *Bible: The Story of the King James Bible* (Oxford: Oxford University Press, 2010), pp. 113–14.

[38] Campbell, *Bible*, p. 108.

means unwelcome, standards.[39] Future Stuart monarchs would retain and refine this English pattern as a template for overseeing and eventually transforming the other churches of the British Isles.

The Articles of Perth

Jacobean debate on ecclesial reformation thus came in waves. The next major surge came out of Scotland in 1617. Devout adherents of each national church recognized the other as a threat, but whereas debate over the Millenary Petition revealed that English ecclesiastics had much to celebrate in their new king, James' reign caused a growing number of Scots to look still more warily upon the Church of England. Once in England, James rapidly became an enthusiastic convert who looked upon the Church of England as the ecclesiastical model for the church in his northern kingdom.[40] At the Hampton Court Conference, James had unapologetically vowed, "I will have one Doctrine and one discipline, one Religion in substance, and in ceremonie."[41] To accomplish his goal, the king had to bring the Scottish and English churches into greater conformity with one another. The House of Commons Journal indicates that on April 13, 1604, during his first Parliament in England, the king called for the union of crowns, explaining that "at his death," he wished "to leave One Worship to God:—One Kingdom, intirely governed:—One Uniformity in Laws." He called this "Reformation of Ecclesiastical Discipline."[42] In a Scottish context, the word "discipline" pertained to church order as much as moral matters or ritual directives, meaning that, at the very least, as early as 1604 James desired a uniform ecclesiastical hierarchy across his British kingdoms. After gentler modes of persuasion proved ineffective earlier in the reign, James turned more insistent. His Scottish opponents responded by becoming more defiant.

A focused attempt at creating unity between the English and Scottish churches began in 1616 when James proposed the Five Articles of Perth. They aimed for significant alterations in Scottish church practice by enjoining upon it devotional practices maintained in the Church of England but rejected in Scotland since 1560. The first article required communicants to receive the sacrament while kneeling. The second allowed the sick to receive communion at home. The third required that infant baptism generally take place in the local parish, excepting only

---

[39] Cromartie, "King James," pp. 61–4.

[40] I owe the terminology of conversion to Alan R. MacDonald, "James VI and I, the Church of Scotland, and British Ecclesiastical Convergence," *The Historical Journal*, Vol. 48, No. 4 (Dec., 2005), pp. 885–903, at p. 900.

[41] Barlow, *Svmme and Svbstance*, p. 71.

[42] "House of Commons Journal Volume 1: 13 April 1604," in *Journal of the House of Commons: Volume 1, 1547–1629* (London: His Majesty's Stationery Office, 1802), p. 171. BHO.

cases of emergency. The fourth article gave bishops a greater pastoral role in parishes by directing the catechesis of children in preparation for episcopal visitation and confirmation. The fifth and final article introduced Christmas, Good Friday, Easter, Ascension, and Pentecost into the Scottish calendar.[43]

The king's push for ecclesial convergence intensified between May and August 1617, when he returned to Scotland for the first and only time since leaving for England. During his progress around the country, James' entourage worked to publicly justify the king's conviction that religious and political unity mutually reinforced one another. On July 13, 1617, the royal chaplain Robert Wilkinson preached before the king and others worshiping at St. Andrews. His chosen text was Psalm 133:1, "Behold how good and pleasant it is for brethren to dwell together in one."[44] Seemingly conciliatory, Wilkinson used France, and especially the papacy,[45] as mutual enemies of England and Scotland, to portray the two British kingdoms as united. But the congratulatory political content of the sermon was belied by his extended discussions of the need for ecclesiastical unity. Commenting on the impossibility of peace with Catholics, Wilkinson informed his audience, "if we agree not first in religion, all other agreement is horrible in the eyes of God."[46] While many attendees may have believed the same, Wilkinson's larger purpose was to defend English liturgical practices then in contention among the Scots. He hedged his apologetic by promising that he would not "meddle with other Churches," and then explained that, unlike the Scottish Presbyterian preference for the black Geneva gown, "wee of the Church of England do serue and minister to God in white, & yet we neither reuiue the dead rites of the Iewes, nor termporize with the popish Churches." Rather, white clerical garb had Biblical warrant in the Apocalypse, where it signified "purenesse and integrity."[47] Other justifications followed. The first apologetic was for bishops; "peace among men is when the superiours gouerne iustly ... when they whom God hath placed aboue, are obeyed as Bishops, and they beneath are respected as brethren."[48] Shortly thereafter, Wilkinson quoted the apostle Paul to vindicate his view that it was "lesse hainous to sacrifice to Idols, then to breake the peace."[49] This reference to idolatry may have touched upon more than one issue. Scottish Presbyterians not only considered kneeling at the communion idolatrous, but religious artwork as well. The Articles of Perth enjoined the former, and in 1616 James controversially

---

[43] Regional variations nonetheless existed in the celebration of holy days and subsequent revisions to the Book of Common Order sometimes added, and sometimes removed, the same. See Nigel Yates, *Preaching, Word and Sacrament: Scottish Church Interiors 1560–1860* (London: T&T Clark, 2009), pp. 11–12.

[44] Robert Wilkinson, *Barwick Bridge: Or England and Scotland Covpled* (London, 1617; STC 25652), p. 1.

[45] Wilkinson, *Barwick Bridge*, pp. 24, 41 (France), 5, 17, 41–2 (the papacy).

[46] Wilkinson, *Barwick Bridge*, p. 17.   [47] Wilkinson, *Barwick Bridge*, p. 26.

[48] Wilkinson, *Barwick Bridge*, p. 27.   [49] Wilkinson, *Barwick Bridge*, p. 35.

had artwork of the apostles placed in Holyrood palace,[50] along with an altar and an English-style prayer closet.[51] With the exception of John Spottiswoode,[52] Archbishop of St. Andrews, Scottish churches did not follow the king's lead.[53] But much like the king, Wilkinson defined ecclesiastical peace in strictly English terms.

Ratifying the Articles of Perth occupied James for many more years than originally anticipated. The General Assembly of the Scottish Kirk accepted the Articles in 1618, but the Scottish Parliament did not approve them until 1621. Throughout Scotland, however, pockets of resistance could be found. Upset was especially aroused by the imposition of a new devotional style surrounding communion. The Articles of Perth directed:

> notwithstanding that our church hath used since the reformation of religion to celebrate the holy communion to the people sitting, by reason of the great abuse of kneeling used in the idolatrous worship of the sacrament by the papists, yet seeing all memory of bypast superstitions is past, in reverence of God and in due regard of so divine a mystery, and in remembrance of so mystical an union as we are made partakers of, the assembly thinketh good, that the blessed sacrament be celebrated hereafter, meekly and reverently upon their knees.[54]

Kneeling ran directly counter to Scottish religious developments more than a half century earlier. William Cowper, bishop of Galloway and a defender of the Articles, described kneeling as "The hardest point of all."[55] Other Scots, including Archbishop Spottiswoode, protested against the Articles. For supporters like Cowper, the Articles restored to the Scottish church a degree of reverence long missing. For critics, the exact opposite was true. Instead of reverence, idolatry had returned. According to the minister David Calderwood, the "English patterne" filled the Scottish church with not only "strange novelties" but "erroneous doctrine."[56] For the duration of his reign, James wrote repeatedly to his Scottish ministers, insisting that they enforce the Articles.[57] Doing so resulted in the

---

[50] MacDonald, "James VI and I," pp. 894–5.
[51] Simon Thurley, "The Stuart Kings, Oliver Cromwell and the Chapel Royal 1618–1685," *Architectural History*, Vol. 45 (2002), pp. 238–74, at p. 241.
[52] Andrew Spicer, "'Laudianism' in Scotland? St Giles' Cathedral, Edinburgh, 1633–39: A Reappraisal," *Architectural History*, Vol. 46 (2003), pp. 95–108, at pp. 102–4.
[53] Yates, *Preaching, Word and Sacrament*, p. 42.
[54] Gerald Bray (ed.), *The Anglican Canons, 1529–1947* (Woodbridge and Rochester: The Boydell Press, 1998); "The Five Articles of Perth, 25 August 1618," pp. 823–4, at p. 823, n. 1.
[55] William Cowper, *The Life and the Death of the Reverend Father, and Faithfull Seruant of God, Mr William Cowper* (London, 1619; STC 5945), sig. D2 v.
[56] David Calderwood, *A Solvtion of Doctor Resolvtvs, His Resolvtions for Kneeling* (Amsterdam, 1619; STC 4364). sig. A2 r–v.
[57] Laura A.M. Stewart, "The Political Repercussions of the Five Articles of Perth: A Reassessment of James VI and I's Religious Policies in Scotland," *The Sixteenth Century Journal*, Vol. 38, No. 4 (Winter, 2007), pp. 1013–36, at p. 1031.

prosecution of at least forty-eight ministers for nonconformity,[58] and thirty Scottish ministers were deprived of their offices between 1618 and the king's death in 1625.[59] The Articles of Perth divided the Scottish church from within, and regardless of the intent stated through sermons or royal overtures, some Scots were alienated still further from English religious practice.[60]

Debate over kneeling rapidly became a topic of dispute that freely crossed the Anglo-Scottish border. In a Lenten sermon before the king in 1618, John Buckeridge, bishop of Rochester, underscored the political aim of the Articles of Perth. "All his Kingdomes must be obedient to his *venite*, and ioyne together, not onely in *vnitate*, in the vnitie and substance of Religion, and worship of God, but also *in vniformitate*, in vniformitie of outward order and ceremony of Gods seruice." This included "Adoration, and Prostration and kneeling, which are not ceremonies, but parts of Diuine worship."[61] The printed version of Buckeridge's sermon further expanded upon the theme of "Diuine worship" by including "A Discovrse Concerning Kneeling at the Communion," a treatise of more than two hundred pages. Like the Articles of Perth and Wilkinson's sermon, Buckeridge understood the gestures of English worship as an earthly imitation of heavenly precedent. The bishop's arguments were soon picked up and debated by both Episcopalians and Presbyterians in Scotland. Calderwood attacked Buckeridge's position in several works,[62] while David Lindsay, bishop of Brechin, defended the English bishop against his Scottish opponent.[63] In England, Thomas Morton, the bishop of Chester, defended kneeling, vestments, and the sign of the cross by writing against "Non-conformists."[64] In Scotland, however, opposing the Articles entailed opposing not only England as a land of spiritual bondage but the Church of England's Scottish supporters as well. Rejecting the new ceremonies, the Scottish layman Thomas Dighton exhorted his readers to remain steadfast in their defiance, for "then shall we see these Inchanters, and witches children with their goddesse *Conformity*, sent home againe to Egypt."[65] For some, kneeling was

---

[58] Laura A.M. Stewart, "'Brothers in Treuth': Propaganda, Public Opinion and the Perth Articles Debate in Scotland," in Ralph Houlbrooke (ed.), *James VI and I: Ideas, Authority, and Government* (Aldershot and Burlington: Ashgate, 2006), pp. 151–68, at p. 151.

[59] MacDonald, "James VI and I," p. 901.

[60] Alan R. MacDonald, "Consultation and Consent under James VI," *The Historical Journal*, Vol. 54, No. 2 (Jun., 2011), pp. 287–306, at pp. 301–2.

[61] John Buckeridge, *A Sermon Preached before His Majeistie... Touching Prostration, and Kneeling in the Worship of God* (London, 1618; STC 4005), p. 8.

[62] Calderwood, *Perth Assembly*, e.g., pp. 38, 49, 51, 57, 58, 61, 62; David Calderwood, *A Defence of Our Arguments Against Kneeling* (Amsterdam, 1620; STC 4354), p. 36.

[63] David Lindsay, *A Trve Narration of All the Passages of the Proceedings in the Generall Assembly of the Church of Scotland* (London, 1621; STC 15657), e.g., pp. 71, 98, 143. The pagination in this work is not sequential; these references are all found in the second part, "The Examination of the Oath Discussed," which begins after p. 136, which concludes the first pagination sequence.

[64] Thomas Morton, *A Defence of the Innocencie of the Three Ceremonies of the Chvrch of England* (London, 1618; STC 18179), addresses "Non-conformists" on its title page and throughout.

[65] Thomas Dighton, *Certain Reasons of a Private Christian Against Conformitie to Kneeling in the Very Act of Receiving the Lord's Supper* (Leiden, 1618; STC 6876), p. 142.

an act of divinely authored reverence; for others, it recalled ancient Israel but demanded a new Exodus. For all involved, the union made kneeling and other devotional practices inescapably political.

Conflict over the Articles of Perth soon intertwined with historical and confessional debate over the Scottish Reformation and the meaning of "Reformed" churches. Rooted in Scottish historiographical habits, the first of Perth's articles referred to "the reformation of religion." In the ensuing dispute, multiple Scots used and adapted the same phrase, regardless of whether they supported or opposed the Articles.[66] Dating "our reformation" to 1560,[67] Calderwood offered an especially detailed discussion of Scottish ecclesiastical history. The Scots' reformation made their church unique, "so evidentilie blessed with happie successe and sensible experience of Gods greatest benefits by the space of 58 yeares, and aboue, so that wee may boldlie say to the praise of God that no Church hath injoyed the trueth and puritie of religion in larger libertie."[68] Each of the Perth articles undermined that reformation in some way, but kneeling and holy days were the principal offenses.[69] In order to show that kneeling destabilized "the uniforme and constant order of this Kirke, since the reformation," Calderwood detailed the many subsequent dates when the General Assembly and even James VI had endorsed the ceremonial restrictions of 1560.[70] Holy days were treated in the same way. "From the beginning of the Reformation to this present yeare of our Lord 1618. the Kirk of Scotland hath diverse waies condemned the observation of all holy dayes, the Lords day onely excepted."[71] Calderwood again offered a chronology of repeated ratifications, each of which followed 1560 as the *annus mirabilis*.

All of this raised an important question: Was the Church of England a Reformed church? Calderwood had little difficulty showing numerous points of agreement between the Church of Scotland and other Reformed churches in Europe, but he argued that outside of this international agreement stood three other Christian groups. By kneeling to receive the Eucharist, each was guilty of violating the Second Commandment's prohibition of idolatry. "The Papists kneele

---

[66] Among supporters see, e.g., Cowper, *The Life and the Death*, sig. [A4]; Lindsay, *A True Narration*, is a point-by-point response to Calderwood, but never rejects Calderwood's understanding of history. Calderwood further developed his arguments in David Calderwood, *The Speach of the Kirk of Scotland to her Beloved Children* (Amsterdam, 1620; STC 4365).

[67] Calderwood, *Perth Assembly*, p. 19; discussions of the Scottish Reformation are found at, e.g., pp. 11, 25–6, 33, 63, 89.

[68] Calderwood, *Perth Assembly*, pp. 18–19; at p. 25, he writes of "Nine and fifty yeares practice and custome universally commended." Perth Assembly was published in 1619; these two calculations indicate that Calderwood saw 1560 as *annus mirabilis*. He likely began composing the work in 1618, finishing it the following year.

[69] Calderwood's *Perth Assembly* is 101 pages; 30 pages are devoted to kneeling, and 24 pages to holy days. Confirmation receives 9 pages, while private baptism and communion (articles 2 and 3, respectively) receive joint treatment in just over 5 pages.

[70] Calderwood, *Perth Assembly*, p. 33.   [71] Calderwood, *Perth Assembly*, p. 63.

in the act of receaving, because they beleue verily, that the bread is transubstantiate into Christs body." Similarly, "The *Lutheran* kneeleth upon his supposition of consubstantiation, and Christs reall presence by consubstantiation." Calderwood described the English as "A third sort" who "kneele for reverence to the Elements." Conceding scholastic theological differences between the three groups, he still arrived at the same conclusion: "this also is Idolatry."[72] Bishop Lindsay endorsed Calderwood's rejection of Lutheran Eucharistic theology, but countered that their error "should not debarre them from the Communion of the Reformed Churches."[73] Here was a less restrictive definition of "Reformed," and Lindsay explicitly applied it to the Church of England, naming Buckeridge part of "the communion of well reformed churches."[74] But their disagreement only reveals the depth of fracture occasioned—or, perhaps, revealed—by the Articles of Perth. It is notable that at least one Scottish bishop looked upon the Church of Scotland as historically closer to other Reformed churches than the Church of England. Bishop Cowper described the Scottish church as his "Mother" and the French Huguenots as a "Sister Church," but he designated the Church of England with no familial language, describing it only as "glorious with many Crownes of Martyrdome."[75] Perhaps Cowper agreed with Calderwood's assessment that the Church of England was "in the midest betwixt the Romane and reformed Kirks."[76] Scotland's reformation, so clearly and readily dated, placed the Church of Scotland in a unique relationship with other Reformed churches, of which—according to some Scots—the Church of England was not one.

The Luther Centenary

Recent scholarship has suggested that, in England, "Protestant" became an increasingly common self-descriptor only during James' reign,[77] but English perceptions of sixteenth-century religious history did not thereby track with developing evangelical historiographical traditions elsewhere. An especially clear example comes from 1617, when German Protestants observed a three-day Luther "jubilee." Theological faculty at the University of Wittenberg originally proposed October 31 as the date for commemoration, but the prince elector of Saxony,

---

[72] Calderwood, *Perth Assembly*, p. 46; see also p. 17, where "English ceremonies" are described as the entry point to "Lutheranisme, and Papistry."
[73] Lindsay, *A True Narration*, the second part, p. 141.   [74] Lindsay, *A True Narration*, p. 143.
[75] Cowper, *The Life and Death*, sig. D3.   [76] Calderwood, *Perth Assembly*, p. 86.
[77] See esp. Peter Marshall, "The Naming of Protestant England," *Past and Present*, No. 214 (Feb., 2012), pp. 87–128. Also helpful are Debora Shuger, "A Protesting Catholic Puritan in Elizabethan England," *Journal of British Studies*, Vol. 48, No. 3 (Jul., 2009), pp. 587–630; Isaac Stephens, "Confessional Identity in Early Stuart England: The 'Prayer Book Puritanism' of Elizabeth Isham," *Journal of British Studies*, Vol. 50, No. 1 (Jan., 2011), pp. 24–47; Calvin Lane, "John Milton's Elegy for Lancelot Andrewes (1626) and the Dynamic Nature of Religious Identity in Early Stuart England," *Anglican and Episcopal History*, Vol. 85, No. 4 (Dec., 2016), pp. 468–91.

Johann Georg I, wanted the jubilee celebrated in "solemnity and gratitude."[78] He expanded the theologians' vision by extending the jubilee to encompass the feasts of All Saints (Nov. 1) and All Souls (Nov. 2). This placed Luther's act on par with celebrations that commemorated the righteous dead in all Christian times and places. Festivals celebrating the German evangelical were not unknown among Lutherans, but despite the academic theological focus of many of Luther's own writings, by the early seventeenth century he was also understood as a national hero and wonder-working saint. Although hailed as "our German apostle and third Elijah,"[79] some popular texts claimed that Luther had fulfilled centuries-old prophecies, while others attributed miraculous powers to him, such as the ability to foresee the future.[80] For the Wittenberg faculty, the selection of October 31 was fully intentional; it emphasized Luther's theological opposition to indulgences by focusing on the popular—but possibly legendary—story that exactly one century earlier, he had nailed his Ninety-Five Theses to the castle church door in Wittenberg.[81] Reformed theologians in the Palatinate recommended a joint cele-bration across Protestant confessional lines, and held their own celebrations concurrently.[82] But Lutheran territories within and beyond the Holy Roman Empire followed the lead of Johann Georg I, slowly elevating the Luther centenary into a defining feature of the festive culture of international Lutheranism.

When the Luther jubilee reached England's shores the following year, English interest was underwhelming. Only one work was published on point, *The Dvke of Saxonie His Ivbilee*, a confessionally idiosyncratic pamphlet comprised of three texts, each of which advanced a distinct understanding of Luther. The first, a set of liturgical directions composed by Johann Georg I with his theological counsel-ors,[83] communicated the prince's vision for the jubilee, which identified Luther as an apocalyptic figure first prophesied in the Old Testament. The prince elector directed clergy in his territory to preach twice and celebrate communion each day between October 31 and November 2. Specific prayers and Scripture passages were appointed for use, each of which the prince elector glossed for his ministers.

---

[78] Quoted in Marianne Carbonnier-Burkard, "Reformation Jubilees: A Protestant Construction," in Petra Bosse-Huber, Serge Fornerod, Thies Gundlach, and Gottfried Locher (eds.), *Reformation: Legacy and Future* (Geneva: World Council of Churches Publications, 2015), pp. 183–96, at p. 184. Robert Kolb, *Martin Luther as Prophet, Teacher, and Hero: Images of the Reformer, 1520–1620* (Grand Rapids: Baker Books, 1999), pp. 126–34, believes that the impetus came from the Reformed.

[79] Quoted in Kolb, *Martin Luther*, p. 130.

[80] Kolb, *Martin Luther*, p. 129; for Lutheran miracle culture more generally, particularly that surrounding Luther, see R.W. Scribner, "Incombustible Luther: The Image of the Reformer in Early Modern Germany," *Past & Present*, No. 110 (Feb., 1986), pp. 38–68. Transformations of relics in Lutheran culture are studied in Ulinka Rublack, "Grapho-Relics: Lutheranism and the Materialization of the World," *Past and Present* (2010), Supplement 5, pp. 144–66.

[81] For the origins and early development of this possibly apocryphal event, see Peter Marshall, *1517: Martin Luther and the Invention of the Reformation* (Oxford: Oxford University Press, 2017), esp. ch. 2.

[82] Marshall, *1517*, pp. 89–90.

[83] Thomas Albert Howard, *Remembering the Reformation: An Inquiry into the Meanings of Protestantism* (Oxford: Oxford University Press, 2017), pp. 14–15.

For example, on October 31, the reading was a passage from Daniel 12. The prince expressly identified the pope as the Antichrist and Luther as the fulfillment of Daniel's prophetic vision of deliverance.[84] Readings for the subsequent days were much the same, drawing upon the Revelation of St. John in the New Testament and Exodus in the Old. For the prince and his co-religionists, Luther was the subject of a distinctly—and combatively—Protestant memory and thanksgiving.

A different understanding of Luther came from the pamphlet's second text, a partisan outline of Christian history from 1517 to 1610 entitled *A Chronology of the Gospels Ivbilee*. Originally printed in Heidelberg, the text reveled in its Reformed confessional orientation,[85] celebrating iconoclasm and commenting extensively on Reformed history. Unlike Johann Georg I, whose Luther jubilee revolved around Luther, this work placed Luther at the beginning of a linear narrative that soon encompassed the Swiss evangelical and Huguenot movements. Matching the prince elector in apocalyptic tenor, the *Chronology* opened, "In the yeare 1517. the first wound was inflicted vpon Antichrist, in a disputation at *Wittenberge* against Indulgences."[86] Within the space of barely a page, the *Chronology* turned to celebrate Swiss history, elaborating that in 1528, "the truth of the reformed doctrine triumph in the disputation at *Berne*, vpon which followed the reformation of many famous Churches."[87] The remainder of the text encompassed later Reformed history. From this perspective, Luther was a catalyst, but nothing more.

The English translator of these two works offered yet a third view of Luther. In the introduction, 1517 remained important, but the translator further wrote, "Now wee and all Gods people wheresoeuer, make up all but one body, the Church (which is Zion) the requickening and recollecting of whose members was in part, by Luther effected."[88] The qualifier should be emphasized: "in part." Instead of granting any kind of primacy to Luther, the translator maintained the historical vision of John Foxe, developing their Elizabethan source by claiming that this line of prophets had not ended with Luther but continued directly into the present. The most recent was Marco Antonio de Dominis, the Archbishop of Spalato who had left his archiepiscopal see and defected from Roman Catholicism, entering England and its episcopal church in 1616 (although he later returned to Roman Catholicism). Praising divine providence, the editor enthused that God "raised *Wickleff* from their Schooles, *Iohn Husse* from their Pulpits, *Martin Luther* from their Cloysters, and now *Marke Antony* from their Archiepiscopall Chaire."[89] This distinctly English historiography, with its repeated and continuing

---

[84] Anonymous, *The Dvke of Saxonie His Ivbilee* (London, 1618; STC 14656), pp. 3–4.

[85] Anonymous, *Dvke of Saxonie His Ivbilee*, p. 11.

[86] Anonymous, *Dvke of Saxonie His Ivbilee*, p. 8.

[87] Anonymous, *Dvke of Saxonie His Ivbilee*, p. 9.

[88] Anonymous, *Dvke of Saxonie His Ivbilee*, sig. A2.

[89] Anonymous, *Dvke of Saxonie His Ivbilee*, sig. [A4] r–v.

acts of providential intervention, could not portray Luther as inflicting "the first wound" in an apocalyptic battle. Johann Georg I made Luther the apocalyptic axis of recent deliverance, and the *Chronology* made the Luther the apocalyptic starting point for recent history; but for the anonymous English translator, Luther was simply one figure among many others, past no less than present.

Luther's purported import did not become a subject of sustained debate in England for another five years, but it took an impetus other than his centenary to bring the German evangelical to the attention of English religious controversialists. That catalyst was the conversion of Mary Villiers, countess of Buckingham, to Catholicism in 1622. George, her son, was the king's favorite, which put her new religious convictions perilously close to the center of political power. Her conversion also came at a time when anti-Catholic feeling was on the increase in England due to international developments, notably the beginning of what became the Thirty Years' War, and the failure of George Villiers and Prince Charles to secure a dynastic union between England and Spain. The countess embraced Catholicism due to the evangelistic efforts of John Percy, better known as Fisher the Jesuit, an energetic English convert to Catholicism. Between 1605 and 1610, Fisher had been involved in a small controversy about Roman Catholicism and its relation to the Church of England. His apologetic work, *A Treatise of Faith*, published pseudonymously in 1605 under the initials A.D., attracted replies by the clergymen Anthony Wotton and John White. None of these texts proved popular or had long-term influence, although White's response, entitled *The Way to the True Church* (1608), saw a second impression in 1610. Only with the countess of Buckingham's conversion did Fisher become a figure of major domestic interest.

On June 27, 1623, Fisher participated in a theological conference with Daniel Featley and Francis White, apologists for the Church of England. Featley quickly published his account of the conference as *The Fisher Catched in His Owne Net*. Initially a short, twenty-eight-page pamphlet, a much-expanded version of more than five hundred pages was published in 1624 with the slightly different title *The Romish Fisher Cavght and Held in His Owne Net*.[90] According to Featley, the conference primarily concerned the visibility of the Church. Fisher chose the topic, and in scholastic style, set forth two questions for dispute: "Whether the Protestant Church was in all ages visible, and especially in the ages going before Luther: 2. And whether the names of such visible Protestants in all ages can be shewed and proued out of good Authors."[91] Despite the request of M. Sweet, another Jesuit in attendance, that "all bitter speeches be forborne,"[92] the conversation quickly devolved. Each group demanded that the other side offer

---

[90] Daniel Featley, *The Fisher Catched in His Owne Net* (London, 1623; STC 10732); Daniel Featley, *The Romish Fisher Cavght and Held in His Owne Net* (London, 1624; STC 10738.3).
[91] Featley, *The Fisher*, p. 5.   [92] Featley, *The Fisher*, p. 7.

a list of historical witnesses to justify its particular version of Christianity, but neither would do so until the other side first offered the same.[93] After several rounds back and forth, Featley averred that "The Protestant Church was so visible, that the names of those who taught and beleeued the doctrine thereof, may be produced in the first hundred yeares, and second, and third, and fourth, & sic de caeteris [etcetera]."[94] Beginning with Christ and the apostles, he offered names from the pre-Constantinian church: Ignatius of Antioch, Justin Martyr, Clement of Alexandria, and Cyprian.[95] Featley refused to continue until Fisher offered his own set of names for the same time period, but Fisher declined to do so and the conference dissolved.[96]

In their debate, theological dispute mapped historiographical disparity. By placing Luther as the historical pivot at the very beginning of the discussion, Fisher depended upon the Catholic heresiology already made familiar by Catholic polemicists since the reign of Mary I. Featley, however, wanted to emphasize the early church, "especially in the first 600 yeares."[97] In his expanded edition of 1624, Featley further developed the point, alleging that Fisher "would haue the *Opponents* begin first with the last age, and so ascend vpwards," thus enabling Fisher to "lurke in the darke and muddy age next before *Luther*," far from "the cleare streame of Antiquity."[98] By beginning with the apostolic and post-apostolic church, Featley's historiography moved in the opposite direction. But this did not cause Featley to simply set aside "Protestant" as a self-descriptor. In an addendum entitled "Of the denomination *Protestant*," Featley argued that because Protestant doctrine was identical with early Christian doctrine, the name Protestant was but a synonym for a number of other words, such as "Berengarians," "Henricians," "Lollards," "Hussites," "Gospellers," and "Christians."[99] However curious and even unbelievable it might seem today, Featley's attempt at defining Protestantism without reference to Luther was, within his English context, fully reasonable; like Foxe and the translator of the Luther jubilee texts, Featley saw no need to elevate Luther above other, allegedly prophetic and even apocalyptic figures. He denied the validity of the Catholic question, "Where was your church before Luther?" The German evangelical was axiomatic only for Lutherans and their Catholic opponents.

Multiple authors followed Featley's lead and cited his work with approval,[100] consistently rejecting the importance that Catholic apologists ascribed to

---

[93] Featley, *The Fisher*, pp. 10, 13, 21.   [94] Featley, *The Fisher*, p. 23.
[95] Featley, *The Fisher*, pp. 23–4.   [96] Featley, *The Fisher*, pp. 24–5.
[97] Featley, *The Fisher*, p. 7.   [98] Featley, *The Romish Fisher*, p. 36.
[99] Featley, *The Romish Fisher*, sig. L2* v–[L4*] r, at sig. L3*.
[100] Thomas Bedford, *Luthers Predecessours: Or an Answere to the Qvestion of the Papists: Where was Your Church before Luther?* (London, 1624; STC 1787), pp. 2–3; Alexander Cooke, *Saint Avstins Religion* (London, 1624; STC 6059), sig. A2.

Luther.[101] Despite the appearance of more than a dozen works against Fisher in the mid-1620s, only William Laud's account of the conference was reprinted throughout the century; first appearing in 1624, it was expanded and reprinted twice in 1639, and again in 1673 and 1686. More common was the sudden surge and rapid dissolution of theological disputation. Richard Bernard's 1623 work *Looke beyond Luther* represents such apologetics well. It bore the explanatory subtitle "Or an Answere to that Qvestion, so often and so insvltingly proposed by our Aduersaries, asking vs; *Where this our Religion was before* Luthers *time?*"[102] Bernard returned to this question throughout the volume,[103] and his collective answers proved popular enough to see a second impression in 1624. The main body of *Looke beyond Luther* consisted of six arguments concerning English belief; each argument began with a syllogism intended to show that English orthodoxy— which Bernard, like others, freely identified as "Protestant"—predated Catholic belief. Two of the six sections were apologetic: the fourth, which appealed to contemporary Catholic practice as a covert argument for English orthodoxy, and the last, which claimed that God was "the Author, and continuall Preseruer of our Religion, against all oppositions."[104] The other four sections appealed to history: the origins and content of the Bible (section one), martyrs ancient and modern (section two), the early Church (section three), and Bede's *Ecclesiastical History* (section five). Each argument claimed that Protestantism predated Luther because it was synonymous with early Christian orthodoxy. In Bernard's words, "Protestants are of the Catholike Church, though no Romanists."[105] Like so many of his contemporaries, Bernard identified the parameters of Catholic ortho- doxy as having been codified in the first six hundred years of Christian history.[106] His rejection of the Catholic heresiological emphasis upon Luther reflected pre- existing English assumptions. For the English, Luther really was a figure of minor consequence.

The print history of Luther's writings in England during these years follows the same pattern. James' reign saw published only three works by Luther. The first, in 1615, was his commentary on the fifteen gradual Psalms,[107] and his commentary on Galatians was printed one year later.[108] The German Elijah's centenary did not inspire the English to print or translate anything. It was not until 1624, amidst the debates between Fisher and his opponents, that the third work appeared, a

---

[101] For general background on these debates, see S.J. Barnett, "Where Was Your Church before Luther? Claims for the Antiquity of Protestantism Examined," *Church History*, Vol. 68, No. 1 (Mar., 1999), pp. 14–41.

[102] Richard Bernard, *Looke beyond Luther* (London, 1623; STC 1956.7).

[103] Bernard, *Looke beyond Luther*, e.g., sig. A3v, pp. 1, 2, 12, 24–8, 35, 37, 38.

[104] Bernard, *Looke beyond Luther*, p. 35.   [105] Bernard, *Looke beyond Luther*, p. 41.

[106] Bernard, *Looke beyond Luther*, pp. 24–5, 31, 43; Cooke, *Saint Avstins Religion*, contains the same focus on Christian antiquity.

[107] Martin Luther, *A Commentarie vpon the Fifteene Psalmes* (London, 1615; STC 16976).

[108] Martin Luther, *A Commentarie of M. Doctor Martin Luther vpon the Epistle of S. Paul to the Galathians* (London, 1616; STC 16973).

translation of select prayers and Biblical commentaries. Entitled *Every-dayes Sacrifice*,[109] these were the only writings by Luther printed in the 1620s, and in 1629 the work saw its second and final impression. If Luther defined Protestantism, then the Luther centenary should have aroused considerable interest among those English who increasingly identified themselves as "Protestant." But the Luther centenary was effectively dead on arrival.

Jacobean Historiography

"To conclude, search the Scriptures, studie the Fathers, and read the Antiquaries."[110] These words, originally written against Fisher, highlight the importance of historical research and writing to seventeenth-century religious disputation. Quite unlike religious writers in Scotland, who identified 1560 as the year of their reformation, English authors neither possessed nor advanced a comparable historiographical schema. Tudor ecclesiastical history failed to occupy an analogous axiomatic position in England. The contrast between the two British nations is well underscored by the 1619 printing in England of Paolo Sarpi's history of the Council of Trent; translated into English in 1620, the work detailed the debates about *reformatio* that took place before, during, and after the council. And yet, Sarpi's work had little to no immediate impact upon English historiography and spurred no attempt at comparing Catholic considerations of Tridentine conciliar *reformatio* with an English reformation.[111] However, as this chapter has already shown, there were sporadic mentions of reformation in England. The Hampton Court Conference offered several instances. In their pamphlet before the conference, the University of Oxford alleged that Puritans intended to "depraue and slaunder, not only the Communion booke, but the whole estate of the Church, as it standes reformed by our late Soueraigne."[112] And, as also noted, James saw England as sharing in a broad, international trend of monarchical reformation—a trend that Scotland refused. But such descriptions were comparatively rare, and should not obscure the more consistent fact that discussions of a discreetly demarcated Tudor religious "reformation" appeared, at most, idiosyncratically.

Where such discussions did appear, they were often at variance with our own historiographical assumptions. In his *Rervm Anglicarvm* (1616), translated in 1630 under the title *Annales of England*, Francis Godwin, later bishop of Hereford, wrote about the reigns of Henry VIII, Edward VI, and Mary I. He

---

[109] W.R.S., *Every-dayes Sacrifice* (London, 1624; STC 6398).

[110] Cooke, *Saint Avstins Religion*, sig. A3.

[111] For a full analysis of Sarpi, see Jaska Kainulainen, *Paolo Sarpi: A Servant of God and State* (Leiden and Boston: Brill, 2014).

[112] The University of Oxford, *The Answere*, sig. ¶3 v.

discussed "Reformation in point of religion" under Edward,[113] but as far as Godwin was concerned, it was fully accomplished by the end of 1547. In his work, the Prayer Books of 1549 and 1552 did not even receive a mention.[114] John Hayward, who authored *The Life and Raigne of King Edward the Sixth*, the first stand-alone study on Edward, never used "reformation" to describe religious developments during the boy king's reign. However, and despite the example found in Godwin, it was unusual at the time to associate Edward's reign with reformation. By not doing so, Hayward tracked with earlier authors; he did not, as some contemporary scholarship argues,[115] push against a preexisting historiographical tradition. In fact, there was no such tradition, because Jacobean authors inherited from earlier historiography no conception of Tudor ecclesial reformation "in head and in members." Simply stated, "reformation" was not yet an organizing category for English historical self-understanding.

Jacobean authors were instead preoccupied with the question of sacrilege.[116] Concerns about the Church of England and its material wellbeing were voiced quite early in James' reign, with Roger Fenton preaching against simony and sacrilege at Paul's Cross on March 18, 1604/5.[117] Sermons on point recurred throughout the reign,[118] and some works further attained minor popularity. In 1613, Henry Spelman published *De Non Temerandis Ecclesiis, A Tracte of the Rights and Respect Due Vnto Chvrches*. He published an expanded edition in 1616 that, after his death, was expanded yet again by his clerical associate Jeremy Stephens; Spelman's son Clement published a further expansion in 1668, which was reprinted in 1676. Finally, and although it remained in manuscript form during Spelman's lifetime, *The History and Fate of Sacrilege*, a lengthy study and analysis partially written with Stephens, was published posthumously in 1698. Spelman's comparatively slight output should not obscure his long-term influence.

---

[113] Francis Godwin, *Rervm Anglicarvm Henrico VIII. Edwardo VI. Et Maria Regnantibus, Annales* (London, 1616; STC 11945); the English edition, translated by Morgan Godwin, is Francis Godwin, *Annales of England* (London, 1630; STC 11947), p. 217. Except where noted, all citations come from the 1630 translation.

[114] Godwin, *Annales of England*, pp. 217–18.

[115] See, e.g., Dale Hoak, "Edward VI," *ODNB*; Diarmaid MacCulloch, *The Boy King: Edward VI and the Protestant Reformation* (Berkeley and Los Angeles: The University of California Press, 1999), pp. 206–8; Stephen Alford, *Kingship and Politics in the Reign of Edward VI* (Cambridge: Cambridge University Press, 2002), pp. 15–18.

[116] Much helpful background material on sacrilege may be found in Graham Parry, *The Arts of the Anglican Counter-Reformation: Glory, Laud and Honour* (Woodbridge and Rochester: The Boydell Press, 2006), ch. 9; see also Alexandra Walsham, *The Reformation of the Landscape: Religion, Identity, & Memory in Early Modern Britain & Ireland* (Oxford: Oxford University Press, 2011), esp. pp. 283–93.

[117] Roger Fenton, *A Sermon of Simonie and Sacrilege* (London, 1604; STC 10801).

[118] See Samuel Gardiner, *The Scovrge of Sacriledge* (London, 1611; STC 11580); Roger Gostwick, *The Anatomie of Ananias: Or, Gods Censure against Sacrilege* (London, 1616; STC 12100); James Sempill, *Sacrilege Sacredly Handled* (London, 1619; STC 22186).

Sacrilege had two historiographical functions. First, narratives of sacrilege aligned seemingly chaotic historical events with the moral clarity of divine order. Those who defied this order therefore defied God. Taking the early Church as his model, Spelman argued that through consecration, "both Church and Church-livings were thus solemnely delivered into Gods possession; and therefore all ages, Councels and Fathers (that ever I yet have met with) account them holy and inviolable things."[119] In the Old Testament, Spelman believed, "the Temple was sanctified unto *three functions.*" First, it was the locus of "the *Divine presence*"; second, atonement was accomplished through the sacrifice of animals; third was "simple worship, prayer, and doctrine."[120] Spelman concluded, "We read not therefore, that Christ reformed any thing in the other two functions of the *Temple*; for they were now, as at an end. But because this third function was for ever to continue to his Church: therefore he purgeth it of that that prophaned it, restoreth it (as he did marriage) to the original sanctitie."[121] Christians were to give the same reverence to churches that Jews showed to the Temple in Jerusalem. In new material appended to the 1616 edition, Spelman detailed how, throughout history, vengeance was visited upon those who spoiled consecrated places. Later expansions of his text added still further information about the history of divine retribution. Other Stuart authors also tracked accounts of divine intervention, and although specific details were sometimes at variance, they all agreed with Hayward's claim that preternatural events "were seene either as messengers or signes of some imminent and eminent euill."[122] If sacrilege produced material losses difficult to relocate, the shamefulness of sacrilege remained easy to find, and its presence was a key factor in treating Tudor ecclesiastical history as a topic for critical evaluation, rather than uncritical celebration.

The second function of sacrilege was thus critique. Whereas modern historians see iconoclasm as a direct function of Protestant belief, "sacrilege" carried a particular value judgment for Stuart authors that distanced their conception of orthodoxy from the perceived excesses of the Tudor past. Stuart analyses of Tudor England discussed and denounced spoliation, with Henry VIII and the Duke of Northumberland identified as the principal culprits. Importantly, authors did not connect sacrilege with any particular confessional orientation. Like Spelman, Godwin noted instances of judgment against those who spoiled the kingdom, and he found evidence of sacrilege well before the English break with Rome. In 1525, "the Pope consenting," Cardinal Wolsey "demolished fourty Monasteries of meaner note, and conferred the lands belonging to them, on these his new

---

[119] Henry Spelman, *De Non Temerandis Ecclesiis* (Oxford, 1646; Wing/S4919A), p. 10.

[120] Spelman, *De Non Temerandis Ecclesiis*, pp. 14–15.

[121] Spelman, *De Non Temerandis Ecclesiis*, p. 16.

[122] John Hayward, *The Life and Raigne of King Edward the Sixth*, ed. Barrett L. Beer (Kent: The Kent State University Press, 1993), p. 168.

Colledges."[123] Four of the men who participated in this act suffered grizzly deaths—two were murdered, a third was hung, and a fourth committed suicide—while the fifth, "before that a wealthy man, sunke to that low ebbe, that he after begged his bread." Drawing readers' attention to the point, Godwin explained, "I could wish, that by these and the like examples, men would learne to take heed how they lay hands on things consecrated to God."[124] Godwin described Wolsey's fall from Henry's grace as a direct consequence of spoliation, which then had a further negative effect upon the kingdom, because Wolsey was, in fact, a check upon the king's own greed. Godwin offered a long list of Henry's failures, beginning with "Lust, Tyrannie, and Avarice," and concluding with "the Church (or rather the Common-wealth) horribly spoiled and robbed of her Patrimony."[125] Throughout the remainder of his *Annales* on Henry, Godwin detailed sacrilege upon sacrilege,[126] but he distinguished it from the rough (or, iconoclastic) correction of alleged religious error. He criticized monks and nuns for spreading "superstition, wherewith the Divine Worship had by them beene polluted," but he also lamented the loss of monasticism, which was "instituted according to the pious example of antient Fathers."[127] Henry's church was hardly Catholicism without the pope. It was victor as much as victim.

Some historians recognized the interplay of confessional debate and icono-clasm, but they believed the relationship more sporadic than the consensus found in contemporary scholarship. According to Godwin, the Church became "Prey" during Edward's reign, because "the infancy of the King in this incertaine ebbe and flow of Religion, made her opportune to all kinde of sacriledge."[128] Northumberland cast an especially long shadow, not least because of the theft of church goods to pay off the king's debts. According to Hayward, commissioners were sent throughout the kingdom to make inquiry into the wealth of churches—ranging from jewels, gold, and silver, to artwork, paten and chalices—"the residue to be applied to the benefit of the King."[129] As the king lay upon his deathbed, Northumberland was "sottishly mad with ouer great fortune,"[130] precisely because religion was not his motivation. Godwin connected religious conviction to spoli-ation only when discussing churches outside of England. "I would the residue of the Reformed Churches of Christendome had not beene pared so neere the quicke by *precise hands*, that but some few of them might in this kinde be paralleled with ours."[131] Neither Godwin nor Hayward connected evangelical theology to the spoliation of churches during Edward's reign. Hayward discussed Edwardian religious debates only by way of criticizing the decisions of the king's council. "I will not deny but that some change in religion is often expedient and sometimes

[123] Godwin, *Annales*, p. 67.   [124] Godwin, *Annales*, p. 67.
[125] Godwin, *Annales*, p. 97; see also p. 113.
[126] Godwin, *Annales*, pp. 135, 145, 161, 166–7, 194, 207.   [127] Godwin, *Annales*, p. 175.
[128] Godwin, *Annales*, p. 224.   [129] Hayward, *King Edward the Sixth*, p. 158.
[130] Hayward, *King Edward the Sixth*, p. 173.   [131] Godwin, *Annales*, p. 225.

necessary," he wrote, but "this must be done with a soft and tender hand."[132] In this, Edward's regime manifestly failed, first by removing images long reverenced, and second by selling off church lands. The former act was met with insurrection, while the latter "enriched many, and enobled some, and thereby made them firme in maintaining the change."[133] Hayward blamed the wider populace for its inability to understand that the substance of religion remained, but he did not thereby absolve the boy king's government. Among Jacobean authors, William Camden was unusual in identifying domestic religious dissent as the major culprit behind sacrilege. Like Bancroft and Hooker, he wrote that those who took their lead from Calvin's Geneva "encreased every where, through a certaine obstinate wilfulnesse in them, indiscretion of the Bishops, and secret Favour of certaine Noblemen which gaped after the wealth of the Church: which sect began presently to be knowne by the envious name of *Puritans*."[134] Camden, like Godwin, believed that the queen sought to defend the Church of England, but both praised James for decisively preventing further spoliation.[135]

Unburdened by an earlier historiographical consensus concerning sixteenth-century religious history, the assumptions and conclusions of Jacobean historical writing often contrast with our own. It is easy but inaccurate to portray their work as obfuscation or mythmaking, for the writings of Godwin, Hayward, and their contemporaries instead reflect a historical understanding that mapped Jacobean religious culture more broadly. An especially vivid example comes from their analyses of sixteenth-century Europe. As already seen, especially in the earlier discussion of Fisher, Jacobean writers often operated with a broadly patristic frame of reference that, however partisan, connected the Church of England to Christian antiquity without any reference to contemporaneous religious disputation elsewhere. Just as the Luther centenary proved unimportant to Jacobean religious practice, Luther was of comparatively little import to Jacobean historiography. Some of this was due to the widespread dislike of Henrician sacrilege, which preoccupied many authors, but even in broader analyses of the much-married king, Luther was not identified as the catalyst for religious developments in England. In his *Annales* on Henry VIII, Godwin introduced Luther only in 1521, by way of Henry's *Assertio Septem Sacramentorum*. Notably, Godwin's understanding of Luther was sometimes quite poor. By his own admission, Godwin did not know the origins of Luther's turn to the religious life. "It is reported, how truly I know not, that retreating himselfe in the fields, his companion with whom he then discoursed, was suddenly stricken dead with thunder. He therupon falling into due consideration of the vncertainetie of death, and of iudgment, left the study of the Ciuill Law, to which he then applied himselfe,

---

[132] Hayward, *King Edward the Sixth*, p. 67.   [133] Hayward, *King Edward the Sixth*, p. 69.
[134] Camden, *Annales*, p. 90.   [135] Camden, *Annales*, p. 17; Godwin, *Annales*, p. 224.

and renouncing the world, betooke himselfe to a Cloister."[136] Other elements of Luther's career were reported with greater accuracy, such as his frequent use of abusive language,[137] his dispute with Erasmus over the freedom of the will,[138] and his death in 1546.[139] Godwin was equally uncertain about Luther's influence upon English religious thought, writing only that Archbishop Cranmer was "thought to have beene seasoned with the leaven of that doctrine."[140] Henry, however, deeply opposed Lutheranism, and strove throughout his reign to communicate the same at home and abroad—or so Godwin believed.[141]

Godwin attributed the division of Christendom not to Luther but to high politics. Pope Julius II received especially harsh treatment. "This Pope more like to that CAESAR, whose Name hee bare, then PETER, from whom hee would faine deriue his Succession, that like another NERO, sitting still he might from on high be a spectator, while the whole world was on fire."[142] Godwin even described Julius II as "the Incendiarie of Chrstendome."[143] Yet, Christian princes were also to blame. In his narrative on the year 1520, and thus before his introduction of Luther, Godwin opined, "there is seldom any heed to be giuen to the Agreement of Princes, where they are tied by no other bands (as of Religion, Affinity, or manifest Vtility) than that weake one of their plighted Troth, those foule dissentions, and bloudy wars which afterwards rent all Christendome, and opened a way for that common enemy of our Faith [re: the Turks], may be a *sufficient example.*"[144] Religious change was, in fact, nothing to celebrate. Despite lamenting "the deuout follie of many preceding ages,"[145] the bishop also concluded that "New opinions (especially in matters of Religion) are of themselues alwayes odious."[146] Luther's theology was briefly mentioned, but only as background for understanding Charles V's sack of Rome. Godwin believed that those who participated in the sack were "for the most part seasoned with LVTHERS doctrine" and that this made them "passionate enemies to the Sea of *Rome,*"[147] but it was the sack itself that "made way for that great alteration which afterward hapned in the estate of the Church."[148] The undermining of papal authority, combined with the conniving territorialism of princes, produced a crisis in authority that cut across the lines of theological demarcation.

If our historiographical habits are understood as normative, Stuart interpretations offer, at best, an unusual reading of sixteenth-century European history. The same is true of their analyses of Tudor religious change. An especially notable example comes from their discussions of liturgy, which consistently homogenized their subject matter. To explain the Book of Common Prayer, Hayward quoted Edward's own words to the Devonshire rebels. "If the service were good in Latine,

[136] Godwin, *Annales*, p. 49.   [137] Godwin, *Annales*, pp. 49–50.
[138] Godwin, *Annales*, p. 71.   [139] Godwin, *Annales*, p. 202.   [140] Godwin, *Annales*, p. 117.
[141] Godwin, *Annales*, pp. 133, 163.   [142] Godwin, *Annales*, p. 9.
[143] Godwin, *Annales*, p. 26.   [144] Godwin, *Annales*, p. 44.   [145] Godwin, *Annales*, p. 41.
[146] Godwin, *Annales*, p. 49.   [147] Godwin, *Annales*, p. 80.   [148] Godwin, *Annales*, p. 58.

it remaines so in English, for nothing is altered but to make you vnderstand what is said. In like sort the masse with great judgment and care was reduced to the same manner as Christ left it, as the Apostles vsed it, as the ancient Fathers receaued, practised and left it."[149] Hayward did not distinguish between the liturgical revisions of 1549 and 1552. Both Godwin and Hayward discussed the Church of England's purification from "superstition,"[150] but Godwin also left liturgical matters vague. He praised the restoration of utraquism, vernacular liturgy, and the marriage of clergy, and he supported the removal of images, private confession, and masses for the dead. But as already noted, Godwin never discussed the Prayer Books as such.

Hayward and Godwin identified constructive religious change with the first part of Edward's reign. Edwardian iconoclasm was thus associated with Northumberland's later presidency. Each author bifurcated Edwardian history in the same way, and by praising Somerset rather than Northumberland, they followed an interpretive framework first advanced by John Foxe.[151] In Godwin's narrative, when Somerset stood on the scaffold awaiting execution, he took refuge in just one facet of his legacy: "In this do I reioice, in this only do I triumph: beseeching him, that his Church in this Realme being now reformed according to the Institution of the antient Primitive, the Members therof may conforme their lives to the purity of its received Doctrine."[152] Northumberland, however, was very different. According to Hayward, he was "almost dissolute" and "highly aspiring, not forebearing to make any mischiefe the meanes for attaining his ambitions endes."[153] As in sixteenth-century historiography, few vices remained as damning as ambition, which seventeenth-century authors also used to explain the downfall of once-great figures.[154] Northumberland thus had only "the appearances of virtues,"[155] and as Edward laid upon his deathbed, Northumberland's "power was dreadful, for as he was easy to enterteine displeasure, so was he strong to reteine it, a cunning dissembler for a tyme, but a sure paymaster in the end."[156] Hayward concluded his narrative with Edward's death, but Godwin continued his Annales through the accession of Elizabeth in 1558. After the failed attempt at placing Jane upon the throne, Northumberland was exposed as having "ripped vp the acts of former times" and commanding others to act "vniustly, cruelly, or

---

[149] Hayward, King Edward the Sixth, p. 79.
[150] Godwin, Annales of England, p. 217; Hayward, King Edward the Sixth, p. 67.
[151] For a fuller analysis of this historiographical development, see Benjamin M. Guyer, "'Of Hopes Great as Himselfe': Tudor and Stuart Legacies of Edward VI," in Estelle Paranque (ed.), Remembering Queens and Kings of Early Modern England and France: Reputation, Reinterpretation, and Reincarnation (Cham: Palgrave Macmillan, 2019), pp. 73–91.
[152] Godwin, Annales of England, p. 250.   [153] Hayward, King Edward the Sixth, p. 45.
[154] See, e.g., Francis Bacon, The History and Reign of King Henry the Seventh, ed. Jerry Weinberger (Ithaca and London: Cornell University Press, 1996), pp. 28, 60, 88; Herbert of Cherbury, The Life and Raigne of King Henry the Eighth (London, 1649; Wing/H1504), e.g., pp. 56, 110, 407.
[155] Hayward, King Edward the Sixth, p. 45.   [156] Hayward, King Edward the Sixth, p. 176.

amisse in the Raigne of King EDWARD."[157] Godwin alleged that Northumberland's religious language was but a "pretext" and a "thing pretended,"[158] an accusation brought full circle at the time of his execution, when Northumberland returned to Catholicism. As Chapters 4 and 5 will show, later Stuart authors consistently divided Edward's reign in 1550, thus restricting salutary religious developments to Somerset's protectorate.

Stuart historical writers also applied confessional labels to English religion in ways unfamiliar today. In the original 1616 edition of his work, as in the second impression of 1628, Godwin did not use "Protestant" to describe the English church under Henry or Edward. Hayward was no different. "Protestant" appeared only twice in his work, but in both instances, it denoted those "beyond the seas," the "Germaine Protestants."[159] Perhaps illustrating growing comfort with the term as a confessional self-descriptor, "Protestant" entered Godwin's work through its 1630 translation by the bishop's son, Morgan. "Protestant" appeared multiple times in the English edition. Writing of Cardinal Pole's early opposition to Henry, Godwin recorded Pole's accusation that, "it is said that the seeds of Turkism [re: Islam] were disseminated throughout England and Germany" ("Turcicum semen per Angliam atque Germaniam dissipatum esse dicit"). Morgan's translation contained a parenthetical aside, in which Pole alleged "that Turcisme (meaning the Protestant Religion) had found entertainement in England and Germany."[160] Morgan's terminological addition created a confessional link across distant geographical regions, but his father's narrative offered no identical set of connections.

Reflecting a preoccupation with domestic developments, Morgan's occasional liberties with translation also created confessional links across the reigns of Henry, Edward, and Mary. Protestants were first named when Morgan translated a marginal note placed beside his father's account of the burning of Robert Barnes, Thomas Gerard, and William Jerome. The original text read, "Both the papal theologians and our own were punished" ("Plectuntur simul theologi Pontificij & nostrates"); Morgan translated this as "Protestants and Papists alike persecuted."[161] Morgan maintained this tendency later in the text as well. Writing of the tumultuous transition between the reigns of Edward and Mary, he denoted two ministers "Protestant," thereby distinguishing them from the Marian episcopate, despite his father having not done so.[162] In two other instances, the addition of "Protestant" reveals much about Morgan's understanding of the interrelationship between the Church of England, Protestant churches elsewhere, and

---

[157] Godwin, *Annales*, p. 270.
[158] Godwin, *Annales*, pp. 266 ("pretext"), 270 ("thing pretended").
[159] Hayward, *King Edward the Sixth*, pp. 125 ("those beyond seas"), 163 ("Germaine Protestants").
[160] Godwin, *Annales*, p. 156; Godwin, *Rervm Anglicarvm*, p. 64.
[161] Godwin, *Annales*, p. 177; Godwin, *Rervm Anglicarvm*, p. 72.
[162] Godwin, *Annales*, p. 276; Godwin, *Rervm Anglicarvm*, p. 110.

Christian orthodoxy. First, the bishop originally wrote that shortly before Northumberland's condemnation, "the people were now well accustomed to purer doctrine" ("plebs puriori doctrinae iam bene assueta"). Morgan changed "purer doctrine" ("puriori doctrinae") to "the Protestant Religion."[163] Second, in his translation of Cardinal Pole's death, Morgan wrote that under the influence of the papacy, Pole had persecuted "Protestants." In the original text, the bishop identified the victims only as "professors of the true religion" ("verae religionis professores").[164] The semantic shift matters, but its novelty is easily missed today given our own historiographical habits. In the end, the Godwins portrayed the English church as an international paragon, and not as a passive recipient of Luther's doctrine. Morgan faithfully rendered his father's original closing sentiment: "our Church (which she [re: Elizabeth] found much distracted) transcends all others of the Christian world" ("ecclesia vero nostra (cuius statum Eliz. valde perturbatum offendit) inter florentissimas vniversi orbis iam palmam ferat").[165] The Church of England was the great wonder of Christendom—and its "Protestant" convictions a world apart.

The term "Protestant" appeared more frequently in studies of Elizabeth's reign, but here again idiosyncratically when compared with our own usage. Camden's *Annales* set the standard for later accounts of the Virgin Queen, and distinguished firmly between the papacy and Protestants. Like other Jacobean authors, he gave an antiquarian orientation only to the latter.

> In the first beginning of her Raigne, she applyed her first care (howbeit with but a few and those her inwardest Counsailours,) to the restoring of the Protestants Religion, which both by her instruction from her tender yeeres, and by her owne judgement, shee verily perswaded her selfe to be the truest, and most consonant to the sacred Scriptures, and the sincerity of the primitive Church.[166]

According to Camden, Elizabeth's conception of Protestantism was conciliatory, unifying disparate portions of the English kingdom. She directed "that Preachers should abstaine from questions controverted in Religion," not least because when she ascended the throne, "the people [were] distracted with different opinions in Religion."[167] Stuart writers believed the queen Protestant, but one who hovered above confessional division. Only a small portion of Hayward's work on Elizabeth was posthumously printed in 1636, but like Camden he portrayed the queen steering a course between conflicted religious convictions by restraining public

---

[163] Godwin, *Annales*, p. 276; Godwin, *Rervm Anglicarvm*, p. 110.
[164] Godwin, *Annales*, p. 337 (mispage as 340); Godwin, *Rervm Anglicarvm*, p. 133.
[165] Godwin, *Annales*, p. 341; Godwin, *Rervm Anglicarvm*, pp. 134–5.
[166] Camden, *Annales*, p. 3.   [167] Camden, *Annales*, pp. 3, 4.

preaching on contentious matters. Hayward wrote that Elizabeth admitted Catholics and Protestants into her council, and that "All these the Queene ruled with such moderation, as neither was shee obnoxious unto any of them, and all devoted and addicted to her."[168] A more detailed portrait of her religious practice came from Camden's *Annales*. With encomiastic joy, he reported that the queen often said "she had rather talke with God devoutly by prayer, then heare others speake eloquently of God." The queen observed Lent, maintained holy days, and reverenced "the Crosse, the blessed Virgin, and the Saints," expecting others to do the same.[169] Elizabeth's political wisdom was inseparable from the breadth and depth of her religious devotion.

The queen's religious convictions nonetheless brought about two sizable political difficulties. It set her opposite the papacy, and placed her into a sometimes-uncomfortably close relationship with Protestants abroad, primarily by way of Scotland. Both developments raised the possibility of rebellion. With the threat of papal excommunication came the threat of invasion from any number of directions. Camden identified Catholics in Scotland, Ireland, France, and Spain as the more immediate threats early in the reign, but with the overthrow of Mary, Queen of Scots, a new confessional enemy arose. Deploying phraseology familiar from authors such as Bancroft and Hooker, Camden wrote that in 1558, "under a glorious pretext of reforming Religion, and maintaining the liberty of *Scotland*," Scottish Protestants "began to disturbe the Quiet of the Land."[170] He named Buchanan and Knox as the chief ideologues, referencing and dissenting both from Knox's *First Blast of the Trumpet Against the Monstrous Regiment of Women*, and from "that damned Dialogue, *De jure Regni apud Scotos*, wherin is maintained, that the people have right to create and depose Kings."[171] Although Elizabeth's council encouraged the establishment of Protestantism in Scotland, Camden detected acute political tension in the queen's dealings with her northern neighbor. He explicated the international effects of the British debate over the Scots' right to depose their queen by analyzing disagreement over the political doctrine of John Calvin. "Queen *Elizabeth*, read not without indignation, and tacitly condemned," the argument "that the Scottish people are aboue their Kings; yea, and by the authority of *Calvin*, that popular Magistrates are ordained euery where to moderate the lust of kings, and that it is lawfull for them to restraine bad Kings by imprisonment, and to depose them."[172] Opposing Protestant political

---

[168] John Hayward, *The Life and Reigne of King Edward the Sixth, With The Beginning of the Reigne of Queene Elizabeth* (London, 1636; STC 12999), p. 461.

[169] Camden, *Annales*, p. 7.   [170] Camden, *Annales*, p. 73.

[171] Camden, *Annales*, pp. 79 (Buchanan); 23, 79 (Knox). The complete text of Hayward's *Annals* was not published until 1840, but it reveals that he saw Knox as the principal instigator of vandalism and civic unrest. See John Hayward, *Annals of the First Four Years of the Reign of Queen Elizabeth*, ed. John Bruce (London: The Camden Society, 1840), pp. 41–2.

[172] Camden, *Annales*, p. 132.

theology in Scotland necessitated opposing Protestant political theology else-where. Here was neither confessional parity enabling Anglo-Scottish unity, nor membership in an international Reformed communion. If Elizabeth transcended theological disputation in England, she could not extricate herself from its broader British entanglements. Her most effective resort was to cut such disputations off at their source. But in this, she and her immediate successors failed.

4

This Present Reformation in *England*

From Civil Wars to Apologetic Consensus, 1625–60

For now nonconformity in the daies of King *Edward* was conceived, which afterward in the Reign of Queen *Mary* (but beyond Sea at *Frankford)* was born; which in the Reign of Queen *Elizabeth* was nursed, and weaned; which under King *James* grew up a young youth, or tall stripling; but towards the end of King *Charles* His Reign, shot up to the full strength, and stature of a man, able, not onely to coap with, but conquer the Herarchie its adversary'

Thomas Fuller (1655)[1]

Introduction

Amidst considerable political violence, "reformation" acquired a new meaning in England under Charles I. It was not an inevitable development. A coherent historiography of the English Reformation was hardly in process by the mid-1630s. During the first fifteen years of his reign, only a small number of English controversialists referred to a vaguely defined "first reformation" of the Church of England, and even then, they did so rarely. As calls for "reformation" resounded throughout the British Isles during the civil wars of the 1640s, a novel historiography took root and "English Reformation" entered the historical lexicon. The next decade then saw a small but growing number of works that presented mid-sixteenth-century religious history as "the English Reformation,"[2] "our English Reformation,"[3] or, most simply, as "our Reformation."[4] Influenced and inspired

---

[1] Thomas Fuller, *The Church-History of Britain* (London, 1655; Wing/F2416), Book VII, p. 401, n. 23.

[2] Charles I and Alexander Henderson, *The Papers Which Passed at New-Castle* (London, 1649; Wing/C2535), p. 16; Henry Ferne, *Of the Division Between the English and Romish Church upon the Reformation* (London, 1655; Wing/F796), p. 38.

[3] Henry Hammond, *A View of the New Directorie* (Oxford, 1645; Wing/H612), p. 6; Anonymous, *A Brief View and Defence of the Reformation of the Church of England by King Edward and Q Elizabeth.* (London, 1654; Wing/B4655), p. 68.

[4] Edward Boughen, *An Account of the Church Catholick* (London, 1653; Wing/B3812), p. 17; Fuller, *The Church-History*, Index, sig. [¶¶4].

How the English Reformation was Named: The Politics of History, c. 1400–1700. Benjamin M. Guyer, Oxford University Press. © Benjamin M. Guyer 2022. DOI: 10.1093/oso/9780192865724.003.0005

by the works discussed in Chapter 3, mid-seventeenth-century apologists argued that reformation in Scotland opposed the monarchy, but that in England, the monarchy supported reform; in Scotland, reformation was violent, but in England, peaceful. The "English Reformation" began as a historiographical apologetic intended to justify the Caroline regime and the Church of England against their shared opponents. It was a historiographical development with the most immediate of short-term causes but the most enduring of long-term consequences.

In many ways the climax of the book, this chapter covers the chaotic reign of Charles I. The opening section, "Ecclesiastical Convergence," narrates the transformation of the British churches after the death of James VI and I, noting how liturgical changes and canon law sought to inhibit the likelihood that something like the Scottish Reformation might occur in any of the other British kingdoms. Before turning to civil war and its aftermath, the chapter then considers how English authors discussed England's "first reformation" under Charles, concluding that the ubiquity of the phrase indicates less consensus than is generally assumed. The remaining sections look at how apocalyptic fears and militant realities formed the backdrop for the dawn of historiography on the English Reformation. With "reformation" a veritable battle cry among many Scots and their English supporters, the first histories of the English Reformation painted a portrait of sixteenth-century religious history diametrically opposite the bloodshed of the 1640s and oppression of the 1650s. "Our English Reformation," a polemical label directed against the militant "reformation" of the civil wars, gave rise the following decade to sustained historical analyses by authors such as Thomas Fuller and Peter Heylyn.

Ecclesiastical Convergence

Charles I continued his father's pursuit of a British ecclesiastical convergence. Unlike James VI and I, the new king lived to see incommensurable understandings of reformation tear this vision apart. On both sides of the Anglo-Scottish border, the king and his supporters pushed for royal control of reformation, a conviction that placed them opposite those who took their lead from the Scottish Reformation of the previous century. Closer to home but no less difficult, Charles inherited an English church increasingly at odds with itself. During his first decade on the throne, major disputes erupted over theological and liturgical matters,[5] and

---

[5] The order of topics listed here maps the chronology of recent historiographical interest. Scholarship on so-called "Arminianism" rapidly declined after 2000; since then, it has focused more on the liturgical—including the architectural and devotional—features of the Caroline church. However, the two topics are often fused together, such that the terminology used in discussions the

royal proclamations proved incapable of stemming the tides of controversy. There is no reason to believe that Charles favored religious change for its own sake; his earliest directives on point maintained the Jacobean status quo. In June 1626, the king issued "A Proclamation for the establishing of the Peace and Quiet of the Church of England." He repudiated "the least innouation" and commanded church leaders:

> that from hencefoorth they cary themselues so wisely, warily, and conscionably, that neither by Writing, Preaching, Printing, Conferences, or other wise, they raise any doubts, or publish, or maintaine any new inventions or opinions concerning Religion, then such as are clearly grounded, and warranted by the Doctrine and Discipline of the Church of *England*, heretofore published, and established by authoritie.[6]

The king's proclamation is notable only for its quotidian content. Religious uniformity remained strategic; a divided Church of England could not provide a template for the other British churches. If seen in the context of ecclesiastical convergence, Charles' focused pursuit of domestic uniformity makes considerable sense.

Following paternal precedent, the Caroline court treated the Church of England as the template for the Scottish and Irish churches. Between the mid-1620s and the late 1630s, ecclesiastical convergence surged forward across the Stuart kingdoms. In July 1626, the king began restoring church lands in Scotland; like his father, he directed the Scottish bishops to enforce the Articles of Perth,[7] and the Scottish episcopate and Privy Council retained almost all of the personnel appointed by James.[8] Working through William Laud, Archbishop of Canterbury, and Thomas Wentworth, Lord Lieutenant of Ireland, the same project became a central feature of the Irish ecclesiastical landscape. As Laud

---

former is carried over into the latter. A helpful overview of this historiographical shift is Anthony Milton, "Arminians, Laudians, Anglicans, and Revisionists: Back to Which Drawing Board?," *The Huntington Library Quarterly*, Vol. 78, No. 4 (Winter, 2015), pp. 723–43.

[6] Charles I, *A Proclamation for the Establishing of the Peace and Quiet of the Church of England* (London, 1626; STC 8824). In his influential monograph on English "Arminianism," Nicholas Tyacke interpreted this proclamation as a proscription of Calvinism, although he conceded that "the proclamation as printed does not mention Arminianism by name." However, as Tyacke also noted, nothing in Charles' words indicates a concern to address or inhibit any specific theological doctrine or school of thought. See Nicholas Tyacke, *Anti-Calvinists: The Rise of English Arminianism c. 1590–1640*, new ed. (Oxford: Clarendon Press, 1990), pp. 48, 157; Nicholas Tyacke, "Archbishop Laud," in Kenneth Fincham (ed.), *The Early Stuart Church, 1603–1642* (Stanford: Stanford University Press, 1993), pp. 51–70, at pp. 65–6.

[7] Leonie James, *"This Great Firebrand": William Laud and Scotland 1617–1645* (Woodbridge and Rochester: The Boydell Press, 2017), p. 28; for the proclamation on church lands, see Charles I, *By the King* (Edinburgh, 1626; STC 21970).

[8] Sally Tuckett, "The Scottish Bishops in Government, 1625–1638," in Sharon Adams and Julian Goodare (eds.), *Scotland in the Age of Two Revolutions* (Woodbridge and Rochester: The Boydell Press, 2014), pp. 59–78.

wrote to Wentworth in 1638, "but for Ireland, it hath been ever reformed by and to the Church of England."[9] The Archbishop wrote in a similar fashion about making the Church of Scotland more congruous with its southern neighbor,[10] thus revealing much about how the royal court envisioned the interrelationship of the British churches. Unity and uniformity were, at least ideally, two sides of a pan-British ecclesiastical coinage.

In both Ireland and Scotland, canon law revision came first. Ireland's new canons were ratified in 1634, and in both form and content, they largely followed the English canon law.[11] The first Irish canon was entitled "Of the agreement of the church of England and Ireland, in the profession of the same Christian Religion."[12] Affirming an identical understanding of doctrine and sacramental practice, the canon stated, "Wee doe receive and approve the Booke of Articles of Religion" promulgated under Elizabeth in 1562.[13] This brought the Irish church, for the first time, into formal confessional agreement with the Church of England.[14] The next canon, entitled "The Kings Supremacy in Causes Ecclesiasticall to be maintained," decreed that papal power "is for most just causes, taken away and abolished."[15] The doctrine of monarchy contained here came directly from England's second canon, and simply applied its claims to Ireland. As in England, it now became an excommunicable offense to maintain in Ireland "that the Kings Majestie hath not the same authority in causes Ecclesiasticall, that the godly Kings had amongst the Iewes, and Christian Emperours in the Primitive Church."[16] The third canon legislated for the Book of Common Prayer, the fourth canon for the maintenance of the episcopal hierarchy, and the fifth canon against schisms. Like the first ten English canons, the first five Irish canons concluded by excommunicating those who dissented from their contents. Unified around faith and liturgy, the English and Irish churches were now also unified in their understanding of royal and ecclesiastical authority.

Canon law revision proceeded apace in Scotland the following year. The new canons aligned the Church of Scotland with its neighbor churches in Ireland and,

---

[9] William Laud, *The Works of the Most Reverend Father in God, William Laud, D.D.,* 7 Vols., ed. William Scott and James Bliss (Oxford: John Henry Parker, 1847–1860; repr. Hildesheim and New York: Georg Olms Verlag, 1977), Vol. 4, p. 544. For a fuller discussion of this letter, see John McCafferty, *The Reconstruction of the Church of Ireland: Bishop Bramhall and the Laudian Reforms, 1633–1641* (Cambridge: Cambridge University Press, 2007), pp. 59–60, and 69–70 for the reappearance of this same desire elsewhere in Laud's correspondence.

[10] James, *"This Great Firebrand,"* pp. 99, 136.

[11] McCafferty, *Reconstruction of the Church of Ireland,* pp. 75–108, provides a magisterial overview.

[12] Church of Ireland, *Constitvtions and Canons Ecclesiasticall* (Dublin, 1635; STC 14265), Canon I, p. 9.

[13] Church of Ireland, *Constitvtions and Canons Ecclesiasticall,* Canon I, p. 10.

[14] McCafferty, *Reconstruction of the Church of Ireland,* pp. 73–5; for the 1615 Irish Articles, see pp. 12–13, 63–8.

[15] Church of Ireland, *Constitvtions and Canons Ecclesiasticall,* Canon II, pp. 10–11.

[16] Church of Ireland, *Constitvtions and Canons Ecclesiasticall,* Canon II, p. 11.

more importantly (if controversially), England. And, as with the English and Irish canons, the Scottish canons directed the excommunication of those who rejected royal authority, the episcopal hierarchy, or the Book of Common Prayer.[17] However, quite unlike their Irish counterpart, which made no concessions to the Catholic population of Ireland, the Scottish canons made select concessions to Scottish Protestants. The new canon law made no mention of the Thirty-Nine Articles, and made further concession to those who objected to the word "priest" by substituting "presbyter." In other ways, the Scottish canons were less compromising. They sought to split the difference between Catholic and Presbyterian approaches to the Eucharist, identifying the former with "*the adoration of the Bread*" and the latter with "*the unreverend communicating, and not discerning of those holie Mysteriee.*" Following the Articles of Perth, the canon resolved that "the holie Sacrament of the Lord's Supper bee receaved with the bowing of the knee; to testifie the devotion and thankfulnesse of the Receavers, for that most excellent Gift."[18] The canons also restricted ordination to those who "first subscrybe, to bee obedient to the Canons of the Church,"[19] effectively preventing hardline Protestants from entering holy orders. The King James/Authorized Version of the Bible became the only translation allowed,[20] and following the requirements of the English canons, every parish was ordered to place a font for baptism in its historic position, near the entrance of the church.[21] Upon completion, the canon laws of England, Ireland, and Scotland overlapped on forty-one individual canons.[22] This was a remarkable and hitherto unattained degree of convergence. In the contest between supporters and opponents of English episcopacy and ceremonies, advocates of Reformed norms emerged the clear losers.

The Irish and Scottish canons differed significantly in the amount of space that each dedicated to ecclesiastical authority. The final Irish canon, a mere paragraph in length, concluded that the "Nationall Synod" of the Irish church was "the representative body of the Church of Ireland, in the name of Christ, and by the Kings authority," and that its determinations, once "ratified & confirmed," were binding.[23] The Scottish canons spent far more time upon ecclesiastical authority, dedicating more than two pages to the topic. After directing the bishops to call diocesan synods twice each year, the king was identified as having sole authority to

---

[17] Church of Scotland, *Canons and Constitvtions Ecclesiasticall* (Aberdeen, 1636; STC 22055), chs. I.2 and I.3, p. 8.

[18] Church of Scotland, *Canons and Constitvtions Ecclesiasticall*, ch. VI.6, p. 21.

[19] Church of Scotland, *Canons and Constitvtions Ecclesiasticall*, ch. II.10, p. 11.

[20] Church of Scotland, *Canons and Constitvtions Ecclesiasticall*, ch. XVI.1, p. 31.

[21] Church of Scotland, *Canons and Constitvtions Ecclesiasticall*, ch. XVI.2, p. 31; for fonts, see Kenneth Fincham and Nicholas Tyacke, *Altars Restored: The Changing Face of English Religious Worship, 1547–c. 1700* (Oxford: Oxford University Press, 2010), pp. 48–51 (Elizabethan debates), 245 (Jacobean placement).

[22] McCafferty, *Reconstruction of the Church of Ireland*, p. 113.

[23] Church of Ireland, *Constitvtions and Canons Ecclesiasticall*, Canon C, p. 113.

call a national synod. This directly affected the Church of Scotland's autonomy, and the new canons further denied "that it is lawfull for anie Presbyter, or Layman, joyntlie, or severallie, to make Rules, Orders, or Constitutions, in causes Ecclesiasticall." It concluded by warning:

> But for-as-much as no reformation in Doctrine or Discipline, can bee made perfect at once in anie Church; THEREFORE it shall and may be lawfull, for the Church of *SCOTLAND*, at anie tyme, to make Remonstrance to His Majestie, or His Successoures, what they conceaue fit to bee taken in farther consideration, in, and concerning the Premisses. And if the King shall therevpon declare his lyking, and approbation, then both Clergie and Lay shall yeeld their obedience, without incurring the Censure afore-sayde, or anie other. But it shall not bee lawfull for the Bishops themselues, in a *NATIONALL SYNOD*, or otherwyse, to alter anie Rubricke, Article, Canon Doctrinall, or Disciplinarie, what-so-ever; vnder the payne aboue mentioned, and HIS MAJESTIE's farther displeasure.[24]

With such strictures, the Scottish Reformation of 1560 was unrepeatable. The canons granted to bishops the impetus for proposing reformation, but the right of reformation to the king alone. Here was an understanding of ecclesiastical authority that the king's opponents would soon contest in diverse ways on both sides of the Anglo-Scottish border.

The 1635 canons paved the way for introducing a new Scottish liturgy. In Ireland, the new canon law accompanied a renewed push for the liturgical use of Irish rather than English, but instead of creating a new Book of Common Prayer, the Irish liturgies of 1608 remained standard. In Scotland, however, there was no Prayer Book, and in 1637 the first Scottish Book of Common Prayer was ratified. It also depended upon English precedent, but the new service book was presented as neither an English imposition nor a Caroline innovation. The Preface noted that James VI and I strove "to work this uniformitie in all his Dominions" but that death prevented him from doing so. Charles I, "not suffering his Fathers good purpose to fall to the ground," continued, and had now completed, James' project.[25] Reflecting a political and theological conviction shared by father and son, the Preface of the new Prayer Book concluded with a significant but subversive appeal to the sixteenth century. Working within the historiographical framework shared by all Scots, whether of Presbyterian or Episcopalian persuasion, the sixteenth century was held up as a distinct moment of reformation. "Our first Reformers were of the same minde with us, as appeareth by the ordinance they made, that in all the Parishes of the Realme, the Common prayer should be read

---

[24] Church of Scotland, *Canons and Constitvtions Ecclesiasticall*, ch. VIII.4, p. 25.
[25] Church of Scotland, *The Booke of Common Prayer* (Edinburgh, 1637; STC 16606), sig. a3.

weekly on Sundaies, and other Festivall dayes." Citing John Knox, the Preface promised, "We keep the words of the historie; *Religion was not then placed in rites and gestures, nor men taken with the fancie of extemporarie prayers.*"[26] Perhaps this was a concession to Scottish sensibility; it was certainly the pursuit of a usable past. The publication of the new liturgy marked two full decades of attempts, under two successive kings, of transforming the Scottish kirk.

Historiographical Divergence

Before analyzing the semantics of "reformation" during and after the civil wars, we need to study Caroline conceptions of sixteenth-century religious history. In line with the historiography discussed in Chapter 3, between 1625 and 1640, only a scattering of references were made to a reformation initiated by one or another of the Tudor monarchs. Tudor historiography changed under Charles only to the extent that it was increasingly illuminated by Elizabethan romanticism. The second portion of William Camden's *Annales* appeared in 1627 and was translated into English in 1629. The entirety of Camden's work was published in 1630, with subsequent editions printed in 1634 and 1635. Elizabeth was, without question, the most popular Tudor. By way of comparison, and as noted in Chapter 3, John Hayward's study of Edward VI saw only two editions, first in 1630 and then again in 1636, and the second edition contained additional material on Elizabeth. But no one published a standalone study of Henry VIII. In the early 1630s, Edward Herbert of Cherbury began researching what ultimately became his *Life and Raigne of King Henry the Eighth*,[27] but such interest in the much-married king was rare. During Charles' reign, Shakespeare's play *All is True*, also known as *King Henry VIII*, saw but one performance, which took place in 1628.[28] Even here, the Virgin Queen overshadowed all. The play concluded with the birth of Elizabeth. In the last scene, Archbishop Cranmer prophesied that she would be "A pattern to all princes,"[29] and that "Truth shall nurse her;/Holy and heavenly thoughts still counsel her."[30] Due at least in part to Camden's popularity, whatever its mode of presentation—theological, historical, or dramatic—interest in Elizabeth dominated and defined early Caroline approaches to Tudor history.

---

[26] Church of Scotland, *The Booke of Common Prayer*, sig. a3 v.

[27] Christine Jackson, "'It Is Unposssible to Draw His Picture Well Who Hath Severall Countenances': Lord Herbert of Cherbury and *The Life and Reign of King Henry VIII*," in Thomas Betteridge and Thomas S. Freeman (eds.), *Henry VIII and History* (Farnham and Burlington: Ashgate Publishing, 2012), pp. 135–49.

[28] William Shakespeare, *King Henry VIII*, ed. Gordon McMullan (London: Bloomsbury, 2000), pp. 8–17.

[29] Shakespeare, *King Henry VIII*, 5.4.22, p. 429.

[30] Shakespeare, *King Henry VIII*, 5.4.28–5.4.29, p. 430.

Recent scholarship has focused on Caroline uses of the phrase "first reformation,"[31] primarily by discussing "Laudianism,"[32] which purportedly aimed to reverse the devotional and doctrinal changes of the previous century.[33] It is consistently assumed today that "first reformation" was a polemical historiographical label used by "Laudian" partisans to distinguish an earlier, more "Catholic" set of religious developments from a later, more "Protestant" successor. But this is quite wrong. The seemingly transparent phrase "first reformation" actually signified something less coherent than is commonly assumed. This becomes clear by analyzing not the meaning of "reformation," but the meaning of "first." Although it could refer to one's position in a series, "first" often denoted moral priority. As far back as 1552, Richard Huloet's definition of "first" included "first example or paterne," which he further defined as "Archetypus, Prototypon, Prototypum."[34] Importance rather than numerical order was just as central to Thomas' *Dictionarium*, which defined *primus* as "First, best, principall; or chiefe, more esteemed, more excellent."[35] So too, John Rider's dictionary offered not only *primo* but *principalis* as part of the definition of "first."[36] These denotations held for decades, as reflected by the continued reprinting of both Thomas' and Rider's dictionaries. Consequently, "first reformation" is better understood as a *moral* appeal. Early Caroline references to Tudor history were apologetic uses of the past, rather than well-developed historical narratives. By aiming at prescriptive rather than strictly descriptive ends, they traversed the same rhetorical road as earlier authors such as John Foxe.

[31] Anthony Milton, *Laudian and Royalist Polemic in Seventeenth-century England: The Career and Writings of Peter Heylyn* (Manchester: Manchester University Press, 2007), pp. 83–91; Calvin Lane, *The Laudians and the Elizabethan Church: History, Conformity and Religious Identity in Post-Reformation England* (London and New York: Routledge, 2013), esp. ch. 3; Fincham and Tyacke, *Altars Restored*, pp. 156–7.

[32] An especially influential overview of "Laudianism" is Peter Lake, "The Laudian Style: Order, Uniformity and the Pursuit of the Beauty of Holiness in the 1630s," in Fincham, *The Early Stuart Church*, pp. 161–85; more subtle is Anthony Milton, "The Creation of Laudianism: A New Approach," in Thomas Cogswell, Richard Cust, and Peter Lake (eds.), *Politics, Religion and Popularity in Early Stuart Britain: Essays in Honour of Conrad Russell* (Cambridge: Cambridge University Press, 2002), pp. 162–84. The most substantive analysis of "Laudianism" is now Fincham and Tyacke, *Altars Restored*, esp. chs. 4–7.

[33] Diarmaid MacCulloch, "The Myth of the English Reformation," *Journal of British Studies*, Vol. 30, No. 1 (Jan., 1991), pp. 1–19, has been especially influential. The title of Graham Parry, *The Arts of the Anglican Counter-Reformation: Glory, Laud and Honour* (Woodbridge and Rochester: The Boydell Press, 2006), states this position most clearly, treating "Laudianism" as an Anglican "counter-reformation," akin to the Tridentine response to sixteenth-century evangelicals. More recently, Fincham and Tyacke, *Altars Restored*, repeatedly write of a "Laudian reformation," e.g., pp. 158, 177, 189, 208, 231, 274, 284, 306, 334.

[34] Richard Huloet, *Abcedarivm Anglico Latinvm* (London, 1552; STC 13940), sig. M.ii.

[35] Thomas Thomas, *Dictionarium Linguae Latinae et Anglicanae* (Cambridge, 1587; STC 24008), sig. Aaa iiij.

[36] John Rider and Francis Holyoake, *Riders Dictionarie* (London, 1612; STC 21033), sig. L5 v.

Invocations of "first reformation" were usually made without chronological specificity or elaboration.[37] Addressing disputes over "Arminianism,"[38] George Carleton wrote that "The *Church* [of] *England* was *reformed* by the helpe of our learned and Reuerend *Bishops*, in the daies of King Edward the sixt, and in the beginning of the Raigne of Queene *Elizabeth*."[39] Although an apparently historical claim, Carleton primarily used his work to pursue moral suasion. Leaping more than a millennium backward in time, he elaborated that the Church of England had returned to a more pristine form of Christian orthodoxy, defined with principal reference to St. Augustine.[40] Arguing that early Christian belief was identical with the doctrinal consensus held by Thomas Cranmer, Martin Bucer, and Peter Martyr Vermigli, Carleton explained that under James and Charles, "the Doctrine of our Church doth not differ" from that taught by "worthy Bishops who were in the first reformation."[41] The prescriptive denotation of "first" animated his appeal, not chronology, and still less any belief in a "first" as opposed to a "second" reformation. Carleton's summary had some influence, and the lawyer William Prynne quoted it three years later in *The Chvrch of Englands Old Antithesis to New Arminianism*.[42] Prynne agreed that Vermigli, Bucer, and Augustine were the theological authorities that grounded what he, too, termed "first reformation."[43] But even more so than Carleton, Prynne connected "first reformation" to an expansive portrait of antiquity. He cited Vincent of Lerins, Leo the Great, and Bernard of Clairvaux,[44] and described Bede, Anselm, Bradwardine, and Wyclif as key doctrinal authorities for "the Primatiue Church of *England*."[45] Here too, "first reformation" signified the return of the English church to something earlier and

---

[37] See, e.g., William Prynne, *The Perpetuitie of a Regenerate Mans Estate* (London, 1626; STC 20471), pp. 223–4; Henry Burton, *A Tryall of Priuate Devotions* (London, 1628; STC 4157), sig. ¶2 v; J.A. of Ailward, *An Historicall Narration of the Iudgement of Some Most Learned and Godly English Bishops, Holy Martyrs, and Others* (London, 1631; STC 4), sig. A2 v.

[38] Because we await a thorough study of the semantics of Arminianism in early Stuart England, I am hesitant to use the term. A similar note of caution may be found in Keith Stanglin, "'Arminius Avant La Lettre': Peter Baro, Jacobus Arminius, and the Bond of Predestinarian Polemic," *Westminster Theological Journal*, Vol. 67, No. 1 (Spring, 2005), pp. 51–74. For a recent general overview of Arminius studies, see Keith Stanglin, "The New Perspective on Arminius: Notes on a Historiographical Shift," *Reformation & Renaissance Review*, Vol. 11, No. 3 (2009), pp. 295–310. A good introduction to Arminius' theology is Keith D. Stanglin and Thomas H. McCall, *Jacob Arminius: Theologian of Grace* (Oxford: Oxford University Press, 2012). I am unconvinced that "Arminian" is a helpful descriptive label for any theological position in early Stuart England. Consequently, in what follows I do not use the term except when quoting contemporaries.

[39] George Carleton, *An Examination of... the Doctrines of the Church of England* (London, 1626; STC 4633), p. 4.

[40] Carleton, *An Examination*, p. 5; Augustine's import and authority are emphasized throughout, esp. in chs. 3 and 7.

[41] Carleton, *An Examination*, p. 5.

[42] William Prynne, *The Chvrch of Englands Old Antithesis to New Arminianisme* (London, 1629; STC 20457), p. 127.

[43] Prynne, *Chvrch of Englands Old Antithesis*, e.g., pp. 52, 128, 130.

[44] Prynne, *Chvrch of Englands Old Antithesis*, p. 1, n. a (Vincent); p. 140 (Leo); sig. ¶2, n. m (Bernard).

[45] Prynne, *Chvrch of Englands Old Antithesis*, p. 120.

more pure. The Church of England's doctrine was "anciently receiued" and its teachers were "the Ancient and Moderne Reformers of the Church."[46] Prynne's diverse appeals to figures who lived centuries apart underscores that the coherence of "first reformation" was predicated upon its function as a righteous exhortation.

Neither Carleton nor Prynne were "Laudians," but the "Laudians" used "first reformation" in the exact same way, conflating the prescriptive with the descriptive. An especially well-known example comes from the speech given by Archbishop Laud at the 1637 condemnation of Prynne, Henry Burton, and John Bastwick for seditious libel.[47] Laud's oration exemplifies the influence that the recent historiography of Elizabethan England had upon Caroline culture. Denying that the Church of England had experienced religious innovation under Charles, the archbishop claimed that "my *care of this Church*" was guided by "the *Rules* of its *first Reformation*."[48] In particular, he defended devotional practices—in this case, bowing at the name of Jesus—by citing the Virgin Queen's injunctions. Because the practice was supported "by *Authority* in the very *beginning* of the *Reformation*," bowing was "therefore no *Innovation now*."[49] It may seem curious that Laud identified Elizabeth's reign with the "*beginning* of the *Reformation*," but in doing so he fused the moral meaning of "first" with the enthusiasm for Elizabeth found in contemporary authors such as Camden. Consistent practice across the intervening decades was less important than the splendor of Gloriana, who was now elevated to a singular position. The archbishop was not averse to arguments of a more diachronic nature, but these complimented rather than obviated his normative use of the past. Responding to the allegation that it was "Popery" to set the communion table where the altar once stood, Laud explained that "in the *Kings Royall Chappels*, and *divers Cathedrals*, the *Holy Table* hath ever since the *Reformation* stood at the *upper end* of the *Quire*, with the *large* or *full side* towards the *people*."[50] Here Laud emphasized continuous usage since an earlier (if undefined) point in time, meaning that in his speech, reformation was both moral pattern and historical event. Precedent, whether understood as past custom or as moral exemplar, set the bounds of Laud's apologetic framework. Revealing a paradigm quite alien to our own, those who looked wistfully upon the Elizabethan past saw no inconsistency in oscillating between these two seemingly disparate meanings.

There was only one instance between 1625 and 1640 when "first reformation" denoted a diachronically discreet event. In his 1629 *Europae Specvlvm*, an

---

[46] Prynne, *Chvrch of Englands Old Antithesis*, pp. 13, sig. A3.

[47] For general background, see Lane, *Laudians and the Elizabethan Church*, pp. 91–6.

[48] William Laud, *A Speech Delivered in the Starr-Chamber* (London, 1637; STC 15306), p. 4; repr. Laud, *Works*, Vol. 6, pp. 35–70, at p. 42. I follow the orthography of the original, which the nineteenth-century editor of Laud's *Works* altered to Victorian norms.

[49] Laud, *Speech*, p. 32; Laud, *Works*, Vol. 6, p. 52.

[50] Laud, *Speech*, p. 53; Laud, *Works*, Vol. 6, p. 59.

anti-Catholic apologetic primarily directed against monasticism, Edwin Sandys distinguished between a "first Reformation under King Edward" and a "second Reformation by her Majestie."[51] However, the difference between these was not that one reformation was more "Catholic" and the other more "Protestant," but that Catholics, following the directives of the papacy, became more divisive and disruptive under Elizabeth. Early on, "in the first Reformation under King Edward, the Praelates and Clergie having before under King Henry discarded the Pope, did easilie joyne with the Protestants, though not in theyr opinions, yet in the publike service of God in the Churches, being indifferentlie composed and offensiue to neither part."[52] However, a decade later, "in the second Reformation by her Majestie, not a Bishop of his [the pope's] could be perswaded to come to our Churches."[53] Some of Sandys' general assumptions about sixteenth-century religious history will appear familiar today. He identified Scripture as "the foundation of the Reformation,"[54] and further held that "The first and chiefe meanes whereby the *Reformers* of *Religion* did prevaile in all places, was their singular assiduitie and dexteritie in *Preaching*, especially in great Cities and Palaces of Princes."[55] But the apparent import of Sandys' words should not be overstated. Even if he entertained a historiographical framework similar to that of many scholars today, his distinction between a "first" and "second" reformation did not catch on. The phrase "second reformation" yields no other hits in the database Early English Books Online.

However, Sandys had comparatively little interest in detailing two discreet reformations. He was, like Francis Godwin, more concerned to show that the Church of England was the paragon for all others in Christendom. Sandys believed that Catholics' continued efforts at domestic evangelization were due to the pristine nature of English Christianity. England was "the only Nation that tooke the right way of iustifiall Reformation, in comparison of other who haue runne headlong rather to a tumultuous innovation."[56] Sandys' targets went unnamed, and although it is difficult to avoid the sense that he was hitting out at Presbyterian sympathizers, his solution was clear: "that alteration which hath beene in England, was brought in with peaceable and orderly proceeding, by general consent of the Prince and whole Realme representatiuely assembled in solemne Parliament, a great part of their owne Clergie according and conforming themselues unto it."[57] He spared no effort in further detailing praiseworthy English particulars. With "no LVTHER no CALVIN the square of theyr Faith," the Church of England embarked upon a uniquely conciliatory path that could have united the nation's Catholics and Protestants together in a single church. A long

[51] Edwin Sandys, *Europae Specvlvm* (London, 1629; STC 21718), pp. 107–8.

[52] Sandys, *Europae Specvlvm*, p. 107.   [53] Sandys, *Europae Specvlvm*, p. 108.

[54] Sandys, *Europae Specvlvm*, p. 117.   [55] Sandys, *Europae Specvlvm*, pp. 77.

[56] Sandys, *Europae Specvlvm*, p. 214.   [57] Sandys, *Europae Specvlvm*, p. 214.

list of ecclesiastical virtues followed. Unlike some other churches, in the Church of England:

> the succession of Bishops and vocation of Ministers continued; the dignity and state of the Clergie preserved; the honour and solemnity of the service of God not abased; the more auncient usages of the Church not cancelled; in summe, no humour affecting contrarietie, but a charitable endeavour rather of conformity with the Church of Rome, in whatsoever they thought not gain saying to the expresse Law of God, which is the onely approvable way in all meere Reformations[.][58]

Continuing a wide range of Jacobean themes and emphases, "reformation" remained a fundamentally moral exhortation—in the present case, to become like the Church of England. None of this was a "Laudian" argument.

Nonetheless, it may be helpful to analyze the views of a "Laudian." Some of the first extended historical works on the English Reformation would later come from the pen of Peter Heylyn, a chaplain to Charles I, who began his writing career in the last years of James' reign. His writings therefore bear comment. Over the course of his many publications, Heylyn's historical research produced surprisingly fluid—and sometimes inconsistent—conclusions. His works often doubled as polemics directed against contemporary political developments, as well as the historical and theological conclusions of various authors with whom he disagreed. In his early work *Mikrokosmos*, which was first published in 1621 and saw eight editions by 1639,[59] Heylyn described Henry VIII's reign in terms reminiscent of Nicholas Udall. The Tudor king "banished the vsurped supremacy of the Popes, and beganne the first reformation of religion; though formerly he had written a book against *Luther*, for which the Pope intituled him *Defender of the Faith*." Udall had penned his Preface as an exhortation to Edward VI to follow in his father's footsteps, and Heylyn described the boy king as doing so. "Edward VI, a most vertuous and religious Prince perfected the reformation began by his father."[60] Royal father and son together bequeathed a religious standard to later generations. By thus describing the relationship between the reigns of Henry and Edward, Heylyn fully tracked with Godwin's *Annales* and other contemporary authors, who often homogenized events that are today seen as quite different.[61] Heylyn did not maintain the terminological trajectory of "reformation" with Elizabeth, but he believed that Elizabeth walked the same path as her familial

---

[58] Sandys, *Europae Specvlvm*, p. 214.

[59] Anthony Milton, "Peter Heylyn (1599–1662), Church of England Clergyman and Historian," *ODNB*.

[60] Peter Heylyn, *Mikrokosmos* (London, 1625; STC 13277), p. 489.

[61] George Jenney, *A Catholike Conference* (London, 1626; STC 14497), pp. 128–9; Henry Burton, *For God, and the King* (Amsterdam, 1636; STC 4142), p. 95.

predecessors. She "reduced religion to its primitiue purity," and transcending religious division, she "succored" warring religious factions abroad, "the *Scots* against the *French*, the *French Protestants* against the *Catholiques*, and both against the *Spaniard*."[62] Here we see the same basic story told by Camden and Hayward. In the mid-1620s, Heylyn shared the historiographical assumptions and conclusions of his contemporaries.

A very different analysis of reformation came more than a decade later when Heylyn wrote *A Briefe and Moderate Answer*, a comparatively lengthy response to the sermons that had resulted in Burton's condemnation for seditious libel. In the *Answer*, Heylyn broke with the brief but unoriginal summary found in his earlier *Mikrokosmos*. As he now told the story, "the first reformation of religion" took place under Edward rather than his father.[63] And, instead of completing Henry's religious work, the boy king now failed, and Elizabeth brought reformation to its glorious conclusion. Heylyn offered no explanation for his changed perspective, but two recent historiographical developments should be noted. First, the second edition of Hayward's study of Edward VI was printed one year before the *Answer*. Although not cited at the time, Hayward became a recurrent authority in Heylyn's later works. In fact, Heylyn summarized Edwardian history in terms remarkably reminiscent of Hayward: "the case stood thus. King *Edward* being a *Minor* about nine yeares old, at his first comming to the crowne; there was much heaving at the Church, by some great men which were about him, who purposed to inrich themselves with the spoyles thereof."[64] Second, perhaps yielding to the enthusiasm for all things Elizabethan, Heylyn now wrote that salutary religious change fully emerged under the Virgin Queen, whose reformation drew upon select earlier legal and religious developments. She revived Henry VIII's prosecution of *praemunire* and his rejection of papal supremacy,[65] and restored the liturgy used by her brother.[66] Like so many others, Heylyn homogenized the differences between the 1549, 1552, and 1559 Prayer Books, only noting the removal, under Elizabeth, of the anti-papal curse used during Edward's reign.[67] Heylyn concluded, "we have found no novelty, nothing that tends to Innovation in the worship of God but a reviver and continuance onely of the antient usages which have beene practiced in this Church since the reformation, and were commended to it from the purest ages."[68] Elizabethan and patristic history, now conflated, became the primary court of appeal. Heylyn's new narrative of reformation thus remained prescriptive, even if now advanced with slightly greater historical detail.

---

[62] Heylyn, *Mikrokosmos*, p. 489.
[63] Peter Heylyn, *A Briefe and Moderate Answer* (London, 1637; STC 13269), p. 78.
[64] Heylyn, *Briefe and Moderate Answer*, p. 100.
[65] Heylyn, *Briefe and Moderate Answer*, pp. 94–5 (praemunire), 97–100 (on papal and royal supremacy).
[66] Heylyn, *Briefe and Moderate Answer*, e.g., pp. 138, 148.
[67] Heylyn, *Briefe and Moderate Answer*, pp. 157–8.
[68] Heylyn, *Briefe and Moderate Answer*, p. 140.

Reformation Now

Between the late 1630s and the early 1650s, "reformation" was primarily used in England to denote current events. It is no exaggeration to describe "reformation" as the keyword of a long civil war decade. In 1641 alone, readers, however invested or casual, could peruse petitions for and against reformation,[69] parliamentary sermons and speeches on point,[70] *apologiae* against these,[71] and rebuttals of the same.[72] Regardless of who deployed it and how, "reformation" was central to the vocabulary of competing political visions in the present, whether within, beyond, or across England's borders. The conviction that mid-sixteenth century England experienced a reformation of religion developed as a historical discourse comparatively marginal to this far more widespread usage. This and the next section survey the sometimes-bewildering diversity of non-historiographical uses of "reformation" through the years immediately following the beheading of Charles I. The final two sections of the chapter then circle back around and analyze the emergence, within this same context, of the English Reformation as a historical narrative that doubled as a religious and political apologetic. During its civil wars, England saw an intellectual development analogous to that which occurred almost a century earlier in Scotland, albeit with calculated thematic differences. As seen in Chapter 2, between 1558 and 1560, some Scots used "reformation" to vindicate their chosen course of political action, and afterwards developed an attendant historiography to justify the same. In the 1640s, a small group of English authors followed suit, crafting a distinct historiography that vindicated and furthered their own political interests and commitments.

The Scottish Prayer Book is often portrayed as the catalyst for the civil wars that engulfed all three British kingdoms. But *post hoc* is not *propter hoc*. Appeals to the Scottish Reformation had defined debate over the Articles of Perth, and opponents of the new Scottish canons and liturgy merely applied the same arguments, which had not yet died out,[73] to a new topic of controversy.[74] In Scotland, the militant

---

[69] See, e.g., Anonymous, *The First and Large Petition of the Citie of London* (London, 1641; Wing/ F973), also known as the "Root and Branch" petition. The major collection of petitions against reformation was Thomas Aston, *A Collection of Sundry Petitions* (London, 1642; Wing/A4073).

[70] See, e.g., Thomas Ford, *Reformation Sure and Stedfast* (London, 1641; Wing/F1515); Harbottle Grimston, *Master Grimston his Worthy and Learned Speech* (London, 1641; Wing/G2051).

[71] See, e.g., Anonymous, *An Apology for Bishops* (London, 1641; Wing/A3543); Joseph Hall, *An Humble Remonstrance to the High Covrt of Parliament* (London, 1641; STC 12675); Joseph Hall, *A Defence of the Humble Remonstrance* (London, 1641; Wing/H378); Joseph Hall, *A Letter Sent to an Honourable Gentleman* (London, 1641; Wing/H392).

[72] Smectymnuus, *An Answer to a Book Entitvled An Hvmble Remonstrance* (London, 1641; Wing/ M748); Smectymnuus, *A Vindication of the Answer to the Hvmble Remonstrance* (London, 1641; Wing/ M798); John Milton, *Animadversions upon the Remonstrants Defence against Smectymnuus* (London, 1641; Wing/M2089).

[73] See, e.g., David Calderwood, *The Re-Examination of the Two Articles Abridged* (Netherlands, 1636; STC 4363.5).

[74] Laura A.M. Stewart, *Rethinking the Scottish Revolution: Covenanted Scotland, 1637–1651* (Oxford: Oxford University Press, 2016), pp. 38–43, describes a "culture of dissent."

apocalypticism and polemical vocabulary found in Knox's *Historie* surged to the fore in public debate. Scots upset by the new liturgy called it "popish,"[75] and they composed and adopted the National Covenant in response. The National Covenant consisted of the 1580 Confession of Faith of the Kirk of Scotland, a discussion of subsequent parliamentary acts on religion, an essay against the 1637 Prayer Book, and a concluding justification. The Covenant declared that:

> all and sundrie, who either gainesaies the Word of the Evangell, received and approved as the heads of the Confession of Faith, professed in Parlament, in the yeare of God 1560 ... or that refuses the administration of the Holy Sacraments, as they were then ministrated to bee no members of the said Kirk within this Realme and true Religion, presently professed.[76]

Supporters believed that the National Covenant returned the country to the purity of its 1560 reformation.[77] One of the Covenant's authors, Archibald Johnston, Lord Wariston, enthused that "The Kirk of *Scotland* after the reformation of Religion did by degrees attaine to as great perfection both in doctrine & discipline as any other reformed kirk in *Europe*."[78] Wariston attacked the Scottish bishops, who he believed were agents of both Catholicism and Arminianism,[79] and like other Covenanters, Wariston described the new Covenant as a means of "preservation."[80] The connection between "reformation" and "preservation" was new, and would soon emerge in English Presbyterian documents as well. By returning the Scottish Reformation to the forefront of national consciousness, and by now positioning it against the idolatry allegedly shared by Catholics, Arminians, and the Scottish bishops, the National Covenant all but demanded another reformation "by force of arms."

The National Covenant helped transform a national argument into a national rebellion. Upset with recent religious changes became defiance, and rapidly spiraled into armed revolt as the Covenanters set about uprooting all recent English influence upon the Scottish church. On November 21, 1638, the General Assembly of the Church of Scotland convened with the king's permission but

---

[75] Joong-Lak Kim, "The Scottish-English-Romish Book: The Character of the Scottish Prayer Book of 1637," in Michael J. Braddick and David L. Smith (eds.), *The Experience of Revolution in Stuart Britain and Ireland: Essays for John Morrill* (Cambridge: Cambridge University Press, 2011), pp. 14–32; John R. Young, "The Covenanters and the Scottish Parliament, 1639–51: The Rule of the Godly and the 'Second Scottish Reformation'," in Elizabeth Boran and Crawford Gribben (eds.), *Enforcing Reformation in Ireland and Scotland, 1550–1700* (Aldershot: Ashgate, 2006), pp. 131–58.

[76] Church of Scotland, *The Confession of Faith, of the Kirk of Scotland* (Amsterdam, 1638; STC 22026.8), pp. 8–9.

[77] Alexander Henderson, *The Protestation* (Edinburgh, 1638; STC 21904); Archibald Wariston, *A Short Relation of the State of the Kirk of Scotland Since the Reformation of Religion* (Edinburgh, 1638; STC 22039), sigs. B3 v–B4 r.

[78] Wariston, *A Short Relation*, sig. A2.

[79] Wariston, *A Short Relation*, sigs. Bv, B3 v; bishops are attacked on literally every page.

[80] Wariston, *A Short Relation*, sigs. C, C3; see also, e.g., Anonymous, *The Beast is Wounded* (Amsterdam, 1638; STC 22032.5), p. 14; Henderson, *The Protestation*, sig. C.

rebelled one week later when ordered to dissolve. Continuing into late December, the Assembly repealed the Articles of Perth,[81] rejected the new canons and liturgy,[82] and abolished the entire episcopate, deposing and excommunicating each bishop by name while declaring their office "pretended."[83] In a remarkable historiographical coup, on December 8 the Assembly determined "Episcopacie to have been abjured by the Confession of Faith, 1580. And to be removed out of this Kirk."[84] Charles saw these actions as treasonous, and even before the General Assembly dissolved itself, the king had revived the late Elizabethan hermeneutic of suspicion. In his proclamation of December 8, he described his opponents as operating "under colour and pretext of religion."[85] With Scotland's subsequent invasion of northern England, the Scots' religiously animated revolt spilled over the border and became the defining feature of English political life for more than two decades.

The ensuing civil wars saw durable descriptive habits yield imaginative stasis. "Reformation" invoked a wide range of apocalyptic images and ideas, and monsters again populated contested discursive horizons. Monstrosity signified deformation, reformation its right reordering. But as in more immediately recognizable political languages, so too in those more esoteric; however vivid the literary spectacle, competing visions and values proved incommensurable. Some authors marshaled Biblical inspiration as invective. Multiple works referenced the endtimes Beast found in the New Testament Book of Revelation.[86] On the eve of the first Bishops' War, in a pamphlet violently entitled *The Beast is Wounded*, the anonymous author described the National Covenant as "a wonderfull deliverance," praying in a marginal note, "Such a *deliverance* God grant England."[87] Adopting Knox's apocalyptic disdain for episcopacy, the pamphleteer described bishops as agents of the Beast and claimed that they allied themselves with the Antichrist.[88] The immensely popular *Souldiers Catechisme*, which went through

---

[81] The Church of Scotland General Assembly, *The Principall Acts...At Glasgow the xxi. of November 1638* (Edinburgh, 1639; STC 22049), pp. 10–11, 27–30.

[82] The Church of Scotland General Assembly, *The Principal Acts*, pp. 12–13.

[83] The Church of Scotland General Assembly, *The Principal Acts*, pp. 14–19.

[84] The Church of Scotland General Assembly, *The Principal Acts*, pp. 19–27, at p. 19; Conrad Russell, *The Fall of the British Monarchies 1637–1642* (Oxford: Clarendon Press, 1990), pp. 53–4; on the need for caution concerning this erroneous historiographical claim, see Stewart, *Rethinking the Scottish Revolution*, e.g., pp. 123–4, 127, 141.

[85] Charles I, *His Majesties Proclamation in Scotland* (London, 1639; STC 22001.5), p. 3.

[86] E.g., John Lilburne, *A Worke of the Beast* (Amsterdam, 1638; STC 15599); Joseph Mede, *The Apostasy of the Latter Times* (London, 1641; Wing/M1590); Anonymous, *The Vntrussing of Above One Hundred Popish Points* (London, 1642; Wing/U103); Thomas Brightman, *Reverend Mr. Brightmans Iudgement* (London, 1642; Wing/B4684A); Iohn Vicars, *Behold Romes Monster* (London, 1643; Wing/V294); for a broad overview, see David Cressy, "Lamentable, Strange, and Wonderful: Headless Monsters in the English Revolution," in Laura Lunger Knoppers and Joan B. Landes (eds.), *Monstrous Bodies/Political Monstrosities in Early Modern Europe* (Ithaca and London: Cornell University Press, 2004), pp. 40–63.

[87] Anonymous, *The Beast is Wounded*, p. 4; the prayer is found in n. a.

[88] Anonymous, *The Beast is Wounded*, pp. 5 n. b (frogs); 4 n. c, 5 n. c (Beast); 11 n. c (Antichrist).

seven editions between 1644 and 1645,[89] offers another example. Soldiers gave telling answers in response to the question, "What is it that you chiefly aime at in this warre?" They first responded, "the Pulling down of Babylon," and then continued, "the suppression of an Antichristian Prelacy, consisting of Archbishops, Bishops &c." The *Catechisme*'s third justification for war was "the Reformation of a most corrupt, lazie, infamous, superstitious, soule-murdering Clergie."[90] Here and elsewhere, the great keyword of the decade—"reformation"— appeared. Royalists were much the same. Appealing to high and low culture alike by drawing upon monstrosity, a text authored by the otherwise unidentified Mercurius Melancholicus advanced its argument with the delightfully polemical title *Mistris Parliament Brought to Bed of a Monstrous Childe of Reformation*.[91] In a declaration bordering upon the confessional, Melancholicus had Parliament inform the reader, "in stead of *Reforming* I have *Deformed*, and in stead of repairing I have pulled down."[92] Even the king described his opponents with apocalyptic imagery: "the Devil of Rebellion, doth commonly turn himself into an Angel of Reformation; and the old Serpent can pretend new Lights."[93] Across numerous works, metaphor gave way to metonymy as "the old Serpent" reappeared wearing guise upon guise, page after page.

Many English works described contemporary events as the instantiation of reformation. In 1642, the front cover of the anonymously authored *Good Newes from the Assembly in Scotland* explained that its contents were "Exhibited to this Parliament in England, concerning this present Reformation in *England*." The author praised "The Confession of Faith, and Reformation of the Kirk of Scotland," especially its new, strictly Presbyterian polity, against "the ambition and usurpation of Prelates."[94] The descriptive distinction between England and Scotland was key; Scotland already had its Reformation, whereas England had "this *present* Reformation." The author believed that a shared Anglo-Scots religious project would soon be completed, thus aligning England with its northern neighbor. John Milton similarly identified political unrest with reformation. The front cover of his controversial 1643 pamphlet *The Doctrine and Discipline of Divorce* advertised its contents as "Seasonable to be now thought on in the Reformation intended."[95] As with many earlier works, "reformation" could also

---

[89] Richard Bagwell, "Ram, Thomas (1564–1634), Church of Ireland bishop of Ferns and Leighlin," rev. Alan Ford, *ODNB*.

[90] Robert Ram, *The Souldiers Catechisme* (London, 1644; Wing/R196), p. 9.

[91] Mercurius Melancholicus, *Mistris Parliament Brought to Bed of a Monstrous Childe of Reformation* (London[?], 1648; Wing/M2281).

[92] Melancholicus, *Mistris Parliament*, p. 7.

[93] Charles I, *Eikon Basilike*, ed. Jim Daems and Holly Faith Nelson (Ontario: Broadview Editions, 2006), p. 186.

[94] Anonymous, *Good Newes*, p. 1.

[95] John Milton, *The Doctrine and Discipline of Divorce* (London, 1643; Wing/M2108).

justify those acts of religious and political violence that brought reformation to pass. In "An Ordinance for the further demolishing of Monuments of Idolatry and Superstition," the Commons decreed in 1644 that the destruction of "Organs, Images, and all manner of Superstitious Monuments," would help "accomplish the blessed Reformation so happily begun."[96] That same year, the *Souldiers Catechism* proclaimed that "God hath put the Sword of Reformation into the Souldiers hand."[97] Royalists were, yet again, no different. As the king sat imprisoned in 1648, Jordan Thomas' anonymously published broadside *The Anarchie* carried the subtitle "Or the blest Reformation since 1640."[98] Sung "To a Rare New Tune" with "thankes to the Powers below," *The Anarchie* sardonically commended the most chaotic of political messages. In the second stanza, a cacophony of voices sang, "Truth's the spell made us rebell," while the fourth stanza concluded with the more ominous exhortation, "Let's all be Kings." For its English proponents, reformation was the current goal. For their opponents, reformation was the most disruptive of immediately tangible realities. In the throes of civil war, reformation was a contest for the present, not the past.

As Parliament came apart in 1643 and the Lords progressively joined the king in Oxford, the House of Commons remained in London, where Presbyterian convictions defined its aims. In a bid at securing religious unity, the Commons created the Westminster Assembly, describing its goal, in words familiar to historians today, as "a further & more perfect Reformation, then yet hath bin attained."[99] On September 25, the remainder of the English Parliament ratified *A Solemne League and Covenant for Reformation, and Defence of Religion*, a text composed by the Westminster Assembly with aid from Scottish Covenanters. Although usually referred to in abbreviated form as the "Solemn League and Covenant," the document's central thematic emphasis is found in the title's clarion call "for Reformation"—a point recognized by its principal opponents. When the king issued his response, he attacked the Covenant by name as the *Solemne League and Covenant for Reformation*.[100] Scottish themes are easily seen in the text. Just as "preservation" and "reformation" were synonymous in the National Covenant and its *apologiae*, the same two words now defined the relationship of religion in Scotland to that in the other Stuart kingdoms. The *Solemn League and Covenant for Reformation* called for "the preservation of the Reformed Religion in the Church of *Scotland*," but for "the reformation of

---

[96] The Parliament of England and Wales, *Two Ordinances of the Lords and Commons Assembled in Parliament* (London, 1645; Wing/E2408A), p. 3.

[97] Ram, *The Souldiers Catechism*, p. 21.

[98] Thomas Jordan, *The Anarchie, Or the Blest Reformation* (London[?], 1648; Wing/J1019B).

[99] The Parliament of England and Wales, *An Ordinance of the Lords and Commons...for the Calling of an Assembly of Learned, and Godly Divines* (London, 1643; Wing/E1952D), sig. A2.

[100] Charles I, *Proclamation Forbidding the Tendring or Taking of a Late Covenant, Called, A Solemn League and Covenant for Reformation, &c.* (Oxford, 1643; Wing/C2658).

Religion in the Kingdoms of *England* and *Ireland*."[101] Printed and reprinted through the end of the decade, the *Solemn League and Covenant for Reformation* became the central religious manifesto of the civil wars. Its presence was ubiquitous, and its demands inescapable.

The king described the *Solemn League and Covenant for Reformation* as "nothing else but a Trayterous and Seditious Combination against Vs, and against the established Religion and Lawes of this Kingdome."[102] He recognized that the Commons and Covenanters had together created a united front against his rule, although they believed that their rebellion would ultimately save the king from his own, evil counselors. Charles was not alone in his perception. Other responses to the *Solemn League and Covenant for Reformation* described it as impious, unlawful, and treasonous,[103] and readers did not miss its threat to episcopacy.[104] Writing from Oxford, Henry Ferne argued that each supporter of the Covenant "doth in conscience allow and approve the Scots Discipline and Government, and withall binds himselfe to endeavor the advancement of the same, by bringing this Kingdome to an Uniformity with them."[105] Placing blame squarely upon Presbyterian shoulders, Ferne believed that the Covenanters and their allies sought "by force of Armes to compell the King to the Reformation pretended herein."[106] Through the end of the decade, still other attacks upon the Covenant would be published by figures such as the English clergyman John Gauden,[107] the University of Oxford,[108] and John Bramhall, bishop of Derry.[109] Anti-Scottish suspicion, present among some English since Elizabeth's reign, became a defining norm among royalists.[110]

---

[101] Westminster Assembly, *A Solemne League and Covenant for Reformation, and Defence of Religion* (London, 1643; Wing/S4442aA), p. 4.

[102] Charles I, *Proclamation*.

[103] See, e.g., Anonymous, *Worse & Worse* (Oxford, 1643; Wing/W3611); Anonymous, *The Iniqvity of the Late Solemn League, or Covenant Discovered* (London, 1643; Wing/I190); Supreme Council of Confederate Catholics, *Admonitions by the Svpreame Covncell of the Confederat Catholicks of Ire[l]and* (Waterford, 1643; Wing/A593A).

[104] Henry Ferne, *The Unlawfulnesse of the New Covenant* (Oxford, 1643; Wing/F24), p. 2; Joseph Hall, *The Lawfvlnes and Vnlawfvlnes of an Oath or Covenant* (London, 1643; Wing/H388), esp. pp. 6–7; John Theyer, *Aerio-Mastix, Or,A Vindication of the Apostolicall and Generally Received Government of the Church of Christ by Bishops* (Oxford, 1643; Wing/T889).

[105] Ferne, *Unlawfullnesse of the New Covenant*, pp. 1–2.

[106] Ferne, *Unlawfullnesse of the New Covenant*, p. 3.

[107] Gauden, *Certaine Scrvples and Doubts of Conscience* (London, 1645; Wing/G345); at pp. 6–9, Gauden notes the threat to episcopacy.

[108] The University of Oxford, *Reasons of the Present Judgment of the Vniversity of Oxford* (London, 1647; Wing/S623, S623A, S624, S625).

[109] John Bramhall, *A Fair Warning, to Take Heed of the Scottish Discipline* (London, 1649; Wing/B4222, B4223, B4223A, B4223B).

[110] Anonymous, *A Briefe Discovrse, Declaring the Impiety and Unlawfulnesse of the New Covenant with the Scots* (Oxford, 1643; Wing/B4580); Anonymous, *The Scots Policie: To Assassinate Our English Monarchy* (London, 1647; Wing/S2029); Anonymous, *The Scots Treacherous Designes Discovered* (London, 1647; Wing/S2030).

The fundamental issue for the king was, as seen in the Scottish canons of 1635, not reformation as such but authority. In a letter written on July 23, 1642, Charles promised the General Assembly of the Scottish Kirk, "We will endeavor a Reformation in a fair and orderly way, and where a Reformation is setled, We resolve with that authority wherewith God hath vested Us, to maintain and defend it in Peace and Libertie."[111] *Eikon Basilike* (Greek for *The Royal Image*), the king's posthumous but popular collection of political reflections and religious medita-tions,[112] maintained the same position. The king punctuated *Eikon Basilike* with references to reformation; many were negative,[113] few were positive,[114] and in a lengthy repudiation of the *Solemn League and Covenant for Reformation*, the king parried with his own literary *coup de grâce*.[115] His enemies were animated by *"pretensions of Piety and Reformation."*[116] Like much of the controversial litera-ture published in the 1640s, *Eikon Basilike* recapitulated older material. The king's book resounded with the thematic echoes of Elizabethans such as Bancroft and Hooker, but even in the face of death, and quite unlike his Elizabethan forerun-ners, Charles explicitly denoted reformation as a fundamental *good*. The twentieth section of *Eikon Basilike*, entitled "Upon the Reformations of the Times," began with the long-familiar contrast between reformed and deformed. "No Glory is more to be envied than that, of due Reforming either Church or State, when deformities are such, that the perturbation and novelty are not like to exceed the benefit of Reforming."[117] Charles urged the cultivation of Christian habits, writing that moderation, counsel, and Christian charity defined true reformation. Disorder, whether through iconoclasm or other forms of violence, was antithetical to the wellbeing of both church and state, "since they leave all things more deformed, disorderly, and discontented, than when they began, in point of Piety, Morality, Charity, and good Order."[118] When the king turned to pray for "Christian and charitable Reformation,"[119] in one stroke he both defended his own authority and emphasized the failure of his opponents to maintain the cardinal Christian virtue.

[111] Charles I, *A True Copy of His Maiesties Letter* (London, 1642; Wing/C2837), p. 4.

[112] Andrew Lacey, *The Cult of King Charles the Martyr* (Woodbridge and Rochester: The Boydell Press, 2003), p. 81, notes that in 1649 alone, thirty-nine editions were published. Authorship of *Eikon Basilike* has long been a point of dispute. For a full discussion, see Charles I, *Eikon Basilike*, pp. 16–21; I fully accept Daems and Nelson's description of the work as "a heteroglossic, collaborative royalist effort" (p. 21). For the sake of ease, I ascribe the work to the king, recognizing that the full extent of his authorship may never be fully ascertained.

[113] Charles I, *Eikon Basilike*, pp. 78, 86, 98, 99, 109, 117–18, 151.

[114] Charles I, *Eikon Basilike*, p. 188, locates the right of reformation with the king; pp. 155–9 contrasts right reformation with rebellion; pp. 135, 157, 158 draw upon the classic contrast of "reformed" and "deformed."

[115] Charles I, *Eikon Basilike*, pp. 114–21.

[116] Charles I, *Eikon Basilike*, p. 120; italics in original.   [117] Charles I, *Eikon Basilike*, p. 155.

[118] Charles I, *Eikon Basilike*, p. 157.   [119] Charles I, *Eikon Basilike*, p. 159.

"Reformation" without End

The king's beheading on January 30, 1648/9 deprived Episcopalians of their political focus, but otherwise did little to alter the thematic emphases that had suffused public discourse for more than a decade. Relations between the Scottish Covenanters and their English allies had since deteriorated, and the king's brutal death only furthered the divide. When Scottish Covenanters declared their loyalty to Charles II but the Rump Parliament did not, the stage was set for a military showdown. Oliver Cromwell's subsequent martial imposition of English rule upon both Scotland and Ireland created an Anglo-centric "British" identity but otherwise did little to resolve long-standing religious disputes. Reformation now became a topic of debate between those who had previously united against the king. Problematically for Presbyterians, a third religious option had emerged. Derided as "Independents" but preferring the term "Congregationalist,"[120] these English Protestants drew upon a marginal line of Elizabethan theological argument and rejected all forms of ecclesiastical leadership beyond the local, individual congregation. Incapable of reaching any conclusion over whether reformation should entail Presbyterian or Congregationalist organization, the successively short-lived governments of the 1650s fudged the question by endorsing religious toleration for all Christians—with three important exceptions: "this Liberty be not extended to Popery or Prelacy, nor to such as under the profession of Christ, hold forth and practise Licentiousness."[121] Catholics comprised less than 2 percent of the English population, but those who favored "Prelacy"—the episcopal order of the Church of England—were much larger in number. The Cromwellian Protectorate is often portrayed as confessionally tolerant because of its minimalist theological criteria,[122] but by excluding such a significant number of English Christians, the Protectorate is better understood as allowing Presbyterians and Congregationalists to pursue their own respective reformations within a political structure defined by confessional oligarchy. Those who opposed either form of reformation were subject to legal reprisals and political exclusion.

The debate between Presbyterians and Congregationalists highlights the semantic confusion that haunted "reformation." Each group continued to look upon reformation as a contest in the present. Shortly after the king's death,

---

[120] Hunter Powell, *The crisis of British Protestantism: Church Power in the Puritan Revolution, 1638–44* (Manchester: Manchester University Press, 2015), pp. 10–11.

[121] Oliver Cromwell, *The Government of the Common-Wealth* (London, 1653; Thomason/E.1063 [5]), p. 43, n. XXXVII.

[122] See, e.g., Barry Coward, *The Cromwellian Protectorate* (Manchester: Manchester University Press, 2002), p. 40; Lacey, *The Cult of King Charles*, p. 57; Andrew Bradstock, *Radical Religion in Cromwell's England: A Concise History from the English Civil War to the End of the Commonwealth* (London and New York: I.B. Tauris, 2011), p. xiii; a better perspective remains Blair Worden, "Toleration and the Cromwellian Protectorate," in W.J. Sheils (ed.), *Persecution and Toleration* (Oxford: Basil Blackwell, 1984), pp. 199–246.

Presbyterians in Lancaster composed *A Solemn Exhortation*. The authors' aim was the creation of a national Presbyterian structure. They alleged that Congregationalists were bound not only by "a common hatred to Reformation," but by their "expectation and endeavors for a legal Toleration, and an assuming of liberty in Religion for the present, the fruitful mother of all Atheism, Error, false Religion, and Profaneness."[123] The Presbyterians of Lancaster concluded their work by calling the nation to "stand fast to our solemn League and Covenant."[124] Countering Presbyterian scruples with an argument for congregational autonomy, the Northamptonshire minister Richard Resbury published *The Tabernacle of God with Men*. According to Resbury, "The true way of Reformation amongst us, in this; that persons fit matter of the Church, joyne together in Church fellowship, chuse Officers with Cautions formerly laid down, and so forme Congregations into a disciplinary State, exercising discipline among themselves, leaving out the rest."[125] For Congregationalists, reformation would be a pressing need for as long as it remained unaccomplished, a perception that continued through at least the end of the decade.[126] Presbyterian reformation had no place for such autonomy, but to Presbyterians' chagrin, Congregationalism persevered beyond the 1650s.

Congregationalist arguments against Presbyterians also aimed north of the border. John Milton wrote *The Tenure of Kings and Magistrates* in 1649 both to justify the regicide and to decry Scottish Covenanters' support for Charles II. The *Tenure* offered a very simple but powerful historical argument: the regicide of Charles I was no different than what Scottish Protestants had accomplished the previous century. According to Milton, regicide and rebellion were central Protestant tenets. About halfway through his text, he began a select roll call of historical events, "all Protestant and chiefly Presbyterian."[127] The most important figure was John Knox, "a most famous Divine and the reformer of *Scotland* to the Presbyterian discipline."[128] Milton believed that Knox and his allies, once they concluded that Mary was a tyrant, sought to "reform all things according to the original institution of Common-welths."[129] Milton's key charge against his Presbyterian contemporaries lay precisely here: "And to let the world know that the whole Church and Protestant State of *Scotland* in those purest times of

---

[123] Anonymous, *A Solemn Exhortation* (London, 1649; Wing/S4440), p. 8.

[124] Anonymous, *A Solemn Exhortation*, p. 16.

[125] Richard Resbury, *The Tabernacle of God with Men: Or, the Visible Church Reformed* (London, 1649; Wing/R1136A), p. 45.

[126] See, e.g., Anonymous, *Reformation Or, The Progress Thereof in Some Foot-steps of it in The Congregational Way of Churches in England, From the Year of Our Lord, 1640* (London, 1659; Wing/R743A).

[127] John Milton, *The Tenure of Kings and Magistrates* (London, 1649; Wing/M2181), p. 26.

[128] Milton, *Tenure of Kings and Magistrates*, p. 26.

[129] Milton, *Tenure of Kings and Magistrates*, p. 27.

reformation were of the same beleif, three years after, they met in the feild *Mary* thir lawful and hereditary Queen, took her prisoner yeilding before fight, kept her in prison, and the same yeare deposd her."[130] As if this were not enough, Milton continued his discussion with an accusation of hypocrisy. "But what need these examples to Presbyterians, I meane to those who now of late would seem so much to abhorr deposing, whenas they to all Christendom have giv'n the latest and the liveliest example of doing it themselves."[131] Presbyterian loyalty to Charles II was not merely capitulation but a refusal of Presbyterianism's own first principles. In presenting Scottish history thus, Milton made an eminently English argument, one that Presbyterians may have dissented from, but which supporters of episcopacy had long maintained.

Royalists looked dimly upon their situation in the early 1650s. The king's violent death only solidified their widespread perception that reformation, understood as rebellion, defined the previous decade. Supporters of the king and the episcopal church echoed the arguments of works such as *Eikon Basilike*, joining to these their own outrage over Charles' execution. Henry King's *An Elegy Upon the Most Incomparable K. Charls the I* portrayed Charles as a second Christ, a typological image that he complimented by casting the king's enemies as Judas Iscariot, who betrayed Jesus for thirty pieces of silver. As the king piled on his accusations, he lamented, "Brave *Reformation*! And a through one too,/Which to enrich Your selves must All undo."[132] Just as Jesus was handed over, so was Charles, and the pattern of first-century Jerusalem was typologically reenacted in seventeenth-century England. In a similar vein, the anonymously authored pamphlet *Women Will Have Their Will, Or Give Christmas His Due* portrayed a fictional dialogue between the characters M^{ris} Custome and M^{ris} New-Come. The latter lived "in *Reformation*-Alley, neer *Destruction*-Street," while the former was a pious Christian who only desired the devout celebration of the recently banned holy day of Christmas.[133] Reformation, the author argued, had brought the nation into a devotional no-man's land. Another anonymously authored pamphlet linked religious custom with heresiology and its attendant fears of political anarchy. Entitled *Newes From Powles, Or the New Reformation of the Army*, it recounted an instance of sacrilege by the New Model Army officer Hugh Peters, who had baptized a colt in St. Paul's, London. The author portrayed the mock baptism as the most scandalous act in a much larger catalogue of sacrilegious exploits. The tract began, however, with a rhetorical question:

[130] Milton, *Tenure of Kings and Magistrates*, p. 27.
[131] Milton, *Tenure of Kings and Magistrates*, p. 29.
[132] Henry King, *An Elegy Upon the Most Incomparable K. Charls the I* (London, n.d.; Wing/K499), p. 11.
[133] Anonymous, *Women Will Have Their Will, Or Give Christmas His Due* (London, 1649; Wing/W3327).

Have we not a blessed *Reformation* indeed, and a sound Religion established, when Horses goe to Church, and Lectures of Treason, Warre and discord are read instead of the Gospel of PEACE and Glad tidings of Salvation, where Warres Horn-book is taught in stead of holy Scripture, and the blessed Sacrament of Baptisme of no more esteem then a mock to christen beasts; Is not this the *Desolation* of *Abomination* in the Holy Place?[134]

Whether through polished couplets or more rough-hewn prose, the Church of England's apologists repudiated "this present reformation" of the 1640s in terms both sweeping and impassioned. But a historiographical counter-argument was still needed.

Our English Reformation

The earliest extended discussions of "our *English* Reformation"[135] were composed during the 1640s as an apologetic move intended to vindicate both the monarchy and the Church of England against their detractors. Nonetheless, many English located the origins of their religious and political disputes in the sixteenth century. With the onset of war, censorship broke down and numerous works originally composed under Edward and Elizabeth were rapidly republished. John Ponet's *Shorte Treatise of Politike Power* was reprinted in 1639 and 1642,[136] some of Martin Marprelate's tractates reappeared,[137] and the first complete printing of Knox's *Historie of the Reformation of the Church of Scotland* took place in 1644.[138] The University of Oxford republished its reply to the Millenary Petition in 1641,[139] and the same year saw the republication of John Foxe's *Acts and Monuments*.[140] Archbishop Bancroft's *Dangerous Positions* was reprinted in 1640,[141] and 1648 saw the first appearance of the sixth and eighth books of

---

[134] Anonymous, *Newes from Powles, Or the New Reformation of the Army* (London, 1649; Wing/ N990), p. 3; "the Desolation of Abomination" is a reference to the Biblical book of Daniel (9:27, 11:31, 12:11). The phrase is also found in the New Testament (Matt. 24:15–16, Mark 13:14, Luke 21:20–1), and similar references are found in the apocryphal/deuterocanonical book I Maccabees (1:54, 6:7). In all instances, it refers to the profanation of the Temple in Jerusalem.

[135] Hammond, *New Directorie*, p. 6.

[136] John Ponet, *A Shorte Treatise of Politike Power* (London, 1639; STC 20179); John Ponet, *A Short Treatise of Politiqve Power* (London, 1642; Wing/P2804B).

[137] Martin Marprelate, *A Dialogue* (Amsterdam[?], 1640; STC 6805.3); Martin Marprelate, *Reformation No Enemie* (London[?], 1641; Wing/R741), which was also published as *Hay Any Worke for Cooper* (London[?], 1642; Wing/H1205).

[138] John Knox, *The Historie of the Reformation of the Church of Scotland* (London, 1644; Wing/ K739).

[139] The University of Oxford, *The Humble Petition of the Ministers of the Church of England* (Oxford [?], 1641; Wing/H3562).

[140] John Foxe, *Acts and Monuments* (London, 1641; Wing/F2035).

[141] Richard Bancroft, *Dangerous Positions and Proceedings* (London, 1640; STC 1345).

Richard Hooker's *Of the Lawes of Ecclesiasticall Politie*.[142] Well-worn themes rapidly became the warp and weft of print culture. For many contemporaries, the road to civil war began a century earlier, and cut across intellectual cultures both high and low.

The long 1640s saw competing historiographies advanced by diverse religious and political contingents. Proponents of reformation did not look fondly back upon a Tudor reformation later undermined by Stuart, and specifically Caroline or "Laudian," innovations. They instead identified Charles and his father as guilty of maintaining an older rejection of reformation. This shared perspective did not map later political allegiances. In the longest of his early pamphlets, simply entitled *Of Reformation*, Milton argued that beginning with Henry VIII, the Tudor monarchs successively hindered reformation of the English church. Under Edward VI, "a complete *Reform* was not effected," and under Elizabeth "*Religion* attain'd not a perfect reducement."[143] Parliament heard the same perspective in a sermon on June 15, 1641, when Thomas Ford called for a new Josiah, "a very reforming Prince" who "had a right spirit in way of Reformation."[144] However, the Josiah in question was not a new Edward VI.[145] Ford, like Milton, believed that Edward's reformation was a betrayal, and that recent history had only continued the same trajectory. Noting "the succession of Queen *Elizabeths* reformation through King *Iames* his Raigne, and our gracious King *Charles*," Ford nonetheless complained that "from perfection in Reformation, we have beene often stopped."[146] For those such as Milton and Ford, such arguments were not subversive uses of "reformation," but the surest of means for rectifying failures past and present.

The Westminster Assembly's attempted imposition of Presbyterian discipline upon England came with a supporting historiography in the *Directory for the Publique Worship of God*, the intended replacement for the Book of Common Prayer. It first mooted, in fully developed form, the idea that reformation happened in sixteenth-century England by degrees. The Preface of the *Directory* positioned the Westminster Assembly as the true inheritor of Tudor liturgical change. Unnamed Edwardian religious figures were described as "our first Reformers" and "Excellent Instruments raised by God to begin the purging and

---

[142] Richard Hooker, *Of the Lawes of Ecclesiasticall Politie; The Sixth and Eighth Books* (London, 1648; Wing/H2635).

[143] John Milton, *Of Reformation Touching Church-Discipline in England* (London, 1641; Wing/M2134), pp. 9 (Edward VI), 15 (Elizabeth).

[144] Ford, *Reformation Sure and Stedfast*, p. 3.

[145] For an overview of Edward's posthumous legacies through the early eighteenth century, see Benjamin M. Guyer, "'Of Hopes Great as Himselfe': Tudor and Stuart Legacies of Edward VI," in Estelle Paranque (ed.), *Remembering Queens and Kings of Early Modern England and France: Reputation, Reinterpretation, and Reincarnation* (Cham: Palgrave, Macmillan, 2019), pp. 73-91.

[146] Ford, *Reformation Sure and Stedfast*, p. 11.

building of his House."[147] But this was all; the first reformers had only begun their work. They failed to complete it and their successors failed to do the same. Sounding Scottish notes of complaint, the Preface averred that the liturgy composed under Edward VI, with its retention of "many unprofitable and burdensome Ceremonies," had caused offense not only to "the Godly at home; but also to the Reformed Churches abroad."[148] The liturgies of 1549, 1552, and 1559 were thus again homogenized, but the Westminster Assembly, operating in tandem with Scottish Covenanters, aimed to fulfill the allegedly unmet aspirations of a long-dead generation. Using a phrase familiar in contemporary scholarship, the Assembly denoted its work "further Reformation," and audaciously claimed that "were they [the first Reformers] now alive, they would joyn with us in this work."[149] Later publications by the Assembly continued in this vein. In a 1644 public letter sent to Reformed churches throughout Europe, the Westminster Assembly, together with commissioners from the Church of Scotland, described their work as "a more thorow Reformation of Religion" that sought a "perfect Reformation" and "right Reformation"—descriptors that revealed their own negative assessment of Tudor religious history.[150] As noted in Chapter 2, current scholarship anachronistically overemphasizes the importance of the phrase "further reformation" when analyzing Elizabethan religious debates. Some historians have rightly noted that "further reformation" was a prime religious goal during the 1640s,[151] but it must be emphasized that in its original usage, "further reformation" was not an attempt at developing the historiography of an earlier "English" Reformation. In truth, the demand for "further reformation" needed no such historiography. Its call was strictly supersessive.

Loyalty to the Church of England spurred the development of a very different argument, but composing a new historiography was hardly an obvious move. It came only in fits and starts because defending an English Reformation also required defining it—but no agreed-upon definition yet existed. An important first step came in 1645, when Peter Heylyn authored *Parliaments Power, In Lawes for Religion*.[152] Heylyn's pamphlet developed out of his published responses to two earlier developments. In *The Rebells Catechism* (1643), he joined many of the

---

[147] Westminster Assembly, *A Directory for the Publique Worship of God* (London, 1644; Wing/D1544), p. 6.

[148] Westminster Assembly, *Directory*, p. 2.   [149] Westminster Assembly, *Directory*, p. 6.

[150] Westminster Assembly, *A Letter from the Assembly of Divines in England, and the Commissioners of the Church of Scotland* (London, 1644; Wing/W1443A), pp. 1 ("a more thorow Reformation of Religion"), 4 ("perfect Reformation"), 8 ("right Reformation").

[151] See, e.g., Russell, *The Fall of the British Monarchies*, e.g., pp. 110, 203, 331, 400; Conrad Russell, *The Causes of the English Civil War* (Oxford: Clarendon Press, 1990), esp. pp. 220–6; John Adamson, *The Noble Revolt: The Overthrow of Charles I* (London: Weidenfeld & Nicolson, 2007), e.g., pp. 120, 123, 327, 412, 469.

[152] Peter Heylyn, *Parliaments Power, In Lawes for Religion* (Oxford, 1645; Wing/H1730). Previous analyses of *Parliaments Power* may be found in Milton, *Laudian and Royalist Polemic*, pp. 128–9; Lane, *Laudians and the Elizabethan Church*, pp. 152–5, analyzes Heylyn's third edition of 1657.

king's supporters in writing against the *Solemn League and Covenant for Reformation*;[153] and, after Archbishop Laud's execution on January 10, 1644/5, Heylyn wrote a short account of the archbishop's "death and sufferings."[154] Both works named the Scots as the prime instigators of England's civil wars,[155] but *The Rebells Catechism* made the unusual step of rescuing "reformation" from its widespread association, particularly among royalists, with rebellion. As discussed in Chapter 2, the Elizabethan "Homily Against Disobedience and Wilful Rebellion" had rendered rebellion synonymous with reformation, laying the groundwork for a hermeneutic of suspicion that continued into the 1640s. Heylyn used the Homily against Disobedience throughout the *Catechism*,[156] allowing "reformation" to retain its politically disruptive denotation. However, he also divided the history of English rebellions into one of two historiographical categories, those that happened "in times of *Popery*" and those that happened "since the *Reformation*."[157] Building on his work from 1637, Heylyn described the Reformation as a clearly demarcated event, and used *The Rebells Catechism* to further underscore the difference between England and several other nations, including Scotland. When his imagined interlocutor cited "France, Holland, Scotland, [and] Germany" as justifiable instances of armed resistance, Heylyn responded, "I am sorry for the *Protestant* Religions sake, that you have furnished me with so many examples of Rebellions since the Reformation."[158] The *Catechism* was first and foremost an argument against resistance. Some reformations were rebellions, but not all.

Parliaments Power, his next key work, fused Heylyn's historical interests with his political and religious commitments, but also offered a still further revision of sixteenth-century religious history. Whereas Elizabeth's regime had been at the forefront of Heylyn's argument against Burton, in 1645 Henry VIII and Edward VI were now elevated to equal status. Heylyn yet again offered no explanation for his changed perspective, but instead traced a single narrative through the reigns of all three monarchs: reformation was the work of the clergy. As if borrowing from John Foxe, whom he cited repeatedly with approval,[159] Heylyn portrayed the reformation of the English church as a typological pattern that proceeded through a series of three steps. The first step jointly comprised the rejection of papal power and the restoration of royal supremacy; translation of the Bible into the vernacular was the second step, and the reformation of doctrine was the third and final step. First accomplished under Henry, the same pattern repeated itself in the reigns of

---

[153] Peter Heylyn, *The Rebells Catechism* (Oxford, 1643; Wing/H1731A).
[154] Peter Heylyn, *A Briefe Relation of the Death and Svfferings of the Most Reverend and Renowned Prelate and L. Archbishop of Canterbvry* (Oxford, 1644; Wing/H1685).
[155] Heylyn, *A Briefe Relation*, pp. 3, 7; Heylyn, *The Rebells Catechism*, p. 7.
[156] Heylyn, *The Rebells Catechism*, pp. 2, 10, 29.
[157] Heylyn, *The Rebells Catechism*, p. 7; the latter phrase also appears at p. 9.
[158] Heylyn, *The Rebells Catechism*, p. 9.
[159] Heylyn, *Parliaments Power*, e.g., pp. 7, 9, 11, 21, 25.

Edward and Elizabeth,[160] rendering their respective reformations identical with that of their father. It is inaccurate to claim that Heylyn "deplored much of what the English Reformation had done,"[161] or that, beginning in the 1640s, he "may have felt more freedom to slay some of the sacred cows of earlier Reformation history."[162] In *Parliaments Power*, we see quite the opposite; Heylyn not only offered a broad history of the English Reformation but an impassioned defense of it as well. Wholly opposite the Westminster Assembly, which worked with its allies in Parliament against the monarch and the bishops, Heylyn's English Reformation was led by the episcopate and supported by the monarchy. Heylyn hoped to save the Reformation of the sixteenth century from the rogue reformation of his own day.

The historical narrative in *Parliaments Power* doubled as an argument against the developing ecclesial realities of the 1640s. Heylyn repeatedly emphasized that under Henry, Edward, and Elizabeth, Parliament's involvement in religious matters had only led to errors and missteps.[163] Discussing the reign of Henry VIII, he lamented, "long it was not I confesse before the *Parliament* put in for a share, and claimed some interest in the worke [of Reformation]; but whether for the better or the worse, I leave you to judge."[164] As under the Tudors, so too under the Stuarts, Parliament interfered in spiritual matters wholly beyond its ken. But earlier history was more than just a Platonic pattern; it was also an indictment of the present. Under Edward VI, "the Protector and the rest of the Kings Counsell being fully bent for a *Reformation*, thought it expedient that one uniform, quiet and godly Order should be had throughout the Realm."[165] In the context of a civil war often justified in the name of reformation, portraying Edwardian religious change as "uniform, quiet and godly" was unflinchingly polemical, and said at least as much about Heylyn's own time as it did about his stated subject matter. By doing so, Heylyn broke decisively with the conclusions of Hayward, who had noted and criticized Edwardian disorder, but Heylyn also maintained some older historiographical assumptions. Like earlier authors, he perceived Somerset's protectorate as morally and spiritually superior to Northumberland's presidency. And, he built on Godwin, Hayward, and Camden, each whom had lamented sacrilege, just as each had identified greed as the great sin that haunted the latter half of Edward's reign. In the closing pages of *Parliaments Power*, Heylyn brought the argument full circle, writing, "'Tis true, indeed, that many *Members* of both Houses in these latter Times, have been very ready to imbrace all businesses which are offered to them, out of a probable hope of drawing the managery of all Affaires as well *Ecclesiasticall* as *Civill* into their own hands."[166] Long primed by earlier authors to

---

[160] Heylyn, *Parliaments Power*, pp. 16–18.   [161] MacCulloch, "English Reformation," p. 4.
[162] Milton, *Laudian and Royalist Polemic*, p. 229.
[163] Heylyn, *Parliaments Power*, pp. 8, 12, 13, 33–4.   [164] Heylyn, *Parliaments Power*, p. 8.
[165] Heylyn, *Parliaments Power*, p. 21.   [166] Heylyn, *Parliaments Power*, p. 33.

see 1550 as the year that divided Edward's reign between pious renewal and opportunistic abuse, Heylyn's evocations of greed enabled his readers to associate the upset of the 1640s with the worst developments in Edwardian England. Parliamentary opposition to true reformation, initially witnessed under Henry VIII and repeated under his son, had recurred yet again under Charles I. Still more damningly, the most impious excesses of Edward's reign were now repeated by those whom Heylyn cast as Northumberland's successors.

There was nothing inherently novel about attributing to the clergy the lead in the reformation of religion. Almost twenty years earlier, and as already seen in this chapter, George Carleton had written that "The *Church* [of] *England* was *reformed* by the helpe of our learned and Reuerend *Bishops*, in the daies of King Edward the sixt, and in the beginning of the Raigne of Queene *Elizabeth*."[167] William Prynne—no friend of conformist clergy—had agreed and borrowed Carleton's own words,[168] but neither author offered any substantive historical detail to vindicate their point. *Parliament's Power* is notable because Heylyn took an otherwise undeveloped commonplace and redirected it against the king's opponents. No less importantly, his new historiography had an immediate effect upon Charles I. After the king was executed, the royalist printer Richard Royston published correspondence between Charles I and Alexander Henderson, a leading Scottish Covenanter. Originally composed between May and July 1646, the correspondents focused exclusively upon church government. Their letters were lengthy and learned mini-treatises, and Royston's running headers throughout the volume designated the letters as "papers." In "*His* MAJESTIES *Second Paper*," the late king wrote, "it was onely the *King and Clergy*, who made the *Reformation*, the *Parliament* meerly serving to help give the *Civill Sanction*."[169] The latter clause either echoed or borrowed directly from Heylyn, who wrote that ejecting the pope was "commended only to the care of the *Parliament*, that it might have the force of a Law by a *civill Sanction*."[170] However, Heylyn's influence was not total. Unlike *Parliaments Power*, which placed Henry, Edward, and Elizabeth on equal footing, Charles wrote that "no man who truely understands the *English Reformation*, will derive it from *Henry the Eight*; for he onely gave the occasion; it was his *Sonne* who began, and Q. *Elizabeth* that perfected it."[171] At the time, this historiographical disparity was unexplored, but as Chapter 5 will show, it became important after the Restoration. Chronological differences aside, the popularity of Charles' writings in the wake of his beheading helped to widely disseminate both his use and his departure from Heylyn. In 1649 alone, the king's correspondence with

---

[167] Carleton, *An Examination*, p. 4.   [168] Prynne, *Chvrch of Englands Old Antithesis*, p. 127.
[169] Charles I and Alexander Henderson, *The Papers*, p. 20.
[170] Heylyn, *Parliaments Power*, p. 2.
[171] Charles I and Alexander Henderson, *The Papers*, pp. 16–17.

Henderson also appeared in two editions printed at the Hague,[172] and was further incorporated into a new domestic edition of *Eikon Basilike* and its French translation.[173] Bloodshed yielded the beginnings of a historiographical watershed.

The English Reformation

The developments just sketched saw further refinement in the mid-1650s. Before then, however, discussions of the English Reformation took an unexpected but sharply apologetic turn directed against Roman Catholicism.[174] In *Parliaments Power*, Heylyn briefly sought to counter the widespread Catholic allegation, made by Nicholas Sanders and others, that the Church of England "had none but *Parliament Bishops*, and a *Parliament-Clergy*."[175] Using *Parliaments Power* as a response to such criticisms allowed Heylyn to recapitulate the Elizabethan argument that nonconforming Protestants were as much a threat to the state as nonconforming Catholics. After Charles II fled to the European continent and settled in France, the situation in England changed in two ways. First, attempting to secure international support, the new king promised legal toleration to Catholics.[176] Second, living in Catholic France made the exiled court subject to proselytization, and a small number of English converted to Catholicism in the 1650s.[177] Back in England, the printing press saw a surge in the publication of Catholic apologetics. A small amount of this literature extended its influence beyond the 1650s, such as Henry Turberville's *Manuel of Controversies*, which was first printed in 1654 and then reprinted in 1671 and 1686. When it came to serious discussions of Catholicism, the 1650s stood a world apart from the 1640s. With the Church of England proscribed, its supporters now had to again address Catholic criticisms of Tudor religious history.

A number of episcopal clergy, including Edward Boughen, John Bramhall, Henry Ferne, and Henry Hammond,[178] published rebuttals against these and other Catholic works. But genuinely new responses to Catholic challenges were, at best, rare, and when they discussed the English Reformation, they revealed that

---

[172] Charles I and Alexander Henderson, *The Papers Which Passed at New-Castle* (The Hague, 1649; Wing/C2154); Charles I, *King Charles the 1st's Defence of the Church of England* (The Hague, 1649; Wing/C2291A).

[173] Charles I, *Eikon Basilike* (London, 1649; Wing/E304); Charles I, *Eikon Basilike* (The Hague, 1649; Thomason/E.1255[1]).

[174] Ferne, *Of the Division*, p. 38.

[175] Heylyn, *Parliaments Power*, sig. A3 v; further attacks on Sanders are at pp. 31, 32.

[176] Ronald Hutton, *Charles II: King of England, Scotland, and Ireland* (Oxford: Clarendon Press, 1989), pp. 85–99.

[177] Hutton, *Charles II*, p. 119.

[178] On Hammond and Bramhall, see Mark F.M. Clavier, "The Role of Custom in Henry Hammond's 'Of Schism' and John Bramhall's 'A Just Vindication of the Church of England'," *Anglican and Episcopal History*, Vol. 76, No. 3 (Sept., 2007), pp. 358–86.

its developing historiography was not yet common intellectual currency. Ferne and Boughen's apologetic writings recapitulated much older material. Each responded to the Catholic question, "Where was your church before Luther?"[179] Like earlier English authors, neither Ferne nor Boughen attributed any special import to the German evangelical. Quoting Archbishop Laud, Boughen answered, "Where was our Church before *Luther*? It was just there, where yours is now. One and the same Church still, no doubt of that. One in *substance*; but not one in condition of state and purity."[180] Ferne was almost identical, writing that "The Church in *England* before the Reformation was their Church,"[181] but had subsequently "cast off those corruptions."[182] In mid-seventeenth century England, apologists still denied the Luther-centric historiography advanced through Catholic heresiology. Despite their agreement on Luther's comparative unimportance, Ferne and Boughen otherwise shared little sense of the precise chronology of sixteenth-century ecclesiastical history. In 1655, in a second, expanded edition of his work, Ferne sounded much like Udall, writing that "upon that Reformation or Ejection of the Popes usurped power, arose the first division of the English and Romish Church."[183] Boughen could not have been more dissimilar. He dated the schism between the English and Roman churches to the excommunication of Elizabeth in 1570, when "that terrible Bull of *Pius Quintus* came thundering out."[184] Greater chronological coherence was a project for future works by other authors.

Boughen and Ferne made a shared antiquarian appeal across their *apologiae*, but their passing historical interests should not occlude the fundamentally prescriptive nature of their endeavour. Boughen argued that the Eucharist was the fundamental matter of contention between the English and Roman churches. Because the Roman church refused giving the cup to the laity, it had "gone against the sense and practice of the Primitive Church."[185] Boughen went so far as to judge Rome guilty of "maiming the blessed *Eucharist*,"[186] perverting it into a *"halfe communion."*[187] Consequently—and quite remarkably—he asked, "What efficacy then can your half Sacrament be of?"[188] Because the English church had returned to ancient practice, "our Reformation is not after any new, or lately invented model; it is according to the ancient course and canons of the Church; and therefore justifiable."[189] Rome, not England, was therefore guilty of a twofold schism—the first with the pattern of early Church, and the second with those churches who had restored "the ancient course." Ferne made a similar argument. "They, when We and all Nations called for Reformation, remained incorrigible;

---

[179] Ferne, *Of the Division*, pp. 6–13; Boughen, *Church Catholick*, pp. 29, 30, 36.
[180] Boughen, *Church Catholick*, p. 29.   [181] Ferne, *Of the Division*, p. 6.
[182] Ferne, *Of the Division*, p. 8.   [183] Ferne, *Of the Division*, p. 21.
[184] Boughen, *Church Catholick*, p. 57.   [185] Boughen, *Church Catholick*, p. 12.
[186] Boughen, *Church Catholick*, p. 42.   [187] Boughen, *Church Catholick*, p. 56.
[188] Boughen, *Church Catholick*, p. 12.   [189] Boughen, *Church Catholick*, p. 17.

We did our duty, they would not doe theirs."[190] To vindicate the Church of England's actions, Ferne developed a detailed theology of the relationship between local and international churches. Insofar as a national church maintained the consensus of prior centuries, it had the right to reform itself. "And this is considerable in the English Reformation," he wrote, "which as it was upon publick Judgement of a Nationall Church in Provinciall Synods, so will it not prove a dissenting from the Catholike Church, or definitions of true Generall Councils."[191] *Reformatio* was a return to the practices of a purer age. A more precise reading of sixteenth-century religious history was of secondary import.

By the time of Oliver Cromwell's death on September 3, 1658, a series of other works had been published that advanced more detailed historical analyses. Not all were of immediate import; Herbert of Cherbury's voluminous study of Henry VIII, published shortly after the regicide of Charles I, had no immediate impact and will be analyzed in Chapter 5. Of the authors discussed in the remainder of this chapter—Peter Heylyn, Thomas Fuller, and an unidentified, anonymous contributor—Heylyn was the most active. In 1653, he published an expanded edition of *Parliaments Power* under a new title, *The Way of Reformation of the Church of England Declared and Justified.*[192] Heylyn is not currently recognized as the text's author; as with *Parliaments Power*, he also published this edition anonymously, but new material aside, the work is identical with its predecessor. In 1657, Heylyn carried his additions over into a third edition that he expanded even further. It was published under his own name and with the slightly altered title *The Way and Manner of the Reformation of the Church of England Declared and Justified.*[193] Thomas Fuller's discussion of the English Reformation appeared in 1655 as part of his much larger work *The Church-History of Britain.* Although it saw a second edition in 1656 and was read, cited, and even anthologized for more than a decade, *The Church-History* was not reprinted in full until the nineteenth century.[194] Finally, two unattributed works appeared in 1654. One was entitled *A Brief View and Defence of the Reformation of the Church of England by King Edward and Q. Elizabeth*; the other bore the same title, but with "Short" replacing "Brief."[195] The two works are otherwise identical but the author remains unknown.

---

[190] Ferne, *Of the Division*, p. 23.   [191] Ferne, *Of the Division*, p. 38.

[192] Anonymous (Peter Heylyn), *The Way of Reformation of the Church of England, Declared and Justified* (London, 1653; Wing/W1164).

[193] Peter Heylyn, *The Way and Manner of the Reformation of the Church of England Declared and Justified* (London, 1657; Wing/H1746).

[194] W.B. Patterson, *Thomas Fuller: Discovering England's Religious Past* (Oxford: Oxford University Press, 2018), pp. 256–7.

[195] Anonymous, *A Short View and Defence of the Reformation of the Church of England by King Edward and Q. Elizabeth* (London, 1654; Wing/S3638). It may be of further interest to note that the title page of *A Brief View* indicates that it was printed for Simon Miller, while the cover of *A Short View*

When read together, these studies reveal the slow coalescence of a shared historiographical perspective that nonetheless remained fluid enough to incorporate more recent apologetic concerns. Heylyn's 1653 additions to *Parliaments Power* were heavily indebted to contemporary anti-Catholic apologetics. In "The Publisher to the Reader," which prefaced *The Way of Reformation*, the "clamour of the *Papists*" was described as "never more insisted on, then it hath been lately."[196] Fuller was equally concerned to address Catholic denials of the Church of England's legitimacy. In section "R" of the Index to his *The Church-History*, he referred those interested in "*Our* REFORMATION" to look at a short two-page discussion in Book V, which covered the reign of Henry VIII.[197] There Fuller explained the matter quite simply. "Three things are Essential to justifie the *English Reformation*, from the *scandal of Schisme*, to shew, that they had 1. Just *cause* for which 2. True *authority* by which 3. Due *moderation* in what"—and with a bracket that connected all three points together, he concluded each with the phrase "they deceded from *Rome*."[198] The cause was justified by a return to "*Scripture* and *Primitive practice*" in controverted matters; the authority was that of a national church, because "the most *regular way*, was by order from a *Free* and *Generall Councell*, but here alas no hope thereof"; and finally, the Church of England's moderation "disclaimed onely the *ulcers* and *sores*, not what was *sound* of the *Romish Church*, retaining still what was *consonant* to *Antiquity*, in *the Four first Generall Councels*."[199] As with so much other apologetic literature, Fuller's response to Catholic critics emphasized continuity with a prior golden age, enabling "reformation" to retain its moral valence.

Our third, anonymous historian was unconcerned with Catholicism, but presented the moral content of reformation in terms no less attractive than those used by Fuller and Heylyn. Internal evidence reveals that *A Brief View and Defence* was written during the 1640s. The author repeatedly used the present tense to describe Charles I, for example, as "our Soveraign Lord the King that now is."[200] The basic argument of the work was simple: reformation necessarily produces peace. The text connected Edward VI and Charles I with earlier Christian kings such as Constantine and Edward the Confessor, and with ancient Israelite leaders such as king Josiah and the governor Zerubbabel.[201] Like other models of princely piety committed to tranquility, Constantine called Nicaea "for setling the peace of the

reveals that it was printed by "A.M.," who worked with Miller on other works at the time. See Anonymous, *A Brief View and Defence of the Reformation of the Church of England by King Edward and Q. Elizabeth* (London, 1654; Wing/B4655).

[196] Heylyn, *The Way of Reformation*, sig. A2.
[197] Fuller, *The Church-History*, Index, sig. [¶¶4].
[198] Fuller, *The Church-History*, Book V, p. 194, ¶. 25.
[199] Fuller, *The Church-History*, Book V, pp. 194, ¶¶. 26, 27; 195, ¶. 32.
[200] Anonymous, *A Brief View*, p. 52; for other references to Charles I as presently reigning, see pp. 45, 60.
[201] Anonymous, *A Brief View*, pp. 19, 28 (Edward the Confessor), 7 (Josiah), 53 (Zerubbabel).

Church in matter of Religion."[202] The author continued, "The same course took the Church of *England* in the daies of *Edw*. 6. or rather *Edw*. the Saint, when Christian Religion was overwhelmed with Popery and Superstition, by restoring it in that Reformation to the truth of the Primitive times."[203] A continual succession of reforming and peace-loving monarchs then followed from Elizabeth to Charles,[204] "until this present unhappy War began."[205] It was hardly ironic to the author that the coherence of England's reformation was revealed by the willingness of its opponents to use violence. Here too was an attack on the Parliament of the 1640s, for "when the first Statute of Reformation was Enacted in the Parl. of 2. *Ed*. 6. There was not during the Sitting of that Parliament the brandishing of a Sword, the ratling of a Spear, a Drum Beating, a Canon roaring, or a Trumpet sounding an Alarm for Warre."[206] The author concluded, however, that the Long Parliament was ultimately identical with earlier misguided and even heretical figures. Henry VIII, Mary I, and the Anabaptists, like Boniface VIII and the Arian emperors of the fourth century, were all singled out for their use of coercive violence.[207] Enemies of peace were enemies of reformation.

A Brief View and Defence was thus written, like the works of Heylyn and Fuller, with a view to the author's present. Fuller first stated his intent to write *The Church-History* in 1642, but his research agenda became more intensive after the execution of the king.[208] Looking back from a vantage point in the early 1650s, Fuller used the outcome of the civil wars to trace the origins of religious nonconformity, which he described as "the saddest difference that ever happened in the *Church of England.*" Although often considered less combative than Heylyn,[209] Fuller was no less inclined toward pointed explanations. As the epigraph of this chapter shows, Fuller traced the origins of recent conflict back to Edward's reign; "nonconformity" grew in the decades that followed, aiming to "conquer the Herarchie its adversary."[210] The retrospective nature of Fuller's narrative reveals an important fact. The burgeoning historiography of the English Reformation was not only rooted in two discrete pasts—that of the sixteenth century and that of the 1640s—but in their perceived intersection, which culminated in regicide, the consequences of which many felt no less intensely years later.

Explaining the origins of nonconformity, Fuller stood apart from Heylyn and the author of *A Brief View and Defence*. The latter two looked ambivalently upon

---

[202] Anonymous, *A Brief View*, p. 6.   [203] Anonymous, *A Brief View*, pp. 6–7.
[204] Anonymous, *A Brief View*, pp, 49–52; other discussion on the centrality of peace can be found on, e.g., sig. A4 v, pp. 1, 60.
[205] Anonymous, *A Brief View*, p. 52.   [206] Anonymous, *A Brief View*, pp. 52–3.
[207] Anonymous, *A Brief View*, pp. 53 (Henry), 9–10, 24–5 (Mary), sig. A4 (Anabaptists), 29 (Boniface VIII), 54 (Arian emperors).
[208] Patterson, *Thomas Fuller*, pp. 155–6.
[209] Milton, *Laudian and Royalist Polemic*, pp. 174–5; Patterson, *Thomas Fuller*, pp. 189–90.
[210] Fuller, *The Church-History*, Book VII, p. 401, n. 23.

John Calvin, partially blaming him for recent evils. Fuller, despite granting that some sixteenth-century English refugees were influenced by time spent in continental Europe, proffered a more domestic explanation for religious dissent. He summarized the differences in the Church of England with a two-column chart (see Table 4.1) that compared conformity with its converse:

Here is a good example of how historiography of the sixteenth century often resounded with the clarion echoes of a more immediate past. In his third point on nonconformity, Fuller used agrarian language that sounded much like the Root and Branch petition of 1641, thus rendering Edwardian nonconformists identical with opponents of the Caroline regime. In *The Church-History*, Edwardian-era agitation burst forth in full, bitter bloom as civil war.

Heylyn looked elsewhere to explain the outcome of the civil wars. Further developing the concern of Bancroft and Hooker with Geneva, Heylyn was conflicted about Calvin's political thought. In *The Stumbling-Block of Disobedience and Rebellion* (1658), Heylyn gave full vent to his tangle of admiration and frustration. The subtitle of the work, "Cunningly laid by *Calvin* in the Subjects way, Discovered, Censured, and Removed," gives a more negative valence to its subject matter than the prose itself. The book is concerned with Calvin's classical scholarship; writing against Calvin's acceptance of magisterial revolt in Book IV of

Table 4.1. Summary of the differences in the Church of England

Founders of Conformity	Founders of Non-Conformity
1. Such as remained here all the Reign of King *Henry the eighth*, and *weathered* out the tempest of His tyrannie at open Sea, partly by a politick compliance, and partly by a cautious concealment of themselves.	1. Such as fled hence beyond the Seas, chiefly into *Germany*, where, living in States, and Cities of popular Reformation, they suck'd in both the aire, and discipline of the place they lived in.
2. These, in the daies of King *Edward the sixt*, were possessed of the best preferments in the land.	2. These, returning late into *England*, were at a losse for meanes, and maintenance, onely supported with the reputation of being *Confessors*, rendring their *patience* to the *praise*, and their *persons* to the *pity* of all conscientious people.
3. And retained many ceremonies practiced in the *Romish Church*, conceiving them to be antient, and decent in themselves.	3. And renounced all ceremonies practiced by the Papists, conceiving, that such ought not onely to be clipt with the sheers, but to be shaved with a raizor; yea, all the stumps thereof to be pluckt out.
4. The authority of *Cranmer*, and activity of *Ridley* headed this party; the former being the highest, the latter the hottest in defence of conformity.	4. *John Rogers*, Lecturer in S. *Pauls*, and Vicar of S. *Sepulchres*, with *John Hooper*, afterwards Bishop of *Glocester*, were Ring-leaders of this party.

Source: Thomas Fuller, *The Church-History of Britain*, Book VII, p. 402, ¶. 24

the *Institution*,[211] Heylyn argued primarily on philological and historical grounds that the Genevan reformer misunderstood Greek and Roman history. The work opened with ambivalence. "Some *Writers* may be likened unto *Jeremies Figs*, of which the Prophet saith, that if they were *good*, they were *very good*; if *evil*, *very evil*, such as could *not be eaten they were so evil*."[212] Heylyn's first example was "*Origen* amongst the Ancients," who "*where he did well, none could do it better*, and *where he failed at all, no man erred more grossly*."[213] The very next example was Calvin. Heylyn praised Calvin's "*Doctrine of Obedience* unto Kings and Princes,"[214] writing that the "credit and authority of the man was deservedly great amongst the people where he lived." But he then voiced concern. Calvin was "in short time of such authority and esteem in the world abroad, that his works were made the only rule to which both *Discipline* and *Doctrine* was to be conformed."[215] However, and again like Bancroft and Hooker, the problem was less Calvin than those who came after him.[216] Where Calvin wrote well, as in his exhortation to political obedience, they ignored his prose. Where he wrote poorly, as in his justification of magisterial rebellion, they followed all too quickly.

There is no basis in *The Stumbling-Block* for the popular stereotype of "Laudians" as sermon-denigrating, ceremony-loving clericalists. "Anti-Calvinism," if the phrase is of any value, should here be given a political valence. Heylyn offered no discussion of sacraments or devotional practices, and no evident longing for a return to the pre-Reformation English church. It was Fuller, not Heylyn, who tried to counter Calvin's influence among the opponents of the Prayer Book,[217] and it was the author of *A Brief View and Defence* who attacked Calvin's Presbyterian discipline. If episcopacy were abandoned, the latter claimed, three things would happen: "1. The King must of necessity lose of his authority. 2. The people of their Liberty. 3. The Common Law of its jurisdiction."[218] Heylyn's alleged "anti-Calvinism" was of a different sort. If a confused political theology was Calvin's greatest offense, his next greatest offense was his betrayal—according to Heylyn—of the Protestant cause. As if inverting Milton's argument in *The Tenure of Kings and Magistrates*, Heylyn alleged that the doctrine of justified rebellion was "the scandal and the hinderance of the *Reformation*." Heylyn lamented that "many of the chief *Reformers* by their heat and violence had given too great advantage to the publick Enemy; and made the *Protestant* Religion to be much suspected."[219] Drawing from a range of French and English authors, Heylyn invited his readers to "Witness the Civil wars of

---

[211] Peter Heylyn, *The Stumbling-Block of Disobedience and Rebellion* (London, 1658; Wing/H1736), sig. a v.

[212] Heylyn, *Stumbling-Block*, p. 2; a marginal note indicates the Biblical passage as Jeremiah 24:4.

[213] Heylyn, *Stumbling-Block*, pp. 2–3.   [214] Heylyn, *Stumbling-Block*, p. 3.

[215] Heylyn, *Stumbling-Block*, p. 3.   [216] Heylyn, *Stumbling-Block*, p. 4.

[217] Fuller, *The Church-History*, Book XI, p. 222–3, ¶. 8, n. 3; Heylyn, *The Way and Manner*, p. 31, notes only in passing Calvin's dislike of the 1549 liturgy.

[218] Anonymous, *A Brief View*, p. 42.

[219] Heylyn, *Stumbling-Block*, p. 130; the same argument is found at pp. 24, 33–4.

France, the revolt of *Holland*, the expulsion of the Earl of *East-Friezland* out of the City of *Embden*, the insurrections of the *Scots*, the tumults of *Bohemia*, the commotions of *Brandenbourg*, the translation of the Crown of *Sweden* from the King of *Pole* to *Charles* Duke of *Finland*, the change of Government in *England*." In each locale, Calvin's followers brought rebellion with them. Heylyn channeled Bancroft when he concluded that the "Presbyterian or *Cavlinian* partie in those several States" all acted "under pretence of *Reformation*."[220] Having sought to save the English Reformation from a rogue Parliament the previous decade, Heylyn now strove to save Calvin from his most enthusiastic supporters.

The differences between Fuller and Heylyn should not obscure the considerable agreement between them, much of which they shared with the author of *A Brief View and Defence*. All three believed in the normative nature of the first four ecumenical councils,[221] and that the conciliar model begun under Constantine was rightly adopted by England's national church in the sixteenth century.[222] Each further drew upon earlier historical works. *A Brief View and Defence* echoed Godwin's view that Edward's "first reformation" happened in 1547, during the boy king's first year on the throne.[223] Heylyn drew on Spelman,[224] and Camden informed his understanding of the Scots' rebellion.[225] The influence of Hayward's historiography is also evident. Like both Hayward and Camden, the same anonymous author portrayed Elizabeth as wholly transcending the confessional divisions of her day.[226] Finally, and again like Hayward, *A Brief View and Defence* indicated no knowledge of the variations between the Prayer Books of 1549, 1552, and 1559. Rather, their complex history appeared much more simply: "ancient Liturgies" were revived in 1549, made "compleat and perfect" in 1552, and finally "restored" by Elizabeth.[227] Heylyn described the relationship between the first two liturgies in equally simple terms. The first was drafted "by *the ayd of the Holy Ghost himself*," while the latter was "made fully perfect."[228] Fuller noted that the first Prayer Book was "brought under a review" after Calvin's complaint and then again under Elizabeth, but offered no detailed analysis of liturgical change.[229] Unlike Hayward, Fuller and our anonymous author entertained an especially warm view of Protector Somerset, and a correspondingly negative understanding of Northumberland.[230] Across these works we see the instantiation of a historiographical norm.

---

[220] Heylyn, *Stumbling-Block*, p. 137.
[221] Heylyn, *The Way and Manner*, p. 62; Fuller, *The Church-History*, Book V, p. 195, ¶. 32; Anonymous, *A Brief View*, p. 25.
[222] Heylyn, *The Way and Manner*, e.g., pp. 59–60, 80–1; Fuller, *The Church-History*, Book V, pp. 194, ¶. 27, 195, ¶. 32; Anonymous, *A Brief View*, p. 6; see also Patterson, *Thomas Fuller*, p. 205.
[223] Anonymous, *A Brief View*, p. 69.   [224] Heylyn, *The Way and Manner*, e.g., pp. 27, 57, 87.
[225] Heylyn, *Stumbling-Block*, p. 137, n. k.   [226] Anonymous, *A Brief View*, pp. 10, 60.
[227] Anonymous, *A Brief View*, pp. 21, 22, 25.   [228] Heylyn, *The Way and Manner*, p. 31.
[229] Fuller, *The Church-History*, Book VII, p. 386, ¶. 4.
[230] Fuller, *The Church-History*, Book VII, pp. 408, ¶¶. 39, 42 (Northumberland's greed), 410, ¶. 45 (Somerset's nobility); Anonymous, *A Brief View*, p. 20.

5

Reformed Catholics, True Protestants

Tudor Religious History in Restoration England, 1660–85

A Reformed Catholique (properly so called) *is an Apostolical Christian*, or *a Son of the Church of* England: *A true Protestant may* be so too; nay, and many times he *is* so; and many a *Loyal, Orthodox, Reformed Catholique calls* himself so; and (according to the stile of the Age) he may be well enough *said* and *accounted* so to *be*.

Roger L'Estrange (1679)[1]

Introduction

The return of Charles II temporarily submerged the historiographical developments of the mid-1650s beneath a swelling tide of much older theological and political issues. "Reformation" returned with all of its militant and apocalyptic connotations, but unlike in the 1640s, renewed attempts at overthrowing monarchy and episcopacy failed. Greater political stability enabled the first great flourishing of historiography on the English Reformation. Operating under the influence of antiquarian methodology, which privileged the use of primary sources while decrying partisan bias, apologetic concern was generally muted—but hardly abandoned—in the name of scholarly reliability and accuracy. English historians found many points of convergence. All opposed Catholic attacks upon the English church, especially that found in Nicholas Sanders' *De Schismatis*, and all published equally sharp criticisms of nonconformist assaults on liturgy and episcopacy. Most importantly, a growing number agreed that the English Reformation did not begin with Henry VIII, but with Edward VI, and was completed by his sister Elizabeth I. With the restoration of the monarchy and the Church of England in 1660, apologetic uses of the past became accepted as accurate historical depictions.

The chapter opens with how the early 1660s often appeared on the verge of repeating recent political history, as new political and religious pamphlets repeated arguments many decades old. This only changed in 1662, when a new

---

[1] Roger L'Estrange, *The Reformed Catholique: Or, The True Protestant* (London, 1679; Wing/L1289–L1291), pp. 1–2.

How the English Reformation was Named: The Politics of History, c. 1400–1700. Benjamin M. Guyer, Oxford University Press. © Benjamin M. Guyer 2022. DOI: 10.1093/oso/9780192865724.003.0006

oath of conformity was ratified. The stage was thus set for the further refinement of English Reformation historiography. Throughout Charles II's reign, historians largely told the same story sketched in Chapter 4, but with two notable exceptions. First, there was a growing awareness of the differences that emerged under Edward VI over Eucharistic doctrine. Second, Henry VIII was increasingly excised from histories of the English Reformation, leaving it a fundamentally Edwardian-Elizabethan event. The final section of the chapter studies developing perspectives on Martin Luther, noting that even in the late seventeenth century, the English still failed to identify him as a catalyst for Tudor religious change. At the time of Charles II's death in 1685, the Church of England lacked a clearly defined sense of "Protestant" identity.

More Semantics of "Reformation"

English print culture in the early 1660s was hardly different than in the 1640s. As diverse pamphleteers published new works of controversy, older works were also reprinted, enabling the unresolved conflicts of the 1640s to invade the Restoration. Familiarity fed rather than slaked the hunger of the reading public, but if popularity was indicative of confessional preference, then past controversies now witnessed a striking imbalance of loyalties. For example, between 1660 and 1662, *A Directory for the Public Worship of God* and the Book of Common Prayer were both republished, but whereas the former saw one edition,[2] the latter saw more than a dozen,[3] including two Latin translations.[4] The writings of Charles I remained immensely popular; the early years of the Restoration saw his complete works published,[5] several volumes of royal apothegms,[6] and at least three editions of his defense of episcopacy.[7] William Barlow's account of the Hampton Court Conference was reprinted in 1661,[8] and Richard Hooker's complete writings appeared in 1662, with three further editions by 1684.[9] Dovetailing with this print history was the return of approximately 95 percent of the English population

---

[2] Westminster Assembly, *A Directory for the Publique Worship of God* (London, 1660; Wing/ D1553A).

[3] The Church of England, *The Book of Common Prayer* (London, 1660; Wing/B3615–B3617, B3619). Reprints in 1661 are Wing/B3620A–B3621. The 1662 revision saw the following editions that same year: Wing/B3622, B3622A–B3625.

[4] The Church of England, *Liber Precvm Pvblicarvm* (Oxford, 1660; Wing/O922M and O992N).

[5] Charles I, *Basilika* (London, 1662; Wing/C2075 and 2157C).

[6] Charles I, *The Golden Apophthegms of His Royall Maiesty* (London, 1660; Wing/G1012); Charles I, *Effata Regalia* (London, 1661; Wing/C2302).

[7] Charles I, *The Kings Majesties Answer... Concerning Church-government* (London, 1660; Wing/ C2126); Charles I, *His Majesties Finall Answer Concerning Episcopacie* (London, 1660; Wing/C2307); Charles I, *His Majesties Reason* (London, 1661; Wing/C2739).

[8] William Barlow, *The Summe and Substance of the Conference* (London, 1661; Wing/B847).

[9] Michael Brydon, *The Evolving Reputation of Richard Hooker: An Examination of Responses 1600–1714* (Oxford: Oxford University Press, 2006), ch. 3.

to the episcopal church.[10] At the popular level, events of the previous two decades had done much to solidify support for episcopal, liturgical, and monarchical order.

Thematic and rhetorical repetition rapidly became the warp and weft of much print culture. "Reformation," the inescapable keyword of recent decades, surged immediately to the fore, as longstanding differences about liturgy and episcopacy returned to national debate. New pamphlet wars extended across months, sometimes even reaching from one year to the next. There is almost no shortage of possible examples. An early pro-episcopal pamphlet by John Gauden, among the most prolific of conforming controversialists, was rapidly countered by the equally prolific Presbyterian apologist Zachary Crofton.[11] In his *ANAΛYΣIΣ* (*Analysis*; the Greek translates as "Loosing"), Gauden expressed his hope for an "ingenuous *Reformation* of Episcopacy" that would bring bishops into a closer working relationship with presbyters, albeit without sacrificing the former's "*paternal authority.*"[12] Crofton countered in his *ANAΛHΨIS* (*Analepsis*; the Greek translates as "Taking up"), "wherein hath not Episcopacie (by *its silencing and suspending zealous Ministers, excommunicating, imprisoning, banishing, and stigmatizing pious Christians, for no fault at all save endeavouring it*) retarded the progress and perfection of the Reformation?"[13] It was hardly an original argument, but little at the time was. Crofton's *ANAΛHΨIS* saw a fourth edition by 1661, and he also wrote an expanded edition later in 1660 that saw a second edition the following year.[14] By that point, still other participants had become involved,[15] and when Gauden moved on to defend the liturgy in 1661, Crofton followed.[16] Here Gauden primarily inveighed against the "pretensions of *Liberty* and *Reformation*" found in works such as the Westminster Assembly's *Directory.*[17] Crofton, now working with the clergyman Giles Firmin, responded with familiar arguments—that the Book of Common Prayer was too akin to the Roman Catholic mass,[18] and that the

---

[10] N.H. Keeble, *The Restoration: England in the 1660s* (Malden: Blackwell Publishing, 2002), pp. 141–2; David J. Appleby, *Black Bartholomew's Day: Preaching, Polemic and Restoration Nonconformity* (Manchester: Manchester University Press, 2007), p. 37.

[11] John Gauden, *ANAΛYΣIΣ. The Loosing of St. Peters Bands* (London, 1660; Wing/G340); Zachary Crofton, *ANAΛHΨIS* (London, 1660; Wing/C6984).

[12] Gauden, *ANAΛYΣIΣ*, pp. 21 (relationship between bishops and presybters), 18 (authority).

[13] Crofton, *ANAΛHΨIS*, p. 31.

[14] Zachary Crofton, *ANAΛHΨIS ANEΛHΦΘH* (London, 1661; Wing/C6983).

[15] See, e.g., Anonymous, *The Anatomy of Dr. Gauden's Idolized Non-sence and Blasphemy* (London, 1660; Wing/A3055); John Rowland, *A Reply to the Answer of Anonymus* (London, 1660; Wing/R2070); John Russell, *The Solemn League and Covenant Discharg'd* (London, 1660; Wing/R2343).

[16] John Gauden, *Considerations Touching the Liturgy* (London, 1661; Wing/G348); Zachary Crofton and Giles Firmin, *The Liturgical Considerator Considered* (London, 1661; Wing/F956).

[17] Gauden, *Considerations Touching the Liturgy*, p. 4; Gauden names the *Directory* at pp. 6–7, but the entire work is an attack upon the Westminster Assembly's rejection of liturgy.

[18] Crofton and Firmin, *The Liturgical Considerator Considered*, sig. a2, p. 21.

Church of England remained in "the *Infancy of Reformation.*"[19] The political context was new but the confessional positions were not.

There was no shortage of similar arguments elsewhere. *Reasons Shewing the Necessity of Reformation*, published in 1660 "By divers Ministers of sundry Counties in England," advocated "reformation" of five well-worn issues: doctrine, worship, rites and ceremonies, church government, and discipline.[20] The title of John Pearson's response, *No Necessity of Reformation*,[21] made its author's stance clear, as did the title of the anonymously authored *Reasons Shewing that There is No Need of Such a Reformation.*[22] William Hamilton responded to Pearson with *Some Necessity of Reformation*,[23] Pearson defended his pamphlet later in 1660,[24] and the debate continued into 1661 with another anonymous publication, *Defence of the Liturgy of the Church of England.*[25] In 1662, Presbyterians summarized their complaints against the Book of Common Prayer with a nineteen-point document entitled "The Exceptions of the Presbyterian-Brethren, Against some passages in the present Liturgy." Authored primarily by Richard Baxter, the "Exceptions" repeated Elizabethan arguments against such matters as wearing vestments, celebrating holy days, and kneeling to receive the sacrament.[26] "Reformation" appeared here, too. Baxter's proposed replacement for the Book of Common Prayer was entitled *The Reformation of the Liturgy.*[27] Throughout the early 1660s, dozens of new works repeated the arguments and counterarguments of the past century.

In such a politically fractious environment, failed uprisings only confirmed the worst of fears. The months following Charles II's return to England saw a small number of unsuccessful attempts at overthrowing the restored regime. An especially disconcerting rebellion took place on Epiphany (January 6) 1660/1, when Thomas Venner, a member of the apocalyptic Fifth Monarchists sect, led an uprising that targeted both the episcopal church and the monarchy.[28] In their manifesto *A Door of Hope*, reformation was proclaimed with all of the militant

---

[19] Crofton and Firmin, *The Liturgical Considerator Considered*, sig. b2 v.

[20] Anonymous [Cornelius Burges?], *Reasons Shewing the Necessity of Reformation* (London, 1660; Wing/B5678).

[21] John Pearson, *No Necessity of Reformation* (London, 1660; Wing/P1001).

[22] H.S., *Reasons Shewing that There is No Need of Such a Reformation* (London, 1660; Wing/S762).

[23] William Hamilton, *Some Necessity of Reformation* (London, 1660; Wing/H489).

[24] John Pearson, *An Answer to Dr. Burges* (London, 1660; Wing/P993).

[25] Anonymous, *Defence of the Liturgy of the Church of England* (London, 1661; Wing/D817).

[26] Richard Baxter, *The Grand Debate Between the Most Reverend the Bishops, and the Presbyterian Divines* (London, 1661; Wing/B1278A and E3841), pp. 1–12; for Baxter's liturgy more generally, see Glen J. Segger, *Richard Baxter's Reformed Liturgy: A Puritan Alternative to the Book of Common Prayer* (Farnham: Ashgate, 2014); on the Savoy Conference, see Tim Cooper, "Richard Baxter and the Savoy Conference (1661)," *Journal of Ecclesiastical History*, Vol. 68, No. 2 (Apr., 2017), pp. 326–39.

[27] Richard Baxter, *A Petition for Peace with the Reformation of the Liturgy* (London, 1661; Wing/B1342).

[28] Greaves, *Deliver Us from Evil: The Radical Underground in Britain, 1660–1663* (Oxford: Oxford University Press, 1986), pp. 50–65.

connotations discussed in previous chapters. The document described the regicide of Charles I as the "beginning of Reformation,"[29] and Venner called to himself anyone "whoso hath a heart to appear for God, for his Christ, for Reformation, Justice, and Righteousness, for the Cause of Truth, and for the good People of these Nations."[30] With fantastic invective, Venner protested:

> against Popery, Prelacy, Common-prayer, Organs, Superstitions, false, prophane forms of Worship, Idolatrous, Ceremonial, Typical, Antichristian shadows and vanities, such as is Sirplices, Lawn Sleeves, Hoods, Tippets, and such whorish trash and Trinkery, Altars, Bowing, Kneeling, and Worshipping a piece of Wood and Bread, and a Wax Candle (a filthy base Idol) for the true God; against Idolatrous Pictures and Images (the seeds of Superstition and Ignorance)[.]

He concluded the paragraph by naming the pope, bishops, and "Cavaliers."[31] Such language was not rhetorical, but instead offered readers the descriptive clarity of an acutely apocalyptic worldview. It allowed only for a zero-sum religious and political contest—one that Venner lost. He was executed on January 19, 1661.

Drawing upon recent history, apocalyptic discussions of political and religious monstrosity simply read like new iterations of otherwise unoriginal narratives.[32] Fears of disorder, having lingered long on the conceptual landscape, continued to traverse elite and popular intellectual cultures. *Cabala*, a ninety-five-page exposé that contained both a fictional political dialogue and a larger historical analysis, contextualized recent religiously inspired political upsets within a larger history of "247 Plots, *viz.* all the Plots from W[illiam] the Conq[ueror],"[33] each of which had failed. Near the beginning of the dialogue, the character "Orthodox" exclaimed against the character "Scruple," "*Reformation!* it's a *dreadful word*, and in thy mouth imports no less then *ruine* and *desolation*."[34] The author covered a range of familiar but widely castigated figures, such as John Knox,[35] Martin Marprelate,[36] and most recently, Thomas Venner.[37] Presbyterians came off just as badly; they were founded by John Calvin in 1542—the same year, it was noted, in which Ignatius of Loyola founded the Jesuit order.[38] Domestic confessional pluralization undermined the English church, for "all the lesser factions were hid in Presbytery."[39] It was a judgment that doubled as a geographically oriented polit-ical analysis. Scotland, "without which no Rebellion can prosper in *England*,"[40] was just as guilty of destabilizing the three kingdoms.

---

[29] Anonymous, *A Door of Hope* (London, 1661; Wing/D1908), p. 1.

[30] Anonymous, *A Door of Hope*, p. 4.   [31] Anonymous, *A Door of Hope*, p. 4.

[32] For a helpful overview of Anglican apocalyptic through the end of the seventeenth century, see Warren Johnston, "The Anglican Apocalypse in Restoration England," *Journal of Ecclesiastical History*, Vol. 55, No. 3 (Jul., 2004), pp. 467–501.

[33] David Lloyd, *Cabala* (London, 1664; Wing/L2636), p. 66.   [34] Lloyd, *Cabala*, p. 3.

[35] Lloyd, *Cabala*, pp. 3, 64.   [36] Lloyd, *Cabala*, pp. 30, 87.   [37] Lloyd, *Cabala*, p. 91.

[38] Lloyd, *Cabala*, p. 4.   [39] Lloyd, *Cabala*, p. 49.   [40] Lloyd, *Cabala*, pp. 69–70.

Popular pamphlets remained short and to the point, detailing graphic spectacle as political argument. The title page of *The Famous Tragedie of the Life and Death of M^{ris} Rump* told readers that "She was brought to Bed of a Monster," and subsequently birthed "her ugly, deformed, ill-shapen, base-begotten *Brat* or *Imp* of Reformation."[41] The unidentified author maintained the centuries old distinction between *reformatio* and *deformatio*, and had the character Rump lament, "instead of Reforming I have deformed, instead of repairing I have pulled down." As seen in Chapter 4, this was almost word-for-word identical to the complaint expressed by Mercurius Melancholicus in the 1648 pamphlet *Mistris Parliament Brought to Bed of a Monstrous Childe of Reformation*. And, as was common in such literature, disorder in church and state was fully revealed by the body of the infant, which was born "without a head."[42] Formulaic polemic resonated widely because it comprehended so very much, and educated authors inhabited the same social imaginary. Gauden echoed Elizabethan precedent by describing Presbyterians as "zealous Pretenders to *Reformation*,"[43] whose actions led to anarchy.[44] Presbyterian religious aspirations were both "deformed and deforming,"[45] depriving the English church and kingdom of leadership. Gauden perceived an outcome identical to that of our anonymous pamphleteer. "At length they all *nestled* themselves under the popular *Shadow*, or in the spreading *Branches* of an Anti-episcopal, novel, illegal and Headless *Presbytery*."[46] He compared their rejection of episcopacy with "the teeth, tail, and sting of a *Dragon*," and with the apocalyptic beasts described in the Biblical book of Daniel.[47] Still other works did the same.[48] "Reformation" thus remained cloaked in a hermeneutic of suspicion. Across a wide variety of genres—popular pamphlets, sermons, apologetics, and historical works—non-conforming Protestants were alleged to operate under "pretence of Reformation."[49] It was the most powerful of arguments, perhaps because it was among the most familiar. Little had changed in England's polemical topography.

---

[41] Anonymous, *The Famous Tragedie of the Life and Death of M^{ris} Rump* (London, 1660; Wing/F385A).

[42] Anonymous, *The Famous Tragedie*, p. 6.

[43] John Gauden, *A Pillar of Gratitude* (London, 1661; Wing/G366), p. 17; see also pp. 25, 50.

[44] Gauden, *A Pillar of Gratitude*, pp. 7, 18, 52, 53.

[45] Gauden, *A Pillar of Gratitude*, p. 43; see also p. 18.   [46] Gauden, *A Pillar of Gratitude*, p. 18.

[47] Gauden, *A Pillar of Gratitude*, pp. 46–7.

[48] Lloyd, *Cabala*, p. 49, uses Gauden's phrase "hid in Presbytery" to describe factions; Anonymous, *The Rumps Last Will & Testament* (London, 1660; Wing/P106), identifies the Rump as a "Monster" on its title page; the same is true of Gryffith Williams, *The Great Antichrist Revealed* (London, 1660; Wing/W2662), who used the title page to identify the Antichrist with those who "united and combined themselves together by a solemn League and Covenant."

[49] See, e.g., Anonymous, *The Grand Rebels Detected* (London, 1660; Wing/G1511); Anonymous [Zachary Crofton?], *The Scotch Covenant Newly Revived* (London, 1661; Wing/C7002); each work repeats this allegation on its title page. Similar language can be found in, e.g., Thomas Mariott, *Rebellion Unmasked* (London, 1661; Wing/M717), pp. 22–3; Gauden, *Considerations Touching the Liturgy*, p. 29 (mispage as p. 23); Izaak Walton, *The Life of Mr. Rich Hooker*. (London, 1665; Wing/W670), p. 192.

Amidst the comparatively unoriginal but utterly polarized, one new area of conflict emerged. In the early 1660s, debate about the *Solemn League and Covenant for Reformation* was more than just the renewed pursuit of unfulfilled ecclesiastical aspirations from the 1640s; it was also a political debate, because unlike his father, Charles II had accepted the Covenant in an attempt to win back the throne. However, the young king's relationship with Presbyterians proved far more tenuous than the latter wanted to admit.[50] During his exile in Europe, Charles II rarely acceded to Presbyterian scruples,[51] and upon returning to England, he immediately set about restoring the episcopate, reportedly saying that he trusted Catholics more than Presbyterians.[52] Nonetheless, many Presbyterians argued that because Charles II was a covenanted king, the Covenant was binding upon the wider nation. They expected either that he would endorse religious toleration, or that he would finally make England's church Presbyterian. In his popular *ΑΝΑΛΗΨΙS*, Crofton enthused about a forthcoming Presbyterian settlement. Despite the rising popularity of the Church of England, Crofton bluntly asserted that although Presbyterians were a minority, "their confidence may be the greater, for that His most *Sacred Majesty* comes in to make up the number."[53] The Covenant was therefore a matter of *"National Obligation,"*[54] a judgment echoed by various of its other supporters.[55] The *Solemn League and Covenant for Reformation* was a live issue, and one that left unresolved and thus imminent the contests over reformation that had suffused the 1640s and 1650s.

Proponents of episcopacy remained obdurate,[56] and some of the anti-Covenant literature printed in the early 1660s came directly from the years of civil war. Daniel Featley's critique saw its first printing in 1660, having lain in manuscript since the mid-1640s,[57] and an anti-Covenant pamphlet authored in 1643 by John

---

[50] Ronald Hutton, *Charles II: King of England, Scotland, and Ireland* (Oxford: The Clarendon Press, 1989), pp. 50 (on tensions with Presbyterians over his household), 59–60 (on Charles II's use of the Covenants to further secure Scottish loyalty), 90–1 (on tensions between Anglicans and Presbyterians at his exiled court), 141–2 (on his arrest of the leading Scottish Covenanters); Nicole Greenspan, "Charles II, Exile, and the Problem of Allegiance," *The Historical Journal*, Vol. 54, No. 1 (Mar., 2011), pp. 73–103, esp. pp. 92–102.

[51] Hutton, *Charles II*, pp. 72, 148 (on his use of Anglican rites).   [52] Hutton, *Charles II*, p. 148.

[53] Crofton, *ΑΝΑΛΗΨΙS*, p. 26.   [54] Crofton, *ΑΝΑΛΗΨΙS*, p. 27.

[55] See, e.g., Anonymous, *The Anatomy*, pp. 21–8; Theophilus Timorcus, *The Covenanters Plea Against Absolvers* (London, 1660; Wing/G314); Anonymous, *A Declaration of the Presbiterians* (London, 1660; Wing/D739).

[56] On episcopacy generally see, e.g., Kenneth Fincham and Stephen Taylor, "The Restoration of the Church of England, 1660–1662: Ordination, Re-ordination and Conformity," in Stephen Taylor and Grant Tapsell (eds.), *The Nature of the English Revolution Revisited* (Woodbridge and Rochester: The Boydell Press, 2013), pp. 197–232; Benjamin M. Guyer, "'From the Apostles' Time': The Polity of the British Episcopal Churches, 1603–62," in Elliot Vernon and Hunter Powell (eds.), *Church Polity and Politics in the British Atlantic World, c. 1635–66* (Manchester: Manchester University Press, 2020), pp. 17–37, esp. pp. 28–33.

[57] Daniel Featley, *The League Illegal* (London, 1660 Wing/F591).

Gauden appeared as well.[58] The University of Oxford's 1647 refutation of the Covenant was published twice,[59] and John Bramhall's 1649 pamphlet *A Faire Warning for England to Take Heed of the Presbyterian Government of Scotland* appeared both as a stand-alone volume and together with several of his other anti-Presbyterian tractates.[60] Many new works were also published. Charles I sometimes loomed large in this literature, because his murder exemplified the brutal realities of reformation "by force of arms." According to the Episcopalian clergyman John Rowland, the legality of the Covenant was suspect for several reasons: because only a "faction" in Parliament had endorsed it, because violence soon surrounded its adoption, and because Charles I had rejected it.[61] In his *ΑΝΑΛΥΣΙΣ*, Gauden argued against the Covenant on both constitutional and theological grounds. Constitutionally, the Covenant's coercive origins were an *ipso facto* disqualification of its legal status; its proponents had made Charles I a "Martyr,"[62] and the Covenant was *"watered* with the *Kings blood."*[63] Theologically, the Covenant's opposition to episcopacy separated the Church of England from "the *judgement* and *custom* of the *Catholick Church,* in all places and ages (till of later years) from the Apostles days, with whom we ought to keep *communion* in all things of so ancient *tradition,* and *universal observation."*[64] Thematic convergence helped define Episcopalian contributions to this and other debates, but also proved incapable of resolving them.

Resolution ultimately came not from the advancement of better arguments in print, but from the convergence of popular support and government direction. The Church of England wasted no time before beginning the restoration of its hierarchy; five new bishops were consecrated in Westminster Abbey on October 28, 1660. In his consecration sermon, John Sudbury took as his text St. Paul's exhortation that "This is a true saying, If a man desire the Office of a Bishop, he desireth a good work."[65] Sudbury repeated many commonplace convictions; he stressed the mutual relationship between church and state,[66] and unapologetically

---

[58] Anonymous (John Gauden?), *Certaine Scruples and Doubts of Conscience* (London, 1660; Wing/ G346). The original text, published under the same title (London, 1645; Wing/G345), contains no authorial ascription; the 1660 edition contains a prefatory letter signed by John Gauden, and its authorship currently ascribed to him.

[59] The University of Oxford, *Reasons of the Present Judgment of the Universitie of Oxford* (Oxford and London, 1660; Wing/S626 and S627).

[60] John Bramhall, *A Faire Warning for England to Take Heed of the Presbyterian Government of Scotland* (London, 1660/1661; Wing/B4220); John Bramhall, *Three Treatises Concerning the Scotish Discipline* (The Hague, 1661; Wing/T1122).

[61] Rowland, *A Reply,* pp. 4-5 (violence), 17, 23, 43 (royal authority); faction is addressed throughout.

[62] Gauden, *ΑΝΑΛΥΣΙΣ,* p. 5.

[63] Gauden, *ΑΝΑΛΥΣΙΣ,* p. 8; see also Anonymous, *Certain Scrvples and Doubts of Conscience,* esp. p. 13, nn. 1-2.

[64] Gauden, *ΑΝΑΛΥΣΙΣ,* p. 9.

[65] John Sudbury, *A Sermon Preached at the Consecration of the Right Revered Fathers in God* (London, 1660; Wing/S6136), p. 1.

[66] Sudbury, *A Sermon,* pp. 12-13.

averred that "a *Christian* cannot be a *Rebell*, but he must depart from his *Faith* and turn *infidel*, if not in *word*, yet in *deed*."[67] Parochial clarity did not need to wait upon casuistry in either law or theology. Parliament agreed, declared the *Solemn League and Covenant for Reformation* illegal, and ordered its burning in 1661.[68] The king was also active. On March 25, 1661, Charles II appointed a group of bishops to meet with Presbyterian clergy and "an equal number of Learned Divines, of both Perswasions" to discuss possible reforms to the Book of Common Prayer.[69] The king's reference to "both Perswasions" denoted only Presbyterians and Episcopalians; Congregationalists were excluded. The Savoy Conference, so named because it occurred at the Savoy palace, saw unequal outcomes for each confessional group. It united the Church of England around shared confessional and political commitments, and thus proved decisive for the future of Anglicanism both within and beyond England. Presbyterians, however, offered no unified front. Their representatives attended sporadically, if they attended at all,[70] which undermined the persuasiveness of their arguments. In 1662, a revision of the Book of Common Prayer was promulgated along with a new Act of Uniformity, which all clergy were required to take under penalty of suspension from their parishes. The entirety of the Jacobean canon law was revived, as were the Articles of Religion. The reformation of the 1640s had failed.

Defining the English Reformation

Several of the works discussed in the previous section, "More Semantics of 'Reformation'," buttressed their claims with passing references to sixteenth-century ecclesiastical history. Presbyterians and Episcopalians each drew upon the historiographical traditions developed over the previous two decades, marshaling these in support of their respective ecclesial ambitions. The supersessive aims of Presbyterian historiography, first articulated in the mid-1640s, remained central to Presbyterian arguments in the 1660s, but they increasingly emphasized the Presbyterian pursuit of reformation as an agonal *longue durée*. Writing against episcopacy, Crofton commented that "the removal of *Englands* Hierarchy hath been sued for from Queen Elizabeths time, downward unto this day."[71] Baxter made an almost identical comment about liturgy: "these Ceremonies have for above an hundred years been the fountain of manifold evils in this Church and Nation."[72] The Presbyterian delegation at the Savoy Conference situated its

---

[67] Sudbury, *A Sermon*, p. 13.
[68] The Parliament of England and Wales, *The Lords in Parliament Assembled...for Burning of the Instrument or Writing, Called The Solemn League or Covenant* (London, 1661; Wing/E2818A).
[69] Baxter, *The Grand Debate*, sig. A2 v.
[70] Barry Till, "Participants in the Savoy Conference (*act*. 1661)," *ODNB*.
[71] Crofton, *ΑΝΑΛΗΨΙS*, p. 14.   [72] Baxter, *The Grand Debate*, p. 10.

arguments in the same historiographical narrative. Like the 1644 *Directory for the Publique Worship of God*, the second point of "The Exceptions" identified Archbishop Cranmer and the other authors of the Book of Common Prayer as "our first Reformers."[73] By framing their appeal as an argument deeply rooted in the Tudor past, Presbyterians could not conceptualize sixteenth-century developments as the English Reformation, an event completed long ago. Rather, Presbyterians' desired reformation remained an unfulfilled ambition. The failure of Presbyterianism at the Savoy Conference, followed by the ratification of the 1662 Prayer Book and Act of Uniformity, prevented this distinctly Presbyterian historiography from becoming normative for English historical self-understanding.

An especially clear example of the difference between Presbyterian and Episcopalian historiographies comes from Henry Hickman, whose *Plus Ultra, Or Englands Reformation Needing to be Reformed* responded to *Ecclesia Restaurata*, Peter Heylyn's 1661 history of the English Reformation, which will be discussed in further detail later.[74] *Plus Ultra* throws into sharp relief the divergence between Presbyterian and Episcopalian self-understandings. Hickman largely agreed with Heylyn's narrative, which he subversively used to justify his assertion that "Englands *Reformation is sadly defective*."[75] Hickman offered the apocalyptic prognostication that "much of that you [re: Heylyn] have laid into the foundation of the Reformation of the Church of *England* (though you and others judge it gold, silver, precious stones) will be found wood, hay and stubble, when he appeareth, who is like a refiners fire."[76] Like other Presbyterians, he too identified the religious leaders of Edwardian England only as "our first Reformers."[77] Here was no lauding of the Edwardian church but instead the criticism that under Henry's son, "the Reformation had gone as far forward as ever it went."[78] Presbyterians such as Hickman did not look to simply strip away recent "Laudian" developments; nor did they advocate returning to an alleged Reformed consensus that held sway under either Edward or Elizabeth. England had needed three reformations, Hickman argued, the first "in point of Doctrine," the second in "Discipline" and the third in "Worship," but he believed that only the first of these was accomplished during Edward's reign.[79] He thus attacked both the episcopate and the liturgy throughout *Plus Ultra*, although the latter received greater attention. In the Book of Common Prayer, Hickman saw vestiges of Catholicism; where conformists saw antiquity, he saw corruption.[80] As already noted in this chapter, and as already seen in earlier chapters, such arguments were

---

[73] Baxter, *The Grand Debate*, p. 3.
[74] Henry Hickman, *Plus Ultra, or, Englands Reformation, Needing to be Reformed* (London, 1661; Wing/H1913).
[75] Hickman, *Plus Ultra*, sig. A2 v.   [76] Hickman, *Plus Ultra*, p. 24.
[77] Hickman, *Plus Ultra*, pp. 15, 35.   [78] Hickman, *Plus Ultra*, p. 20.
[79] Hickman, *Plus Ultra*, p. 12.
[80] Hickman, *Plus Ultra*, e.g., pp. 15–16, 30, 44; see also 13, 16, 20, 27, 36 (against ceremonies), 21, 22, 23 (against Cranmer), 15, 22, 23, 26, 36 (against Ridley).

wholly mundane, but they well underscore the fact that Presbyterians and Episcopalians had come to articulate fundamentally incompatible understandings of the past.

For Episcopalians, on the other hand, the English Reformation was a past event completed a full century prior, and historical works published between the early 1660s and the early 1680s offered increasingly detailed analyses of it. All attained some level of popularity, sometimes extending well into the eighteenth century. Herbert of Cherbury's *Life and Raigne of King Henry the Eight*, first published in 1649, was republished in 1672, and then again in 1682 and 1683; it saw five further editions when it was included in White Kennett's popular multi-volume *History of England* (1706), and yet another edition appeared in 1741. Anthony Sparrow's 1661 volume *A Collection of Articles* was reprinted in 1671, 1675, 1684, and 1699. Peter Heylyn's *Ecclesia Restaurata*, his most sustained analysis to date of sixteenth-century religious history, was first published in 1661 and reprinted in 1670 and 1674. Gilbert Burnet's *The History of the Reformation of the Church of England* had a more complicated print history and eventually comprised three parts. The first, which studied the reign of Henry VIII, appeared in 1679; the second, which encompassed the reigns of Edward, Mary, and Elizabeth, appeared two years later. A one-volume edition that contained both parts appeared in 1681 and was republished in 1683. An abridgment appeared twice in 1682 and again in 1683, and the same year saw a French translation, with a further Latin translation in 1686. The entire work was then republished in 1715, when Burnet added a third part, and various of its volumes and abridgments appeared with regularity into the 1730s. By then, still other multi-volume histories had been written on point, but they exceed the scope of the present study.

Current scholarship generally draws sharp divisions between these works and authors,[81] but in fact, all shared significant degrees of apologetic, chronological, and methodological overlap. The ideological should not be allowed to overshadow the historiographical; whatever an individual author's political or theological commitments, each was also committed to participating in what had become a burgeoning academic discourse. The normative and prescriptive concerns across these histories were, as with much other controversial material of the time, rote.

---

[81] Diarmaid MacCulloch, "The Myth of the English Reformation," *Journal of British Studies*, Vol. 30, No. 1 (Jan., 1991), pp. 1–19; J.A.I. Champion, *The Pillars of Priestcraft Shaken: The Church of England and its Enemies 1660–1730* (Cambridge: Cambridge University Press, 1992), chs. 2 and 3, esp. pp. 75–76, n. 89; Andrew Starkie, "Contested Histories of the English Church: Gilbert Burnet and Jeremy Collier," *The Huntington Library Quarterly*, Vol. 68, Nos. 1–2 (Mar., 2005), pp. 335–51; Tony Claydon, *Europe and the Making of England 1660–1760* (Cambridge: Cambridge University Press, 2007), ch. 2; Christine Jackson, "Lord Herbert of Cherbury and the Presentation of the Henrician Reformation in his *Life and Raigne of King Henry the Eighth*," *The Seventeenth Century*, Vol. 28, No. 2 (2013), pp. 139–61, at p. 155, contrasts Herbert of Cherbury with Heylyn and Burnet. Anthony Milton, *Laudian and Royalist Polemic in Seventeenth-century England* (Manchester: Manchester University Press, 2007), pp. 197–204, 228–33, compares and contrasts Heylyn less with his contemporaries than with earlier authors.

Anti-Presbyterian and anti-Catholic *apologiae* traversed thematic terrain a century old. Herbert of Cherbury,[82] Peter Heylyn,[83] and Gilbert Burnet[84] each explicitly named Nicholas Sanders as a major opponent. Even where he went unnamed, his influence was easy to detect. According to Anthony Sparrow, it was a "notorious slander" by "some of the Roman perswasion" that "her [the Church of England's] Reformation hath been altogether Lay and Parliamentary." He countered that, "the Reformation of this Church was orderly and Synodical by the Guides and Governours of souls, and confirmed by Supream Authority."[85] It was at once both an ecclesial and a political argument, and one made just as forcefully by other authors. In *Ecclesia Restaurata*, Heylyn retained his earlier opposition to Parliament's influence in religious matters, and Burnet was equally concerned to emphasize that the Church of England's religion was not the mere determination of Parliament.[86] By the 1670s, when Burnet began working on his *Reformation*, attacking Sanders was a historiographical habit and, arguably, a veritable rite of passage. Burnet concluded the first part of his *Reformation* with a lengthy appendix entitled, "Errors and Falshoods in Sander's Book of the English Schism."[87] It was the longest and most systematic attack on Sanders' work yet printed, and it brought Burnet public acclaim. In 1680, both houses of Parliament offered their public thanks to Burnet for his work.

English historians demarcated the chronology of the English Reformation in largely similar ways. As the next section, "Debating the English Reformation," will further detail, Sparrow, Heylyn, and Burnet all refrained from locating Henry's reign as the beginning of the English Reformation. They instead detailed the reigns of Henry's children, crafting a shared historiographical perspective that emphasized the differences between the Church of England and its domestic opponents. Even where their chronologies parted ways, one finds the same ideological commitment against religious dissent. Heylyn concluded his work not in 1563, when he claimed that "Religion and the State" were "fortified and secured" under Elizabeth,[88] but in 1566, "when the Puritan Faction had began to disturb her [the Church of England's] Order."[89] Sparrow's editorial work consisted of compilation rather than commentary, but he shared Heylyn's concern with confessional definition by including two seminal anti-Puritan texts, Elizabeth's 1573 "Proclamation against the despisers or breakers of the orders

---

[82] Herbert of Cherbury, *The Life and Raigne of King Henry the Eight* (London, 1649; Wing/H1504), e.g., pp. 258–9, 358, 386, 437, 569–70, 572–3.

[83] Peter Heylyn, *Ecclesia Restaurata* (London, 1674; Wing/H1703), p. 294.

[84] Gilbert Burnet, *The History of the Reformation of the Church of England* (London, 1681; Wing/B5798), Part I, sig. (b); Book II, pp. 41–4, 86, 113–14, 149, 153; Book III, p. 356.

[85] Anthony Sparrow, *A Collection of Articles* (London, 1661; Wing/C4093A), sig. [*4].

[86] Burnet, *History of the Reformation*, Part II, Preface, sig. [b2].

[87] Burnet, *History of the Reformation*, Part I, Book III, pp. 271–304.

[88] Heylyn, *Ecclesia Restaurata*, p. 332.   [89] Heylyn, *Ecclesia Restaurata*, p. 346.

prescribed in the book of Common Prayer,"[90] and the Jacobean canon law. When Burnet published the second part of his *Reformation* in 1681, he concluded his narrative of Elizabeth's "settlement" of religion with a paragraph on the divisions that developed within the English church. The queen was "moderate and wise," but others less so, and their continued agitation remained a threat, "unless our Lawgivers do vigorously apply themselves to it."[91] Burnet's *History of the Reformation* joined Heylyn's *Ecclesia Restaurata* and Sparrow's *Collection of Articles* by drawing a firm line of division between the Church of England and nonconformists.

These works further witness to the rapid adoption of shared methodological standards. Drawing upon professional norms then current in antiquarian research, which vaunted academic neutrality over personal religious conviction,[92] historical works now purported to distinguish between an author's theological views and their methodological commitments, effectively—at least ideally— separating the prescriptive (the confessional) from the descriptive (the historical). The instantiation of antiquarian norms is seen clearly in two ways. One is through explicit appeals to dispassionate scholarship. In his Epistle Dedicatory, Herbert of Cherbury informed his reader that "I have endeavoured to set down the truth impartially."[93] Peter Heylyn did the same in the introduction to *Ecclesia Restaurata*.

> I am to let thee know, that in the whole Carriage of this Work I have assumed unto my Self the Freedom of a *Just Historian*, concealing nothing out of Fear, nor speaking any thing for Favour: delivering nothing for a Truth without good Authority; but so delivering the Truth, as to witness for me that I am neither biassed by Love or Hatred,(*) nor overswayed by Partiality and corrupt Affections.[94]

In the margin of the page, Heylyn revealed the source of his parenthetical asterisk as the first-century Roman historian Tacitus, whose claim to impartial historical reporting was widely taken as a model for historical writing among antiquarians.[95] In 1679, when Burnet complained of Heylyn that "*either he was very ill informed,*

---

[90] Sparrow, *A Collection of Articles*, pp. 227–8.

[91] Burnet, *History of the Reformation*, Part II, Book III, p. 407.

[92] Anthony Grafton, *What Was History? The Art of History in Early Modern Europe* (Cambridge: Cambridge University Press, 2007); the same principles were applied to biography, as seen in Jessica Martin, *Walton's Lives: Conformist Commemorations and the Rise of Biography* (Oxford: Oxford University Press, 2001).

[93] Herbert of Cherbury, *King Henry the Eighth*, sig. A2 v; see also Christian Jackson, "'It Is Unpossible to Draw His Picture Well Who Hath Several Countenances': Lord Herbert of Cherbury and *The Life and Reign of King Henry VIII*," in Thomas Betteridge and Thomas S. Freeman (eds.), *Henry VIII and History* (Farnham and Burlington: Ashgate Publishing, 2012), pp. 135–49, at pp. 138–9.

[94] Heylyn, *Ecclesia Restaurata*, sig. [a3] v; Tacitus is also cited on p. 48.

[95] Grafton, *What Was History?*, e.g., pp. 5, 71, 184, 201.

or very much led by his Passions,"[96] he witnessed not to a different standard, but to one that was widely shared. In 1681, Burnet similarly affirmed before his readers that "*I know the* Duty *of an* Historian *leads him to write as one that is of neither Party.*"[97] It is not especially interesting to note that Heylyn, Burnet, and others failed to achieve their desired academic neutrality. It is entirely interesting, however, that they tried.

Antiquarian influence is equally evident through the reproduction of extensive primary documentation. Herbert of Cherbury incorporated into his work on Henry VIII dozens of documents, ranging from papal bulls to political treatises. Heylyn transcribed documents within his narrative such as the Articles of Religion, and letters by continental religious leaders, including Calvin,[98] Vermigli,[99] and correspondence between Melanchthon and Cranmer.[100] Unusual in this regard was Sparrow's *A Collection of Articles*, a work akin to what we today would term a document reader on the English Reformation— apparently the first of its kind. Sparrow gathered together nearly two-dozen sources, and aside from his introduction, the work consisted exclusively of primary sources. Some had appeared elsewhere. Fuller and Heylyn both included the complete text of Edward VI's 1547 injunctions, and *Ecclesia Restaurata* contained a lengthy appendix with both the Latin and English editions of the Articles of Religion.[101] Sparrow included these together with a detailed comparison of the Elizabethan Articles and their Edwardian predecessor. He also incorporated a number of other texts too, such as the 1548 English communion office,[102] the visitation articles of Archbishop Cranmer and bishop Ridley,[103] the Elizabethan injunctions,[104] and the liturgy for the Royal Touch.[105]

Burnet outdid all, with each successive volume of his work containing transcriptions of numerous documents. He included almost none of the texts found in Sparrow's collection. Referring to the Edwardian injunctions, Burnet wrote that they were "so often printed, I shall refer the Reader that would consider them more carefully, to the Collection of these and other such curious things by the Right Reverend Father in God *Anthony Sparrow* now Lord Bishop of *Norwich*."[106] Like Sparrow, Burnet also compared the Edwardian and Elizabethan versions of the Articles of Religion, but otherwise preferred previously unpublished material. Those who read Burnet's *History of the Reformation* could peruse for first time the

---

[96] Burnet, *History of the Reformation*, Part I, Preface, sig. (b) v; emphasis in original.
[97] Burnet, *History of the Reformation*, Part II, Preface, sig. [a2] v.
[98] Heylyn, *Ecclesia Restaurata*, pp. 80, 107.
[99] Heylyn, *Ecclesia Restaurata*, pp. 92, 94, 250, 328.   [100] Heylyn, *Ecclesia Restaurata*, p. 108.
[101] Thomas Fuller, *The Church-History of Britain* (London, 1655; Wing/F2416), Book VII, ¶. 3, pp. 372–4; Heylyn, *Ecclesia Restaurata*, pp. 34–6 (Injunctions), 349–68 (Articles).
[102] Sparrow, *A Collection of Articles*, pp. 17–24.
[103] Sparrow, *A Collection of Articles*, pp. 25–31 (Archbishop Cranmer), 33–5 (bishop Ridley).
[104] Sparrow, *A Collection of Articles*, pp. 61–80.
[105] Sparrow, *A Collection of Articles*, pp. 223–4.
[106] Burnet, *History of the Reformation*, Part II, Book I, p. 29.

journal of Edward VI,[107] and multiple documents from Mary's reign, such as Bishop Tunstal's articles of visitation,[108] the Marian liturgy for the consecration of cramp-rings,[109] and the writ for burning Archbishop Cranmer.[110] The collection of documents for Elizabeth was just as expansive, encompassing the liturgy for Matthew Parker's consecration as Archbishop of Canterbury,[111] Parker's Eleven Articles,[112] and the queen's excommunication.[113] Documents such as these enabled readers to peruse sixteenth-century religious history firsthand. It was a commitment shared by all historians of the English Reformation.

Debating the English Reformation

Expertise is sometimes—and perhaps oftentimes—defined less by agreement than bounded disagreement. Two significant areas of academic divergence emerged in Restoration-era scholarship. The first, which pertained to liturgical change under Edward VI, was not a dispute between historians so much as a break with past consensus. The second was about the role of Henry VIII in the English Reformation, although here, too, the primary contrast was dissensus between an earlier and a more recent historiography. Before discussing these, however, a brief word of caution is in order. The previous section, "Defining the English Reformation," outlined the shared frameworks that informed Episcopalian historiography on the English Reformation, but recent scholarship has tended to argue that political ideology drove the differences between Episcopalian historians.[114] It is easy to assume a political orientation behind historical writing, but comparatively difficult to demonstrate. Burnet, for example, wrote during the Exclusion Crisis, but there is no reason to privilege that event as the primary context for his

---

[107] Burnet, *History of the Reformation*, A Collection of Records...Referred to in the Second Part, pp. 3–67.

[108] Burnet, *History of the Reformation*, A Collection of Records...Referred to in the Second Part, pp. 260–5.

[109] Burnet, *History of the Reformation*, A Collection of Records...Referred to in the Second Part, pp. 295–7.

[110] Burnet, *History of the Reformation*, A Collection of Records...Referred to in the Second Part, pp. 300–1.

[111] Burnet, *History of the Reformation*, A Collection of Records...Referred to in the Second Part, pp. 363–5.

[112] Burnet, *History of the Reformation*, A Collection of Records...Referred to in the Second Part, pp. 365–8; the pagination is inconsistent and these should be pp. 369–72.

[113] Burnet, *History of the Reformation*, A Collection of Records...Referred to in the Second Part, pp. 377–9.

[114] Champion, *Pillars of Priestcraft Shaken*, p. 77, proposes clericalism and its converse as the fault line between Heylyn and Burnet. Milton, *Laudian and Royalist Polemic*, pp. 197ff., sees Heylyn's post-1660s publications as directed at the Restoration church and monarchy, while also noting that these works were long in gestation. Claydon, *Europe*, p. 68, reads Burnet's scholarship in the context of the Exclusion Crisis; so does Andrew Starkie, "Henry VIII in History: Gilbert Burnet's *History of the Reformation* (v. 1), 1679," in Betteridge and Freeman, *Henry VIII and History*, pp. 151–63.

History. Earlier historiography on the English Reformation is at least as contextually relevant for understanding the results of Burnet's research. Furthermore, although it may prove difficult to demarcate between the descriptive and the prescriptive, the reality of the latter should not be allowed to overshadow the antiquarian earnestness of the former. Correlation is not necessarily causation.

Beginning with liturgical history, and as seen in Chapter 3, it may be recalled that many decades before the Restoration, the liturgical history of successive Prayer Books was often homogenized. John Hayward had used Edward VI's epistle to the rebels in Devonshire to explain that the English liturgy was a translation of the mass. Those who wrote in the 1640s and 1650s followed the conclusion of Hayward's research, rendering his view a matter of historiographical consensus. However, with Heylyn's *Ecclesia Restaurata*, Restoration historiography embarked upon a significant departure from this longstanding interpretation. In *Ecclesia Restaurata*—for the first time, it would seem—an English historian took seriously the changes in Eucharistic language between 1549 and 1559. Heylyn now advanced a historical narrative in which external theological and political developments influenced changes surrounding the Eucharist within successive Prayer Books.

Heylyn nonetheless advanced his new perspective within the framework of other, long-established assumptions. Following earlier authors, as well as his own work, he still divided Edward's reign between a more moderate if sometimes greedy Somerset,[115] and a sacrilegious Northumberland driven by "Ambition";[116] he still described the first English liturgy as a translation of the mass,[117] and he further believed that the Book of Common Prayer ameliorated Catholics, uniting them in a single church with those of more evangelical inclinations.[118] Perhaps most importantly, and again tracking with earlier scholarship, fidelity to Christian antiquity remained a bright thread of thematic emphasis. Within the context of Somerset's moderate reformation, Heylyn wrote, English bishops such as Nicholas Ridley began their own, independent study of the early Church, and consequently arrived at conclusions that stood apart from other contemporary Christian groups. Catholics maintained transubstantiation, Lutherans held "the Figment of Consubstantiation," and Zwinglians believed in "Signs and Figures, as if there had been nothing else in the blessed *Eucharist*." Ridley, however, "thought it most agreeable to the Rules of Piety, to frame his Judgement to the Dictates of the Ancient Fathers," and thus advocated "a *Real presence* of *Christ's* Body and Blood in the Holy Sacrament as to exclude that Corporal Eating of the same."[119] Ridley

---

[115] Heylyn, *Ecclesia Restaurata*, p. 118.   [116] Heylyn, *Ecclesia Restaurata*, p. 162.
[117] Heylyn, *Ecclesia Restaurata*, pp. 42, 58, 74.   [118] Heylyn, *Ecclesia Restaurata*, pp. 58, 74.
[119] "Real Presence" underwent its own semantic shift in "early modern" England. The term was originally synonymous with the concept of Christ's physical presence in the consecrated elements, but Heylyn deployed "real" *against* corporeal—or, as he also termed it, "carnal"—presence.

soon compelled Cranmer to adopt the same view.[120] The 1549 Book of Common Prayer incorporated this rediscovered patristic doctrine, and the Church of England—uniquely, from Heylyn's point of view—returned to the consensus of Christian antiquity. Discussing the Elizabethan revision, Heylyn noted that the 1549 liturgy identified the consecrated bread and wine as the Body and Blood of Christ, while the 1552 liturgy did not. He denied that any change in doctrine had occurred between these two liturgies, but he did claim that the 1552 revision was intended to pacify evangelical troublemakers, most notably "*Calvin* and his Disciples." In the 1559 revision, "the Revisors of the Book joyned both Forms together, lest under colour of rejecting a *Carnal*, they might be thought also to deny such a *Real Presence* as was defended in the Writings of the Antient Fathers."[121] Even if considered inadequate today, from the standpoint of seventeenth-century scholarship, Heylyn's recognition of liturgical heterogeneity was a real divergence from the homogenizing habits made familiar by the previous generation of historians.

Burnet is often contrasted with Heylyn, but he followed Heylyn's basic lead when writing about the liturgy and shared with Heylyn many of the same, inherited historiographical conclusions. Burnet maintained the bright line of demarcation between Somerset and Northumberland. "*As for the Duke of Northumberland*," he wrote, "*the Reformation is not at all concerned with him,*" but "*The Duke of* Somerset *was indeed more sincere*"—not least because, unlike Northumberland, "*I never find him charged with any personal disorders, nor was he ever guilty of falsehood, of perverting Justice, of Cruelty, or of Oppression.*"[122] The first Prayer Book, furthermore, "left the Office of the Mass as it was, only adding to it that which made it a Communion."[123] Burnet did not explicitly assert that the 1549 liturgy drew Catholics into the Church of England, but he did hold a rosy view of that liturgy's popularity, writing that it was "received over *England* without any opposition,"[124] Mary Tudor excepted.[125] Burnet shared many of the assumptions of his contemporaries and predecessors.

The issue, therefore, is not how Burnet differed from Heylyn or other, earlier writers, but how he built upon and developed their research. Simply stated, Burnet wrote the most detailed historical narrative yet published. For example, he offered readers a helpful overview of the composition and revision of the so-called "Black Rubric," which prescribed kneeling at the communion but rejected adoration of the elements.[126] Burnet's discussion of Eucharistic doctrine further illustrates the point. He too believed that the Church of England was heavily influenced by

---

[120] Heylyn, *Ecclesia Restaurata*, p. 53.   [121] Heylyn, *Ecclesia Restaurata*, p. 283.
[122] Burnet, *History of the Reformation*, Part II, sig. [b2] r–v.
[123] Burnet, *History of the Reformation*, Part II, Book I, p. 64.
[124] Burnet, *History of the Reformation*, Part II, Book I, p. 68.
[125] Burnet, *History of the Reformation*, Part II, Book I, p. 103.
[126] Burnet, *History of the Reformation*, Part II, Book I, pp. 170–1.

antiquity, but he further detailed the view found in *Ecclesia Restaurata* by citing the patristic authors who influenced Cranmer and others involved in liturgical revision. In Burnet's *History*, readers perused summaries of Augustine, Chrysostom, and Theodoret, as well as later figures such as Ratramnus and Alcuin. Burnet then offered a slightly more expansive analysis of the Prayer Book by setting it within a comparative confessional context. Heylyn had summarized Lutheran and Zwinglian theology rather harshly; the Lutheran theology of the Eucharist was a "figment" and Zwinglian sacramental theology was portrayed as inadequately minimalist. Burnet, however, cited the Augsburg and Helvetic confessions, and then—uniquely for the time—compared those documents with what he knew of Greek Orthodoxy.[127] Finally, discussing Elizabeth's reign, Burnet saw in the revised communion service a reflection of the queen's own belief in the corporeal presence of Christ in the Eucharist, a conviction that she shared with the wider nation. He explained, "for the chief design of the Queens Council was, to unite the Nation in one Faith; and the greatest part of the Nation continued to believe in such a Presence."[128] In the end, Burnet composed a highly nuanced overview of Tudor Eucharistic debate, but one that hardly broke with the broad outline found in Heylyn. Historiographical advances are rarely a paradigm shift.

The matter of Henry VIII is more complicated.[129] Chapter 4 noted that between the 1640s and 1650s, a discrepancy appeared in Episcopalian historiography concerning the relationship between Henry VIII and the English Reformation. The most popular recent work that denied Henry's import was Charles I's *Eikon Basilike*, which had seen more than three dozen editions printed since 1649.[130] The martyr king's life and legacy was an important court of appeal for a variety of religious issues from 1660 onward;[131] even if the *Eikon* was not their direct inspiration, a growing number of authors in the 1660s echoed Charles I's assessment. As Edward Stillingfleet wrote in his *Irenicum* (1660), "I meddle not with the times of *Henry 8.* when I will not deny but the first *quickning* of the Reformation might be, but the matter of it was as yet rude and undigested; I date the birth of it from the first setlement of that most excellent Prince *Edward 6.*"[132] The author of *Cabala* shared this view of the English Reformation,[133] as did Thomas Sprat, who

---

[127] Burnet, *History of the Reformation*, Part II, Book I, pp. 104–10.

[128] Burnet, *History of the Reformation*, Part II, Book III, p. 392 (mispage as p. 390).

[129] Two volumes of essays offer much helpful material on the broader afterlives of Henry VIII. See Mark Rankin, Christopher Highley, and John N. King (eds.), *Henry VIII and His Afterlives: Literature, Politics, and Art* (Cambridge: Cambridge University Press, 2009); Betteridge and Freeman, *Henry VIII and History*.

[130] Andrew Lacey, *The Cult of King Charles the Martyr* (Woodbridge and Rochester: The Boydell Press, 2003), p. 81.

[131] See, e.g., Walton, *Mr. Rich. Hooker*, pp. 172–4 (on whether to accept the last three books of Hooker's *Politie*).

[132] Edward Stillingfleet, *Irenicum* (London, 1660; Wing/S5596), p. 385.

[133] Lloyd, *Cabala*, pp. 5–6.

protested against a Catholic interlocutor in 1665 that "it is false that *our English Reformation began upon a shamefull occasion*, or from the extravagance of a private passion."[134] Arguing that Henry only sought as much distance from the pope as the Gallican church of the seventeenth century, Sprat continued, "There is no man of our *Church*, that looks upon his [Henry VIII's] breach with the *Pope*, to have been a *Reformation*."[135] By the mid-1660s, Sprat's assertion was probably true.

Historical works confirm as much. Sparrow divided his *Collection of Articles* into three sections, each of which corresponded to the reign of a particular monarch: Edward VI, Elizabeth I, and James I. Henry VIII's 1536 abrogation of select holy days was the sole Henrician text that appeared—and this only because Elizabeth reissued it in 1560. Heylyn was equally mum on Henry's import. In his dedication to Charles II, Heylyn described his work as "an History *of the* Reformation of the Church of ENGLAND, *with all the Various Fortunes and Successes of it, from the first Agitations in* Religion *under* Henry the Eighth (*which served for a Preamble thereunto*) *until the Legal Settling and Establishment of it by the great* Queen Elizabeth, *of Happy Memory*."[136] Wholly absent here was Heylyn's earlier portrayal of reformation as a typological pattern that began with Henry VIII; *Ecclesia Restaurata* was instead a work of narrative history in which Henry's presence was greatly marginalized as "a Preamble." Edward and Elizabeth now took center stage. Burnet's interest in Henry VIII was equally unoriginal. As he wrote in his Epistle Dedicatory to Charles II, the Reformation "was carried on by a slow and unsteady Progress under King *Henry* the VIII."[137] Burnet devoted an entire volume of his *History of the Reformation* to Henrician England, but as will soon be shown, he did not return the king to a central position in the English Reformation. Henry's role in the English Reformation was, generally speaking, ambivalent.

A minority perspective could nonetheless be found in Herbert of Cherbury's *Life and Raigne of King Henry the Eighth*. Although first published in 1649, it did not become a recurring presence on the literary landscape until its first reprinting in 1672. Herbert opened his work by noting the generally negative view of Henry's reign,[138] but concluded with the more ambivalent judgment that, "With all his crimes yet, he was one of the most glorious Princes of his time."[139] Reformation was just as conflicted in Herbert's work. "Reformation was pray'd, as farre as might bee, in Religion: Though when Particulars were examin'd, it was found, that some diseases therein were like that of *Cancer Occultus*, which Physicians say, It is

---

[134] Thomas Sprat, *Observations on Monsieur de Sorbier's Voyage into England* (London, 1665; Wing/S5035), p. 104.

[135] Sprat, *Observations*, pp. 105–6.   [136] Heylyn, *Ecclesia Restaurata*, sig. A2.

[137] Burnet, *History of the Reformation*, Part I, sig. [A2] v.

[138] Herbert of Cherbury, *King Henry the Eighth*, pp. 1–2.

[139] Herbert of Cherbury, *King Henry the Eighth*, p. 574.

more safe to let alone, than to Cure."[140] Herbert questioned the wisdom of religious innovation,[141] yielding an equivocal judgment on the time period that perhaps reveals the lingering influence of early Stuart historiography. He too lamented sacrilege,[142] and he treated Luther as but one figure among many who sought reformation, instead locating the first stirrings for reformation at Lateran V.[143] The fundamental problem was that reformation had actually produced confusion and division. He complained that "contentious Preachers and factious Schoolmen on all sides would have rather disturb'd the peace of the whole World, then relinquished or retracted one particle of those opinions they had publickly taught their Auditors and Disciples."[144] Henry strove for "a more sober Reformation" than that of his contemporaries,[145] and thus one less factious, but the outcome was the same. Reformation came to England during Henry's reign, but consequently, discord came as well. Here was no ringing endorsement of sixteenth-century religious developments, and this despite the fact that Herbert was no "Laudian."

Although first published in the wake of Charles I's execution, it is difficult to tease political or apologetic meanings out of Herbert's text. Other historical works published after 1660 took a different approach. Heylyn and Burnet both used Henry's reign to advance apologetic projects that took direct aim at Nicholas Sanders' *Schismatis Anglicani*. Heylyn did so by removing Henry from the history of the English Reformation. Burnet took the opposite approach, dedicating his entire first volume to the king's reign. Even so, the goals for both authors were identical, and each produced a work that defended the legitimacy of the Church of England. Despite the fact that Parliament in the 1660s showed immense support for the episcopal church, Heylyn's marginalization of Henry's reign in *Ecclesia Restaurata* fit neatly with his earlier arguments against Parliamentary influence upon religious matters. By setting Henry aside, Heylyn did not have to determine the precise extent of Parliament's role in the English Reformation. There is a significant backstory behind this change, one missed by recent scholarship. In 1659, Heylyn published *Examen Historicum*, which initiated a public dispute with Thomas Fuller over the latter's *Church-History*.[146] Heylyn critiqued diverse details in Fuller's work, but argued extensively against the fifth and sixth books of the *Church-History*, which covered the reign of Henry VIII. Heylyn charged Fuller with inconsistent treatment of Parliament—and for Heylyn this doubled as an

---

[140] Herbert of Cherbury, *King Henry the Eighth*, p. 296; emphasis in original.
[141] Herbert of Cherbury, *King Henry the Eighth*, pp. 58, 292 (on innovation); at p. 157, evangelicals are described as "Innovators."
[142] Herbert of Cherbury, *King Henry the Eighth*, pp. 444, 524; Spelman's work is cited at p. 233.
[143] Herbert of Cherbury, *King Henry the Eighth*, p. 67.
[144] Herbert of Cherbury, *King Henry the Eighth*, p. 406.
[145] Herbert of Cherbury, *King Henry the Eighth*, p. 560.
[146] W.B. Patterson, *Thomas Fuller: Discovering England's Religious Past* (Oxford: Oxford University Press, 2018), pp. 258–64.

inconsistent treatment of the English Reformation itself. It should be kept in mind that Heylyn's argument against Parliament had long been a twofold polemic, striking out at both Presbyterian and Catholic attacks upon the Church of England. According to Heylyn, Parliament sometimes appeared in the *Church-History* as "a joynt Assistant with the King in the Reformation," but at other times, Fuller attributed the work of reformation to the king and Convocation, reducing Parliament's role to confirmation "upon the *Postfact*."[147] Which was it?

Recognizing this as "the main fault" alleged against him,[148] Fuller responded with *The Appeal of Iniured Innocence*, in which he made historical, legal, and theological arguments in his self-defense. Denying that he undermined ecclesiastical authority, Fuller first countered that he held to Christ's promise that "*the Gates of Hell shall not prevail against it.*" He then turned to a legal and historical defense of his allowance for Parliament's role in religious matters. The clergy, he wrote, had both "*consultive*" and "*conclusive*" power, which allowed them to function as representatives of the church and to distinguish between orthodoxy and heresy. Parliament had "*punitive power*," which extended to "Life, Limb, and Estate... that so neither *Royal Prerogative* nor *Subjects Rights* may be injured." Fuller then argued that Convocation's power was more limited than Heylyn wanted to believe. "I distinguish betwixt the power of the *Convocation* had over the *Clergy*, and what they have over the Laity. Over the Estates of the latter, they have no power."[149] The church took the lead in religious matters, but Parliament remained an unavoidable feature of England's ecclesiastical landscape. When Heylyn offered a partial rebuttal to Fuller later that year, he judged Fuller guilty of "denying any power to the Church of making Canons, which are of force to binde the subject till confirmed in Parliament."[150] Although Fuller and Heylyn later reconciled,[151] and although Heylyn cited Fuller's work in *Ecclesia Restaurata*,[152] the two authors had incommensurable understandings of the relationship between church and state, which rendered the past an unstable, possibly unreliable, pattern for the present. One could, however, simply cut Henry VIII—and his parliaments—from the story. And that is precisely what Heylyn did in *Ecclesia Restaurata*. The English Reformation became a much shorter event, begun by Edward VI and settled by Elizabeth I during her first decade on the throne.

The apologetic agenda that informed the first volume of Burnet's *History of the Reformation* was just as committed to defending the legitimacy of the Church of England. Whether because of his later involvement with the Williamite invasion

---

[147] Peter Heylyn, *Examen Historicum* (London, 1659; Wing/H1707), p. 99; he is commenting on Fuller, *The Church-History of Britain*, Book V, ⁋. 52, p. 188.

[148] Thomas Fuller, *The Appeal of Iniured Innocence* (London, 1659; Wing/F2410), Part II, p. 68.

[149] Fuller, *Iniured Innocence*, Part II, p. 68.

[150] Peter Heylyn, *Certamen Epistolare* (London, 1659; Wing/H1687), pp. 359–61, at p. 360.

[151] Patterson, *Thomas Fuller*, p. 264.   [152] Milton, *Laudian and Royalist Polemic*, p. 199.

of 1688, or because of his sometimes-negative comments on other historians,[153] Burnet's *History* has been read as antagonistic toward earlier historiography, but such an interpretation concedes far too much to Burnet's own protests of originality and industry. His dedicatory epistle sounded political themes that were, by 1679, quite old. The Reformation saw "slow and unsteady Progress" under Henry VIII, further "advanced" under his son, "was brought to a full settlement" under Elizabeth, and "defended by the Learned Pen of King *James*." Most importantly, given the political turmoil still so fresh in the minds of so many, "the established frame of it, under which it had so long flourished, was overthrown with your Majestyies blessed Father, who fell with it, and honoured it by his unexempled Suffering for it; and was again restored to its former beauty and order by Your Majesties happy Return."[154] Burnet's *History of the Reformation* was a bulwark for the political and ecclesiastical consensus of his time.

When compared with the general tendency to cut Henry VIII from histories of the English Reformation, Burnet's focus appears odd, and this even moreso given his view that reformation saw only a "slow and unsteady Progress" during that king's reign. Henry's import only becomes clear when read in the light of Burnet's stated apologetic aims. Burnet attacked Sanders throughout the *History of the Reformation*. The *Schismatis Anglicani* not only left "a foul and lasting stain both on the Memory of *Anne Boleyn*, and of her incomparable Daughter Queen *Elizabeth*," but "It also derogates so much from the first Reformers, who had some kind of dependence on Queen *Anne Boleyn*."[155] Studying Henry's reign enabled Burnet to better defend Boleyn, Elizabeth, and the English Reformation, whose legacies he considered inextricable. Burnet rejected Sanders' claim that Henry had intercourse with Boleyn's mother and sister, denied that Anne was the king's daughter, and further castigated Sanders' claim that Boleyn had six fingers and other physical signs of monstrosity. Lest his reader balk at his argument, Burnet laid out the chronology required by Sanders' attack, contrasting it with other documentary and historical evidence that revealed Sanders an untrustworthy narrator.[156] Burnet repeatedly impugned Sanders' integrity and reliability,[157] but this, his first attack, was his most detailed broadside against *Schismatis Anglicani*. Burnet's own descriptions of Boleyn were laudatory, and her virtues were commended.[158] In fact, he claimed that it was precisely the queen's virtues that got her into trouble. "She was of a very cheerful temper, which was not always limited within the bounds of exact decency and discretion."[159] Too good to be

---

[153] Burnet, *History of the Reformation*, Part I, sigs. (b) v–[(b2)].
[154] Burnet, *History of the Reformation*, sig. [A2] v.
[155] Burnet, *History of the Reformation*, Part I, e.g., sig. (b); Book II, pp. 42.
[156] Burnet, *History of the Reformation*, Part I, e.g., sig. (b); Book II, pp. 41–3.
[157] Burnet, *History of the Reformation*, Part I, e.g., sig. (b); Book II, pp. 86, 113–14, 149, 153, 356; Book III, pp. 356, 363.
[158] Burnet, *History of the Reformation*, Part I, Book II, e.g., pp. 132, 152; Book III, p. 204.
[159] Burnet, *History of the Reformation*, Part I, Book III, p. 197.

true, she became the victim of political intrigue. Abandoned amidst her husband's newfound interest in Jane Seymour, other members of the court, "either out of their zeal to Popery, or design to make their fortune,"[160] attacked her reputation. Condemned to death for adultery, Burnet raised the possibility that "there was no legal evidence against the Queen."[161] Her death was fearless, her sufferings unjust. Consequently, neither Elizabeth nor the English Reformation was born of an incestuous union. The descriptive and prescriptive, ideally twain, were truly met.

Protestant England?

How, then, did the increasingly sophisticated historiography of the English Reformation influence English confessional identity? This chapter concludes by analyzing perceptions of Martin Luther and the fluid semantics of "Protestant" in England. Both point to the simple fact that England lacked a clearly defined sense of unity with those other Christian groups now classified as confessionally related. An important factor here is that no one at the time advanced a historical narrative that argued all "Protestant" groups had a shared point of historical origin. The broadly national focus of historical writing on sixteenth-century religious change would have rendered such an approach difficult. In the British Isles, Knox had initiated this process by writing about a discreet reformation in sixteenth-century Scotland, and despite their criticisms of Knox and all that he symbolized, seventeenth-century English historians merely adopted and adapted the same approach to their own kingdom. The title of Burnet's work illustrates the matter perfectly. Whereas Knox entitled his work *The Historie of the Reformation of the Church of Scotland*, Burnet substituted "England" for "Scotland." Reformation was, on each side of the Anglo-Scottish border, a national event rather than the domestic experience of an international transformation.

Consequently, it should not be surprising that English authors in the latter seventeenth century still did not identify Luther as the starting point of English Protestant history. The feature most often mentioned about Luther was not any particular theological doctrine or idea, but his infamous temper.[162] Otherwise, the German Elijah was consistently submerged beneath the broader history of his own times. Several historians followed the interpretation of Herbert of Cherbury, who located a broad revival of knowledge that began in the late fifteenth century. The printing press "had brought in and restored Books and Learning," but had also "been the occasion of those Sects and Schismes which daily appeared in the world,

---

[160] Burnet, *History of the Reformation*, Part I, Book III, p. 198.

[161] Burnet, *History of the Reformation*, Part I, Book III, p. 197.

[162] Herbert of Cherbury, *King Henry the Eighth*, pp. 71, 102; Burnet, *History of the Reformation*, Part II, Book I, p. 104; Edward Stillingfleet, *Several Conferences Between a Romish Priest, a Fanatick Chaplain, and a Divine of the Church of England* (London, 1679; Wing/S5667), p. 119.

but chiefly in *Germany*."[163] As with a number of earlier authors, including but not limited to "Laudians," Herbert saw the Reformation as a mixed good. However novel the interest in the printing press, his interpretation of Luther's import thus tracked with that of earlier decades. Even those more inclined to celebrate the same historical epoch were just as little inclined to find in Luther the inspiration for domestic religious developments. Thomas Sprat similarly located the Reformation within "the *third great Age* of the *flourishing* of *Learning*." The renaissance of knowledge began with "the benefit of *Printing*," which led to an undated sixteenth-century rupture between "the blindness, and stupidity, of the *Roman Fryers*," and "the *Reformation*, which put men upon a stricter inquiry into the Truth of things."[164] Sprat hoped that the Royal Society would arbitrate in natural philosophy just as the Church of England arbitrated in religion, facilitating the need for both open investigation and political stability.[165] His comparison underscores the pervasive presence of Episcopalian historiography within English literary culture, but that same historiography had little place for Luther.

Still other authors made categorical denials of Luther's import, thereby witnessing to the abiding influence of apologetic assumptions first advanced in the early seventeenth century. On the cover page of his 1677 treatise *Origo Protestantium*, the clergyman John Shaw announced his defense of "the Protestant Catholick Religion...wherein PROTESTANCY is demonstrated to be elder than POPERY."[166] Beginning with the Council of Constance and continuing on through the Council of Basel and the Pragmatic Sanction of Bourges, Shaw traced the emergence of "the new *Popish Church*" at the Fifth Lateran Council.[167] The crux of Shaw's historical narrative was apologetic, and located key events before Luther. "Wherefore as the *Papists* frequently, but foolishly propose to us, *Where was your church before* Luther? So we upon the foregoing grounds may more reasonably demand of them, where was your *Popish* Church before *Julius* the Second, and *Leo* the Tenth?"[168] In 1679, Edward Stillingfleet mocked any assumption of Luther's primacy, writing, "it is a foolish thing to imagine that a quarrel between two *Monks* at *Wittemberg* should make such an alteration in the state of *Christendom*."[169] Tracing the origin of religious upheaval long before Luther, Stillingfleet continued, "things had been tending that way a good while before; by the gradual restoration of Learning in these Western parts."[170] He first identified the flight in 1453 of Greek scholars from Constantinople to Italy, which

[163] Herbert of Cherbury, *King Henry the Eighth*, p. 157.
[164] Thomas Sprat, *The History of the Royal-Society of London* (London, 1667; Wing/S5032), p. 22. For a broad analysis of Sprat's work, see John Morgan, "Religious Conventions and Science in the Early Restoration: Reformation and 'Israel' in Thomas Sprat's 'History of the Royal Society' (1667)," *The British Journal for the History of Science*, Vol. 42, No. 3 (Sept., 2009), pp. 321–44.
[165] Sprat, *Royal-Society of London*, p. 371 (mispage as p. 363).
[166] John Shaw, *Origo Protestantium* (London, 1677; Wing/S3032C).
[167] Shaw, *Origo Protestantium*, p. 5.   [168] Shaw, *Origo Protestantium*, p. 8; see also p. 82.
[169] Stillingfleet, *Several Conferences*, p. 116.   [170] Stillingfleet, *Several Conferences*, p. 116.

spurred the increased study of ancient languages in Germany and elsewhere. Two Biblical scholars were singled out for praise, Johann Reuchlin, an expert in both Hebrew and Greek, and Erasmus of Rotterdam, "the Man who awakened mens understandings."[171] The latter was especially important for English religious developments, for "it was not *Luther*, or *Zuinglius* that contributed so much to the Reformation, as *Erasmus*; especially among us in *England*."[172] In academically sophisticated treatises, the fragmentation of Western Christian unity was multi-causal. Reformation existed before—and without—Luther.

One can, however, find a small number of very different perspectives on Luther. After the Restoration, he occasionally appeared in starkly apocalyptic terms. The first instance was in 1664, with the publication of *The Prophecyes of the Incomparable Dr. Martin Luther*,[173] a work reprinted in 1666. A much shorter but similar text, *Dr. Martin Luther's Prophecies*, appeared twice in 1679.[174] Although German Protestants had long ascribed a range of supernatural gifts to Luther, such literature was new in an English context. Yet, four total editions of merely two works hardly indicates a sea change in perception or appreciation. Studying the history of Luther's reputation in the decades after the Restoration thus runs the same risk of confirmation bias noted in Chapter 2, but there do seem to be real, if short-lived, historiographical developments. Peter Heylyn began *Aërius Redivivus*, his heresiological account of Presbyterianism, in the year 1517, "At such time as it pleased God to raise up *Martin Luther*, a Divine of *Saxonie*, to write against the errours and corruptions of the Church of *Rome*."[175] Luther largely faded from the narrative after Heylyn's opening paragraph, but not before Heylyn offered a brief overview of Luther's allegedly patristic theological convictions on the Eucharist and predestination.[176] Like earlier authors, Heylyn knew comparatively little about Luther's own theology, especially on predestination, but even if the opening of *Aërius Redivivus* reveals the continued import of confessional providentialism, after the publication of its second edition in 1672, the work was not reprinted until the nineteenth century.

Equally providential, if more contextually polemical, were discussions of Luther that followed the 1685 accession of James II, England's first Catholic monarch since Mary I. In 1689, Johann Sleidan's *Commentaries* saw its first printing in more than a century, but was republished with the new title *The General History of the Reformation of the Church*. The cover page asserted that this reformation, "from the errors and Corruptions of the Church of Rome," was "begun in

---

[171] Stillingfleet, *Several Conferences*, p. 115.   [172] Stillingfleet, *Several Conferences*, p. 115.
[173] Anonymous, *The Prophecyes of the Incomparable Dr. Martin Luther* (London, 1664; Wing/L3513).
[174] Anonymous, *Dr. Martin Luthers Prophecies* (London, 1679; Wing/L3514).
[175] Peter Heylyn, *Aërius Redivivus* (London, 1672; Wing/H1682), p. 1.
[176] Heylyn, *Aërius Redivivus*, p. 2.

Germany by Martin Luther."[177] Following almost immediately on the heels of the Williamite invasion of 1688, the flight of James II from England appeared as yet another deliverance from Catholicism. And, by that point, a similar perception of Luther's import had become a familiar feature in the popular *Protestant Almanack*. The *Almanack's* front cover had long noted the years that had elapsed since two key dates: "The Incarnation of Jesus Christ" and "Our Deliverance from *Popery* by Queen *Eliz.*" Between these two events, the edition for 1685 added a third, "The Reformation begun by *Luther.*"[178] It might therefore seem that belief in Luther's catalytic import had finally arrived on English shores.

But within just a few years, the same historical description was recast and rewritten. Later editions of *The Protestant Almanack* maintained the dates associated with the incarnation, Luther, and Elizabeth, but progressively included others as well. The 1689 edition added the creation of the world, the gunpowder treason, and the fire of London, and altered its description of Luther to the less sensational claim, "*Martin Luther* wrote against the Pope."[179] That same year the editor, William Winstanley, included his first reference to the evangelization of England, which he dated to the year 190; this was likely a reference to King Lucius, now believed legendary, but whose story was contained in Bede's *Ecclesiastical History*. The date was important for a non-Catholic understanding of the history of English Christianity, as it marginalized the date of the Roman mission that featured so prominently in Bede's work.[180] As the years passed, *The Protestant Almanack* featured an increasingly elaborate calendar of anti-papal events. On the cover of the 1692 edition, Winstanley included "Our Second Deliverance from Popery, by K. *Will* & Q. *Mary*,"[181] and in 1694 added "Our first Deliverance from Popery by K. *Edward* VI,"[182] renumbering the salvific acts under Elizabeth, and William and Mary, accordingly. By the mid-1690s, the front cover of *The Protestant Almanack* recounted a series of deliverances that followed Luther's anti-papal protest, but all underscored a larger narrative point: from its origins to the present, the history of English Christianity was independent of Catholicism. It was chronologically dynamic but ideologically consistent. Revealingly, but again in keeping with habits almost a century old, even warm sentiments toward Luther spurred no surge of interest in his writings. Only two of his works left the English presses between 1660 and 1700, a volume containing excerpts from his

[177] Johannes Sleidanus, *The General History of the Reformation of the Church* (London, 1689; Wing/ S3989).

[178] William Winstanley, *The Protestant Almanack . . . 1685* (London, 1684; Wing/A2229).

[179] William Winstanley, *The Protestant Almanack . . . 1689* (London, 1689; Wing/A2229A).

[180] For a broad overview, see Felicity Heal, "What Can King Lucius Do for You? The Reformation and the Early British Church," *The English Historical Review*, Vol. 120, No. 487 (Jun., 2005), pp. 593–614.

[181] William Winstanley, *The Protestant Almanack . . . 1692* (London, 1692; Wing/A2232).

[182] William Winstanley, *The Protestant Almanack . . . 1694* (London, 1694; Wing/A2234).

commentaries on the Psalms and the First Epistle of Peter,[183] and a sermon on the end times.[184] Like other popular hagiographies, that of England's deliverances from popery took refuge in symbolic appeals to an oftentimes unstudied past. And yet, even here Luther was, more often than not, but one notable figure in a much larger—and much older—history.

The term "Protestant" also failed to unify. Anti-Catholicism was a staple of Anglican apologetics, but it rarely culminated in a conviction of pan-Protestant identity. The historical writings covered in this chapter are a perfect example; they attacked Sanders, but they also attacked domestic dissent. For members of the Church of England, recognizing such groups as confessionally equal would have entailed forgetting, within the space of less than a generation, civil war and its aftermaths. That was unlikely to happen. Pushes for pan-Protestant unity were thus ad hoc, as in the case of the so-called Popish Plot, a conspiracy that began in 1678 and alleged that Catholics were planning to overthrow both king and kingdom. Titus Oates, the principal inventor of the plot, claimed that in 1677, he had learned that Catholics aimed to poison the king, with the hope that James, the king's brother, would inherit the throne and reinstate Catholicism.[185] Catholics would then "Rise and Cut the Throats of 100000. Protestants in *London*."[186] Oates gave his initial testimony before several people, including Sir Edmund Berry Godfrey, a justice of the peace, who was then found murdered that October. Despite the king's own skepticism,[187] Godfrey's death rapidly gave Oates' rumormongering the appearance of truth.

As fears of attempted regicide grew, prescriptively entitled broadsides such as *Protestant Unity* urged the creation of a pan-Protestant defense as "The best Policy to defeat *Popery*, and all its Bloody Practices." According to its opening lines, "Would *England* ever blest and happy be,/It must be done by perfect Unity,/ Let *Protestants* in all things then agree."[188] Here was an attractive message against a shared enemy, and some other contemporary works also urged a speedy resolution to confessional differences.[189] However, even if the Church of England had opened itself to dissenters, there is little reason to believe that the latter would have consistently responded in kind. Just as it was unlikely that Episcopalians would forgive and forget the regicide, it was equally unlikely that nonconformists would suddenly abandon their deeply ingrained habits of apocalyptic invective against episcopacy and liturgy. When faced with the perception of a renewed Catholic threat, divisions and arguments many decades old actually

---

[183] Martin Luther, *A Word in Season* (London 1685; Wing/L3519).
[184] Martin Luther, *The Signs of Christs Coming, and Of the Last Day* (London 1661; Wing/L3516).
[185] Titus Oates, *The Discovery of the Popish Plot* (London, 1679; Wing/O34), p. 2, n. 5.
[186] Oates, *Discovery of the Popish Plot*, p. 24, n. 53.
[187] John Kenyon, *The Popish Plot* (New York: St. Martin's Press, 1972; repr. London: Phoenix Press, 2000), e.g., pp. 85–7, 158.
[188] Anonymous, *Protestant Unity* (London, n.d.; Wing/P3846).
[189] See, e.g., John Humfrey, *The Healing Paper* (London, 1678; Wing/H3680).

returned. In the midst of the Popish Plot, George Fox, the founder of Quakerism, hit out against the Church of England, asking, "you *Protestants*, so called, in other places; how do you call and observe CHRISTMASS Day, CANDLEMASS Day, MICHAELMASS Day, LENT Time, EASTER and WHITSON-Tide, and other the Saints Dayes?"[190] Fox believed that "True Protestants" were "*such as protest against the Pope and the Antichristian Wayes the Papists have set up*,"[191] but unlike the Church of England, Fox understood protest as synonymous with rejection.

In ways that are strange to us today, the meaning of "Protestant" was surprisingly unclear in the last decades of seventeenth-century England. Several authors developed a range of additional terms to try and resolve the confusion. In *Origo Protestantium*, Shaw rendered "Protestant Catholicks" identical with "*English Protestants*," and he distinguished these from "*Puritans*," the latter of whom were defined by "their Principles of *Rebellion* and *Sedition* against the *King*, and their *Schism* against *Bishops*."[192] As the epigraph of the present chapter shows, Roger L'Estrange, censor of the press, added another variation into the mix, distinguishing between the "Reformed Catholique," with whom he identified, and the "True Protestant," whose definition was less clear. "*A Reformed Catholique (properly so called) is an Apostolical Christian, or a Son of the Church of* England: *A true Protestant may* be so too; nay, and many times he *is* so"[193]—but this also suggested that sometimes the "true Protestant" was not. Amidst the Popish Plot, L'Estrange thus cautioned against any plans for Protestant union in England. "Does not our *Saviour* himself tell us that *there shall arise* **False Christs** *and* False Prophets? and why not **False Protestants**?"[194] The "False Protestants" in question were those whom L'Estrange and others termed "Protestant Dissenters." Appealing to the memory of the civil wars, L'Estrange sought to remind his readers that "The *Protestant Dissenters* pretended the same respect for the *King* and *Church*, with the *Royal Party*," but when they thought that popular support would back them, they "took up *Arms against* the *Government*, which they Swore to *Defend*."[195] Shaw had made "English Protestants" synonymous with "Protestant Catholics"; L'Estrange was open to doing the same for "Reformed Catholics" and "True Protestants." Protestant Dissenters, however, could not be trusted. Their religion was as false as their politics.

And such arguments continued on for many more years, even after the Popish Plot was exposed and its fabricators executed. Despite its emphatic clarity, the title

---

[190] George Fox, *Caesar's Due* (London, 1679; Wing/F1753), pp. 31–2.
[191] Fox, *Caesar's Due*, p. 29.   [192] Shaw, *Origo Protestantium*, pp. 53–4.
[193] L'Estrange, *The Reformed Catholique*, pp. 1–2.
[194] L'Estrange, *The Reformed Catholique*, p. 6.
[195] L'Estrange, *The Reformed Catholique*, p. 32.

"True Protestant" resolved nothing. If anything, it only offered up for debate yet another confessional label. Some members of the Church of England were perfectly content to simply abandon the term. The anonymously published 1683 broadside *A True-Protestant-Catechism* defined its subject as "Him that Protesteth against the Abominations of *Popery* and *Tyranny.*" When asked to explain "Popery," the True Protestant spoke of "Conformity to the *Hierarchical* Government and Discipline of the *Church* established by Law"; when asked to define "Tyranny," the True Protestant answered, '"Tis the exercise of *Monarchical Government*, according to the Rights inherent in the Crown, and confirmed by Law."[196] According to the author, True Protestants engaged in "*bloody Villanies*" against a number of people, including "the Sacred Person of the King" and "*Orthodox-Protestants (viz. Church-of-England-men).*"[197] The latter statement, setting "Orthodox-Protestants" against "True Protestants," was not unique in conceding terminological ground to the author's opponents. In 1684, writing against the recently executed regicide theorist Algernon Sidney, the Anglican clergyman William Assheton ascribed all "Anti-Monarchical Tenets" to "the *True-Protestant* PARTY."[198] However, in a mischievous subversion of seemingly set confessional demarcations, Assheton included Catholics, especially Jesuits who justified theories of resistance and regicide, among the True Protestants. When it came to politics, True Protestants could be identified with Catholics, but the Church of England was a third political—and, arguably, confessional—entity.

In the late 1680s, "True Protestant" began to take on a more clearly militant meaning. Shortly after James II came to the throne, there was yet another failed coup against the government. One of the conspirators was Colonel Richard Rumbold, who had served under Oliver Cromwell. From the scaffold, he declared that he had fought for "*Just Rights and Liberties, against Popery and Slavery.*" He also declared that he "*adhered to the True Protestant Religion, detesting the erroneous Opinions of many that called themselves so.*"[199] After 1688, such confessional militancy became central to the literature of "dying speeches," a kind of literary genre in which "True Protestants" were posthumously vindicated through the reproduction of their final words. Rumbold's scaffold speech appeared in 1689 as part of *The Dying Speeches of Several Excellent Persons*, part of a larger push to vindicate nonconformist voices silenced, under whatever circumstances, since the Popish Plot. A follow-up volume, *The Second and Last Collection of the Dying Speeches*, appeared that same year, as did other, thematically identical

---

[196] Anonymous, *A True-Protestant-Catechism* (London, 1683; Wing/T2862), sig. [A] r.

[197] Anonymous, *A True-Protestant-Catechism*, sig. [A] v.

[198] William Assheton, *The Royal Apology* (London, 1684; Wing/A4038); see esp. the comparative chart at p. 60.

[199] Anonymous, *The Dying Speeches of Several Excellent Persons* (London, 1689; Wing/D2957), p. 24.

publications. John Tutchin described his work *A New Martyrology* as "A Compleat History" of "Eminent Martyrs Who fell in the West of England, And elsewhere, From the Year 1678. to 1689."[200] It saw three editions in 1689 alone and a fourth in 1693. As the century closed, there may have been many Protestants in England, but they did not recognize one another as such.

Influential here was the desire of historians, from the 1650s onward, to trace out the sequence of events that culminated in the regicide of Charles I. Genevan and Scottish history loomed large in such explanations, and thereby undercut any sense that Protestants outside the Church of England were inherently trustworthy. Some new arguments rapidly became popular after the Restoration, such as the identification of Presbyterians with the fourth-century heretic Aërius, who denied the authority of bishops.[201] Heylyn's posthumously published *Aërius Redivivus* was the most elaborate genealogy of the alleged Presbyterian revival of Aërian heresy, but the first draft of this new apologetic turn appeared in *Ecclesia Restaurata*. Beginning with liturgical debates in the reign of Edward VI, Heylyn located a line of anti-liturgical and anti-episcopal thought from Zwingli and Calvin through the Marian exiles to the Elizabethan Puritans.[202] Calvin came off quite badly, as an embittered egotist who, having been ignored by Archbishop Cranmer, sought to ingratiate himself with the Edwardian council.[203] In Heylyn's words, Calvin, "thinking nothing to be well done, which either was not done by him, or by his Direction … must needs be meddling in such matters as belonged not to him."[204] Because of Calvin, there was "a continual multiplying of Disorders in all Parts of this Church."[205] *Aërius Redivivus* further elaborated the same story. However, "Laudians" had no monopoly on such claims. Daniel Featley, the Oxford heads, and John Sudbury each made the same identification,[206] and John Gauden went one step further by comparing Presbyterians with not just Aërianism but Islam.[207] Polemical refinement vindicated, rather than altered, the received historiographical consensus. The conclusion of Burnet's *History*, although written in the early 1680s, simply repeated historiographical orthodoxy. Calvin urged "a more compleat Reformation" during Edward's reign,[208] and under the influence of Knox, "a Man of hot temper," Calvin later wrote "somewhat sharply of some things in the *English* Service." In sum, "they began the Breach,

---

[200] John Tutchin, *A New Martyrology* (London, 1689; Wing/T3379).

[201] Aërius is different from Arius, who also lived in the fourth century, but who denied the divinity of Christ.

[202] Heylyn, *Ecclesia Restaurata*, e.g., pp. 78–80.

[203] Heylyn, *Ecclesia Restaurata*, pp. 65, 79–80.   [204] Heylyn, *Ecclesia Restaurata*, p. 80.

[205] Heylyn, *Ecclesia Restaurata*, p. 93.

[206] Featley, *The League Illegal*, pp. 29, 52, 58; The University of Oxford, *Reasons*, pp. 8–9; Sudbury, *A Sermon*, p. 9.

[207] Gauden, *A Pillar of Gratitude*, pp. 32 (Aerianism), 33 (Islam).

[208] Burnet, *History of the Reformation*, Part II, Book I, p. 88.

who departed from that way of Worship, which they acknowledged was both lawful and good." Burnet conceded that "there followed too much animosity on both sides, which were the Seeds of all those differences that have since distracted this Church,"[209] but it is more important that he too laid blame at the feet of Calvin, Knox, and their associates. In this, he was hardly alone.

[209] Burnet, *History of the Reformation*, Part II, Book II, p. 339.

Conclusion

> What is decisive is not to get out of the circle [of understanding], but
> to get into it in the right way.
>
> Martin Heidegger (1927)[1]

To briefly summarize the present volume, "reformation" changed meaning between the fifteenth and seventeenth centuries. Church councils from Constance to Trent aspired to the *reformatio* of Latin Christendom's entire ecclesial body. But as local schism became enduring reality, reformation "by force of arms" emerged as a central goal in Scotland. Consequently, the label "Scottish Reformation" did not originally denote the domestic experience of an international event, much less one led by Luther, but the local success of an apocalyptic rebellion. A century later, the wholly derivative label "English Reformation" entered the historical lexicon as an apologetic argument intended to justify the Church of England against its Scottish opponents and their English sympathizers. We today are the heirs of this historiographical shift, and we have largely taken its descriptive accuracy for granted. But to repeat a point made in the Introduction, if the opponents of Charles I had succeeded, the term "English Reformation" would likely denote the outcome of the religious strife that pervaded the 1640s, rather than the mid-sixteenth century. Because "The English Reformation" denotes mid-Tudor rather than mid-Stuart religious history, it is an inescapably Anglican historiographical category. But how does all of this apply to the broader field of Reformation studies? We are not autonomous knowers, directly studying the past from a privileged or superior vantage point in the present. We are instead embedded inquirers, studying a past "always already" framed and re-framed by the interpretive work of earlier generations.[2] To again quote Herbert Butterfield, "History is not the study of origins; rather it is the analysis of all the mediations by which the past was turned into our present."[3] In now concluding this volume, I propose, in Baconian fashion, several new avenues for historical study. These will neither remove us from nor elevate us above

---

[1] Martin Heidegger, *Being and Time*, trans. Joan Stambaugh, rev. Dennis J. Schmidt (Albany: State University of New York Press, 2010), p. 148.

[2] The phrase "always already" appears throughout Heidegger's *Being and Time*.

[3] Herbert Butterfield, *The Whig Interpretation of History* (New York and London: W.W. Norton & Company, 1965), p. 47.

How the English Reformation was Named: The Politics of History, c. 1400-1700. Benjamin M. Guyer, Oxford University Press. © Benjamin M. Guyer 2022. DOI: 10.1093/oso/9780192865724.003.0007

inherited historiographical norms, but will instead provide new possibilities for inquiry and thus—inescapably partial—understanding.

Beyond Pietist Mythology

At a popular level—whether among scholars, within a given church, or in society at large—sixteenth-century religious change is often interpreted through the multifaceted prism of a pious Protestant mythology. The standard narrative positions 1517 as a watershed year because Martin Luther, according to later and possibly legendary sources,[4] nailed up his Ninety-Five Theses that October. However, I have given no place to this supposedly historical account. Nor have I repeated the popular variant of a Bible-centric reformation, in which Luther played the role of catalyst. Still other mythologies, such as the priesthood of all believers, have been absent from my analysis.[5] And, at no point have I used the hagiographically endearing but historically misleading phrase "the Reformers" to denote an evangelical collective comprised of figures who, in their own lifetimes, sometimes excommunicated one another. To be blunt, we need to set aside such pietist mythology. I suspect that the (purportedly) non-confessional historiography of our own day has unquestioningly accepted an interpretive framework that owes its existence to the prescriptive confessional projects of past generations of hagiographers and heresiologists (who, perhaps ironically, agree on the import of 1517). Although Luther influenced some sixteenth-century religious developments, this is different from how those changes were later historiographically conceptualized.

Going forward, we need to continue uprooting pietist mythology, replacing it with studies of how the vocabulary of *reformatio* was used and disseminated elsewhere in fifteenth- through seventeenth-century Latin Christendom. If Luther did not define references to "reformation," whether during or after his own lifetime, why should he define our own analyses of the same broad time period?

A Long Fifteenth Century

There is a more contextually sensitive approach to the Reformation that notes "reform" movements in the century or so before Luther (although it is not generally shown that these movements described themselves with the term

---

[4] This is thoroughly analyzed in Peter Marshall, *1517: Martin Luther and the Invention of the Reformation* (Oxford: Oxford University Press, 2017).

[5] For an introduction to this problem, see Timothy J. Wengert, "The Priesthood of All Believers and Other Pious Myths." *Institute of Liturgical Studies Occasional Papers* No. 117 (2006). Available online: https://scholar.valpo.edu/ils_papers/117, accessed January 20, 2022. No doubt more work needs to be done.

"reform"). Thus "great men" (or, "great heretics") such as Wyclif, Hus, Savonarola, and Erasmus are portrayed as having unwittingly (or, in the case of Hus, prophetically) laid the groundwork for the German Hercules. One finds elements of this approach in Foxe's *Actes and Monuments*, but the clearest and most concise such statement is probably Beza's *Icones*. I have also dispensed with this narrative because accepting it wholly concedes historical understanding to the confessional projects of various sixteenth-century protagonists.

Going forward, we need to approach fifteenth-century history not as a prelude to Luther or the so-called Protestant Reformation. Rather, if we are concerned with how contemporaries spoke, it should be accepted that councils were the primary locus for discussions and debates about *reformatio*. For Catholics, this remained so after Trent, but even among evangelicals, no one believed that "reformation" was the work of isolated individuals. Furthermore, councils were sometimes massive international events, perhaps even the largest international events of their day. If we want an accurate understanding of that fractious but still influential time period, is it not imperative that we return councils to the central place that they occupied in the social imaginary of "early modern" Europeans?

International Historiographies

The present volume ends just before 1688. In British history, 1688 is important because of the Williamite invasion, subsequently known as the Glorious Revolution. However, 1688 is also important because it saw the publication of the first volume of Veit Ludwig von Seckendorff's *Commentarius Historicus et Apologeticus de Luthernismo sive De Reformatione Religionis Ductu D. Martini Lutheri* (*The Historical and Apologetic Commentary on Lutheranism, or, On the Reformation of Religion Led by Dr. Martin Luther*). On the off chance that it is mentioned today, von Seckendorff's study, which he completed in 1692, is accepted as the point of historiographical demarcation that gave us the Luther-centric narrative now so familiar.[6] Thus the historiography of the Reformation began in the same place as the Reformation itself, among the followers of the German Elijah.

But there is little reason to privilege von Seckendorff this way. In his prologue, he referenced the *Acta Eruditorum* (roughly "Philosophical Transactions"), a German academic journal.[7] Its August 1684 issue contained a review of

---

[6] John W. O'Malley, *Trent and All That: Renaming Catholicism in the Early Modern Era* (Cambridge: Harvard University Press, 2000), p. 19; C. Scott Dixon, *Contesting the Reformation* (Malden and Oxford: Wiley-Blackwell, 2012), p. 9.
[7] For a general overview, see Augustinus Hubertus Laeven, *The "Acta eruditorum" under the Editorship of Otto Mencke (1644–1707): The History of an International Learned Journal between 1682 and 1707*, trans. Lynne Richards (Amsterdam and Maarssen: APA-Holland University Press, 1990).

Jean-Baptiste de Rosemond's 1683 translation of Burnet's *History of the Reformation of the Church of England*.[8] As von Seckendorff explained the apologetic impetus behind his own historical research, he made a passing comment to that review. "I also remember that I read some excellent things about the *Historia Anglica*, edited and annotated by Dr. Burnet, on page 383 of the 1684 *Leipzig Philosophical Transactions*."[9] It may seem like little, but it reveals not only that von Seckendorff was following rather than initiating a trend but that the trend in question partially developed because of earlier British writings about religious reformation.

Going forward, we need to analyze the international dissemination of the histories of local reformations—recognizing, of course, that the histories in question need to explicitly name the events they describe as "reformation." Burnet's work, for example, was later translated into Latin, which made it fully accessible to an international audience.[10] Did Burnet's historiography inspire others, such as von Seckendorff, to look into their own local history and find seemingly analogous events that they, too, then termed "reformation"? More broadly, what if "The Protestant Reformation" developed as a historiographical category not out of local, sixteenth-century adaptations of Luther's soteriological ideas, but from the dissemination and concatenation of diverse national histories fundamentally concerned with adjudicating competing domestic notions of right *reformatio* in the absence of an ecumenical council (or at least, one accepted as such)?

Ending a Chapter of British Historiography

For a generation now, British scholarship has often alleged a "Laudian" revolt against sixteenth-century religious developments and thus the "Protestant"—specifically, Reformed—heritage of England's episcopal church. The chapters in this volume problematize these claims. So-called "Laudians" like Heylyn were among the first to compose histories of the English Reformation, an event that they not only codified but also then defended. However, the ambivalent attachment of many English to sixteenth-century religious history began before "Laudianism." It originated as a defensive maneuver against the apocalyptic threats and sometimes violence wrought by domestic religious dissent—dissent that contemporaries traced, most immediately, to Scotland. In truth, "Laudians" had no monopoly on conflicted analyses of Tudor religious change.

---

[8] Gilbert Burnet, *Histoire de la Reformation de l'Eglise d'Angleterre*, trans. Jean-Baptiste de Rosemond (London, 1683; Wing/B5795).

[9] Veit Ludwig von Seckendorff, *Commentarius Historicus et Apologeticus de Luthernismo sive de reformatione religionis ductu D. Martini Lutheri* (Frankfurt and Leipzig, 1688), sig. b v: "memini etiam tale aliqvid in *Actis Eruditorum Lipsiensibus 1684. p. 383.* ex Historia Anglica a D. Burneto edita annotatum legi."

[10] Gilbert Burnet, *Historia Reformationis Ecclesiae Anglicanae*, trans. Melchior Mittelholzer (Geneva, 1686).

Early eighteenth-century historical publications further bear this out. White Kennett's *A Complete History of England* (1706), which rapidly saw five printings and, in 1719, a new edition,[11] depended quite heavily upon the early Stuart historiography of Tudor England. Kennett reprinted Herbert of Cherbury's history of Henry VIII, used John Hayward's work to cover the reign of Edward VI, excerpted Francis Godwin's discussion of Mary I from the *Annales*, and republished William Camden's study of Elizabeth I. Writing before the "English Reformation" was developed and accepted as a historiographical framework, these four early Stuart authors do not fit the assumed ideological division between "Laudian" and non-"Laudian" approaches to the mid-sixteenth century, but all transmitted to their readers skepticism about the value of Tudor religious change.

Going forward, it is of no descriptive worth to denigrate as "myth" what was, in fact, the first generation of a now-familiar, and long-enduring line of confessional apologetic-cum-historical inquiry. For what is any academic history but well-sourced mythology?

---

[11] Laird Okie, "Kennett, White (1660–1728), historian and bishop of Peterborough," *ODNB*.

Bibliography

Abbreviations

BHO *British History Online.* Available online: https://www.british-history.ac.uk.

CWE Erasmus of Rotterdam. *Collected Works of Erasmus.* Ed. and trans. various. Toronto: University of Toronto Press, 1974–Present.

DEC Norman P. Tanner, S.J. (ed.). *Decrees of the Ecumenical Councils.* 2 Vols. London: Sheed & Ward and Washington, DC: Georgetown University Press, 1990.

FLE Richard Hooker. *The Folger Library Edition of the Works of Richard Hooker.* Ed. W. Speed Hill. 7 Vols. Vols. 1–5, Cambridge: Belknap Press of Harvard University Press, 1977–90; Vols. 6–7, Tempe: Medieval & Renaissance Texts & Studies, 1993–98.

LW Martin Luther. *Luther's Works.* Ed. Jaroslav Pelikan and Helmut T. Lehmann. St. Louis: Concordia Publishing and Philadelphia: Augsburg Fortress Press, 1958–Present.

ODNB *Oxford Dictionary of National Biography.* Oxford: Oxford University Press. Available online: https://www.oxforddnb.com.

ST Thomas Aquinas. *Summa Theologiae.* 61 Vols. Trans. The English Province of the Order of Preachers. Cambridge: Cambridge University Press, 1964–81.

Printed Sources

Adamson, John. *The Noble Revolt: The Overthrow of Charles I.* London: Weidenfeld & Nicolson, 2007.

J.A. of Ailward. *An Historicall Narration of the Iudgement of Some Most Learned and Godly English Bishops, Holy Martyrs, and Others.* London, 1631; STC 4.

Alford, Stephen. *Kingship and Politics in the Reign of Edward VI.* Cambridge: Cambridge University Press, 2002.

Amos, Andrew. *Observations on the Statutes of the Reformation Parliament in the Reign of King Henry the Eighth.* London: V. & R. Stevens, & G.S. Norton and Cambridge: Deighton, Bell and Co., 1859.

Anonymous. *The Anatomy of Dr. Gauden's Idolized Non-sence and Blasphemy.* London, 1660; Wing/A3055.

Anonymous. *An Apology for Bishops.* London, 1641; Wing/A3543.

Anonymous. *The Beast is Wounded.* Amsterdam, 1638; STC 22032.5.

Anonymous. *A Briefe Discovrse, Declaring the Impiety and Unlawfulnesse of the New Covenant with the Scots.* Oxford, 1643; Wing/B4580.

Anonymous. *A Brief View and Defence of the Reformation of the Church of England by King Edward and Q. Elizabeth.* London, 1654; Wing/B4655.

Anonymous. *A Short View and Defence of the Reformation of the Church of England by King Edward and Q. Elizabeth.* London, 1654; Wing/S3638.

Anonymous. *A Declaration of the Presbiterians*. London, 1660; Wing/D739.

Anonymous. *A Door of Hope*. London, 1661; Wing/D1908.

Anonymous. *Dr. Martin Luthers Prophecies*. London, 1679; Wing/L3514.

Anonymous. *The Dvke of Saxonie His Ivbilee*. London, 1618; STC 14656.

Anonymous. *The Dying Speeches of Several Excellent Persons*. London, 1689; Wing/D2957.

Anonymous. *The Famous Tragedie of the Life and Death of M^{ris} Rump*. London, 1660; Wing/F385A.

Anonymous. *The First and Large Petition of the Citie of London*. London, 1641; Wing/F973.

Anonymous. *Good Newes from the Assembly in Scotland*. London, 1642; Wing/G1069A.

Anonymous. *The Grand Rebels Detected*. London, 1660; Wing/G1511.

Anonymous. *The Iniqvity of the Late Solemn League, or Covenant Discovered*. London, 1643; Wing/I190.

Anonymous. *Mar-Martin*. London, 1589; STC 17461.5.

Anonymous. *Newes from Powles, Or the New Reformation of the Army*. London, 1649; Wing/N990.

Anonymous. *A Paraphrase Vppon the Epistle of the Holie Apostle S. Paule to the Romanes*. London, 1572; STC 19137.5.

Anonymous. *The Prophecyes of the Incomparable Dr. Martin Luther*. London, 1664; Wing/L3513.

Anonymous. *Protestant Unity*. London, n.d.; Wing/P3846.

Anonymous. *Reasons Shewing the Necessity of Reformation*. London, 1660; Wing/B5678.

Anonymous. *Reformation Or, The Progress Thereof in Some Foot-steps of it in The Congregational Way of Churches in England, from the Year of Our Lord, 1640*. London, 1659; Wing/R743A.

Anonymous. *The Rumps Last Will & Testament*. London, 1660; Wing/P106.

Anonymous. *The Scots Policie: To Assassinate Our English Monarchy*. London, 1647; Wing/S2029.

Anonymous. *The Scots Treacherous Designes Discovered*. London, 1647; Wing/S2030.

Anonymous. *A Solemn Exhortation*. London, 1649; Wing/S4440.

Anonymous. *A True-Protestant-Catechism*. London, 1683; Wing/T2862.

Anonymous. *The Vntrussing of Above One Hundred Popish Points*. London, 1642; Wing/U103.

Anonymous. *Women Will Have Their Will, Or Give Christmas His Due*. London, 1649; Wing/W3327.

Anonymous. *Worse & Worse*. London, 1643; Wing/W3611.

Anonymous [Cornelius Burges?]. *Reasons Shewing the Necessity of Reformation*. London, 1660; Wing/B5678.

Anonymous [Zachary Crofton?]. *The Scotch Covenant Newly Revived*. London, 1661; Wing/C7002.

Anonymous [Zachary Crofton?]. *Certaine Scrvples and Doubts of Conscience about Taking the Solemn League and Covenant*. London, 1660; Wing/G346.

Anonymous [William Whittingham?]. *A Brieff Discours off the Troubles Begonne at Franckford*. Heidelberg[?], 1574; STC 25442.

Appleby, David J. *Black Bartholomew's Day: Preaching, Polemic and Restoration Nonconformity*. Manchester: Manchester University Press, 2007.

Aquinas, Thomas. "The treatise 'De regimine principum' or 'De regno'." In R.W. Dyson (ed.). *Aquinas: Political Writings*. Cambridge: Cambridge University Press, 2002, pp. 5–52.

Arand, Charles P., Robert Kolb, and James A. Nestingen. *The Lutheran Confessions: History and Theology of the Book of Concord*. Minneapolis: Fortress Press, 2012.

Armitage, David. *The Ideological Origins of the British Empire*. Cambridge: Cambridge University Press, 2000.

Assheton, William. *The Royal Apology*. London, 1684; Wing/A4038.

Aston, Thomas. *A Collection of Sundry Petitions*. London, 1642; Wing/A4073.

Atherton, Ian. "Cathedrals, Laudianism, and the British Churches." *The Historical Journal*, Vol. 53, No. 4 (Dec., 2010), pp. 895–918.

Bacon, Francis. *The History and Reign of King Henry the Seventh*. Ed. Jerry Weinberger. Ithaca and London: Cornell University Press, 1996.

Bagwell, Richard. "Ram, Thomas (1564–1634), Church of Ireland bishop of Ferns and Leighlin." Revised by Alan Ford. *ODNB*. Accessed 17 May 2021.

Baker, Keith Michael. *Inventing the French Revolution: Essays on French Political Culture in the Eighteenth Century*. Cambridge: Cambridge University Press, 1990.

Bale, John. *The Vocacyon of Iohan Bale*. Rome [Wesel?], 1553; STC 1307.

Bale, John (ed.). *The True Historie of the Christen Departynge of the Reuerende Man D. Martyne Luther*. Wesel, 1546; STC 14717.

Bancroft, Richard. *Davngerovs Positions and Proceedings*. London, 1593; STC 1344.5.

Bancroft, Richard. *Dangerous Positions and Proceedings*. London, 1640; STC 1345.

Baret, John. *An Aluearie or Triple Dictionarie*. London, 1574; STC 1410.

Barlow, William. *The Svmme and Svbstance of the Conference*. London, 1604; STC 1456.5.

Barlow, William. *The Summe and Substance of the Conference*. London, 1661; Wing/B847.

Barnett, S.J. "Where Was Your Church before Luther? Claims for the Antiquity of Protestantism Examined." *Church History*, Vol. 68, No. 1 (Mar., 1999), pp. 14–41.

Bately, Janet. "Cawdrey, Robert (b. 1537/8?, d. in or after 1604), Church of England Clergyman and Lexicographer." *ODNB*. Accessed 17 May 2021.

Baxter, Richard. *The Safe Religion*. London, 1657; Wing/B1381.

Baxter, Richard. *The Grand Debate Between the Most Reverend the Bishops, and the Presbyterian Divines*. London, 1661; Wing/B1278A and E3841.

Baxter, Richard. *A Petition for Peace with the Reformation of the Liturgy*. London, 1661; Wing/B1342.

Baxter, Richard. *Full and Easie Satisfaction*. London, 1674; Wing/B1272.

Beall, Stephen M. and John J. Schmitt (eds. and trans.). *Libellus: Addressed to Leo X, Supreme Pontiff*. Milwaukee: Marquette University Press, 2016.

Bedford, Thomas. *Luthers Predecessours: Or an Answere to the Qvestion of the Papists: Where was your Church before Luther?* London, 1624; STC 1787.

Beer, Barrett L. *Rebellion & Riot: Popular Disorder in England during the Reign of Edward VI*. Rev. ed. Kent: The Kent State University Press, 2005.

Bellitto, Christopher M. *Nicolas de Clamanges: Spirituality, Personal Reform, and Pastoral Renewal on the Eve of the Reformation*. Washington, DC: The Catholic University of America Press, 2001.

Bellitto, Christopher M. "The Reform Context of the Great Western Schism." In Joëlle Rollo-Koster and Thomas M. Izbicki (eds.). *A Companion to the Great Western Schism (1378–1417)*. Leiden: Brill, 2009, pp. 303–31.

Bennett, Henry (ed. and trans.). *A Famous and Godly History*. London, 1561; STC 1881.

Bernard, G.W. "The Dissolution of the Monasteries." *History*, Vol. 96, No. 4 (324) (Oct., 2011), pp. 390–409.

Bernard, G.W. *The Late Medieval English Church: Vitality and Vulnerability before the Break with Rome*. New Haven and London: Yale University Press, 2012.

Bernard, G.W. "Henry VIII: 'Catholicism without the Pope?'" *History*, Vol. 101, No. 2 (345) (Apr., 2016), pp. 201–21.

Bernard, Richard. *Looke Beyond Luther*. London, 1623; STC 1956.7.

Beza, Theodore. *Novum Testamentum*. Henricus Stephanus, 1565.

Beza, Theodore. *A Confession of Fayth*. London, 1568; STC 23554.

The Bible: Authorized King James Version with Apocrypha. Ed. Robert Carroll and Stephen Prickett. Oxford: Oxford University Press. 1997.

Bierma, Lyle D. "The Sources and Theological Orientation of the Heidelberg Catechism." In Lyle D. Bierma (ed.). *An Introduction to the Heidelberg Catechism: Sources, History, and Theology*. Grand Rapids: Baker Academic, 2005, pp. 75–102.

Bierma, Lyle D. (ed.). *An Introduction to the Heidelberg Catechism: Sources, History, and Theology*. Grand Rapids: Baker Academic, 2005.

Bietenholz, Peter G. *Historia and Fabula: Myths and Legends in Historical Thought from Antiquity to the Modern Age*. Leiden: Brill, 1994.

Black, A.J. *Monarchy and Community: Political Ideas in the Later Conciliar Controversy 1430–1450*. Cambridge: Cambridge University Press, 1970.

Black, Joseph L. (ed.). *The Martin Marprelate Tracts: A Modernized and Annotated Edition*. Cambridge: Cambridge University Press, 2008.

Black, Robert. "The Donation of Constantine: A New Source for the Concept of the Renaissance?" In Alison Brown (ed.). *Language and Images of Renaissance Italy*. Oxford: Clarendon Press, 1995, pp. 51–85.

Blakeway, Amy. "The Anglo-Scottish War of 1558 and the Scottish Reformation." *History*, Vol. 102, No. 1 (350) (Apr., 2017), pp. 201–24.

Blumenfeld-Kosinski, Renate. *Poets, Saints, and Visionaries of the Great Schism, 1378–1417*. University Park: The Pennsylvania State University Press, 2006.

Blumenthal, Uta-Renate. *The Investiture Controversy: Church and Monarchy from the Ninth to the Twelfth Century*. Philadelphia: University of Pennsylvania Press, 1988.

Boughen, Edward. *An Account of the Church Catholick*. London, 1653; Wing/B3812.

Bradstock, Andrew. *Radical Religion in Cromwell's England: A Concise History from the English Civil War to the End of the Commonwealth*. London and New York: I.B. Tauris, 2011.

Brady, Thomas A., Jr. *German Histories in the Age of Reformations, 1400–1650*. Cambridge: Cambridge University Press, 2009.

Bramhall, John. *A Fair Warning, to Take Heed of the Scottish Discipline*. London, 1649; Wing/B4222, B4223, B4223A, B4223B.

Bramhall, John. *A Faire Warning for England to Take Heed of the Presbyterian Government of Scotland*. London, 1660/1661; Wing/B4220.

Bramhall, John. *Three Treatises Concerning the Scotish Discipline*. London, 1661; Wing/T1122.

Brammall, Kathryn. "Monstrous Metamorphosis: Nature, Morality, and the Rhetoric of Monstrosity in Tudor England." *The Sixteenth Century Journal*, Vol. 27, No. 1 (Spring, 1996), pp. 3–21.

Bray, Gerald (ed.). *The Anglican Canons, 1529–1947*. Woodbridge and Rochester: The Boydell Press, 1998.

Bray, Gerald (ed.). *Tudor Church Reform: The Henrician Canons of 1535 and the Reformatio Legum Ecclesiasticarum*. Woodbridge and Rochester: The Boydell Press, 2000.

Bray, Gerald (ed.). *The Books of Homilies: A Critical Edition*. Cambridge: James Clarke & Co. Ltd., 2015.

Bray, Gerald (ed.). *The Institution of a Christian Man*. Cambridge: James Clarke and Co., 2018.

Brightman, Thomas. *Reverend Mr. Brightmans Iudgement*. London, 1642; Wing/B4684A.

Brooke, Christopher. "Cambridge in the Age of the Puritan Revolution." In Victor Morgan, with Christopher Brooke. *A History of the University of Cambridge, Vol. 2: 1546–1750*. Cambridge: Cambridge University Press, 2004, pp. 464–82.

Brouncker, Edward. *The Curse of Sacriledge*. Oxford, 1630; STC 1025.

Brown, Keith M. "The Reformation Parliament." In Keith M. Brown and Roland J. Tanner (eds.). *The History of the Scottish Parliament, Vol. 1: Parliament and Politics in Scotland, 1235–1560*. Edinburgh: Edinburgh University Press, 2004, pp. 203–31.

Browne, Robert. *A Booke which Sheweth the Life and Manners of all True Christians*. Middelburgh, 1582; STC 3910.3.

Brydon, Michael. *The Evolving Reputation of Richard Hooker: An Examination of Responses 1600–1714*. Oxford: Oxford University Press, 2006.

Buck, Lawrence P. "'Anatomia Antichristi': Form and Content of the Papal Antichrist." *The Sixteenth Century Journal*, Vol. 42, No. 2 (Summer, 2011), pp. 349–68.

Buck, Lawrence P. *The Roman Monster: An Icon of the Papal Antichrist in Reformation Polemics*. Kirksville: Truman State University Press, 2014.

Buckeridge, John. *A Sermon Preached before His Majeistie… Touching Prostration, and Kneeling in the Worship of God*. London, 1618; STC 4005.

Burnet, Gilbert. *The History of the Reformation of the Church of England*. London, 1681; Wing/B5798.

Burnet, Gilbert. *Histoire de la Reformation de l'Eglise d'Angleterre*. Trans. Jean-Baptiste de Rosemond. London, 1683; Wing/B5795.

Burnet, Gilbert. *Historia Reformationis Ecclesiae Anglicanae*. Trans. Melchior Mittelholzer. Geneva, 1686.

Burnett, Amy Nelson. "The Social History of Communion and the Reformation of the Eucharist." *Past & Present*, No. 211 (May, 2011), pp. 77–119.

Burns, J.H. *Lordship, Kingship and Empire: The Idea of Monarchy 1400–1525*. Oxford: Clarendon Press, 1992.

Burns, J.H. and Thomas Izbicki (eds. and trans.). *Conciliarism and Papalism*. Cambridge: Cambridge University Press, 1997.

Burton, Henry. *A Tryall of Priuate Devotions*. London, 1628; STC 4157.

Burton, Henry. *For God, and the King*. Amsterdam, 1636; STC 4142.

Butterfield, Herbert. *The Whig Interpretation of History*. New York and London: W.W. Norton & Company, 1965.

Calderwood, David. *Perth Assembly*. Leiden, 1619; STC 4360.

Calderwood, David. *A Solvtion of Doctor Resolvtvs, His Resolvtions for Kneeling*. Amsterdam, 1619; STC 4364.

Calderwood, David. *A Defence of Our Arguments Against Kneeling*. Amsterdam, 1620; STC 4354.

Calderwood, David. *The Speach of the Kirk of Scotland to her Beloved Children*. Amsterdam, 1620; STC 4365.

Calderwood, David. *The Re-Examination of the Two Articles Abridged*. Netherlands, 1636; STC 4363.5.

Calvin, John. *A Faythful and Moost Godlye Treatyse*. London, 1548; STC 4409.5–4412.

Calvin, John. *An Epistle*. London, 1550; STC 4408.

Calvin, John. *Institutes of the Christian Religion*. 2 Vols. Ed. John T. McNeill. Louisville and London: Westminster John Knox Press, 1960.

Calvin, John et al. *Consensio Mutua in Re Sacramentaria.* Tiguri ex Officina Rodolphi Vuissenbachii, 1551[?].

Camden, William. *Annales Or, the History of the Most Renowned and Victorious Princesse Elizabeth.* London, 1635; STC 4501.

Campbell, Gordon. *Bible: The Story of the King James Version.* Oxford: Oxford University Press, 2010.

Campi, Emidio. "The Consensus Tigurinus: origins, assessment, and impact." *Reformation & Renaissance Review,* Vol. 18, No. 1 (Mar., 2016), pp. 5–24.

Campi, Emidio. "The Myth of the Reformation." In Jan Stievermann and Randall C. Zachman (eds.). *Multiple Reformations? The Many Faces and Legacies of the Reformation.* Tübingen: Mohr Siebeck, 2018, pp. 95–104.

Camporeale, Salvatore I. "Lorenzo Valla's 'Oratio' on the Pseudo-Donation of Constantine: Dissent and Innovation in Early Renaissance Humanism." *Journal of the History of Ideas,* Vol. 57, No. 1 (Jan., 1996), pp. 9–26.

Canning, Joseph. *Ideas of Power in the Late Middle Ages 1296–1417.* Cambridge: Cambridge University Press, 2011.

Capern, Amanda L. "New Perspectives on the English Reformation." *Journal of Religious History,* Vol. 33, No. 2 (Jun., 2009), pp. 235–53.

Carbonnier-Burkard, Marianne. "Reformation Jubilees: A Protestant Construction." In Petra Bosse-Huber, Serge Fornerod, Thies Gundlach, and Gottfried Locher (eds.). *Reformation: Legacy and Future.* Geneva: World Council of Churches Publications, 2015, pp. 183–96.

Carleton, Dudley. *The Speech of Sir Dvdly Carlton.* London, 1618; STC 4629.

Carleton, George. *An Examination of . . . the Doctrines of the Church of England.* London, 1626; STC 4633.

Caxton, William. *Polychronicon.* London, 1482; STC 13438.

Cawdry, Robert. *A Table Alphabeticall.* London, 1609; STC 4884.5.

Champion, J.A.I. *The Pillars of Priestcraft Shaken: The Church of England and its enemies 1660–1730.* Cambridge: Cambridge University Press, 1992.

Charles I. *By the King.* Edinburgh, 1626; STC 21970.

Charles I. *A Proclamation for the Establishing of the Peace and Quiet of the Church of England.* London, 1626; STC 8824.

Charles I. *A Proclamation for the Better Execution of the Office of His Maiesties Exchanger, and Reformation of Sundry Abuses and Fraudes Practised vpon his Maiesties Coyness.* London, 1627; STC 8860.

Charles I. *His Majesties Proclamation in Scotland.* London, 1639; STC 22001.5.

Charles I. *A True Copy of His Maiesties Letter.* London, 1642; Wing/C2837.

Charles I. *Proclamation Forbidding the Tendring or Taking of a Late Covenant, Called, A Solemn League and Covenant for Reformation, &c.* Oxford, 1643; Wing/C2658.

Charles I. *Eikon Basilike.* London, 1649; Wing/E304.

Charles I. *Eikon Basilike.* La Haye [The Hague], 1649; Thomason/E.1255[1].

Charles I. *King Charles the 1st's Defence of the Church of England.* The Hague, 1649; Wing/ C2291A.

Charles I. *The Kings Majesties Answer . . . Concerning Church-government.* London, 1660; Wing/C2126.

Charles I. *The Golden Apophthegms of His Royall Maiesty.* London, 1660; Wing/G1012.

Charles I. *His Majesties Finall Answer.* London, 1660; Wing/C2307.

Charles I. *Effata Regalia.* London, 1661; Wing/C2302.

Charles I. *His Majesties Reason.* London, 1661; Wing/C2739.

Charles I. *Basilika*. London, 1662; Wing/C2075 and 2157C.

Charles I. *Eikon Basilike*. Ed. Jim Daems and Holly Faith Nelson. Ontario: Broadview Editions, 2006.

Charles I and Alexander Henderson. *The Papers Which Passed at New-Castle*. London, 1649; Wing/C2535.

Charles I and Alexander Henderson. *The Papers Which Passed at New-Castle*. The Hague, 1649; Wing/C2154.

Herbert of Cherbury. *The Life and Raigne of King Henry the Eighth*. London, 1649; Wing/H1504.

The Church of England. *Articles Devised by the Kynges Highnes Maiestie*. London, 1536; STC 10033.6.

The Church of England. *Orarium*. London, 1546; STC 16042.

The Church of England. *The Order of Communion*. London, 1548; STC 16457.

The Church of England. *Articles*. London, 1553; STC 10034.

The Church of England. *Catechismus Breuis*. London, 1553; STC 4808.

The Church of England. *The Primer*. London, 1559; STC 16087.

The Church of England. *Orarium*. London, 1560; STC 16089.

The Church of England. *Preces Privatae*. London, 1564; STC 20378.

The Church of England. *Constitvtions and Canons Ecclesiasticall*. London, 1604; STC 10070.

The Church of England. *Liber Precvm Pvblicarvm*. Oxford, 1660; Wing/O922M and O992N.

The Church of England. *The Book of Common Prayer*. London, 1660; Wing/B3615–B3617, B3619; London, 1661; Wing/B3620A–B3621; London, 1662; Wing/B3622, B3622A–B3625.

The Church of Ireland. *Constitvtions and Canons Ecclesiasticall*. Dublin, 1635; STC 14265.

The Church of Scotland. *Confessio Fidei et Doctrinae per Ecclesiam Reformatam Regni Scotiae Professe*. Andreapoli, 1572; STC 22028.

The Church of Scotland. *Canons and Constitvtions Ecclesiasticall*. Aberdeen, 1636; STC 22055.

The Church of Scotland. *The Booke of Common Prayer*. Edinburgh, 1637; STC 16606.

The Church of Scotland. *The Confession of Faith, of the Kirk of Scotland*. Amsterdam, 1638; STC 22026.8.

The Church of Scotland General Assembly. *The Principal Acts . . . At Glasgow the xxi. of November 1638*. Edinburgh, 1639; STC 22049.

Cicill, Edward. *A Speech Made in the Lower Hovse of Parliament*. London, 1621; STC 22087.

Clavier, Mark F.M. "The Role of Custom in Henry Hammond's 'Of Schism' and John Bramhall's 'A Just Vindication of the Church of England'." *Anglican and Episcopal History*, Vol. 76, No. 3 (Sept., 2007), pp. 358–86.

Claydon, Tony. *William III and the Godly Revolution*. Cambridge: Cambridge University Press, 1996.

Claydon, Tony. *Europe and the Making of England, 1660–1760*. Cambridge: Cambridge University Press, 2007.

Cogswell, Thomas, Richard Cust, and Peter Lake, "Revisionism and its Legacies: The Work of Conrad Russell." In Thomas Cogswell, Richard Cust, and Peter Lake (eds.). *Politics, Religion and Popularity in Early Stuart Britain: Essays in Honour of Conrad Russell*. Cambridge: Cambridge University Press, 2002, pp. 1–17.

Cohn, Norman. *The Pursuit of the Millennium: Revolutionary Millenarians and Mystical Anarchists of the Middle Ages*. Rev. and exp. ed. Oxford: Oxford University Press, 1970.

Colley, Linda. *Britons: Forging the Nation 1707–1837.* Rev. ed. New Haven and London: Yale University Press, 2009.

Collinson, Patrick. *The Elizabethan Puritan Movement.* Oxford: The Clarendon Press, 1967.

Collinson, Patrick. *The Religion of Protestants: The Church in English Society 1559–1625.* Oxford: Oxford University Press, 1982.

Collinson, Patrick. "The Jacobean Religious Settlement: The Hampton Court Conference." In Howard Tomlinson (ed.). *Before the English Civil War: Essays on Early Stuart Politics and Government.* London: Macmillan Press, 1983, pp. 27–51.

Collinson, Patrick. *Elizabethan Essays.* London and Rio Grande: The Hambledon Press, 1994.

Cooke, Alexander. *Saint Avstins Religion.* London, 1624; STC 6059.

Cooper, Thomas. *Thesavrvs Lingvae Romanae & Britannicae.* London, 1565; STC 5686.

Cooper, Thomas. *An Admonition to the People of England.* London, 1589; STC 5683.

Cooper, Tim. "Richard Baxter and the Savoy Conference (1661)." *Journal of Ecclesiastical History,* Vol. 68, No. 2 (Apr., 2017), pp. 326–39.

Cosin, John. *A Collection of Private Devotions.* Ed. P.G. Stanwood with Daniel O'Connor. Oxford: Clarendon Press, 1967.

Cosin, Richard. *Conspiracie, for Pretended Reformation.* London, 1592; STC 5823.

Cotgrave, Randle. *A Dictionarie of the French and English Tongues.* London, 1611; STC 5830.

Coward, Barry. *The Cromwellian Protectorate.* Manchester and New York: Manchester University Press, 2002.

Cowper, William. *The Life and the Death of the Reverend Father, and Faithfull Seruant of God, Mr William Cowper.* London, 1619; STC 5945.

Craig, John. "The Growth of English Puritanism." In John Coffey and Paul C.H. Lim (eds.). *The Cambridge Companion to Puritanism.* Cambridge: Cambridge University Press, 2008, pp. 34–47.

Cranmer, Thomas. *Miscellaneous Writings and Letters of Thomas Cranmer.* Ed. John Edmund Cox. The Parker Society/Cambridge University Press, 1846; repr. Vancouver: Regent College Publishing, n.d.

Cranmer, Thomas and Justus Jonas. *Catechismus.* London, 1548; STC 5993.

Cressy, David. *Birth, Marriage, and Death: Ritual, Religion, and the Life-Cycle in Tudor and Stuart England.* Oxford: Oxford University Press, 1997.

Cressy, David. "Lamentable, Strange, and Wonderful: Headless Monsters in the English Revolution." In Laura Lunger Knoppers and Joan B. Landes (eds.). *Monstrous Bodies/ Political Monstrosities in Early Modern Europe.* Ithaca and London: Cornell University Press, 2004, pp. 40–63.

Crofton, Zachary. *ANAΛHΨIS.* London, 1660; Wing/C6984.

Crofton, Zachary. *ANAΛHΨIS ANEΛHΦΘH.* London, 1661; Wing/C6983.

Crofton, Zachariah and Giles Firmin. *The Liturgical Considerator Considered.* London, 1661; Wing/F956.

Cromartie, Alan. "King James and the Hampton Court Conference." In Ralph Houlbrooke (ed.). *James VI and I: Ideas, Authority, and Government.* Aldershot and Burlington: Ashgate, 2006, pp. 61–80.

Cromwell, Oliver. *The Government of the Common-Wealth.* London, 1653; Thomason/ E.1063[5].

Crowley, Robert. *A Briefe Discourse Against the Outwarde Apparell and Ministring Garmentes of the Popishe Church.* Emden[?], 1566; STC 6079.

Cushing, Kathleen G. *Reform and the Papacy in the Eleventh Century: Spirituality and Social Change*. Manchester: Manchester University Press, 2005.

Cust, Richard. *Charles I: A Political Life*. Harlow: Pearson, 2005.

Daston, Lorraine and Katharine Park. *Wonders and the Order of Nature 1150–1750*. New York: Zone Books, 1998.

Davies, C.S.L. "Tudor: What's in a Name?" *History*, Vol. 97, No. 1 (325) (Jan., 2012), pp. 24–42.

Davies, Julian. *The Caroline Captivity of the Church: Charles I and the Remoulding of Anglicanism, 1625–1641*. Oxford: Clarendon Press, 1992.

Dawson, Jane E.A. *Scotland Re-Formed 1488–1587*. Edinburgh: Edinburgh University Press, 2007.

Dawson, Jane E.A. *John Knox*. New Haven and London: Yale University Press, 2015.

Dawson, Jane E.A. (ed.). *Letters from Exile: Documents of the Marian Exile*. Edinburgh: The University of Edinburgh, School of Divinity, 2012. Available online: https://www.marianexile.div.ed.ac.uk/.

Dawson, Jane E.A., Lionel K.J. Glassey and John Knox. "Some Unpublished Letters from John Knox to Christopher Goodman." *The Scottish Historical Review*, Vol. 84, No. 218, Part 2 (Oct., 2005), pp. 166–201.

Decaluwé, Michiel. *A Successful Defeat: Eugene IV's Struggle with the Council of Basel for Ultimate Authority in the Church, 1431–1449*. Brussel: Institut Historique Belge de Rome, 2009.

Decaluwé, Michiel and Gerald Christianson. "Historical Survey." In Michiel Decaluwé, Thomas M. Izbicki, and Gerald Christianson (eds.). *A Companion to the Council of Basel*. Leiden: Brill, 2017, pp. 8–37.

DeSilva, Jennifer Mara. "Pluralism, Liturgy, and the Paradoxes of Reform: A Reforming Pluralist in Early Sixteenth-Century Rome." *The Sixteenth Century Journal*, Vol. 43, No. 4 (Winter, 2012), pp. 1061–78.

Dickens, A.G. and John M. Tonkin, with Kenneth Powell. *The Reformation in Historical Thought*. Cambridge: Harvard University Press, 1985.

Dighton, Thomas. *Certain Reasons of a Private Christian Against Conformitie to Kneeling in the Very Act of Receiving the Lord's Supper*. Leiden, 1618; STC 6876.

Dixon, C. Scott. *Contesting the Reformation*. Malden and Oxford: Wiley-Blackwell, 2012.

Dodds, Gregory D. *Exploiting Erasmus: The Erasmian Legacy and Religious Change in Early Modern England*. Toronto: University of Toronto Press, 2009.

Dudley, John. *The Sayinge of John Late Duke of Northumberlande Uppon the Scaffolde*. London, 1553; STC 7283.

Duffy, Eamon. *The Stripping of the Altars: Traditional Religion in England 1400–1580*. Second ed. New Haven and London: Yale University Press, 2005.

Duffy, Eamon. *Fires of Faith: Catholic England under Mary Tudor*. New Haven and London: Yale University Press, 2009.

Duguid, Timothy. "The 'Troubles' at Frankfurt: A New Chronology." *Reformation & Renaissance Review*, Vol. 14, No. 3 (Dec., 2012), pp. 243–68.

Edward VI. *Inivnccions*. London, 1547; STC 10089.

Edward VI. *A Proclamation Against the Vnreuerent Disputers and Talkers of the Sacramente of the Body and Blood of Christ*. London, 1547; STC 7812.

Edward VI. *A Message Sent by the Kynges Maiestie, to Certain of His People, Assembled in Deuonshire*. London, 1549; STC 7506.

Elizabeth I. *Iniunctions*. London, 1559; STC 10099.5.

Elizabeth I. *Articles for the Due Execution of the Statutes of Apparell, and for the Reformation of the Outragious Excesse Thereof.* London, 1562; STC 7947.

Elizabeth I. *A Proclamation Against Certaine Seditious and Schismatical Bookes and Libels.* London, 1588; STC 8182.

Elyot, Thomas. *The Dictionary.* London, 1538; STC 7659.

The English Congregation at Geneva. *The Forme of Prayers and Ministration of the Sacraments.* Geneva, 1556; STC 16561.

Erasmus of Rotterdam. *Enchiridion.* London, 1533, 1534, 1541, 1544, 1548, 1552; STC 10479–10480, 10482–10486.

Erasmus of Rotterdam. *An Epistell of the Famous Doctor Erasm[us] of Roterdame.* London, 1533; STC 10488.7.

Erasmus of Rotterdam. *The Dialoge Betwene Iulius the Seconde, Genius, and Saynt Peter.* London, 1534; STC 14841.5.

Erasmus of Rotterdam. *The Dyaloge Bytwene Iullius the Seconde, Genius, and Saynt Peter.* London, 1535; STC 14842.

Erasmus of Rotterdam. *A Shorte Recapitulacion or Abrigement of Erasmus Enchiridion.* Abr. Miles Coverdale. London, 1545; STC 10488.

Erasmus of Rotterdam. *The First Tome or Volume of the Paraphrase of Erasmus vpon the Newe Testament.* Trans. Nicholas Udall. London, 1548; STC 2854.3.

Erasmus of Rotterdam. *An Epistle... Concernynge the Veryte of the Sacrament of Christes Body, and Bloude.* London, 1549; STC 10490.

Evenden, Elizabeth and Thomas S. Freeman. *Religion and the Book in Early Modern England: The Making of John Foxe's "Book of Martyrs".* Cambridge: Cambridge University Press, 2011.

Fairfield, Leslie P. *John Bale: Mythmaker of the English Reformation.* West Lafayette: Purdue University Press, 1976; repr. Eugene: Wipf & Stock Publishers, 2006.

Featley, Daniel. *The Fisher Catched in His Owne Net.* London, 1623; STC 10732.

Featley, Daniel. *The Romish Fisher Cavght and Held in His Owne Net.* London, 1624; STC 10738.3.

Featley, Daniel. *The League Illegal.* London, 1660; Wing/F591.

Fenton, Roger. *A Sermon of Simonie and Sacrilege.* London, 1604; STC 10801.

Ferne, Henry. *The Unlawfulnesse of the New Covenant.* Oxford, 1643; Wing/F24.

Ferne, Henry. *Of the Division Between the English and Romish Church upon the Reformation.* London, 1652; Wing/F795.

Ferne, Henry. *Of the Division Between the English and Romish Church upon the Reformation.* London, 1655; Wing/F796.

Field, John and Thomas Wilcox et al. *An Admonition to the Parliament.* Leiden[?], 1617; STC 10849.

Fincham, Kenneth. "William Laud and the Exercise of Caroline Ecclesiastical Patronage." *Journal of Ecclesiastical History,* Vol. 51, No. 1 (Jan., 2000), pp. 69–93.

Fincham, Kenneth. "The Restoration of Altars in the 1630s." *The Historical Journal,* Vol. 44, No. 4 (Dec., 2001), pp. 919–40.

Fincham, Kenneth. "'According to Ancient Custom': The Return of Altars in the Restoration Church of England." *Transactions of the Royal Historical Society,* Sixth Series, Vol. 13 (2003), pp. 29–54.

Fincham, Kenneth and Peter Lake. "The Ecclesiastical Policy of King James I." *Journal of British Studies,* Vol. 24, No. 2 (Apr., 1985), pp. 169–207.

Fincham, Kenneth and Stephen Taylor. "The Restoration of the Church of England, 1660–1662: Ordination, Re-ordination and Conformity." In Stephen Taylor and Grant

Tapsell (eds.). *The Nature of the English Revolution Revisited: Essays in Honour of John Morrill.* Woodbridge and Rochester: The Boydell Press, 2013, pp. 197–232.

Fincham, Kenneth and Nicholas Tyacke. *Altars Restored: The Changing Face of English Religious Worship, 1547–c. 1700.* Oxford: Oxford University Press, 2007.

Fleming, Martha H. (ed.). *The Late Medieval Pope Prophecies: The Genus nequam Group.* Tempe: Arizona Center for Medieval and Renaissance Studies, 1999.

Fletcher, Anthony and Diarmaid MacCulloch. *Tudor Rebellions.* Sixth ed. London and New York: Routledge, 2016.

Ford, Thomas. *Reformation Sure and Stedfast.* London, 1641; Wing/F1515.

Fox, George. *Caesar's Due.* London, 1679; Wing/F1753.

Foxe, John. *Acts and Monuments.* London, 1641; Wing/F2035.

Foxe, John. *The Unabridged Acts and Monuments Online or TAMO.* HRI Online Publications, Sheffield, 2011. Available online: https://www.johnfoxe.org.

Freeman, Thomas S. "'The Reformation of the Church in this Parliament': Thomas Norton, John Foxe and the Parliament of 1571." *Parliamentary History*, Vol. 16, No. 2 (Jun., 1997), pp. 131–47.

Freeman, Thomas S. "Hands Defiled with Blood: Henry VIII in Foxe's 'Book of Martyrs'." In Thomas Betteridge and Thomas S. Freeman (eds.). *Henry VIII and History.* Farnham and Burlington: Ashgate, 2012, pp. 87–118.

Fritze, Ronald H. "Root or Link? Luther's Position in the Historical Debate over the Legitimacy of the Church of England, 1558–1625." *Journal of Ecclesiastical History*, Vol. 37, No. 1 (Apr., 1986), pp. 288–302.

Fudge, Thomas A. *The Magnificent Ride: The First Reformation in Hussite Bohemia.* Aldershot and Brookfield: Ashgate, 1998.

Fuller, Thomas. *The Church-History of Britain.* London, 1655; Wing/F2416.

Fuller, Thomas. *The Appeal of Iniured Innocence.* London, 1659; Wing/F2410.

Gadamer, Hans-Georg. *Truth and Method.* Second, rev. ed. Trans. Joel Weinsheimer and Donald G. Marshall. London and New York: Continuum, 2004.

Gardiner, Samuel. *The Scovrge of Sacriledge.* London, 1611; STC 11580.

Gauden, John. *Certaine Scrvples and Doubts of Conscience.* London, 1645; Wing/G345.

Gauden, John. *ΑΝΑΛΥΣΙΣ. The Loosing of St. Peters Bands.* London, 1660; Wing/G340.

Gauden, John. *Certain Scruples and Doubts of Conscience.* London, 1660; Wing/G346.

Gauden, John. *Considerations Touching the Liturgy.* London, 1661; Wing/G348.

Gauden, John. *A Pillar of Gratitude.* London, 1661; Wing/G366.

Gehring, David Scott. *Anglo-German Relations and the Protestant Cause: Elizabethan Foreign Policy and Pan-Protestantism.* London and New York: Routledge, 2013.

Gehring, David Scott. "From the Strange Death to the Odd Afterlife of Lutheran England." *The Historical Journal*, Vol. 57, No. 3 (Sept., 2014), pp. 825–44.

Gilby, Anthony. *An Admonition to England and Scotland.* In John Knox, *The Appellation of Iohn Knox.* Geneva, 1558; STC 15063, pp. 59–77.

Gilby, Anthony. *To My Louynge Brethren.* Emden[?], 1566; STC 10390.

Godwin, Francis. *Rervm Anglicarvm Henrico VIII. Edwardo VI. Et Maria Regnantibus, Annales.* London, 1616; STC 11945.

Godwin, Francis. *Annales of England.* London, 1630; STC 11947.

Goodare, Julian. "How Archbishop Spottiswoode Became an Episcopalian." *Renaissance and Reformation/Renaissance et Réforme*, Vol. 30, No. 4 (Fall/Automne, 2006/2007), pp. 83–103.

Goodman, Christopher. *How Superior Powers Oght to be Obeyd.* Geneva, 1558; STC 12020.

Gootjes, Nicolaas H. *The Belgic Confession: Its History and Sources*. Grand Rapids: Baker Academic, 2007.

Gordon, John. *Eirenokoinonia: The Peace of the Commvnion of the Chvrch of England*. London, 1612; STC 12056.

Gostwick, Roger. *The Anatomie of Ananias: Or, Gods Censure against Sacrilege*. London, 1616; STC 12100.

Grafton, Anthony. *What Was History? The Art of History in Early Modern Europe*. Cambridge: Cambridge University Press, 2007.

Greaves, Richard L. *Deliver Us from Evil: The Radical Underground in Britain, 1660–1663*. Oxford: Oxford University Press, 1986.

Greenspan, Nicole. "Charles II, Exile, and the Problem of Allegiance." *The Historical Journal*, Vol. 54, No. 1 (Mar., 2011), pp. 73–103.

Greschat, Martin. *Martin Bucer: A Reformer and His Times*. Trans. Stephen E. Buckwalter. Louisville and London: Westminster John Knox Press, 2004.

Grimston, Harbottle. *Master Grimston His Worthy and Learned Speech*. London, 1641; Wing/G2051.

Gunther, Karl. "The Marian Persecution and Early Elizabethan Protestants: Persecutors, Apostates, and the Wages of Sin." *Archiv für Reformationsgeschichte*, Vol. 107, No. 1 (2016), pp. 137–64.

Guyer, Benjamin M. "The Protestant Reformation—A Review Article." Review no. 2254. *Reviews in History* (Jun., 2018). Available online: https://reviews.history.ac.uk/review/2254.

Guyer, Benjamin M. "'Of Hopes Great as Himselfe': Tudor and Stuart Legacies of Edward VI." In Estelle Paranque (ed.). *Remembering Queens and Kings of Early Modern England and France: Reputation, Reinterpretation, and Reincarnation*. Cham: Palgrave Macmillan, 2019, pp. 73–91.

Guyer, Benjamin M. "'From the Apostles' Time': The Polity of the British Episcopal Churches, 1603–62." In Elliot Vernon and Hunter Powell (eds.). *Church Polity and Politics in the British Atlantic World, c. 1635–66*. Manchester: Manchester University Press, 2020, pp. 17–37.

Guyer, Benjamin M. "'Sacrifices of Laud, Praise, and Thanksgiving': The Eucharist in Classical Anglican Formularies." In Daniel J. Handschy, Donna R. Hawk-Reinhard, and Marshall E. Crossnoe (eds.). *A Eucharist-Shaped Church: Prayer, Theology, Mission*. Lanham: Fortress Press/Lexington Books, 2022.

H.S. *Reasons Shewing that There is No Need of Such a Reformation*. London, 1660; Wing/S762.

Hacket, Roger. *A Learned Sermon Handling the Qvestion of Ceremonies*. London, 1605; STC 12588.

Hacket, Roger. *A Sermon Principally Entreating of the Crosse in Baptisme*. London, 1606; STC 12591.

Haigh, Christopher. *English Reformations: Religion, Politics and Society under the Tudors*. Oxford: Oxford University Press, 1993.

Haigh, Christopher. "Where was the Church of England, 1646–1660?" *The Historical Journal*, Vol. 62, No. 1 (Mar., 2019), pp. 127–47.

Hall, Basil. "Martin Bucer in England." In D.F. Wright (ed.). *Martin Bucer: Reforming Church and Community*. Cambridge: Cambridge University Press, 1994, pp. 144–60.

Hall, Joseph. *A Defence of the Humble Remonstrance*. London, 1641; Wing/H378.

Hall, Joseph. *An Humble Remonstrance to the High Covrt of Parliament*. London, 1641; STC 12675.

Hall, Joseph. *A Letter Sent to an Honourable Gentleman.* London, 1641; Wing/H392.

Hall, Joseph. *The Lawfvlnes and Vnlawfvlnes of an Oath or Covenant.* London, 1643; Wing/H388.

Hamm, Berndt. "Farewell to Epochs in Reformation History: A Plea." *Reformation & Renaissance Review*, Vol. 16, No. 3 (Nov., 2014), pp. 211–45.

Hammond, Henry. *A View of the New Directorie.* Oxford, 1645; Wing/H612.

Harkins, Robert. "Elizabethan Puritanism and the Politics of Memory in Post-Marian England." *The Historical Journal*, Vol. 57, No. 4 (Dec., 2014), pp. 899–919.

Hartley, T.E. (ed.). *Proceedings in the Parliaments of Elizabeth I*, Vol. 1: 1558–1581. London and New York: Leicester University Press, 1981.

Harvey, Margaret. "Ecclesia Anglicana Cui Ecclesiastes Noster Christus Vos Prefecit: The Power of the Crown in the English Church During the Great Schism." In Stuart Mews (ed.). *Religion and National Identity: Papers Read at the Nineteenth Summer Meeting and the Twentieth Winter Meeting of the Ecclesiastical History Society.* Oxford: Basil Blackwell, 1982, pp. 229–41.

Harvey, Margaret. "England, the Council of Florence and the End of the Council of Basel." In Giuseppe Alberigo (ed.). *Christian Unity: The Council of Ferrara-Florence 1438/39–1989.* Leuven: Peeters Publishers, 1991, pp. 203–25.

Harvey, Margaret. *England, Rome and the Papacy 1417–1464: The Study of a Relationship.* Manchester and New York: Manchester University Press, 1993.

Haugaard, William P. *Elizabeth and the English Reformation.* Cambridge: Cambridge University Press, 1968.

Hawthorne, Nathaniel. *The Scarlet Letter and Other Writings.* Ed. Leland S. Person. New York and London: W.W. Norton & Company, 2005.

Hayward, John. *The Life and Reigne of King Edward the Sixth, With The Beginning of the Reigne of Queene Elizabeth.* London, 1636; STC 12999.

Hayward, John. *Annals of the First Four Years of the Reign of Queen Elizabeth.* Ed. John Bruce. London: The Camden Society, 1840.

Hayward, John. *The Life and Raigne of King Edward the Sixth.* Ed. Barrett L. Beer. Kent: The Kent State University Press, 1993.

Heal, Felicity. "What Can King Lucius Do for You? The Reformation and the Early British Church." *The English Historical Review*, Vol. 120, No. 487 (Jun., 2005), pp. 593–614.

Healey, Robert M. "John Knox's 'History': A 'Compleat' Sermon on Christian Duty." *Church History*, Vol. 61, No. 3 (Sept., 1992), pp. 319–33.

Heidegger, Martin. *Being and Time.* Trans. Joan Stambaugh. Rev. Dennis J. Schmidt. Albany: State University of New York Press, 2010.

Henderson, Alexander. *The Protestation.* Edinburgh, 1638; STC 21904.

Henry VIII. *An Epistle.* London, 1538; STC 13081.

Heylyn, Peter. *Mikrokosmos.* London, 1625; STC 13277.

Heylyn, Peter. *A Briefe and Moderate Answer.* London, 1637; STC 13269.

Heylyn, Peter. *The Rebells Catechism.* Oxford, 1643; Wing/H1731A.

Heylyn, Peter. *A Briefe Relation of the Death and Svfferings of the Most Reverend and Renowned Prelate The L. Archbishop of Canterbvry.* London, 1644; Wing/H1685.

Heylyn, Peter. *Parliaments Power, In Lawes for Religion.* Oxford, 1645; Wing/H1730.

Heylyn, Peter. *The Way of Reformation of the Church of England, Declared and Justified.* London, 1653; Wing/W1164.

Heylyn, Peter. *The Way and Manner of the Reformation of the Church of England Declared and Justified.* London, 1657; Wing/H1746.

Heylyn, Peter. *The Stumbling-Block of Disobedience and Rebellion*. London, 1658; Wing/ H1736.

Heylyn, Peter. *Certamen Epistolare*. London, 1659; Wing/H1687.

Heylyn, Peter. *Examen Historicum*. London, 1659; Wing/H1707.

Heylyn, Peter. *Aërius Redivivus*. London, 1672; Wing/H1682.

Heylyn, Peter. *Ecclesia Restaurata*. London, 1674; Wing/H1703.

Hickman, Henry. *Plus Ultra, or, Englands Reformation, Needing to be Reformed*. London, 1661; Wing/H1913.

Hicks, Michael. "Stafford, Thomas (c. 1533–1557), Rebel." *ODNB*. Accessed May 17, 2021.

Higgins, Iohn (ed.). *Hvloets Dictionarie*. London, 1572; STC 13941.

Highley, Christopher. "'A Pestilent and Seditious Book': Nicholas Sander's *Schismatis Anglicani* and Catholic Histories of the Reformation." *The Huntington Library Quarterly*, Vol. 68, Nos. 1 & 2 (Mar., 2005), pp. 151–71.

Holt, Mack P. *The French Wars of Religion, 1562–1629*. Second ed. Cambridge: Cambridge University Press, 2005.

Holyoake, Francis. *A Sermon of Obedience*. Oxford, 1610; STC 13622.

Hooker, Richard. *Of the Lawes of Ecclesiasticall Politie; The Sixth and Eighth Books*. London, 1648; Wing/H2635.

Hooper, John. *An Ouersight... vpon the Holy Prophete Jonas*. London, 1550; STC 13763.

Horie, Hirofumi. "The Lutheran Influence on the Elizabethan Settlement, 1558–1563." *The Historical Journal*, Vol. 34, No. 3 (Sept., 1991), pp. 519–37.

Hornbeck II, J. Patrick. *Remembering Wolsey: A History of Commemorations and Representations*. New York: Fordham University Press, 2019.

Horne, Robert. *Certain Homilies of M. Ioan Calvine Conteining... an Apologie of Robert Horne*. Rome [Wesel?], 1553; STC 4392.

Houliston, Victor. "Fallen Prince and Pretender of the Faith: Henry VIII as Seen by Sander and Persons." In Thomas Betteridge and Thomas S. Freeman (eds.). *Henry VIII and History*. Farnham and Burlington: Ashgate, 2012, pp. 119–34.

Howard, Thomas Albert. *Remembering the Reformation: An Inquiry into the Meanings of Protestantism*. Oxford: Oxford University Press, 2016.

Huggarde, Miles. *The Displaying of the Protestantes*. London, 1556; STC 13558.

Hugget, Anthony. *A Diuine Enthymeme of True Obedience*. London, 1615; STC 13909.

Huloet, Richard. *Abcedarivm Anglico Latinvm*. London, 1552; STC 13940.

Humfrey, John. *The Healing Paper*. London, 1678; Wing/H3680.

Hutton, Ronald. *Charles II: King of England, Scotland, and Ireland*. Oxford: Clarendon Press, 1989.

Hyland, William Patrick. "Reform Preaching and Despair at the Council of Pavia-Siena (1423–1424)." *The Catholic Historical Review*, Vol. 84, No. 3 (Jul., 1998), pp. 409–30.

Inhabitant of Rochill. *The Reformed Catholicque, against the Deformed Jesuit*. [Netherlands?], 1621; STC 4830.5.

Innocent III. *Between God & Man: Six Sermons on the Priestly Office*. Trans. Corrine J. Vause and Frank C. Gardiner. Washington, DC: The Catholic University of America Press, 2004.

Israel, Jonathan I. *The Dutch Republic: Its Rise, Greatness, and Fall 1477–1806*. Oxford: Clarendon Press, 1995.

Jackson, Christine. "It Is Unpossible to Draw His Picture Well Who Hath Severall Countenances': Lord Herbert of Cherbury and *The Life and Reign of King Henry VIII*." In Thomas Betteridge and Thomas S. Freeman (eds.). *Henry VIII and History*. Farnham and Burlington: Ashgate, 2012, pp. 135–49.

Jackson, Christine. "Lord Herbert of Cherbury and the Presentation of the Henrician Reformation in his *Life and Raigne of King Henry the Eighth.*" *The Seventeenth Century*, Vol. 28, No. 2 (2013), pp. 139–61.

James VI and I. *A Proclamation for Reformation of Great Abuses in Measures*. London, 1603; STC 8317.

James VI and I. *By the King*. London, 1604; STC 8361.

James VI and I. *Basilicon Doron*. In Johann P. Sommerville (ed.). *King James VI and I: Political Writings*. Cambridge: Cambridge University Press, 1994, pp. 1–61.

James, Leonie. *"This Great Firebrand": William Laud and Scotland, 1617-1645*. Woodbridge and Rochester: The Boydell Press, 2017.

Jeanes, Gordon P. *Signs of God's Promise: Thomas Cranmer's Sacramental Theology and the Book of Common Prayer*. London and New York: T & T Clark, 2008.

Jenney, George. *A Catholike Conference*. London, 1626; STC 14497.

Jewel, John. *An Apology of the Church of England*. Ed. John E. Booty. Charlottesville: University Press of Virginia, 1963; repr. New York: Church Publishing, 2002.

Jones, Norman L. "An Elizabethan Bill for the Reformation of the Ecclesiastical Law." *Parliamentary History*, Vol. 4, No. 1 (Dec., 1985), pp. 171–87.

Jordan, Thomas. *The Anarchie, Or the Blest Reformation*. London[?], 1648; Wing/J1019B.

Josephus. *The Jewish War*. Trans. H. St.J. Thackeray. Loeb Classical Library 210. Cambridge and London: Harvard University Press, 1928.

Kainulainen, Jaska. *Paolo Sarpi: A Servant of God and State*. Leiden and Boston: Brill, 2014.

Kamen, Henry. *The Spanish Inquisition: An Historical Revision*. Third ed. London: Weidenfeld & Nicolson, 1997.

Keeble, N.H. *The Restoration: England in the 1660s*. Malden and Oxford: Blackwell Publishing, 2002.

Kenyon, J.P. *The Popish Plot*. New York: St. Martin's Press, 1972; repr. London: Phoenix Press, 2000.

Kenyon, J.P. "Revisionism and Post-Revisionism in Early Stuart History." *The Journal of Modern History*, Vol. 64, No. 4 (Dec., 1992), pp. 686–99.

Kenyon, J.P. (ed.). *The Stuart Constitution 1603–1688: Documents and Commentary*. Cambridge: Cambridge University Press, 1969.

Kess, Alexandra. *Johann Sleidan and the Protestant Vision of History*. Aldershot and Burlington: Ashgate, 2008.

Kesselring, K.J. *The Northern Rebellion of 1569: Faith, Politics, and Protest in Elizabethan England*. New York: Palgrave Macmillan, 2007.

Ketley, Joseph (ed.). *The Two Liturgies, A.D. 1549 and A.D. 1552*. Cambridge: The Parker Society/The University Press, 1844; repr. Eugene: Wipf & Stock Publishers, 2006.

Kim, Joong-Lak. "The Scottish-English-Romish Book: The Character of the Scottish Prayer Book of 1637." In Michael J. Braddick and David L. Smith (eds.). *The Experience of Revolution in Stuart Britain and Ireland: Essays for John Morrill*. Cambridge: Cambridge University Press, 2011, pp. 14–32.

King, Henry. *An Elegy Upon the Most Incomparable K. Charls the I*. London, n.d.; Wing/K499.

Kirby, W.J. Torrance. *Richard Hooker, Reformer and Platonist*. Aldershot and Burlington: Ashgate, 2005.

Kirby, W.J. Torrance. "Consensus Tigurinus, 1549." *Reformation & Renaissance Review*, Vol. 18, No. 1 (Mar., 2016), pp. 34–44.

Kneupper, Frances Courtney. *The Empire at the End of Time: Identity and Reform in Late Medieval German Prophecy*. Oxford: Oxford University Press, 2016.

Knighton, C.S. "Barlow, William (d. 1613)." *ODNB*.

Knoppers, Laura Lunger. *Constructing Cromwell: Ceremony, Portrait, and Print 1645–1661*. Cambridge: Cambridge University Press, 2000.

Knox, John. *The Copie of a Letter*. Wesel, 1556; STC 15066.

Knox, John. *The Appellation of Iohn Knox*. Geneva, 1558; STC 15063.

Knox, John. *The Historie of the Reformation of the Church of Scotland*. London, 1644; Wing/K739.

Knox, John. *The History of the Reformation of the Church of Scotland*. In David Laing (ed.). *The Works of John Knox*. 6 Vols. Edinburgh: The Wodrow Society, 1846.

Knox, John. *The History of the Reformation of the Church of Scotland*. Ed. William Croft Dickinson. 2 Vols. New York: Philosophical Library, 1950.

Knox, John. *Knox: On Rebellion*. Ed. Roger A. Mason. Cambridge: Cambridge University Press, 1994.

Kolb, Robert. *Martin Luther as Prophet, Teacher, and Hero: Images of the Reformer, 1520–1620*. Grand Rapids: Baker Academic and Carlisle: Paternoster Press, 1999.

Kolb, Robert and Timothy Wengert (eds.). *The Book of Concord: The Confessions of the Evangelical Lutheran Church*. Minneapolis: Fortress Press, 2000.

Kouri, E.I. *Elizabethan England and Europe: Forty Unprinted Letters from Elizabeth I to Protestant Powers*. London: Bulletin of the Institute of Historical Research, 1982.

Kuhn, Thomas. *The Structure of Scientific Revolutions*. 50th Anniversary ed. Chicago and London: The University of Chicago Press, 2012.

L'Estrange, Roger. *The Reformed Catholique: Or, The True Protestant*. London, 1679; Wing/L1289–L1291.

Lacey, Andrew. *The Cult of King Charles the Martyr*. Woodbridge and Rochester: The Boydell Press, 2003.

Ladner, Gerhart B. *The Idea of Reform: Its Impact on Christian Thought and Action in the Age of the Fathers*. Cambridge: Harvard University Press, 1959.

Laeven, Augustinus Hubertus. *The "Acta eruditorum" under the Editorship of Otto Mencke (1644–1707): The History of an International Learned Journal between 1682 and 1707*. Trans. Lynne Richards. Amsterdam & Maarssen: APA-Holland University Press, 1990.

Lake, Peter. *Moderate Puritans and the Elizabethan Church*. Cambridge: Cambridge University Press, 1982.

Lake, Peter. "Lancelot Andrewes, John Buckeridge, and Avant-garde Conformity at the Court of James I." In Linda Levy Peck (ed.). *The Mental World of the Jacobean Court*. Cambridge: Cambridge University Press, 1991, pp. 113–33.

Lake, Peter. "The Laudian Style: Order, Uniformity and the Pursuit of the Beauty of Holiness in the 1630s." In Kenneth Fincham (ed.). *The Early Stuart Church, 1603–1642*. Stanford: Stanford University Press, 1993, pp. 161–85.

Lakoff, George and Mark Johnson. *Metaphors We Live By*. Chicago and London: The University of Chicago Press, 2003.

Lane, Calvin. *The Laudians and the Elizabethan Church*. London and New York: Routledge, 2013.

Lane, Calvin. "John Milton's Elegy for Lancelot Andrewes (1626) and the Dynamic Nature of Religious Identity in Early Stuart England." *Anglican and Episcopal History*, Vol. 85, No. 4 (Dec., 2016), pp. 468–91.

Laud, William. *A Speech Delivered in the Starr-Chamber*. London, 1637; STC 15306.

Laud, William. *The Works of the Most Reverend Father in God, William Laud, D.D.* 7 Vols. Ed. William Scott and James Bliss. Oxford: John Henry Parker, 1847–60; repr. Hildesheim and New York: Georg Olms Verlag, 1977.

Levin, Carole. "Elizabeth's Ghost: The afterlife of the Queen in Stuart England." *Royal Studies Journal*, Vol. 1, No. 1 (2014), pp. 1–16.

Lilburne, John. *A Worke of the Beast*. Amsterdam, 1638; STC 15599.

Lindsay, David. *A Trve Narration of All the Passages of the Proceedings in the Generall Assembly of the Church of Scotland*. London, 1621; STC 15657.

Lloyd, David. *Cabala*. London, 1664; Wing/L2636.

Loach, Jennifer. "The Function of Ceremonial in the Reign of Henry VIII." *Past & Present*, No. 142 (Feb., 1994), pp. 43–68.

Loach, Jennifer. *Edward VI*. Ed. George Bernard and Penry Williams. New Haven and London: Yale University Press, 1999.

Logan, F. Donald. "The Henrician Canons." *The Bulletin of the Institute of Historical Research*, Vol. 47, No. 1 (May, 1974), pp. 99–103.

Lucas, Peter J. (ed.). *John Capgrave's Abbreuiacion of Cronicles*. Oxford: The Early English Text Society and Oxford University Press, 1983.

Luther, Martin. *Here After Ensueth a Propre Treatyse of Good Works*. London, 1535; STC 16988.

Luther, Martin. *A Very Excellent and Sweet Exposition*. London, 1537, 1538; STC 16999, 17000.

Luther, Martin. *The Last Wil and Last Confession*. Wesel[?], 1543; STC 16984.

Luther, Martin. *A Frutfull Sermon...vpon the. XVIII. Chapi. of Mathew*. London, 1548; STC 16983.

Luther, Martin. *A Frutefull and Godly Exposition and Declaracion of the Kyngdom of Christ and of the Christen Lybertye*. London, 1548; STC 16982.

Luther, Martin. *A Ryght Notable Sermon...vppon the Twenteth Chapter of Iohan*. Ispwich, 1548; STC 16992.

Luther, Martin. *A Commentarie of M. Doctor Martin Luther vpon the Epistle of S. Paul to the Galathians*. London, 1575; STC 16965; 16966 [1577], 16967 [1580], 16968, 16969 [1588], 16970 [1602]; 16973 [1616].

Luther, Martin. *A Treatise, Touching the Libertie of a Christian*. London, 1579; STC 16995, 16996.

Luther, Martin. *A Commentarie vpon the Fifteene Psalmes*. London, 1615; STC 16976.

Luther, Martin. *The Signs of Christs Coming, and Of the Last Day*. London 1661; Wing/L3516.

Luther, Martin. *A Word in Season*. London 1685; Wing/L3519.

Luther, Martin. *D. Martin Luthers Werke: Kritische Gesamtausgabe*. Vol. 50. Weimar: Hermann Böhlaus Nachfolger, 1914.

Luttikhuizen, Frances. *Underground Protestantism in Sixteenth Century Spain: A Much Ignored Side of Spanish History*. Göttingen: Vandenhoeck & Ruprecht, 2017.

Lyly, John. *Rhythmes against Martin Marre-Prelate*. London, 1589; STC 17465.

MacCulloch, Diarmaid. "The Myth of the English Reformation." *Journal of British Studies*, Vol. 30, No. 1 (Jan., 1991), pp. 1–19.

MacCulloch, Diarmaid. *Thomas Cranmer*. New Haven and London: Yale University Press, 1996.

MacCulloch, Diarmaid. *The Boy King: Edward VI and the Protestant Reformation*. Berkeley and Los Angeles: University of California Press, 1999.

MacDonald, Alan R. "James VI and I, the Church of Scotland, and British Ecclesiastical Convergence." *The Historical Journal*, Vol. 48, No. 4 (Dec., 2005), pp. 885–903.

MacDonald, Alan R. "Consultation and Consent under James VI." *The Historical Journal*, Vol. 54, No. 2 (Jun., 2011), pp. 287–306.

Maltby, Judith. *Prayer Book and People in Elizabethan and Early Stuart England.* Cambridge: Cambridge University Press, 1998.

Mansfield, Bruce. *Phoenix of His Age: Interpretations of Erasmus c. 1550–1750.* Toronto: University of Toronto Press, 1979.

Mariott, Thomas. *Rebellion Unmasked.* London, 1661; Wing/M717.

Marprelate, Martin. *A Dialogue.* Amsterdam[?], 1640; STC 6805.3.

Marprelate, Martin. *Reformation No Enemie.* London[?], 1641; Wing/R741.

Marprelate, Martin. *Hay Any Worke for Cooper.* London[?], 1642; Wing/H1205.

Marshall, Peter. "(Re)defining the English Reformation." *The Journal of British Studies,* Vol. 48, No. 3 (Jul., 2009), pp. 564–86.

Marshall, Peter. "John Calvin and the English Catholics, c. 1565–1640." *The Historical Journal,* Vol. 53, No. 4 (Dec., 2010), pp. 849–70.

Marshall, Peter. "The Naming of Protestant England." *Past and Present,* No. 214 (Feb., 2012), pp. 87–128.

Marshall, Peter. *1517: Martin Luther and the Invention of the Reformation.* Oxford: Oxford University Press, 2017.

Marshall, Peter. *Heretics and Believers: A History of the English Reformation.* New Haven and London: Yale University Press, 2017.

Martin, Jessica. *Walton's Lives: Conformist Commemorations and the Rise of Biography.* Oxford: Oxford University Press, 2001.

Mary I and Philip I. *A Copie of a Letter wyth Articles.* London, 1553; STC 9182.

Mary I and Philip I. *By the Kyng and the Quene.* London, 1556; STC 7868.3.

Mary I and Philip I. *By the Kyng and the Quene.* London, 1557; STC 7875.

Mary I and Philip I. *A Proclamation ... Agaynste Thomas Stafforde.* London, 1557; STC 7874.

Mason, Francis. The Avthoritie of the Chvrch in Making Canons and Constitutions Concerning Things Indifferent. London, 1607; STC 17595.

Mason, Roger A. and Martin S. Smith (eds.). *A Dialogue on the Law of Kingship among the Scots: A Critical Edition and Translation of George Buchanan's De Iure Regni apud Scotos Dialogos.* Aldershot and Burlington: Ashgate, 2004.

Mayer, T.F. "Sander [Sanders], Nicholas (c. 1530–1581), Religious Controversialist." *ODNB.* Accessed May 17, 2021.

Mayes, Benjamin T.G. *Counsel and Conscience: Lutheran Casuistry and Moral Reasoning After the Reformation.* Göttingen: Vandenhoeck & Ruprecht, 2011.

McCafferty, John. *The Reconstruction of the Church of Ireland: Bishop Bramhall and the Laudian Reforms, 1633–1641.* Cambridge: Cambridge University Press, 2007.

McDermott, Peter L. "Nicholas of Cusa: Continuity and Conciliation at the Council of Basel." *Church History,* Vol. 67, No. 2 (Jun., 1998), pp. 254–73.

McEntegart, Rory. *Henry VIII, The League of Schmalkalden, and the English Reformation.* Woodbridge and Rochester: The Boydell Press, 2002.

McGinnis, Paul, and Arthur Williamson. "Radical Menace, Reforming Hope: Scotland and English Religious Politics, 1586–1596." *Renaissance and Reformation/Renaissance et Réforme,* Vol. 36, No. 2 (Spring, 2013), pp. 105–30.

McGrath, Alister. *In the Beginning: The Story of the King James Bible and How It Changed a Nation, a Language, and a Culture.* New York: Anchor Books, 2001.

McGrath, Alister. *Iustitia Dei: A History of the Christian Doctrine of Justification.* Third ed. Cambridge: Cambridge University Press, 2005.

Mede, Joseph. *The Apostasy of the Latter Times.* London, 1641; Wing/M1590.

Melancholicus, Mercurius. *Mistris Parliament Brought to Bed of a Monstrous Childe of Reformation*. London[?], 1648; Wing/M2281.

Melanchthon, Philip. *A Newe Work Concernyng Both Partes of the Sacrament*. London, 1548; STC 17795–17796.

Melanchthon, Philip and Martin Luther. *Of Two Wonderful Popish Monsters*. London, 1579; STC 17797.

Melanchthon, Philip et al. *The Confessyon of the Fayth of the Germaynes*. London, 1536, 1538; STC 908, 909.

Merritt, J.F. "The Cradle of Laudianism? Westminster Abbey, 1558–1630." *Journal of Ecclesiastical History*, Vol. 52, No. 4 (Oct., 2001), pp. 623–46.

Milbourne, Richard. *Concerning Imposition of Hands*. London, 1607; STC 17917.

Milton, Anthony. *Catholic and Reformed: The Roman and Protestant Churches in English Protestant Thought, 1600–1640*. Cambridge: Cambridge University Press, 1995.

Milton, Anthony. "The Creation of Laudianism: A New Approach." In Thomas Cogswell, Richard Cust, and Peter Lake (eds.). *Politics, Religion and Popularity in Early Stuart Britain: Essays in Honour of Conrad Russell*. Cambridge: Cambridge University Press, 2002, pp. 162–84.

Milton, Anthony. *Laudian and Royalist Polemic in Seventeenth-century England: The Career and Writings of Peter Heylyn*. Manchester: Manchester University Press, 2007.

Milton, Anthony. "Arminians, Laudians, Anglicans, and Revisionists: Back to Which Drawing Board?" *The Huntington Library Quarterly*, Vol. 78, No. 4 (Winter, 2015), pp. 723–43.

Milton, Anthony. "Peter Heylyn (1599–1662), Church of England Clergyman and Historian." *ODNB*. Accessed May 17, 2021.

Milton, Anthony (ed.). *The British Delegation and the Synod of Dort (1618–1619)*. Woodbridge and Rochester: The Boydell Press, 2005.

Milton, John. *Animadversions upon the Remonstrants Defence against Smectymnuus*. London, 1641; Wing/M2089.

Milton, John. *Of Reformation Touching Church-Discipline in England*. London, 1641; Wing/M2134.

Milton, John. *The Doctrine and Discipline of Divorce*. London, 1643; Wing/M2108.

Milton, John. *The Ivdgement of Martin Bucer, Concerning Divorcement*. London, 1644; Wing/B5270.

Milton, John. *The Tenure of Kings and Magistrates*. London, 1649; Wing/M2181.

Minnich, Nelson H. *The Fifth Lateran Council (1512–1517)*. Aldershot and Brookfield: Variorum, 1993.

Minnich, Nelson H. "Councils of the Catholic Reformation: A Historical Survey." In Gerald Christianson, Thomas M. Izbicki, and Christopher M. Bellitto (eds.). *The Church, the Councils, and Reform: The Legacy of the Fifteenth Century*. Washington, DC: The Catholic University of America Press, 2008, pp. 27–59.

Montagu, Richard. *A Gagg for the New Gospell?* London, 1624; STC 18038.

Morgan, John. "Religious Conventions and Science in the Early Restoration: Reformation and 'Israel' in Thomas Sprat's 'History of the Royal Society' (1667)." *The British Journal for the History of Science*, Vol. 42, No. 3 (Sept., 2009), pp. 321–44.

Morrill, John. "The Religious Context of the English Civil War." *Transactions of the Royal Historical Society*, Vol. 34 (1984), pp. 155–78.

Morrill, John. "Revisionism's Wounded Legacies." *The Huntington Library Quarterly*, Vol. 78, No. 4 (Winter, 2015), pp. 577–94.

Morton, Thomas. *A Defence of the Innocencie of the Three Ceremonies of the Chvrch of England.* London, 1618; STC 18179.

Moyn, Samuel. *The Last Utopia: Human Rights in History.* Cambridge and London: The Belknap Press of Harvard University Press, 2010.

Muller, Richard. *Post-Reformation Reformed Dogmatics: The Rise and Development of Reformed Orthodoxy, ca. 1520 to ca. 1725.* Second ed. 4 Vols. Grand Rapids: Baker Academic, 2003.

Muller, Richard. *Christ and the Decree: Christology and Predestination in Reformed Theology from Calvin to Perkins.* New ed. Grand Rapids: Baker Academic, 2008.

Muller, Richard. "Demoting Calvin: The Issue of Calvin and the Reformed Tradition." In Amy Nelson Burnett (ed.). *John Calvin, Myth and Reality: Images and Impact of Geneva's Reformer.* Eugene: Cascade Books, 2011, pp. 3–17.

Nash, Thomas. *An Almond for a Parrat.* London, 1589; STC 534.

Nash, Thomas. *A Countercuffe Giuen to Martin Iunior.* London, 1589; STC 19456.5.

Nicholas of Cusa. *The Catholic Concordance.* Ed. and trans. Paul E. Sigmund. Cambridge: Cambridge University Press, 1991.

Nicholas of Cusa. *Writings on Church and Reform.* Trans. Thomas M. Izbicki. Cambridge and London: Harvard University Press, 2008.

O'Day, Rosemary. *The Debate on the English Reformation.* London: Routledge, 1986.

O'Malley, John W. *Trent and All That: Renaming Catholicism in the Early Modern Era.* Cambridge and London: Harvard University Press, 2000.

O'Malley, John W. *Trent: What Happened at the Council.* Cambridge and London: The Belknap Press of Harvard University Press, 2013.

Oakley, Francis. *The Conciliarist Tradition: Constitutionalism in the Catholic Church 1300–1870.* Oxford: Oxford University Press, 2003.

Oates, Titus. *The Discovery of the Popish Plot.* London, 1679; Wing/O34.

Oberman, Heiko. *Luther: Man between God and the Devil.* New Haven and London: Yale University Press, 1989.

Oberman, Heiko, Daniel E. Zerfoss, and William J. Courtenay (eds.), *Defensorium Obedientiae Apostolicae et Alia Documenta.* Cambridge: The Belknap Press of Harvard University Press, 1968.

Oecolampadius, Johann. *A Sarmon, of Ihon Oecolampadius, to Yong Men, and Maydens.* London, 1548; STC 18787.

Okie, Laird. "Kennett, White (1660–1728), Historian and Bishop of Peterborough." *ODNB.* Accessed May 17, 2021.

Olde, John. *The Acquital or Purgation of the Moost Catholyke Christen Prince, Edwarde the. VI.* Waterford, 1555; STC 18797.

Olson, Jeannine E. "The Flight from France of Nicolas des Gallars: Archival Discoveries on His Interlude in Geneva (1568–1571) with Beza and the 'Histoire Ecclésiastique Des Eglises Reformées au Royaume de France'." *Bibliothèque D'Humanisme Et Renaissance,* T. 77, No. 3 (2015): 573–603.

Ozment, Steven. *The Age of Reform 1250–1550: An Intellectual and Religious History of Late Medieval and Reformation Europe.* New Haven and London: Yale University Press, 1980.

Paravicini-Bagliani, Agostino. *The Pope's Body.* Trans. David S. Peterson. Chicago and London: The University of Chicago Press, 2000.

Park, Katharine and Lorraine J. Daston. "Unnatural Conceptions: The Study of Monsters in Sixteenth- and Seventeenth-Century France and England." *Past & Present,* No. 92 (Aug., 1981), pp. 20–54.

Parker, Geoffrey. *Imprudent King: A New Life of Philip II*. New Haven and London: Yale University Press, 2014.

The Parliament of England and Wales. *An Ordinance of the Lords and Commons... for the Calling of an Assembly of Learned, and Godly Divines*. London, 1643; Wing/E1952D.

The Parliament of England and Wales. *Two Ordinances of the Lords and Commons Assembled in Parliament*. London, 1645; Wing/E2408A.

The Parliament of England and Wales. *The Lords in Parliament Assembled... for Burning of the Instrument or Writing, Called The Solemn League or Covenant*. London, 1661; Wing/E2818A.

Parry, Graham. *The Arts of the Anglican Counter-Reformation: Glory, Laud and Honour*. Woodbridge and Rochester: The Boydell Press, 2006.

Patterson, W.B. *James VI and I and the Reunion of Christendom*. Cambridge: Cambridge University Press, 1997.

Patterson, W.B. *William Perkins and the Making of a Protestant England*. Oxford: Oxford University Press, 2014.

Patterson, W.B. *Thomas Fuller: Discovering England's Religious Past*. Oxford: Oxford University Press, 2018.

Pauck, Wilhelm (ed.). *Melanchthon and Bucer*. Philadelphia: The Westminster Press, 1969.

Pearson, John. *An Answer to Dr. Burges*. London, 1660; Wing/P993.

Pearson, John. *No Necessity of Reformation*. London, 1660; Wing/P1001.

Pemble, William. *Vindiciae Gratiae*. London, 1627; STC 19591.

Perkins, William. *A Reformed Catholike*. Cambridge, 1598; STC 19736.

Pettegree, Andrew. "Print Workshops and Markets." In Ulinka Rublack (ed.). *The Oxford Handbook of the Protestant Reformations*. Oxford: Oxford University Press, 2017, pp. 373–89.

Piccolomini, Aeneas Sylvius. *De Gestis Concilii Basiliensis Commentariorum Libri II*. Ed. and trans. Denys Hay and W.K. Smith. Rev. ed. Oxford: Clarendon Press, 1992.

Pocock, J.G.A. *Virtue, Commerce, and History: Essays on Political Thought and History, Chiefly in the Eighteenth Century*. Cambridge: Cambridge University Press, 1985.

Pocock, J.G.A. *The Discovery of Islands: Essays in British History*. Cambridge: Cambridge University Press, 2005.

Pocock, J.G.A. "Present at the Creation: With Laslett to the Lost Worlds." *International Journal of Public Affairs*, Vol. 2 (2006), pp. 8–17.

Pocock, J.G.A. *Political Thought and History: Essays on Theory and Method*. Cambridge: Cambridge University Press, 2009.

Ponet, John. *An Apologie*. Strasbourg, 1555; STC 20175.

Ponet, John. *A Shorte Treatise of Politike Pouuer*. Strasbourg, 1556; STC 20178.

Ponet, John. *A Shorte Treatise of Politike Power*. London, 1639; STC 20179.

Ponet, John. *A Short Treatise of Politiqve Povver*. London, 1642; Wing/P2804B.

Powell, Hunter. *The crisis of British Protestantism: Church Power in the Puritan Revolution, 1638–44*. Manchester: Manchester University Press, 2015.

Prior, Charles W.A. "Ecclesiology and Political Thought in England, 1580–c. 1630." *The Historical Journal*, Vol. 48, No. 4 (Dec., 2005), pp. 855–84.

Prior, Charles W.A. *A Confusion of Tongues: Britain's Wars of Reformation 1625–1642*. Oxford: Oxford University Press, 2012.

Prudovsky, Gad. "Can We Ascribe to Past Thinkers Concepts They Had No Linguistic Means to Express?" *History and Theory*, Vol. 36, No. 1 (Feb., 1997), pp. 15–31.

Prynne, William. *The Perpetuitie of a Regenerate Mans Estate*. London, 1626; STC 20471.

Prynne, William. *The Chvrch of Englands Old Antithesis to New Arminianisme*. London, 1629; STC 20457.

Pucci, Michael S. "Reforming Roman Emperors: John Foxe's Characterization of Constantine in the *Acts and Monuments*". In David Loades (ed.). *John Foxe: An Historical Perspective*. Aldershot and Brookfield: Ashgate, 1999, pp. 29–51.

Ram, Robert. *The Souldiers Catechisme*. London, 1644; Wing/R196.

Ramelli, Ilaria L.E. and David Konstan. *Terms for Eternity: Aiônios and Aïdios in Classical and Christian Texts*. Piscataway: Gorgias Press, 2013.

Rankin, Mark, Christopher Highley, and John N. King (eds.). *Henry VIII and His Afterlives: Literature, Politics, and Art*. Cambridge: Cambridge University Press, 2009.

Redworth, Glyn. *The Prince and the Infanta: The Cultural Politics of the Spanish Match*. New Haven and London: Yale University Press, 2003.

Resbury, Richard. *The Tabernacle of God with Men: Or, the Visible Church Reformed*. London, 1649; Wing/R1136A.

Rex, Richard. *The Lollards*. Basingstoke and New York: Palgrave Macmillan, 2002.

Rider, John and Francis Holyoake. *Riders Dictionarie*. London, 1612; STC 21033.

Rider, John and Francis Holyoake. *Riders Dictionarie*. London, 1659; Wing/R1443.

Ritchie, Pamela. "Marie de Guise and the Three Estates, 1554–1558." In Keith M. Brown and Roland J. Tanner (eds.). *Parliament and Politics in Scotland, 1235–1560*. Edinburgh: Edinburgh University Press, 2004, pp. 179–202.

Rollo-Koster, Joëlle. *Avignon and its Papacy, 1309–1417: Popes, Institutions, and Society*. Lanham: Rowman & Littlefield, 2015.

Rose, Jacqueline. *Godly Kingship in Restoration England: The Politics of the Royal Supremacy, 1660–1688*. Cambridge: Cambridge University Press, 2011.

Rowland, John. *A Reply to the Answer of Anonymus*. London, 1660; Wing/R2070.

Rublack, Ulinka. "Grapho-Relics: Lutheranism and the Materialization of the World." *Past and Present* (2010), Supplement 5, pp. 144–66.

Rublack, Ulinka (ed.). *The Oxford Handbook of the Protestant Reformations*. Oxford: Oxford University Press, 2017.

Russell, Alexander. *Conciliarism and Heresy in Fifteenth-Century England: Collective Authority in the Age of the General Councils*. Cambridge: Cambridge University Press, 2017.

Russell, Conrad. *The Causes of the English Civil War*. Oxford: Clarendon Press, 1990.

Russell, Conrad. *The Fall of the British Monarchies 1637–1642*. Oxford: Clarendon Press, 1990.

Russell, John. *The Solemn League and Covenant Discharg'd*. London, 1660; Wing/R2343.

Ryrie, Alec. "The Strange Death of Lutheran England." *The Journal of Ecclesiastical History*, Vol. 53, No. 1 (Jan., 2002), pp. 64–92.

Ryrie, Alec. *The Origins of the Scottish Reformation*. Manchester: Manchester University Press, 2006.

Ryrie, Alec. "The Slow Death of a Tyrant: Learning to Live without Henry VIII, 1547–1563." In Mark Rankin, Christopher Highley, and John N. King (eds.). *Henry VIII and His Afterlives: Literature, Politics, and Art*. Cambridge: Cambridge University Press, 2009, pp. 75–93.

Ryrie, Alec. "Prologue: When Did the English Reformation Happen? A Historiographical Curiosity and Its Interpretative Consequences." *Études Épistémè* 32 (2017). Available online: https://journals.openedition.org/episteme/1845.

Sander, Nicholas. *Rise and Growth of the Anglican Schism*. Trans. David Lewis. London: Burns and Oates, 1877.

Sandys, Edwin. *Europae Specvlvm*. London, 1629; STC 21718.

Saunders, Austen. "The Hacket Rebellion and Henry Arthington's Manuscript Annotations to his own Pamphlet." *The Review of English Studies*, New Series, Vol. 64, No. 266 (Sept., 2013), pp. 594–609.

Schofield, A.N.E.D. "England, the Pope, and the Council of Basel." *Church History*, Vol. 33, No. 3 (Sept., 1964), pp. 248–78.

Schofield, John. *Philip Melanchthon and the English Reformation*. Aldershot and Burlington: Ashgate, 2006.

Scholz, Maximilian Miguel. *Strange Brethren: Refugees, Religious Bonds, and Reformation in Frankfurt, 1554–1608*. Charlottesville and London: University of Virginia Press, 2022.

Scribner, Bob, Roy Porter, and Mikuláš Teich (eds.). *The Reformation in National Context*. Cambridge: Cambridge University Press, 1994).

Scribner, R.W. "Incombustible Luther: The Image of the Reformer in Early Modern Germany." *Past & Present*, No. 110 (Feb., 1986), pp. 38–68.

Seckendorff, Veit Ludwig. *Commentarius Historicus et Apologeticus de Luthernismo Sive De Reformatione Religionis Ductu D. Martini Lutheri*. Frankfurt and Leipzig, 1688.

Seed, John. *Dissenting Histories: Religious Division and the Politics of Memory in Eighteenth-Century England*. Edinburgh: Edinburgh University Press, 2008.

Segger, Glen J. *Richard Baxter's* Reformed Liturgy: *A Puritan Alternative to the* Book of Common Prayer. Farnham and Burlington: Ashgate, 2014.

Selwyn, David G. (ed.). *The Library of Thomas Cranmer*. Oxford: The Oxford Bibliographical Society, 1996.

Sempill, James. *Sacrilege Sacredly Handled*. London, 1619; STC 22186.

Shagan, Ethan H. *Popular Politics and the English Reformation*. Cambridge: Cambridge University Press, 2003.

Shagan, Ethan H. *The Rule of Moderation: Violence, Religion and the Politics of Restraint in Early Modern England*. Cambridge: Cambridge University Press, 2011.

Shakespeare, William. *King Henry VIII*. Ed. Gordon McMullan. London: Bloomsbury, 2000.

Shapin, Steven. *The Scientific Revolution*. Chicago and London: The University of Chicago Press, 1996.

Shaw, John. *Origo Protestantium*. London, 1677; Wing/S3032C.

Shriver, Frederick. "Hampton Court Re-visited: James I and the Puritans." *Journal of Ecclesiastical History*, Vol. 33, No. 1 (Jan., 1982), pp. 48–71.

Shuger, Debora. "A Protesting Catholic Puritan in Elizabethan England." *Journal of British Studies*, Vol. 48, No. 3 (Jul., 2009), pp. 587–630.

Skinner, Quentin. *The Foundations of Modern Political Thought*. 2 Vols. Cambridge: Cambridge University Press, 1978.

Skinner, Quentin. *Visions of Politics*. 3 Vols. Vol. 1: Regarding Method. Cambridge: Cambridge University Press, 2002.

Sleidanus, Johannes. *A Famovse Cronicle of Oure Time, Called Sleidanes Commentaries* (London, 1560; STC 19848).

Sleidanus, Johannes. *Martin Luther's Declaration to His Countrimen*. London, 1643; Wing/L3511.

Sleidanus, Johannes. *The General History of the Reformation of the Church*. London, 1689; Wing/S3989.

Smectymnuus. *An Answer to a Book Entitvled An Hvmble Remonstrance*. London, 1641; Wing/M748.

Smectymnuus. *A Vindication of the Answer to the Hvmble Remonstrance*. London, 1641; Wing/M798.

Smuts, R. Malcolm. "States, Monarchs and Dynastic Transitions: The Political Thought of John Hayward." In Susan Doran and Paulina Kewes (eds.). *Doubtful and Dangerous: The Question of Succession in Late Elizabethan England*. Manchester: Manchester University Press, 2014, pp. 276–94.

Sparrow, Anthony. *A Collection of Articles*. London, 1661; Wing/C4093A.

Spelman, Henry. *De Non Temerandis Ecclesiis*. Oxford, 1646; Wing/S4919A.

Spicer, Andrew. "'Accommodating of Thame Selfis to Heir the Worde': Preaching, Pews and Reformed Worship in Scotland, 1560–1638." *History*, Vol. 88, No. 3 (291) (Jul., 2003), pp. 405–22.

Spicer, Andrew. "'Laudianism' in Scotland? St Giles' Cathedral, Edinburgh, 1633–39: A Reappraisal." *Architectural History*, Vol. 46 (2003), pp. 95–108.

Spinks, Bryan D. "Treasures Old and New: A Look at Some of Thomas Cranmer's Methods of Liturgical Compilation." In Paul Ayris and David Selwyn (eds.). *Thomas Cranmer: Churchman and Scholar*. Woodbridge and Rochester: The Boydell Press, 1993, pp. 175–88.

Spinks, Bryan D. "Durham House and the Chapels Royal: Their Liturgical Impact on the Church of Scotland." *Scottish Journal of Theology*, Vol. 67, No. 4 (Nov., 2014), pp. 379–99.

Spinks, Bryan D. *The Rise and Fall of the Incomparable Liturgy: The Book of Common Prayer, 1559–1906*. London: SPCK, 2017.

Sprat, Thomas. *Observations on Monsieur de Sorbier's Voyage into England*. London, 1665; Wing/S5035.

Sprat, Thomas. *The History of the Royal-Society of London*. London, 1667; Wing/S5032.

Stanglin, Keith D. "'Arminius Avant La Lettre': Peter Baro, Jacobus Arminius, and the Bond of Predestinarian Polemic." *Westminster Theological Journal*, Vol. 67, No. 1 (Spring, 2005), pp. 51–74.

Stanglin, Keith D. "The New Perspective on Arminius: Notes on a Historiographical Shift." *Reformation and Renaissance Review*, Vol. 11, No. 3 (2009), pp. 295–310.

Stanglin, Keith D. and Thomas H. McCall. *Jacob Arminius: Theologian of Grace*. Oxford: Oxford University Press, 2012.

Stapleton, Paul J. "Pope Gregory and the Gens Anglorum: Thomas Stapleton's Translation of Bede." In Christopher Cobb (ed.), *Renaissance Papers (2008)*. Rochester: Camden House and Woodbridge: Boydell & Brewer, 2009, pp. 15–34.

Starkie, Andrew. "Contested Histories of the English Church: Gilbert Burnet and Jeremy Collier." *The Huntington Library Quarterly*, Vol. 68, No. 1–2 (Mar., 2005), pp. 335–51.

Starkie, Andrew. "Henry VIII in History: Gilbert Burnet's History of the Reformation (v. 1), 1679." In Thomas Betteridge and Thomas S. Freeman (eds.). *Henry VIII and History*. Farnham and Burlington: Ashgate, 2012, pp. 151–63.

Stephen, Jeffrey. *Scottish Presbyterians and the Act of Union 1707*. Edinburgh: Edinburgh University Press, 2007.

Stephens, Isaac. "Confessional Identity in Early Stuart England: The 'Prayer Book Puritanism' of Elizabeth Isham." *Journal of British Studies*, Vol. 50, No. 1 (Jan., 2011), pp. 24–47.

Stewart, Laura A.M. "'Brothers in Treuth': Propaganda, Public Opinion and the Perth Articles Debate in Scotland." In Ralph Houlbrooke (ed.). *James VI and I: Ideas, Authority, and Government*. Aldershot and Burlington: Ashgate, 2006, pp. 151–68.

Stewart, Laura A.M. "The Political Repercussions of the Five Articles of Perth: A Reassessment of James VI and I's Religious Policies in Scotland." *The Sixteenth Century Journal*, Vol. 38, No. 4 (Winter, 2007), pp. 1013–36.

Stewart, Laura A.M. "Power and Faith in Early Modern Scotland." *The Scottish Historical Review*, Vol. 92, No. 234, Supplement: The State of Early Modern and Modern Scottish Histories (Apr., 2013), pp. 25–37.

Stewart, Laura A.M. *Rethinking the Scottish Revolution: Covenanted Scotland, 1637–1651.* Oxford: Oxford University Press, 2016.

Stillingfleet, Edward. *Irenicum*. London, 1660; Wing/S5596.

Stillingfleet, Edward. *Several Conferences Between a Romish Priest, a Fanatick Chaplain, and a Divine of the Church of England.* London, 1679; Wing/S5667.

Stow, John. *The Chronicles of England.* London, 1580; STC 23333.

Strauss, Gerald (ed. and trans.). *Manifestations of Discontent in Germany the Eve of the Reformation.* Bloomington and London: Indiana University Press, 1971.

Streete, Adrian. "Christian Liberty and Female Rule: Exegesis and Political Controversy in the 1550s." In Victoria Brownlee and Laura Gallagher (eds.). *Biblical Women in Early Modern Literary Culture, 1550–1700.* Manchester: Manchester University Press, 2015, pp. 59–74.

Stump, Phillip H. *The Reforms of the Council of Constance (1414–1418).* Leiden: Brill, 1994.

Stump, Phillip H. "The Council of Constance and the End of the Schism." In Joëlle Rollo-Koster and Thomas M. Izbicki (eds.). *A Companion to the Great Western Schism (1378–1417).* Leiden: Brill, 2009, pp. 395–442.

Sudbury, John. *A Sermon Preached at the Consecration of the Right Revered Fathers in God.* London, 1660; Wing/S6136.

Supreme Council of Confederate Catholics. *Admonitions by the Svpreame Covncell of the Confederat Catholicks of Ire[l]and.* Waterford, 1643; Wing/A593A.

Sylvester, Richard S. and Davis P. Harding (eds.). *Two Early Tudor Lives.* New Haven and London: Yale University Press, 1962.

Taylor, Charles. *Modern Social Imaginaries.* Durham and London: Duke University Press, 2003.

Theyer, John. *Aerio-Mastix, Or, A Vindication of the Apostolicall and Generally Received Government of the Church of Christ by Bishops.* Oxford, 1643; Wing/T889.

Thiry, Steven. "'In Open Shew to the World': Mary Stuart's Armorial Claim to the English Throne and Anglo-French Relations (1559–1561)." *English Historical Review*, Vol. CXXXII, No. 559 (Dec., 2017), pp. 1405–39.

Thomas, Thomas. *Dictionarium Linguae Latinae et Anglicanae.* Cambridge, 1587; STC 24008.

Thomson, John A.F. *Popes and Princes 1417–1517: Politics and Polity in the Late Medieval Church.* London: George Allen & Unwin, 1980.

Thurley, Simon. "The Stuart Kings, Oliver Cromwell and the Chapel Royal 1618–1685." *Architectural History*, Vol. 45 (2002), pp. 238–74.

Tierney, Brian (ed.). *The Crisis of Church and State 1050–1300.* Toronto: University of Toronto Press and the Medieval Academy of America, 1988.

Till, Barry. "Participants in the Savoy conference (*act.* 1661)." *ODNB*. Accessed May 17, 2021.

Timorcus, Theophilus. *The Covenanters Plea Against Absolvers.* London, 1660; Wing/G314.

Todd, Margo. "'All One with Tom Thumb': Arminianism, Popery, and the Story of the Reformation in Early Stuart Cambridge." *Church History*, Vol. 64, No. 4 (Dec., 1995), pp. 563–79.

Toon, Peter. "The Parker Society." *The Historical Magazine of the Protestant Episcopal Church*, Vol. 46, No. 3 (Sept., 1977), pp. 323–32.

Tuckett, Sally. "The Scottish Bishops in Government, 1625–1638." In Sharon Adams and Julian Goodare (eds.). *Scotland in the Age of Two Revolutions*. Woodbridge and Rochester: The Boydell Press, 2014, pp. 59–78.

Tutchin, John. *A New Martyrology*. London, 1689; Wing/T3379.

Tyacke, Nicholas. *Anti-Calvinists: The Rise of English Arminianism c. 1590–1640*. New ed. Oxford: Clarendon Press, 1990.

Tyacke, Nicholas. "Archbishop Laud." In Kenneth Fincham (ed.). *The Early Stuart Church, 1603–1642*. Stanford: Stanford University Press, 1993, pp. 51–70.

Tyacke, Nicholas. *Aspects of English Protestantism c. 1530–1700*. Manchester and New York: Manchester University Press, 2001.

Tyacke, Nicholas. "The Puritan Paradigm of English Politics, 1558–1642." *The Historical Journal*, Vol. 53, No. 3 (Sept., 2010), pp. 527–50.

Tyndale, William. *The Practyse of Prelates*. London, 1549; STC 24467.

University of Oxford. *The Answere of... the Vniversitie of Oxford*. Oxford, 1603; STC 19011.

University of Oxford. *The Humble Petition of the Ministers of the Church of England*. Oxford[?], 1641; Wing/H3562.

University of Oxford. *Reasons of the Present Judgment of the Vniversity of Oxford*. London, 1647; Wing/S623, S623A, S624, S625.

University of Oxford. *Reasons of the Present Judgment of the Universitie of Oxford*. Oxford and London, 1660; Wing/S626 and S627.

Valla, Lorenzo. *A Treatyse of the Donation or Gyfte and Endowme[n]t of Possessyons, Gyuen and Graunted vnto Syluester Pope of Rhome, by Constantyne Emperour of Rhome*. London, 1534; STC 5641.

Valla, Lorenzo. *On The Donation of Constantine*. Trans. G.W. Bowersock. Cambridge and London: Harvard University Press, 2007.

Van Engen, John. "Multiple Options: The World of the Fifteenth-Century Church." *Church History*, Vol. 77, No. 2 (Jun., 2008), pp. 257–84.

Van Engen, John. "A World Astir: Europe and Religion in the Early Fifteenth Century." In J. Patrick Hornbeck II and Michael van Dussen (eds.). *Europe After Wyclif*. New York: Fordham University Press, 2017, pp. 11–45.

Vicars, Iohn. *Behold Romes Monster*. London, 1643; Wing/V294.

Vidmar, John, O.P. *English Catholic Historians and the English Reformation, 1585–1954*. Brighton and Portland: Sussex Academic Press, 2005.

von Wied, Hermann. *Einfaltigs Bedencken*. Cologne, 1543.

von Wied, Hermann. *A Simple, and Religious Consultation*. London, 1547; STC 13213.

von Wied, Hermann. *The Right Institucion of Baptisme*. London, 1548; STC 13211.

von Wied, Hermann. *The Right Instytucion of Baptisme*. London, 1549; STC 13212.

von Wied, Hermann. *A Brefe and a Playne Declarayion of the Dewty of Maried Folkes*. London, 1553; STC 13208.

de Voragine, Jacobus. *The Golden Legend: Readings on the Saints*. Trans. William Granger Ryan. Princeton: Princeton University Press, 2012.

W.R.S. *Every-dayes Sacrifice*. London, 1624; STC 6398.

Walsham, Alexandra. "'Frantick Hacket': Prophecy, Sorcery, Insanity, and the Elizabethan Puritan Movement." *The Historical Journal*, Vol. 41, No. 1 (Mar., 1998), pp. 27–66.

Walsham, Alexandra. *The Reformation of the Landscape: Religion, Identity, & Memory in Early Modern Britain & Ireland*. Oxford: Oxford University Press, 2011.

Walsham, Alexandra, Bronwyn Wallace, Ceri Law, and Brian Cummings (eds.). *Memory and the English Reformation*. Cambridge: Cambridge University Press, 2020.

Walton, Izaak. *The Life of Mr. Rich. Hooker*. London, 1665; Wing/W670.

Wariston, Archibald. *A Short Relation of the State of the Kirk of Scotland Since the Reformation of Religion*. Edinburgh, 1638; STC 22039.

Watkins, John. "'Old Bess in the Ruff': Remembering Elizabeth I, 1625–1660." *English Literary Renaissance*, Vol. 30, No. 1 (Winter, 2000), pp. 95–116.

Webb, Diana. *Pilgrimage in Medieval England*. London and New York: Hambledon Continuum, 2000.

Wendel, François (ed.). *Martini Bvceri Opera Latina, Volumen XV: De Regno Christi Libri Dvo 1550*. Paris-VIᵉ: Presses Universitaires de France, 1955.

Wengert, Timothy J. "The Priesthood of All Believers and Other Pious Myths." *Institute of Liturgical Studies Occasional Papers*. 117 (2006). Available online: https://scholar.valpo.edu/ils_papers/117.

Westminster Assembly. *A Solemne League and Covenant for Reformation, and Defence of Religion*. London, 1643; Wing/S4442aA.

Westminster Assembly. *A Directory for the Publique Worship of God*. London, 1644; Wing/D1544.

Westminster Assembly. *A Letter from the Assembly of Divines in England, and the Commissioners of the Church of Scotland*. London, 1644; Wing/W1443A.

Westminster Assembly. *A Directory for the Publique Worship of God*. London, 1660; Wing/D1553A.

Whitaker, E.C. *Martin Bucer and the Book of Common Prayer*. Essex: The Alcuin Club, 1974.

White, Micheline. "The Psalms, War, and Royal Iconography: Katherine Parr's *Psalms or Prayers* (1544) and Henry VIII as David." *Renaissance Studies*, Vol. 29, No. 4 (Sept., 2015), pp. 554–75.

White, Peter. *Predestination, Policy and Polemic: Conflict and consensus in the English Church from the Reformation to the Civil War*. Cambridge: Cambridge University Press, 1992.

Whitford, David M. "The Papal Antichrist: Martin Luther and the Underappreciated Influence of Lorenzo Valla." *Renaissance Quarterly*, Vol. 61, No. 1 (Spring, 2008), pp. 26–52.

Whittingham, William et al. (eds.). *The Bible*. Geneva, 1560; STC 2093.

Wilkins, David. *Concilia Magnae Britanniae et Hiberniae*. 4 Vols. London, 1737; ESTC T138837.

Wilkinson, Robert. *Barwick Bridge: Or England and Scotland Covpled*. London, 1617; STC 25652.

William Durande of Mende. *The Rationale Divinorum Officiorum*. Prologue and Book I. Trans. Timothy M. Thibodeau. New York: Columbia University Press, 2007.

Williams, Gryffith. *The Great Antichrist Revealed*. London, 1660; Wing/W2662.

Winship, Michael P. "Puritans, Politics, and Lunacy: The Copinger-Hacket Conspiracy as the Apotheosis of Elizabethan Presbyterianism." *The Sixteenth Century Journal*, Vol. 38, No. 2 (Summer, 2007), pp. 345–69.

Winstanley, William. *The Protestant Almanack... 1685*. London, 1684; Wing/A2229.

Winstanley, William. *The Protestant Almanack... 1689*. London, 1689; Wing/A2229A.

Winstanley, William. *The Protestant Almanack... 1692*. London, 1692; Wing/A2232.

Winstanley, William. *The Protestant Almanack... 1694*. London, 1694; Wing/A2234.

Worden, Blair. "Toleration and the Cromwellian Protectorate." In W.J. Sheils (ed.). *Persecution and Toleration*. Oxford: Basil Blackwell, 1984, pp. 199–246.

Yates, Nigel. *Preaching, Word and Sacrament: Scottish Church Interiors 1560–1860*. London and New York: T&T Clark, 2009.

Young, John R. "The Covenanters and the Scottish Parliament, 1639–51: The Rule of the Godly and the 'Second Scottish Reformation'." In Elizabeth Boran and Crawford Gribben (eds.). *Enforcing Reformation in Ireland and Scotland, 1550–1700*. Aldershot and Burlington: Ashgate, 2006, pp. 131–58.

Younger, Neil. "How Protestant was the Elizabethan Regime?" *English Historical Review*, Vol. CXXXIII, No. 564 (Oct., 2018), pp. 1060–92.

Zwingli, Ulrich. *A Brief Rehersal of the Death, Resurrectio[n], & Ascension of Christ*. London, 1561; STC 26135.

Zwingli, Ulrich. "Vpon the Euchariste." In Anonymous. *A Paraphrase Vppon the Epistle of the Holie Apostle S. Paule to the Romanes*. London, 1572; STC 19137.5, fos. 68r–69r.

Index

For the benefit of digital users, indexed terms that span two pages (e.g., 52–53) may, on occasion, appear on only one of those pages.

Henry VIII 10, 12–13, 23–4, 26–36, 38–41, 47,
86–7, 89–90, 121, 152–3, 163–4, 166–7,
169–70
in *A Brief View* (Anonymous) 147–8
in Catholic historiography 63–8
in Dissenting historiography 139
in Burnet, Gilbert 162, 170–4
in Erasmus of Rotterdam (Udall) 35, 126–7,
144–5
in Foxe, John 72–3
in Fuller, Thomas 147, 149, 171–2
in Godwin, Francis 104–9, 111–12
in Heylyn, Peter 126–7, 141–4, 170–2
in Sandys, Edwin 124–5
in Sparrow, Anthony 170
See also Herbert of Cherbury
Herbert of Cherbury 121, 146, 162–5, 170–2,
174–5, 187
Heylyn, Peter 116, 126–7, 140–4, 146–51, 161–5,
167–72, 176, 181–2, 186
Hooker, Richard 82–5, 88–9, 113–14, 134,
138–9, 149–50, 153–4
Huggarde, Miles 49, 75

Indulgences 20–1, 26–7, 98–100

James VI and I 10–11, 85–98, 107–8, 115–18,
120–1, 123–4, 170, 172–3

Knox, John 1–2, 10–11, 47–8, 50–7, 60–1, 68,
74–7, 79–80, 82–3, 86, 89, 113–14, 120–1,
128–31, 136–9, 156, 174, 181–2

Lateran V, *see* Fifth Lateran Council
Laud, William 102–3, 117–18, 124, 140–1, 144–5
Laudianism (historiographical label) 122, 150–1,
161–2, 170–1, 181–2, 186–7
Liturgy
at the Fifth Lateran Council 21
in Latin 42–3
See also Book of Common Prayer
Luther centenary 86–7, 98–104, 108–9
Luther, Martin 1–2, 5–6, 8–10, 13, 18–19, 21–2,
25–6, 38–9, 41, 70–1, 74–5, 86–7, 98–104,
108–9, 111–12, 126–7, 144–5, 152–3, 170–1,
174–8, 183–6
See also Luther centenary
Lutheran (origins of confessional label) 37–8,
58–60

Marian Exiles 48–57, 60–1, 181–2
Martin Marprelate 47, 79–83, 85, 138–9, 156
Mary I 47–51, 53–4, 57, 64–5, 176–7
in *A Brief View* (Anonymous) 147–8

in Catholic historiography 66–7
in Burnet, Gilbert 162, 165–6, 168
in Godwin, Francis 104–5, 111–12, 187
Melanchthon, Philip 18–19, 30–1, 38–41, 58–9,
70–1, 165
Millenary Petition 87–9, 93, 138–9
Milton, John 31–2, 131–2, 136–7, 139, 150–1
Monstrosity 6–8, 13, 17–19, 53–4, 68, 70–1,
113–14, 130–1, 156–7, 173–4
See also Beast (apocalyptic); Pope-Ass

National Covenant 128–33
Northern Rebellion 57–8, 68, 77–8

Olde, John 51–2, 69–70, 72
"Our English Reformers" 82–3
See also English Reformation, "First Reformers"

Piccolomini, Aeneas Sylvius 21–2, 74
Plenitudo potestatis 15–16, 22–3, 25, 64–5
Pole, Reginald (Cardinal) 48, 63–5, 111–12
Ponet, John 48–9, 52–4, 68, 138–9
Pope-Ass 18–19, 21–2, 70–1
Popish Plot 178–81
Presbyterian (church order) 61, 79, 89, 120–1,
125–6, 131–3, 135–7, 139–40, 150–1,
156–60, 176
See also Aërius, *Directory for the Publique
Worship of God*, *Solemn League and
Covenant for Reformation*, Westminster
Assembly
Protestant (confessional label) 1, 102,
as reference to German evangelicals 111, 174–5
as English self-designation 75, 86–7, 98–9,
102–4, 111–13, 174–82
Protestant Reformation (historiographical
label) 1, 8–9, 185–6
Puritan 9, 90–1, 104, 107–8, 163–4, 179, 181–2

Reformatio Legum Ecclesiasticarum see Canon
law, 1552 (England; proposed)
Reformatio Sigismundi 21–4
Reformation
in dictionaries 3–5, 44, 122
as pretence, pretended, pretension,
pretext 77–9, 81–5, 88–9, 113–14, 129–31,
133–4, 150–1, 154–5, 157, 179
See also Council of Basel, Council of
Constance, Council of Trent, Counter-
Reformation (historiographical label),
English Reformation, Fifth Lateran Council,
Protestant Reformation (historiographical
label), Scottish Reformation
Reformation Parliament 27n.116